For years, this has been t
for anyone planning to

"Facts, prices and advice on choosing a ski package, getting around Europe and finding friends to ski with."

-New York Times

"Everything skiers need to know but the weather forecast."

-Robb Report

"Tips and money-saving ideas for skiing in Europe."

-San Francisco Examiner

"Detailed information on lift ticket prices, cross-country facilities, nightlife and more."

-Powder Magazine

"The flavor, feel and personality of each resort."   *-Boston Globe*

"It provides independent evaluation of the ski terrain and offers more extensive information than found in other guides."

-Skier News

"Start your planning with Ski Europe. It includes everything needed to make an educated decision about which slopes to hit."

-PhysiciansFinancial News

"Get it before you ski off."   *-Endless Vacations*

"I've been using Ski Europe since the first edition appeared to select destinations for my club and then to organize the trips."

-RN, Washington DC

"We live about two hours from Chamonix and we love your Ski Europe book."   -JM, Thoiry, France

Other books published by World Leisure

- Skiing America by Charles Leocha
  Annually updated guidebook to North America's best ski resorts
  $21.95
- WomenSki by Claudia Carbone
  Award-winning breakthrough book about why women can't ski like men
  and shouldn't.
  $14.95
- All Terrain Skiing by Dan Egan
  A course of practical on-the-snow exercises designed to take skiers to the
  next level of excellence.Comes with 19 snow-proof take-along cards.
  $24.95
- Getting To Know You – 365 questions and activities
  to enhance relationships by Jeanne McSweeney & Charles Leocha
  A book of intimate questions that get to the heart of successful relationships.
  $6.95
- Getting To Know Kids in Your Life
  by Jeanne McSweeney and Charles Leocha
  Interactive questions and activities to really get to know children for parents,
  aunts, uncles, grandparents and anyone who shares time with 3 to 7 year-olds
  $6.95
- A Woman's ABCs of Life – from those who learned the hard way
  by Beca Lewis Allen
  Inspired advice collected for her daughter helps women expand their lives
  with practical, fun and entering insights about life
  $6.95
- Travel Rights by Charles Leocha
  The book filled with answers to travelers' difficult questions. It saves you
  money and makes travel more hassle-free.
  $9.95
- Great Nature Vacations With Your Kids
  Great Adventure Vacations With Your Kids both by Dorothy Jordon
  Tips and recommendations on choosing the best vacations for both
  yourselves and your kids, and how to get the most out of them.
  Nature outlines trips such asrain forests tours, safaris, desert camping,
  swimming with dolphins and others. Adventure covers white-water
  rafting, backcountry skiing, rick climbing and so on.
  $9.95 and $11.95

All available by calling 1-800-444-2524
or send payment plus $3.75 shipping and handling
to: World Leisure, 177 Paris St. Boston, MA 02128

SKI EUROPE

11th Edition

by Charles A. Leocha

with
William Walker
James Kitfield
Steve Giordano
Glen Putman
Andrew Bill
Cindy Bohl
Christopher Elliott
Lynn Rosen

WORLD LEISURE CORPORATION
Hampstead, NH   Boston, MA

Copyright © 1985, 1986, 1987, 1988, 1989, 1990, 1991, 1992, 1993, 1996, 1998 by World Leisure Corporation

Cover design by Concialdi Design , Frankfort, IL.
Cover photo courtesy of St. Anton Tourist Board, Austria.

Chapter heading illustrations by Len Shalansky,
59 Darling St., Warwick, RI 02886, (401) 738-3215

Distributed to national chains, Ingram, Baker & Taylor, Bookazine in USA by Midwest Trade Books, Inc., 27 W. 20th Street, Suite 1102, New York, NY 10011, Tel. (212) 727-0190, fax (212) 727-0195.

Distributed to independent bookstores, regional chains, and other wholesalers by The Talman Company, 89 Fifth Avenue, New York, NY 10003 Tel. (800) 537-8894, fax (212) 352-1772

Distributed to the trade in U.K. by
Portfolio, Unit 1c, West Ealing Business Centre, Alexandria Road, London W13 0NJ. Tel. (0181) 579-7748, fax (0181)567-0904.

Mail Order, Catalog, other International sales and rights, and Special Sales by World Leisure Corporation, 177 Paris Street, Boston, MA 02128. Tel. (617) 569-1966, fax (617) 561-7654
E-mail: wleisure@aol.com; Internet: www.worldleisure.com

ISBN: 0-915009-59-5   ISSN: 1072-8996
LCCN: 93-643935

Contributors to *Ski Europe* *(11th edition)*

Charlie Leocha has been skiing worldwide for over two decades. He is author of *Skiing America '98*, an annually updated guidebook to North America's top ski resorts. He has skied at virtually evey major international resort. He writes about travel and skiing for scores of magazines and newspapers.

William Walker is one of the founding co-authors of this book. A skiing journalist, he has been writing and living in Germany for over twenty years. He is an editor with European *Stars and Stripes* and writes extensively for international newspapers and magazines.

James Kitfield has been awarded the Gerald R. Ford prize twice for distinguished reporting, and the Jesse H. Neal award for excellence in reporting. His book, *Prodigal Soldiers*, was published by Simon & Schuster. He's not always so serious. He skis whenever and wherever he has a chance. He first met Charlie Leocha dancing in a conga line through a bar in Verbier.

Steve Giordano is a Pacific Northwest writer who contributes to the *Bellingham Herald*, *Adventure Northwest* and *Northwest Skier* magazines. Once a ski patroller, he is president of the Pacific Northwest chapter of the North American Ski Journalists Association (NASJA). Today he switches between his snowboard and his skis depending on his mood, the snow and the company.

Glen Putman is a Los Altos, California freelance writer specializing in articles about travel, food and skiing. His feature articles have appeared in scores of publications. When he can't ski, he heads for the nearest golf course.

Andrew Bill is a writer living in New York. He has scratched a freelance living from travel writing for more than 15 years. He is the force behind *Newsweek's* Best Bars section. He is also director of Thunder Publications, a custom publishing company.

Cindy Bohl is an itinerant snowboarder and well-rounded ski bum living in the backwoods of New Hampshire. She specializes in finding the gnarliest trails and the wildest après-ski action. She visited several resorts in Austria.

Christopher Elliott's writing has appeared in the *Wall Street Journal, The New York Times, The Los Angeles Times* and *Travel Weekly* among numerous other publications. He has authored several books and has been active creating internet publications. He just finished a stint in Germany as a Fulbright Scholar.

Lynn Rosen, a Pacific Northwest-based journalist and Emmy award-winning producer, offered color comentary on the Jungfrau Region with its Jungfraujoch Railroad and the Piz Gloria on the Schilthorn over Mürren, plus traditional Zermatt and modern, boxy Davos.

Bob Hertzka, the creator of Resorts OnLine, an internet resource providing information on destination resorts worldwide at www.resortsonline.com, provided updates on skiing, dining, lodging and nightlife in Zermatt and Lech.

Ski Europe

General Information

Ski Europe

Getting the most out of this guidebook   8

Getting to Europe   12

Getting around Europe   19

Accommodations and Meals   23

European skiing basics

The weather, What to wear,

Snow conditions

Insurance, Important papers,

Telephone basics,

Handling money in Europe,

Ski equipment,

Taking photos in the snow,

Meeting Europeans, Holidays,

Etiquette on the slopes and in the lift lines   28

European après-ski   35

When in the Alps

...a first-timer's guide to skiing Europe   39

Cross-country   42

Valley-to-valley and cross-border skiing in Europe   47

Austria   52

The Arlberg

St. Anton, St. Christoph, Lech, Zürs, Stuben   55

Badgastein   69

Innsbruck   78

Ischgl, Galtür and the Paznaum Valley   78

Kitzbühel/Kirchberg   85

Mayrhofen, Zillertal, Tuxertal   96

Oetztal

Sölden, Hochsölden, Obergurgl, Hochgurgl   99

Saalbach-Hinterglemm   107

Schladming/Ramsau Dachstein-Tauern Region   113

Söll   118

St. Johann im Tirol   122

Zell am See/Kaprun   127

Contents

France 136

Les Arcs, Bourg-St. Maurice 137
Avoriaz/Morzine 143
Chamonix Mont Blanc 148
La Clusaz 155
Flaine 159
La Plagne 163
Megève 171
Les Trois Vallées
Courchevel, Méribel, Les Menuires, Val Thorens 179
Tignes 193
Val d'Isère 198
Germany, Garmisch-Partenkirchen 206
Italy 211
Cervinia 213
Courmayeur 217
Cortina d'Ampezzo 221
Madonna di Campiglio 225
Val Gardena 229
Switzerland 234
Arosa 237
Champéry and the Portes du Soleil 241
Crans-Montana 247
Davos 252
Engelberg 259
Flims Laax Falera 263
Gstaad/Saanenland - Super Ski Region 267
Jungfrau Region
Grindelwald, Wengen, Mürren 273
Klosters 284
Saas-Fee 288
St. Moritz 294
Verbier 301
Zermatt 306
Spain 317
Baqueira/Beret 318
Sierra Nevada 323
Tourist Offices 327

Ski Europe
Getting the most out of this guidebook

Skiing in Europe is the dream of just about every American skier and for British skiers it is normally the most cost effective ski holiday available. Today, with easy flights across the Atlantic and the Channel, and tour packages to dozens of the resorts that nestle in the Alps, the dream is easy to fulfill. This book is designed to help give you the information you'll need to plan your trip and get the most out of it.

For Alpine veterans who return year after year, this book will help you to make your own arrangements, or at least to decide which resorts you want to visit. We believe that you won't find another guide with as many useful numbers and addresses for a European ski vacation.

Time and money

Unfortunately, too many Americans don't seriously consider skiing in Europe. They may seriously dream about it, but dismiss the idea as too costly or too time-consuming. Skiing in Europe is neither.

Consider the average urban skier in the United States: reaching the nearest resort will take him five, six or seven hours, and that travel is normally during the day. If you

---

A disclaimer on pricing

The prices in this book were, to the best of our ability, accurate as of press time. In most cases we obtained 1997/98 prices from the resorts as they were in the process of setting them. Those prices are clearly marked. Otherwise, assume that any prices are approximate.

None of these prices are guaranteed, nor are they official in any sense. All are subject to change at any time and owing to any circumstance, and as noted in each resort chapter, prices do change with the high, low and shoulder seasons each winter. Use the prices here as a guide to planning your best ski vacation.

No hotel, restaurant or ski resort has paid to be included in this book. The recommendations are based on personal visits to each of the resorts mentioned, and judgments based on extensive discussions with year-long residents and returning visitors.

were to head to Europe, you would board a flight in the evening and land the next morning. Transfers to the Alps are only a couple of hours, and this puts you in the resort the following afternoon. Voilà!—on the average, you spend about the same travel time.

As far as money goes, European ski packages average about $1,200 to $1,400 for a week of skiing, including seven nights of first-class lodging, transatlantic airfare, transfers to resorts, breakfast and dinner every day, lift tickets in some cases and all taxes. This is about the same as you would spend taking a vacation to a Rocky Mountain resort from the East Coast or from California.

Also, with the advent of direct flights from the West Coast to Europe and code sharing, time and expense are no longer the major factors they once were for people living in once non-gateway cities.

What's new in this edition

Prices for lift tickets, child care and ski school at virtually every resort have been updated to 1997/98 winter prices. Where new lifts have been installed, descriptions of the skiing have been modified. This year we are once again focusing on the Alps, where the big change has been snowmaking at many of the resorts. Low level slopes are now covered with limited snowmaking to insure that vacationers can ski back into the towns and villages even in poor snow years. Another significant change, especially for families, is the establishment of a Youth or Teenage lift ticket. Now many resorts have created a new ticketing category with prices between those of children and adults. This new pricing category affects youth from 13–18 years in most cases.

Where we have been able to get the internet and e-mail addresses of various resorts, we have included them in the Tourist Information section. We have also set up a web site at **www.worldleisure.com** that will provide updated information on our publications and provide a means of sending us any messages, suggestions for future books and questions.

We have also included basic information on the ski chalets operated by many British ski tour organizers. This information will be an assistance to many of our British readers as well as an eyeopener to our American readers who have no clue about this money-saving concept.

Chapter organization

The resort chapters are in several sections. We begin by sketching the personality of the place, to give you a feel for the overall resort—is it old and quaint or modern and highrise? Clustered at the base of the slopes, or a few miles down the road? Remote and isolated, or around the bend from another resort? Is it family-oriented or catering to singles, walkable with good shuttlebuses or requiring a car, filled with happy, friendly faces or with an aloof herd of "beautiful" skiers?

A detailed description of the mountain layout is next, followed by a mountain rating. We suggest an approach to exploring the mountain based on your abilities, and in the mountain rating we describe what the mountain has to offer for beginner, intermediate or expert; more importantly, this section also suggests which resorts the beginner looking for the mellow might try or the expert looking for the extreme may choose to avoid.

The major ski school programs are outlined, together with prices for group and private lessons.

Lift ticket prices are listed for adults, children and seniors. The price lists in most cases include single-day passes, as well as multiday tickets where available. Where possible we list the 97/98 prices; where no date is noted, assume the prices are from the 96/97 season.

Under Accommodations we list the most luxurious places to stay as well as many of the ski area bargains. In the Apartments section we include accommodations which would be considered condominiums in the U.S.

The dining recommendations always include the best gourmet restaurants in town, where money is no object—but we don't leave out affordable places where a hungry family can chow down and relax. There are also plenty of in-between restaurants suggested. These suggestions have been compiled from interviews with locals and tourists, then combined with our own experiences.

Après-ski/nightlife describes places to go once the lifts begin to close, and where to find entertainment later in the evening. We discuss, for example, which bars are packed with celebrants for immediate après-ski, likewise where to find an inviting, cozy spot in front of a fireplace. We'll help you find pulsing disco on a packed dance floor, or soft music and quiet after-dinner talk.

Details on resort child care facilities are given with prices, times and ages of children accepted.

Activities and facilities, such as tennis and squash, fitness clubs, skating, sleigh rides, hot-air ballooning, curling and festivals, are included under other activities.

Finally, we give detailed getting there instructions on how to reach the resort either by plane, car or train and finish with the most important phone numbers and addresses for tourist information.

Skier ability levels

The level of skiing ability needed to negotiate a particular trail is regularly noted. Because resorts and ski schools use different rating systems, we provide ours to assist you in reading "Where to ski":

Never-evers are just what the name implies, and the term normally sticks with them for the first three to five days on skis.

Beginners have about a week of instruction and can turn and stop more or less when they choose, but still rely on the stem christie and wedge turns.

Lower intermediates can link stem christies and are beginning to make parallel turns.

Intermediates can negotiate any blue trail and can normally more-or-less parallel ski on the smooth stuff; they go back to survival rules when working their way down an expert trail, and definitely struggle in heavy powder and crud.

Advanced skiers can ski virtually any marked trail with carved turns, but are still intimidated by crud, deep heavy powder and super steeps.

Experts can always ski anything, anytime, anywhere. They are few and far between.

Getting in shape

How important is it to be in shape for skiing? Well, we aren't going to lie to you—the higher fitness level you have, the more fun you'll have and the better you'll ski.

But this doesn't mean you have to devote half your life to jogging and hamstring stretches. We won't lie to you about this, either—most of the contributors to this book would never be mistaken for Jane Fonda or Arnold Schwarzenegger, writing being the sedentary profession it is. But we all have learned—sometimes the hard way—that if we get lax about our exercise programs at home, we pay for it when we're doing our on-slope research.

A moderate exercise program—about an hour three to four times a week—is all it takes. Here are some of the key things to include:

• Aerobics. Get that heart pumping so your whole body will process oxygen more efficiently. A good portion of America's skiers—especially those who buy guidebooks— live at or near sea level. Most of the Alpine ski areas range up to a nearly 10,000-foot elevation where the air is thin. Those who lead sedentary lives where the oxygen is plentiful will be exhausted after two or three hours where the oxygen isn't as plentiful. You've spent big money for your ski trip—why waste a minute?

• Flexibility. Stre-e-e-tch those muscles, particularly the ones down the backs of your legs. Sometimes your skis decide to head in different directions, and sometimes your feet stay attached. If your hamstrings or inner-thigh muscles are tight, a fall like that could put you out of commission for the rest of your vacation. If you're learning to snowboard, you need flexibility in your ankles just to be able to stand up on the board. (One of our contributors discovered why the expression "Achilles heel" refers to a vulnerable point after a particularly embarrassing snowboard lesson last season.)

• Strength. Most skiers, even new ones, know that strong leg muscles make skiing a lot easier. Muscles that are just as important, but usually ignored by many skiers, are the ones in your upper body. Have you ever had to push yourself across a long, flat section of the mountain? Have you ever carried 15 pounds of ski equipment from your car or lodge to the chair lift? Have you ever pushed yourself up off the snow after a fall?

Of course, it's important to consult your doctor before going from a completely chairbound lifestyle to a regular exercise program. And it's best to get some professional help regarding the best program for you.

If you can't find a ski-conditioning class in your area, you can take one with your VCR. Several ski-conditioning videos are on the market now, such as Patty Wade's "In Shape To Ski." Wade, a fitness instructor in Aspen, teaches a ski-conditioning class each autumn that many of the locals swear by. Her 60-minute video workout offers a thorough and tough workout (even Patty breathes hard during the workout). You can adjust the pace to your level simply by not doing the exercises as long as she does. In the U.S.A, and Canada call (800) 925-9754 for ordering information if you can't find it at a local video outlet.

For our European and Australian readers

Most of the introduction chapters are written with our North American audience in mind. But the chapters describing the skiing, accommodation, dining and other facets of each resort are totally international. Prices are given in the local currency and most of our observations are cross-cultural (at least across the English-speaking cultures).

If we refer to anything, such as a product or service, that is not available in your country feel free to send us a fax, letter, or e-mail. We will do our best to get back to you with details on how to order it.

You can reach us at:
World Leisure Corporation
177 Paris Street
Boston, MA 02128
(617) 459-1966; fax (617) 561-7654;
Internet: www.worldleisure.com

Getting To Europe

If you are planning to put your own European ski vacation together your first step is to get across the Atlantic. Crossing the ocean and getting to the resort is the major cost to be borne: for example, while transporation to Aspen, Colorado, from New York City constitutes about 37 percent of a typical week's ski vacation budget, the travel segment of a similar ski trip to Austria represents almost 60 percent of the total cost. But transatlantic air travel is also where a clever traveler can save the most money.

If you are a do-it-yourselfer, even the transfer from the airport to the resort can be used to save both time and money if you plan ahead. Remember, though, that there are tradeoffs between cost and convenience: you want to go to Europe to ski and see as much as possible, not to spend endless hours in bus or train stations waiting for connections. It's worth doing a little homework to get the best deal, and a travel agent can help out with the specifics.

After studying pricing at ski resorts and airlines, we feel that the best overall values are available through tour operators. These are not group tours where everyone is herded onto a bus together, but rather tours which take advantage of group discounts. You will fly with friends you choose and will receive coupons or passes for transportation to the resorts. Some operators use buses, others trains, and some even provide rental cars, all for remarkably low prices.

Getting across the Atlantic

Transatlantic airfares have been at all-time lows for several years. There is more capacity and more service from almost every area of the country, which makes getting to

Europe more convenient, easier and less expensive than ever. And, of course, winter air travel works to a skier's advantage, because prices are often 40 to 50 percent lower than in the peak summer months.

A travel agent can be extremely helpful at this stage. But supplement the agent's information by doing some investigating on your own. Airline fare structures are complicated and seem to change daily—even with scheduled airlines. And when charters and group tour flights are included, the options can become phenomenally complex.

Tell the travel agent exactly what you are looking for and explain what you think you should have to pay, based on ads you have seen. The agent will either confirm your opinions or let you know what has changed since your last information. Try to find an agent who will guarantee the lowest possible fare.

These agents often will let you know exactly what is available and then you can make a decision, even if it's to take a more expensive flight based on convenience or better connections. There is no additional cost for using a travel agent; you can only save both time and money by working through a good one.

You have two basic choices for transatlantic air travel:

• Scheduled airlines — There are many advantages in taking a scheduled airline. For one, the airline must adhere to its general schedule. If there is a problem with the aircraft, passengers are normally transferred to a flight on another airline. In emergencies, a scheduled airline offers flexibility with additional flights and interline connections.

Another aspect of their flexibility is the option of landing in one city and leaving from another. Called "Open Jaw" in travel jargon, this type of ticket might let you land in Milan, ski the Italian side of the Matterhorn for a week, ski Austria for the second week, then fly home from Munich. You can also arrange limited stopovers for an additional charge, depending on your ticket, making it easy to squeeze in a few days in Amsterdam, Paris or London on your way to the slopes or on your way back..

It helps to plan your trip as far in advance as possible. You may have to book—and pay—in advance by as much as a month to get special fares that approach the lowest charter prices. Arrival and departure dates must be set in advance, and changes may bring additional charges.

Most tour packagers work with scheduled airlines who sell them blocks of seats at near-charter rates. This saving is passed on to you. By working with a reputable packager through your travel agent you get most of the benefits of the scheduled airline for charter prices.

• Charter flights — These flights are money-savers and in some cases offer excellent connections for skiers. There are some problems with charters. Often you are only guaranteed a flight date rather than a time. The charters also reserve the right to reschedule your flight, cancel it or add fuel charges. Your best protection is to fly with a charter airline that has been in business for some time, one with which your travel agent is familiar.

Try to get some form of flight cancellation insurance in case you don't leave on the planned date, and also get additional medical insurance to cover the cost of an emergency trip home in case of an accident.

Airline considerations

The transatlantic scene has changed dramatically in the past few years. Once upon a time, virtually all flights to the European continent left from New York. Today there are dozens of cities with nonstop and direct flights to Europe's major destinations. You can now make your connections in many other American cities or in Europe.

Code sharing, which started with the KLM/Northwest landmark partnership, has created even more "through connections" that can be booked as direct flights. Code sharing allows airlines to use their designator on a flight even though the flight is operated by another company. For instance, if you purchase a ticket for a KLM flight from Boston to Zürich you will check in at a joint KLM/Northwest counter then board a Northwest jet for the flight from Boston to Amsterdam. The connecting flight will be on a KLM jet from Amsterdam to Zürich. The main "hub" for these KLM/Northwest flights is Amsterdam, with connecting flights to every major airport near the Alps.

Lufthansa uses its hub in Frankfurt, Germany and American Airlines has direct flights to the Alps from their American hubs in Dallas and Chicago. Delta code shares with Swissair and Austrian Air.

Dealing with jet lag

The most unwelcome traveling companion on an overseas ski vacation is jet lag. While there are no cures, following these time-tested suggestions may help ease you into the European time zone.

• Go to bed early and wake up early for three or four days before traveling to Europe. This will allow your body to get a gradual head start in adjusting to European time. At 9 p.m. on the U.S. East Coast, it is 3 a.m. in Western Europe. If you can go to bed around 9 or 10 p.m. for a few days before your trip, you will have to overcome only about three hours of jet lag, not six.

• Try to sleep as much as possible on the plane. Many people take sleep aids and ask flight attendants not to disturb them for meals or drinks. If you have a sleep mask, use it, and cover up with the blanket stowed in the overhead: this helps conserve your body heat and energy.

• Drink as little alcohol as possible, and don't eat very much on the flight; but drink plenty of water, tea or soft drinks to avoid dehydration—cabin air is very dry.

• When you arrive at the resort, take about a two-hour nap in the afternoon or early evening. Be sure to get yourself up, then go out and explore the town, returning to sleep at about 11 p.m. or midnight.

Gateways to the Alps

Zürich, Switzerland

Skiers setting out for virtually any ski resort in Switzerland or western Austria may find themselves in Zürich for a night or two. You might well expect the Swiss banking capital to present a stuffy face to the world; but the real Zürich has managed to marry prosperity and progress to Old-World tradition.

A good place to start is the Bahnhofstrasse, where you'll see a few of those famous Swiss banks and also some of the most exclusive shops—with some of the highest price tags in the country. This is the city's main street, often called the picture window of Switzerland.

If you walk the Bahnhofstrasse you'll eventually come to Bürkliplatz and Lake Zürich. Where the Limmat River flows out from the lake, boat tours offer the best views.

A walk along the shore to your right, through the arboretum, leads past a number of rowing and boating clubs paralleling Mythenquai Street. At 88 Mythenquai, across the boat clubs' parking lot, is an immense greenhouse called the Municipal Collection of Succulents. It is home to 25,000 succulents and cacti. The indoor garden is open weekdays 9–11 a.m. and 1:30–3 p.m.

Back on Bahnhofstrasse, on foot, you'll find the most scenic sections of the old town between Bahnhofstrasse and the Limmat. One of the city's major attractions is the Swiss National Museum, on the shore of the Limmat close to the main train station. The museum chronicles Swiss civilization from prehistoric times to the present. The collection from the Roman era is particularly good.

The most-visited churches are also within walking distance of the central area. Across the Limmat, the Grossmünster 11th-century cathedral is distinguished by its twin towers. The Münster bridge from the cathedral leads to the 12th-century Frauenmünster with the famed stained-glass windows created in this century by Chagall.

A few minutes' walk from the cathedral is Zürich's Kunsthaus, an art museum with an excellent collection of Swiss masters, as well as works by Van Gogh, Cézanne, Renoir, Manet, Degas and Picasso.

Time in Zürich is a pleasant way to get over jet lag. On the Limmat River, the Hotel Zürich/La Résidence has luxury accommodations just a ten-minute ride from the airport. (Tel. 363-6363 or fax 363-6015).

The Dolder Grand Hotel in Zurich is a splendid way to begin or end your ski holiday. Maybe both. The hotel sits high on a hill overlooking Lake Zurich and the Dolderbahn (cog railway) provides free transpor-tation for hotel guests to the Romerhof district and three streetcars that feed into the center of the city. Call (800) 223-6800 for reservations.

If you prefer the backpacking style of travel, stash your skis at Left Luggage either in the airport or train station under the airport, and catch the train into Zürich. Walk across the Limmat to the hip 'n happening Niederdorf section to The City Backpacker Zürich/ Hotel Biber at Schweizerhofgasse 5. It's a bit of a modern and clean youth hostel without the curfew. Most rooms are dormitory style, but there are a few private rooms for SFr65. For bargain basement eating head to the Cafeteria Mensa, up the hill on the University campus.

Niederdorf is where Zürich's citizens ease the stress of world financial responsibilities. Along crowded streets, the old-town section of Zürich pulsates with live jazz, smoky bars, packed discos and scores of restaurants. For a more subdued outing, plan to have an elegant dinner in an old guild house.

Geneva, Switzerland

If your skiing plans are leading you toward the Valais in Switzerland, any of the French Alps, or the Val d'Aosta in Italy, Geneva is an excellent gateway.

This is one of Europe's most beautiful lakeside cities, and any tour should begin with a few moments on the Pont du Mont Blanc, the Mont Blanc bridge, for a panoramic view of the Alps; in clear weather the outline of Mont Blanc crests on the horizon. Then a climb up the north tower of St. Pierre Cathedral gives a superb view of the city, which is built around the contours of a small section of Lac Leman (Lake Geneva). The interior of the cathedral, built over a period of 300 years beginning in the 10th century, offers a stained-glass illumination of Swiss religious art and architecture.

Afterward, walk through the narrow streets surrounding the cathedral and take time to poke through Geneva's best collection of antique stores.

The attractions in Geneva are spread out. A bus tour may help you get an overall feeling for the city. Later, catch a bus or a taxi to the places you want to revisit.

The ill-fated League of Nations, founded after World War I, had its headquarters here in the Palais des Nations. Today this building serves as the European headquarters for the United Nations.

Geneva's greatest park runs along the lake and combines the Mon Repos, Perle du Lac and Villa Barton—all park areas that form a beautiful walking range.

The city's best-known museum is the Art and History Museum, which features collections in archaeology and decorative arts.

For an offbeat fling, check the flea market held on the city's Plaine de Palais Wednesdays and Saturdays.

Frankfurt, Germany

Although Frankfurt certainly is not in the heart of the Alps, skiers occasionally spend a night or two in the business capital on the way to or from an Alpine vacation.

Frankfurt's accessibility is outstanding—only 15 minutes by train or taxi from the airport. Trains leave approximately every 20 minutes and whisk passengers to the central station. From there, it's only a short walk or quick taxi ride to any of the tourist attractions. If your time is very limited, take a cab. The fare to any of the main tourist sites should be no more than $12 to $15.

The Hauptbahnhof, or railway station, is an adventure in itself, a genuine slice of prewar Europe with soaring girders supporting a massive skylight roof that arches above some two dozen tracks and platforms. Stop in and visit the tourist information center, where hostesses will orient you to the city and provide maps and brochures.

From the train station the first destination is the Römerberg, a square near the Main (pronounced mine) River that has been the focus of extensive city renovation efforts in recent years. The gabled facades of the three burghers' houses on the Römer square have come to serve as the symbol of the city and mark the core of the old quarter. Here the Kaisersack, or Imperial Hall, was the site of many celebrations when Holy Roman Emperors were crowned in Frankfurt.

This is the district of the Altstadt, or old city; although the aerial bombings in World War II destroyed nearly 80 percent of the city, many of the oldest buildings have been restored, including historic St. Bartholomew cathedral, the Nikolai church on the Römerberg and the unique, oval Paul's Church across the street.

Close by, for a visitor who wants to do last-minute (or first day) shopping, is the Zeil, Frankfurt's most fashionable pedestrian shopping street. The Hauptwache, a square where Zeil and Rossmarkt meet, reigns as the commercial heart of Frankfurt. Further down the Zeil stands the reconstructed Alte Oper, the old opera house, which rivals the beauty of prewar Dresden buildings. In the same area is the Goethe House and museum honoring Germany's most famous writer.

For nightlife, Sachsenhausen is lively. This district, across a footbridge on the opposite side of the Main River from the Römerberg, bustles with pubs and restaurants, and all pour Apfelwoi, a distinctive apple cider.

Munich, Germany

The Bavarian capital is southern Germany's crown jewel. Munich's greatest attraction is that it rivals any other city in Europe for sheer merrymaking, much of it inspired by the formidable one-liter mugs of beer served morning, noon and night. Spend at least an evening in one of the city's great beer halls.

Every visitor should check out Marienplatz, the main square. At 11 a.m. daily the dancing figures in the town hall Glockenspiel perform. Nearby is the Frauenkirche, or Church of Our Lady. The 450-year-old, onion-shaped domes topping its towers have come to symbolize Munich. The best view of the city is from the 332-foot-high north tower, where on clear days the Bavarian Alps, only 50 miles away, can be seen. For an even better view, though a bit out of the center of the town, visit the 1972 Olympic grounds for an elevator trip up the television tower, which is almost three times higher.

Munich's array of art museums is too extensive to list, but whatever your interest—paintings, ceramics, sculp-ture, ethnology—there should be a collection for you. Of special interest is the Alte Pinakothek, which houses one of the world's greatest art collections, including rooms full of works by Rubens and Dürer.

The Deutsches Museum features a great technical collection rivaling the Smithsonian's, and shouldn't be missed. This museum is a fantasy world of pushbutton fun with machines to crawl through and explore, including an early submarine and classic cars, airplanes and locomotives. The collection seems endless—from replicas of early mines you can explore to a hall full of harpsichords, this museum has every kind of mechanical device and many important inventions. It's a place children (and many adults) never want to leave.

Schloss Nymphenburg with its classic gardens and ornate furnishings is well worth the streetcar ride.

One excursion you may want to take is to Dachau, site of the concentration camp, now preserved as a memorial. It's approximately a 40-minute drive from the city center.

If you have an extra day or two in Munich, consider a bus tour to the castles of Ludwig II, the Dream King—some called him mad—of Bavaria. A particularly good tour is the Royal Castles Tour, promoted by the Bavarian Tourist Board. The luxury bus trip visits Neuschwanstein (inspiration for Disneyland's castle), Linderhof and Herrenchiemsee, three great castles built by Ludwig.

Salzburg, Austria

More than 25 years after Julie Andrews scampered across the Austrian hillsides as Maria von Trapp, Americans still flock to Salzburg for a glimpse at the locations featured in "The Sound of Music." Even in winter, it is one of the city's most popular tours.

The music the Austrians identify with Salzburg flowed from the pen of Wolfgang Amadeus Mozart. For it was here, in a well-preserved building, 9 Getreidegasse, that the famed composer and musician was born in 1756. It is now a fascinating museum that houses numerous artifacts from Mozart's day.

But the Mozart birthplace is only one attraction. The Hohensalzburg Fortress sits regally atop a hill over-looking the city, just as it has for the past 900 years. Salzburg's most recognizable landmark (and the best preserved fortress in Europe) was begun in 1077.

Below its impregnable walls is a labyrinth of narrow streets flanked by spacious plazas, and on every plaza stands a church. For centuries, Salzburg was a principality ruled by Catholic bishops.

Salzburg is best enjoyed by walking to its famous sights—to its huge cathedral (or Dom) bordered on two sides by Residenzplaz and Kapitalplaz, to the Mirabell Palace and gardens on the north side of the Salzach River that splits the old city, or to Nonnburg Abbey where the real Maria von Trapp lived.

Milan, Italy

Most skiers heading for the Italian slopes will land in Milan, the commerce and fashion heart of Italy. The city is only about a two-hour drive from the main Val d'Aosta resorts of Courmayeur and Cervinia. This city is full of surprises and deserves exploration.

One of the jewels of Milan is the majestic white-marble Duomo, or cathedral. The façade, finished in the early 19th century by order of Napoleon, is breathtaking, and tours are organized to allow a walk on the roof where no less than 135 pinnacles and scores of marble statues adorn the cathedral.

Walk through the Galleria, one of the first covered shopping malls, to the La Scala, the most famous opera house in the world. Here you can take a tour and see the gilded splendor of one of the world's great theaters. If you are in Milan for an evening, check into seeing an opera here. The season lasts most of the winter.

The Sforzas castle, built in the mid-1300s, and the park that surrounds it are both fun to explore. The Bera Palace houses an art collection with works by most of the Italian Renaissance masters. Perhaps the jewel of Milan's art treasures is the fresco of The Last Supper, by Leonardo da Vinci, in the Church of Santa Maria delle Grazia.

If you have additional time, a visit to the Leonardo da Vinci Museum, filled with models of Leonardo's great and prophetic inventions, is fascinating.

Lyon, France

The city's Fine Arts Museum houses the most impressive French collection of art outside the Louvre in Paris. Other museums packed into the city include the Museum of Textiles with a wonderful tapestry collection.

The major attraction for tourists is the old town, which is the most extensive grouping of 15th-century and Renaissance buildings in France. A visit to the St. Jean Cathedral, and a walk through the narrow streets past artisans' workshops in old Gothic doorways and medieval courtyards yield a new discovery every few yards. This area is crisscrossed with covered passageways, called traboules, which give access from one street to another and pass through courtyards and old buildings. The old town has over 100 of these unique passages.

Take the cable car to the top of the hill dominating the old town. Here enjoy the basilica and a fabulous view over Lyon. The Greco-Roman Museum houses antiquities such as inscribed Roman tablets, a Gaulish calendar and beautiful mosaics. Outside, the Roman theater is restored.

The marionette, or string-controlled puppet, was created in Lyon. Today, Guignol et Madelon—the French equivalent of Punch and Judy—still perform and poke fun at national and local politics.

Lyon is one of the gourmet centers of France. A meal in one of the city's leading restaurants will be an experience you will savor for some time.

Getting around Europe

Car rental

For the independent skier who wants to get the most out of a European ski vacation, a rental car offers the most flexibility and is a bargain—especially when two skiers share expenses. Rental cars can be picked up directly at the airport upon arrival. Aside from making it a breeze to get to the ski resort, a rental car gives you the freedom to explore the surrounding area or take a short side trip when ski conditions aren't perfect or you just want a break from skiing.

What license do you need?

The driver of the car usually must be at least 19 years old and must have a valid driver's license that has been in effect for at least one year. (The age requirement increases for some more luxurious automobiles.) It is not necessary to have an International Driving Permit when driving in Europe—your home state license is acceptable—but it is a good idea. The AAA issues them, and they are good for a year. Fill out an application and give them two passport-type portrait snapshots. By mail, start the process a month before your departure. If you live near an AAA office, you can accomplish the entire process there, including photos, in less than an hour. International Driving Permits cost $10. Call AAA for details and the location for the nearest office issuing International Driving Permits at (800) AAA-HELP. Remember, even with the International Driving Permit you will still need your U.S. state license as well. Canadians can call (800) 336-HELP for information on the nearest location to pick up an international license.

NOTE: In Europe, especially in the Alpine countries, you need to have what is called a Green Card (carte verte) for insurance. This is provided by rental companies, but it is best to make a quick check of the documents when you pick up your car.

Getting the best rates

If you make reservations two to seven days in advance of your arrival with any of the major car rental companies, you qualify for special European vacation rates. These run about $200 to $250 a week, excluding taxes. (If you're comparing car rentals to possible train travel, this will mean that each person will pay about $400 for a full month's automobile use—plus gasoline, which even in an extreme case shouldn't run more than $200 apiece.) The only requirement for this rate is that you keep the car for at least five days. If you return it before that, you will be charged at the daily rate, which often can cost more than keeping the car the entire week.

While all car rental companies may offer reasonable rates throughout the year for tourism, only Auto Europe (800-223-5555) guarantees that they will find the lowest rate. Auto Europe also can organize camper van rentals, handicap vehicles and chauffeur services.

Drop-off charges

Generally, there are no drop-off charges if a rental car is returned in the country where it was picked up. Some rental companies will allow rental cars to be dropped off in other countries for no drop-off charge if the rental is for at least 21 days. There are some companies that will allow one-way rentals, but only to a limited group of cities. Ask whether your case falls into one of these categories and if not, pick up and drop off in the same country.

Value added taxes (VAT)

Depending on where you pick up the car, you will have to pay an additional value-added tax (VAT), which is significant. Current VATs:

Germany	15.0%	Austria	21.0%
Italy	19.0%	Spain	16.0%
France	20.6%	Switzerland	6.5%

As an example of how VAT can affect the total rental cost, consider a car that lists in the brochure for $200 a week. After the VAT is added it will end up costing from $213 in Switzerland to $242 in Austria.

Collision damage waiver/insurance

If you rent your car with a credit card which provides collision damage waiver (CDW) you have adequate protection. Diners Club, American Express, MasterCard Gold and Business and VISA Gold and Business all provide this coverage automatically **as long as you decline the CDW option on the rental contract.**

This credit card coverage covers the card holder and additional drivers as long as they are correctly signed up properly with the rental company and appear on the contract. Read the fine print. Some credit card companies do not cover your car if you were driving on a dirt road or in the case of hit and run accidents and so on. Check also to see whether this is primary or secondary coverage. Primary coverage is what you want. Secondary coverage only comes into play after your own insurance company pays for damages . . . then the credit card company pays the difference. Most credit card collision damage is primary in Europe, while back in the U.S. it is normally secondary.

In the U.S. most collision insurance coverage applies to rental cars as well as to your own automobile, but in Europe most American coverage is not valid. You should have some form of collision damage insurance. According to Auto Europe the normal rental contract deductibles in Europe range from $2,000 to $5,000.

Even with your credit card coverage, your rental car company may demand a security deposit to cover the deductible until everything is settled. You must, in most cases, settle with your credit card company and then reimburse the rental company. Taking the European collision damage insurance allows you to walk away from any accident without mountains of followup paperwork.

If you are planning on renting a luxury or four-wheel-drive vehicle, check with the credit card to make sure that the car you are renting is insured under their CDW plan.

Rental car operators highly recommend the purchase of CDW for anywhere from $3 to $30 a day depending on the make of car. It makes your life easier in the event of an accident. If you can handle the hassles of doing some of your own accident paperwork during the settlement, credit card companies allow you to save money.

Theft insurance

Collision damage used to include other types of damage such as theft of the vehicle. These days, theft insurance has been separated from collision—you must purchase it separately.

According to Auto Europe many countries have made theft insurance mandatory. Where theft insurance is mandatory it is included in Auto Europe rental charges at a discounted rate.

When theft insurance is not required, we recommend purchasing it even if you are covered for collision through your credit card CDW.

Other charges

Most major airports now assess an airport pickup surcharge.

Additional driver charges of around $22 per rental will be added to your bill if you need to have an extra driver listed on the contract.

Child seats cost approximately $35 per rental.

Heading into Eastern Europe

If you are planning to take a rental car into Eastern Europe make sure to inform the company. Many rental car companies will not allow cars to be brought into Eastern Europe because of high rates of theft. Auto Europe has the largest selection of vehicles available for travel into the former Soviet Bloc, however, rates are higher than regular rentals.

Ask for a ski rack and check your chains

When you make reservations, be sure to tell the agent that you will require a ski rack and chains. Chains are usually provided free when ordered in advance, however in Austria there will be an extra charge. Ski racks cost extra (for example $35 per rental in Austria) in some countries. When you pick up the car, the ski rack will be easy to see, but you'll have to check closer for the chains. Make sure the chains provided are the correct size for the car. You are the one who will be putting the blasted things on, so you should take a great interest in making sure they are the right size. Check the number on the box carefully against the size of the tires. There is nothing more disconcerting than finding out that the chains are one size too small when you are stuck only a few hundred meters from the top of a pass.

Special airline deals

Airlines often offer reduced price cars or "free" cars with many promotions to Europe. You may be able to take advantage of them.

• You normally must travel with another person for the deal.

• Your deal is only for one week, or three days in most cases, and then you begin paying the regular rates—either weekly or daily. These may be high enough to wipe out the original savings if you remain in Europe for a week or two.

• You will have to pay the insurance, taxes, gasoline, and any drop-off charges in most cases.

• Ski racks and snow tires are much harder to come by with these deals.

Autobahn tolls

The superhighway systems in Italy, Spain and France are simply expensive. However, the time they save is normally worth the expense.

NOTE: In Switzerland cars must pay an annual autobahn toll to be permitted on the superhighways. If you rent a car outside of Switzerland and plan to drive on the superhighways, make sure your rental car has the appropriate up-to-date Swiss highway toll sticker before you drive on the Swiss superhighways. The police will not let transgressions go unfined. The hassles can easily ruin a vacation.

Germany has no tolls and no speed limits.

Austria charges about 65¢ per day for a toll sticker payable to the local rental car company.

Taking the train

There are good train transfers from Munich to Garmisch and the Austrian resorts; from Zürich and Geneva to most of the Swiss resorts; and from Milan to some of the Italian resorts. The major problem with rail travel is the hassle of dragging equipment on and off the train, compounded by the usual need to change trains at least once on a trip to an out-of-the-way resort. The Swiss railways are the only ones with a workable luggage transportation system: baggage can be checked in at the train station at Geneva or Zürich airport and then delivered to your resort. The system works in reverse, with the luggage actually checked through to your final destination—New York, London or anywhere. Cost for the service is about SFr10 per piece of luggage.

Unless you are planning to stay in a self-contained Swiss resort such as Zermatt or St. Moritz, we recommend you avoid taking trains in most cases. Four people sharing a car always save money over a train and, in many cases, two people can save money, or they will find the price difference so small that car rental is the way to go.

The Eurailpass and other national train passes are not much good for a ski vacation. It is better to merely purchase a second-class ticket to the resort; remember, since skiing is your object, you probably will not be on the train long enough to justify buying a long-term pass.

Accommodations and meals

Where you sleep, live and eat constitutes the most expensive part of your stay at a European ski resort. Lodging and meals vary widely, not only with the type of hotel or restaurant but also with the season.

Use this guide to select a hotel or apartment that is near the slopes and near the center of town. Or if you want a quiet spot on the outskirts of the village we'll help to point you in the right direction.

Choosing a hotel

If you take a package tour, your decisions are made long before you arrive at the resort. Most of the popular hotels used by tour packagers are included in this guide; the descriptions should help.

If you arrive in a resort without reservations, plan ample time to select a hotel. This means taking about a half hour to check out what the room situation is like.

The local tourist office will steer you in the right direction and will tell you which hotels have rooms available. Ask for three or four recommendations, then check out the rooms in person. In low season—January or April—don't be pressured into taking a room you don't want; in most cases, there are plenty available.

Many times rates at hotels and pensions vary significantly even within the same categories. After choosing where you want to stay, you'll need to decide whether to take full or half board, or only breakfast (see below). Make sure to ask if any reductions are available. You may get a special rate by staying a full week or by staying through Friday night and leaving on Saturday, the day most ski weeks turn over.

Make sure that you understand exactly what the room rate includes. Are the listed prices for the room or are they per person? If you insist on getting clear information at the start, it makes your trip much more pleasant.

Country by country

Hotels in different European countries are organized and run by different standards. These standards affect how the hotels are listed and what amenities you can expect within their various categories.

Accommodation in Italy and France is controlled by a government rating system which is too difficult to explain and often seems to make no sense. Hotels grouped within the same category with similar room rates often vary greatly. Some regulations produce confusion, such as a requirement in Italy that to be classified as first class, a hotel must have at least 40 rooms. Thus, some 36-room hotels with fabulous rooms and perfect service are listed as second class.

Hotels and other accommodations in the mountains are usually far cleaner and the service far superior to what you normally find in the rest of France and Italy.

Switzerland, Austria and Germany are no-nonsense countries. The hotels are clean and neat. The rating system is based on stars, with the highest rating being five stars, which means luxury class. The hotels tend to be accurately rated. In these countries it is actually hard to find a real dive.

One fact of life in the mountains during the winter season is the requirement to take at least two meals, or half pension (see below), in the hotel where you are staying. During high season this requirement is firm, and some hotels may even insist on full pension. The price is well worth it in most cases. In your hotel search, however, ask several locals which hotels or pensions have the best food. This research should also enter into your decision on where to spend your week in the resort.

Season by season

The best season to stay in any resort hotel—and to eat at any restaurant—is low season. This is normally from December 1 through the weekend before Christmas, then again from the weekend after New Year's through the first weekend in February, and again from the end of March through the month of April. The exact dates vary. Be sure to check to see when the low season starts and finishes.

In low season the resorts are not packed to capacity, so the kitchen and hotel staff have time to provide exceptional service. In addition, the on-site facilities, such as sauna, steamroom, pool or exercise room tend to be less crowded.

Pensions

Pensions are usually smaller, family-run affairs that cost significantly less than hotels. The pension guest in many cases feels a part of the family.

Some lodgings have a bath and toilet in the room, others have the bath and toilet down the hall or just next door. Most pensions recommended in this book have rooms available with private bath and toilet. If you do not mind a semi-private arrangement, you can request that type of room and save even more.

Many pensions, especially in the mountains, offer full restaurant service and will include all three meals in the price during the ski season. Many require that you take at least half pension (see below) when you stay for a week. It usually is well worth the price.

Bed & Breakfasts

These are what the name implies: room with breakfast only. Normally, you cannot take lunch or dinner there. This means heading out to discover local restaurants.

The Bed & Breakfast arrangement is often the least expensive in a mountain town, other than staying in private homes or apartments. Do not let yourself be fooled by the low price, though. Remember, you will have to pay for your meals in restaurants, which will add significantly to your costs. Although pensions and hotels may appear to cost more, when meal prices are taken into consideration they may really be a bargain.

Garnis and Bed & Breakfasts (essentially the same thing) do offer several advantages. First, you have a chance to try different restaurants and different styles of cooking during your stay. Second, you can often save money by eating less. Hotel menus include a full meal with all the trimmings and each is priced on the assumption that you eat everything on the daily menu. You may only want to eat a plate of spaghetti and be on your way. In other words, you pay only for what you eat.

"Full pension/full board" or "Half pension/half board" That is the question

Full pension, or full board, means that your hotel will provide breakfast, lunch and dinner each day of your stay.

The meals are served at set times in most hotels and pensions. If you miss the mealtime, the establishment is not required to provide an alternative meal (but some of the better hotels will offer you a meal in a smaller grill rather than in the main dining room).

When you agree to full pension, ask whether the hotel has either a box lunch to take with you or a coupon arrangement with a restaurant on the slopes. If the hotel does not have such an arrangement, you will be required to return to the hotel for every meal, which can really cut into skiing time. (Or, simply forgo the meal even though you are paying for it.) This could be an important consideration when deciding between hotels.

Half pension means that the hotel will offer breakfast, plus one additional meal, normally dinner, every day of your stay. Often referred to as half board, this is often the best arrangement. You are free to eat what you want and where you want during the day while on the slopes. If you plan to go out on the town to dine at a special restaurant, you can arrange to have lunch at the hotel that day and be free for dinner elsewhere.

In high season many hotels require you to take full pension. But in low season you can often get the room at half pension only, or with breakfast only.

The basic meal is all that is included in the full- or half-pension price. Any wine, water, extras, changes from the menu, coffee or liqueurs are billed as extra charges.

What is breakfast?

Depending on where they come from, it's called petit déjeuner, Frühstück, desayuno, or prima colazione. Here is a primer on what you can expect.

In Switzerland, Austria, Germany and Italy's Val Gardena region, breakfast means yogurt, cold cuts, cheese, jams and jellies, butter, rolls and endless coffee or tea. In some hotels, you get boiled eggs and juice—all included in the breakfast with the room.

In France, Spain and most of Italy, breakfast means a basket of rolls, sometimes a few sweet rolls, butter, jam and jelly with coffee or tea. Juice and eggs are almost always extras.

Staying in apartments or chalets

An economical alternative to staying in a hotel, pension or B&B is to take an apartment or chalet. They are often scattered through the town and offer reasonably priced accommodations. It's exactly the same as renting a condominium at a U.S. ski resort.

Apartments are most popular in Switzerland and France, and the Italians are now beginning to get their apartment rental arrangements organized.

They come in all sizes. You can rent a studio, which is perfect for a couple, or an apartment for four, five, six or eight people. The price per person drops considerably as the size increases. These are fantastic bargains: the daily cost can be as low as $15 to $30 per person if two share an apartment.

Units are normally rented with a fully equipped kitchen, all utensils and a dishwasher. Bed linen and a clean-up are sometimes included; in other cases there are charges for them. Check also for a utility fee: it may be included, or you may pay for the electricity used at the end of the stay.

You can cook your own breakfast and as many meals as you want, which will save a lot of money. There is usually a supermarket nearby—often on the ground floor of the building. Grocery prices are about the same as, or slightly higher than, those in a large European city.

If you decide that you would like to stay in an apartment or chalet, contact the resort tourist office and ask for a listing of the units that will be free when you're going to visit. The tourist office will send you a list; make your choice and return the information to the tourist office. You will usually have your confirming correspondence with the owners.

If you arrive with no arrangements, the tourist office will make several calls and send you off to see several apartments and speak with the owners.

The leading apartment and chalet rental firm in the world is Interhome—in some resorts it virtually controls the apartment rentals. Interhome has offices in Britain and in the United States. In the U.K., contact Interhome Ltd., 383 Richmond Road, Twickenham TW1-2EF, United Kingdom; tel. 01-8911294. In the U.S., contact Interhome at 124 Little Falls Road, Fairfield, NJ 07004; tel. (800) 882-6864, fax (201) 808-1742.

Staying in a private home

Private homes at many resorts will rent out rooms. These rooms are normally very inexpensive, with prices ranging between those of a Bed & Breakfast and an apartment. If you are traveling alone, a private home is often the best bargain you can get.

Staying in a private home can give you a better feel for the local scene: you pick up hints on the best places to go on the slopes and in town, and in many cases you will find yourself treated like a friend of the family.

Start at the local tourist office. It has addresses and phone numbers of the families who rent out rooms. The tourist office often will call and make arrangements. Ask to see several rooms and then make your choice.

In some cases, the room price includes breakfast but the arrangements vary from house to house. Expect to pay $15 to $30 a night, depending on the resort and the season.

Make sure that baths or showers are included in the price; if not, ask for the price and the best time of day to take a bath or shower. (Hot water can be at a premium just after the slopes close for the day.)

Staying in British-style ski chalets

Ski Chalets have recently become one of the most popular ways for British skiers to stay and ski in style, without paying whopping hotel rates. What the rest of the skiers of the world haven't yet realized is that they can use them too.

A chalet takes the convenience and informality of an apartment and the amenities and gourmet cuisine of a hotel and lumps them all into one fantastic package. Chalets are often converted private homes or small hotels, fully catered (breakfast, afternoon tea and snack and three-course dinner with wine), and run by professional hosts who cook, clean, and do the shopping. Many are ski-in/ski-out or near the slopes and even employ their own ski guides to get their guests acquainted with the mountain.

Chalets are best suited for young, sociable skiers looking for an easy way to form a group of friends to eat, ski, and party with (some chalets sleep up to 35 people!). Chalet-goers should be easy-going and not too squeamish about sharing bedrooms (there is a charge for unused beds or rooms), but in return you will stay in some of the nicest accommodations around with a group of people who may challenge even your apres-ski and nightlife stamina.

Staying in a chalet, you'll also be able to customize your own vacation. While the meals and service included in the basic price are first-rate, there are a number of extras for you to choose from if the basic package just isn't enough. When you book your vacation, be prepared to specify if you want vegetarian meals, premier service (with even more amenities and gourmet cuisine!), or even, packed lunches for the slopes, etc.

One thing to remember: chalets can be a great alternative for families (with discounts for children and nanny services at an extra charge); however, many of the chalets listed by various travel companies do not accept children under 16 unless you book the entire chalet. If you are travelling with children, you will probably need to look for smaller chalets for your family or inquire about special family chalets that will cater to your needs.

Chalets are available at most major French resorts and at a few Austrian, Swiss, and Italian areas as well. There are a number of tour holiday operators to call or write to for information. Be aware that most prices they will quote include one-week's lodging, food, ski guides plus round-trip airfare from London (or snowtrain from Calais), so be sure to tell the sales agent if you are not travelling from the U.K. All companies below have discounts for large groups and for children. The major tour operators are as follows (individual resort chapters list which ones provide chalets in the area):

Crystal Holidays (Internet: http://www.crystalholidays.co.uk E-mail: travel@crystalholidays.co.uk or Phone: 0181-399-5144) claims to have the largest service, with chalets in almost all resorts in Europe.

Inghams (0181 780 4444; e-mail Travel@inghams.co.uk) has incorporated Bladon Lines Chalets and has an impressively long list of chalets at major ski resorts in France, Austria, Switzerland and Italy.

Simply Ski (0181 642 25641; e-mail ski@simply-travel.com), Chalet World (01952 840 462) and Thomas Cook/Neilson (01733 335513) have chalets for rent at most French resorts and a very limited number in Switzerland and Austria. First Choice (0990 557755) also has chalets in France and Austria.

Ski Mark Warner (0171 393 3168) has a limited number of chalets but a wider selection of chalethotels (larger, more hotel-like but only a little bit more expensive than chalets).

YSE (0181 871 5117) is the place to call in Val d'Isère, with a number of chalets that range from moderately to very expensive.

We mention Ski Chalet availability in each resort, however please refer back to these pages for phone, fax and internet connections.

European skiing basics

What should a skier expect when arriving at a European resort? Culture shock aside, there shouldn't be too many surprises, because the U.S. ski industry has been modeled to a great extent on the long-established European resorts.

In most cases you will be able to ski into the town or village where you are staying. Of course, this doesn't apply if you are staying in a city such as Innsbruck, Salzburg or Interlaken.

The weather

A friend had just arrived in Switzerland from New England the week before Christmas and we were getting ready to go skiing. Her preparations amazed me. She began by putting on lots of bulky clothing: sweaters, a jacket and other Arctic-expedition paraphernalia.

"Whoa," I said. "What are you doing ? You want to be able to move on the mountain, don't you?"

"I don't want to be cold," she replied.

"Well, you'll melt if you dress like that," I said.

After this argument she reluctantly agreed to take off half of the clothing and risked taking my advice to wear only a turtleneck, a sweater and a windbreaker.

The point is this: Skiing in Europe is not a freezing proposition. The weather is very mild in the mountain areas. Even in the coldest sections of the Alps, the winter daytime temperatures hover at around 20 degrees Fahrenheit. Windy days, few and far between, usually herald a coming snowstorm.

What to wear

Try to dress in layers, and because temperatures are relatively mild, you will rarely need more than a ski jacket over a turtleneck shirt. On most days, a turtleneck worn under a light sweater and a windbreaker will be more than enough. Don't underestimate the temperatures, though; they drop rapidly when you're sitting in the wind on a long chair lift ride. Europe's heavy use of T-bar and poma lifts will help keep you warmer, although American skiers may swear at staying on their feet.

Protection from the sun

Europe's resorts are no different from any others when it comes to sun, especially in spring. Sunburn or snow blindness can ruin any vacation, so use sun screen and lip protection, and always wear glasses or goggles. The glasses do not have to be tinted; the glass itself stops most harmful ultraviolet rays. Goggles are even better, especially on overcast days when they help you find trail contours.

General snow conditions

Snow in Europe is not as dry as Utah or Colorado snow, owing to lower elevations and milder climate. Nor is it ice half the time as in New England, because of more constant temperatures.

Generally, the slopes are not as carefully groomed as those in the U.S., and relatively consistent snowfall obviates the need for extensive snowmaking equipment.

The best snowfall seems to take place in January, making both January and February good months for skiing. Plan to go in January if you can, since February and March are also the most expensive times to ski, except for the Christmas, New Year's and Easter holiday periods. The week before Christmas is normally a pretty good time to go, but chancy.

Spring skiing sees the Alps at their finest, with prices at most resorts again at low-season levels. If you want an adventure head off-piste with an instructor for spring skiing. In his company you will learn the best times to ski different areas as the day progresses and the sun warms the snow. The secret is to get onto the run just before you begin breaking through the crust and then move to the next section of the mountain.

Insurance

You really do not need to bring any special documents other than a passport for traveling in Europe. Before you go, take a close look at your health insurance to be certain you are covered in case of an accident. Most policies provide worldwide coverage, some are limited in the case of skiing accidents, and others group skiing accidents under the broad category of "accidental injury," which may mean that your deductible will be waived. Know what coverage you have. If you do not have enough, arrange to buy special ski insurance. Your agent should be able to point you in the right direction.

Several companies offer this insurance and surprisingly (amazing what you can find in the fine print) some credit cards include similar insurance if you purchase your airline ticket or pay for your vacation with the card. In addition, you can purchase ski insurance once you arrive at the resort. *Carte Neige* in France is easy to purchase at most resorts. Local tourist offices have details.

Photocopy important papers

Make a photocopy of your passport pages showing your photo and personal information, and write down your passport number. Also, make photocopies of your airline tickets and the credit cards you'll be taking.

Make two copies: Keep one with you, separate from your passport, tickets and credit cards, and leave the second copy with a friend or relative.

If you somehow lose everything, these backup records will be invaluable. The passport copy will help in getting a replacement at an overseas consulate or embassy. The ticket copy may help in getting a replacement and alerts the airline to look for a stolen ticket with that number. The credit card numbers will make reporting stolen cards and limiting your liability much easier.

Telephones in the Alps

The telephone system in Europe works well, especially in this section of the continent. At the end of each resort section we have included the local prefix for the resort, the equivalent of an area code in the U.S. If you see a number in parentheses preceding another phone number it is normally a town prefix.

The prefixes are normally noted as a zero followed by one to five digits, then after a closed parenthesis or dash, the local number follows. When calling inside the same country, you must dial the entire prefix including the zero; however, when calling the resort from outside that country you would dial the country code, then the prefix without the zero, then the local number.

In France you will notice that there is no city prefix. It is included in the eight digits which make up the number. Only Paris has an additional prefix.

If calling a resort from within Europe, just dial the country code as shown above, including the double zeros. If you are calling the resort from the U.S. you must dial 011, then the country code without the double zeros, then the prefix withour the zero, then the local number.

Country codes are as follows:

Austria:	0043
France:	0033
Germany:	0049
Italy:	0039
Spain:	0034
Switzerland:	0041

If you see phone numbers of varying lengths even within the same resort, it is not necessarily a misprint. In the Alps the phone numbers are not all the same number of digits—in fact, the main number of a hotel often has a different number of digits than its fax number.

Calling from Europe to the U.S.

It is simple to direct-dial from any of these European countries to the U.S. The prefix for the U.S. is 01 in most countries. Then dial the area code and your local number.

It is often easier and also allows you to avoid excessive hotel charges if you use AT&T's USA Direct service, or the similar MCI, LDDS and Sprint World services. They each allow you to call an operator toll-free in the U.S. who will connect you to the U.S. number and either charge the call to your credit card or make a collect call. The charges are always at the maximum operator-assisted rates, which are higher than might be expected when direct dialing from home to Europe, but much less than calling through a European hotel telephone switchboard to the U.S.

Credit cards and travelers checks

Most large resorts and full-fledged hotels accept major credit cards, but don't expect the smaller pensions and hotels to accept them. The normally accepted cards are American Express, Diners Club, Visa and MasterCard (called "Eurocard" in Europe). You can leave store credit cards and Discover cards at home.

Some resorts allow skiers to pay for lift tickets with credit cards but they are few and far between. It is best to come prepared with adequate cash or travelers checks to cover your expenses. American Express offers the best-known travelers checks, but in the Alps almost all are easily exchanged.

In Germany, Switzerland and Austria credit cards are accepted by restaurants and hotels but not with the frequency they are taken in the U.S. In France, Italy and Spain, however, credit cards are accepted for virtually all transactions from car rentals to some taxi cabs.

You can get cash advances in local currency with a MasterCard or Visa at most banks in the Alps. In France and Spain cash machines are the most convenient means of getting Francs or Pesetas and often provide the best exchange rates. But plan ahead—there is a limit on daily withdrawals. So don't wait until the last day when you have to settle your bills to head to the cash machine.

Credit cards often have advantages you wouldn't think about. They offer toll-free numbers for assistance in finding doctors and lawyers should you need them. Most credit cards also have a buyers protection plan that may insure gifts you buy from theft and damage during your travels. And some cards will help with arrangements back home should you have an unfortunate accident.

Changing money

The basic rule of changing money at a bank applies at ski resorts—even more so than in most places. Hotels and restaurants that accept travelers checks almost never give you a rate of exchange equal to the one you can get from a bank. Plan ahead and save yourself the difference. If you want to change a small amount of money, it is often better to exchange it at your hotel, because you normally will not have to pay a minimum exchange fee.

The cash advance service is available from many banks and automatic bank machines as well. Use your credit cards for a cash advance or your bank card. Though you pay a service charge (which you pay to change money anyway), you will be getting the best interbank exchange rate with the credit card. Using a credit card for advances is an advantage when playing the exchange rate game. In fact, if you use your credit card in preference to travelers checks when possible, you save money on exchange fees and often get better exchange rates.

Taking your own equipment

Most airlines will allow you to check your ski equipment onto your flight for no additional charge. However, check with the airline for their policies. Most airlines consider skis and ski boots one piece of luggage and they become part of your three free pieces of luggage. Some airlines, such as Iberia, simply don't take skis.

Upon your arrival in Europe, have a word with the personnel in the baggage-claim area to find out where to pick up your equipment. Skis are often delivered to a separate part of the baggage area.

Renting equipment

You can rent all the equipment you'll need at your resort. Ski rentals—depending on the quality ski you want—range from about $6–$20, with discounts for periods of three days or more and weekly rentals running $33–$75. Bring your own boots, however, because these are extremely important to your comfort. We have yet to find rental boots that are comfortable. If you rent boots, expect to pay $3–$8 a day, or $16–$37 a week, depending on the quality of the boot.

Taking photos in the snow

The best souvenirs of any vacation are the pictures you bring home to share with friends. What's more, photos help you to remember the good times you had, the places you visited and the people you met.

Standard and automatic cameras, however, do not make it easy to take good photographs on ski slopes. The overall brightness of the snow and sky often confuses light meters and automatic exposure systems. Many travelers have returned home with pictures that are washed out and underexposed, or in which the snow looks like a dirty sheet rather than the sparkling whiteness they remembered and hoped to catch on film.

Follow these tips to get the best results when shooting photographs in the snow:

- Try to have the sun somewhere in front of you when you take any picture in the snow. This allows you to capture the glistening sunlight and the texture of the snow.
- If shooting into the sun with a manual camera, close down the camera's f-stop to its smallest aperture (highest number). The sun then appears with a starlike flare effect.
- With a manual camera, remember that additional light is being reflected off the snow. In order to make allowances for this backlight, open the camera's f-stop about two stops. The best solution is to meter directly off the subject or the palm of your hand, then take the picture.
- With an automatic camera, override the automatic feature or select the plus-two f-stop setting.
- Snow heightens the effects of ultraviolet rays. A UV filter helps insure accurate colors. When shooting black-and-white photos, use a yellow, orange or red filter to heighten contrast.
- Your camera gets cold and so does the film. This means slower speeds unless you keep the camera warm. Try to keep it inside your jacket until ready to shoot.

Meeting Europeans

Take along a small notebook for jotting down names and addresses of people you meet at the resorts, or to note special things that you enjoyed and want to pass on to other friends. Don't be afraid to follow up some of the contacts you make on the slopes or at the resorts. Europeans are usually sincere when they invite you to come and see them. They tend to make the invitation out of sincerity rather than an assumed obligation. If you plan to spend some time in Europe or plan to return there, the people you meet can enhance any trip, if you stay in touch.

Resort locals can also add to your knowledge of the country by recommending special ski runs that may be obscure, by suggesting a good wine or hot drink to enjoy after a day of skiing, and by explaining which local specialties you should order in a restaurant or at your hotel.

Christmas, New Year, Fasching and Carnevale

These are major holidays in Europe and are still observed as family affairs for many Europeans. During Christmas and New Years, make sure that you have reservations at a restaurant if your hotel plan doesn't include board. Many smaller pensions and hotels have traditional dinners and often you are expected to wear a jacket and tie for the holiday dinner.

For New Year's Eve, if you are planning to be out for a celebration to ring in the new, make a reservation, or else you may spend it watching CNN on the hotel TV.

Fasching is a period just before lent of merriment, especially during the weekend and Monday and Tuesday before Ash Wednesday. If you are going to be in a resort, you can join in with the locals if you have a costume. Bring something simple or buy face paints and make yourself up for this crazy time.

Etiquette on the slopes

The Austrian Tourist Office lists 10 rules for the slopes, which, although not especially profound, make good sense and should be followed by everyone.

1. Keep equipment in good condition.
2. Do not endanger others or destroy property.
3. Ski in control, keep weather and terrain in mind.
4. It's the uphill skier's responsibility to avoid the skier below him. Give other skiers a good safe margin.
5. After stopping, look around before starting again.
6. Get up quickly after a fall and do not stop in blind spots on the trails.
7. If you walk up a slope, keep to the edge of the run.
8. Obey all signs and markers.
9. You are obliged to help injured skiers. Protect them from further risk and get first aid.
10. If you are in a skiing accident, you are required to furnish identification.

Dealing with European lift lines...or lack of them

One major difference between skiing in Europe and the United States can be seen in lift-line etiquette. In the U.S., lift lines are relatively orderly: a line for singles is maintained along the far right or left, and nearly everyone takes pains to avoid stepping on or skiing over another skier's equipment. The result is that you almost never get jammed together as you move through the lift line.

Not so in Europe. Although the lift lines in various countries on the Continent differ as to the degree of pushy behavior, in general they are a free-for-all. Until you reach the point where barriers have been set up to funnel skiers into the lift, there are no controls. He who moves the fastest and shuffles forward the most aggressively is usually the first to get up the lift. While there is a mild effort not to blatantly trample over each other's skis, you may presume that your equipment will be stepped on no matter what you do or how angry you appear to be.

Here are some tips to handling lift lines:

• Before you enter the line, see whether it turns to the right; if so, go to the far outside left of the line. If the line turns to the left, go to the extreme right. If you have ever tried to turn a sharp corner with skis on, you will understand the wisdom of this. There is no mercy shown in the lift line. Once stuck on the inside of a sharp turn within the barriers, you are in trouble—there is no room to swing your skis. I've seen skiers snap out of their bindings to make the corner.

• If the line is almost straight, get on its outside edge. You will quickly see that the mass of skiers funnel down the narrow barriers on either side. Those who get caught in the middle get squeezed from both sides and move about half as fast as those on the outside of the crowd.

• Another solution is to follow a snowboarder, whose board cuts a wider swath.

• Maintain a sense of humor. It will be tested, especially on weekends and school holidays.

• The best time to ski and avoid crowds is during lunch time. You'll find clear slopes, shorter lift lines and fewer frustrations. In Italy, Spain and France, the lines all but disappear as everyone heads in for a big lunch. The noon-hour difference is not as great in Switzerland and Austria.

European après-ski

Most of my friends begin careful planning of their European ski vacations months in advance. They pore over trail maps analyzing the percentage of beginner or expert *pistes* and calculate the working vertical meters; check into the annual snowfall and altitude; speak with other skiers hoping to learn secret bumps and jumps or discover powder pockets and unmarked trails through the trees; and brush up on their *parlez-vous français* and *sprechen Sie Deutsch*. I never developed the patience nor the consuming interest required to deal with such technical trivia and ski area minutiae. Since most ski area sizes and verticals in Europe dwarf those of U.S. resorts, I figure someone else can spend their time comparing the intermediate-to-advanced run ratios and lift capacities per hour . . . at a recognized European resort it's hard to go wrong. For me, one all-important decision-making factor overshadows all other considerations—how hot is the après-ski action?

Basic après-ski knowledge is as important to a successful vacation as a perfected stem christie. The consummate European ski connoisseur skis tightly packed bumps, then jostles shoulder to shoulder in Austrian bars, foxtrots cheek to cheek in Swiss ballrooms or discos until daybreak in France.

Austria

Austria boasts beer-spilling, dance 'til-you-melt, don't-wait-to-take-off-your-ski-boots après-ski starting as the slopes close. Admittedly, some resorts such as Lech and Zürs are more appropriate for a Quaker meeting, with excitement normally generated by the intonations of a local zither. But for the most part, Austria is where Europe's young skiers gather to ski hard, then pack themselves into mountain huts, town bars and pulsing discos for the night.

The après-ski parties kick off in midafternoon as hundreds of skiers jam themselves into tiny mountain huts lining the runs back into town. These huts, originally designed for a dozen farmers and their cows, heat up when schnapps, beer and wine mix with boisterous and unrestrained singing. Drink orders are by hand signal since verbal communication gets lost in the din. After managing a couple of shots of schnapps and a beer or a *Jägertee* (tea laced with 180-proof Austrian Stroh rum) the true party animal weaves down the last kilometer to town for "tea time." This "tea time" has no resemblance to the Park Lane in London. Here, top tea-time gasthauses are identified by scores of skis—in racks just outside the door, piled in the snow or leaning against the pub walls. Inside it's a Turkish bath. Loud disco music pulses, sweating après-skiers dance and drink in ski suits, and ski boots are a badge of the partygoer who just can't wait.

Between 7 and 8 p.m. the tea parties dissolve as if someone had struck a massive gong: it's time to stagger or dance back to your hotel for dinner. Later, at about 11 p.m., discos begin to crank and friends who may have met at tea time begin to party again until the wee hours.

The best party resorts in Austria, surprisingly, are the least famous. They are packed with blond Scandinavians, young tireless British skiers, uninhibited Dutch, and indefatigable Germans as well as Austrian locals. These young Europeans want both excellent skiing and nightlife at some of Europe's most affordable prices. Names like Saalbach, Ischgl, Mayrhofen, Söll, Kirchberg and Sölden would fill any après-ski honor roll. Among the resorts familiar to American skiers, St. Anton, Zell am See and Kitzbühel are the hottest spots.

Switzerland

In Switzerland après-ski is done with moderation. There is little if any singing in mountain huts; tea-time dances are unheard of; no one would be caught dancing in his ski boots, let alone sweating in public; and there are probably ordinances forbidding indiscriminate piling of skis in front of town bars.

Though arms may not be locked together, bodies don't sway around tables, singing never drowns out your beer order and *Café Fertig* (coffee laced with schnapps and topped with thick cream) is the warm up drink of choice versus the 180-proof Austrian version, Swiss mountain huts offer skiers the first stop on any après-ski safari and a great chance to meet other skiers. In the village, the après-ski scene is more comparable to a normal Friday night bar scene in Boston or Chicago than to revelry at Oktoberfest. There may be a D.J. or a one-man-band, but any dancing is restrained, while friends converse over a normal bar-room roar.

As in Austria, 7 to 8 p.m. is the witching hour—the crowds vanish and most revelers head back to hotel dinners. Discos begin to show signs of life again at about 11 p.m. . . . however, they are not normally crowded, except for weekends. Be that as it may, Switzerland does have its moments. Friends tell stories of me leading a 50-person early-morning snake dance over tables and chairs and behind a Verbier bar to the strains of songs sung by a female impersonator. (I swear I don't remember a thing.)

In Switzerland, unlike Austria, the best nightlife is found in the best known resorts. Quaint Zermatt and ritzy St. Moritz have something for everyone, Davos is quiet but nightlife can be found, and Saas-Fee has one of the best collections of bars and discos. The smaller, less-known towns are quiet . . . very quiet.

Germany

Germany, one would expect, might parallel Austria or Switzerland with its nightlife and après-ski, but the German resorts pale in comparison with Austria's robust exuberance and even fail to match Switzerland's pace. German resorts don't seem to attract the skiers from northern Europe who are on vacation to let it all hang out for a week. Garmisch, Oberstdorf and Berchtesgaden are more day-ski areas for Munich, Augsburg and Stuttgart and are normally filled with families or with singles who pack up and leave at night. Though nightlife in a Bierkeller can occasionally be as powerful as the brew Bavarian fräuleins serve, don't expect to find good times every night unless you are there with your own group.

France

Nightlife in France takes place in a different time zone from the lift operations. It doesn't even begin to commence until about 1 a.m. Disco lights don't dim until 3 or 4 a.m. For years, I never figured out how anyone manages both extreme skiing and serious nightlife in fabled après-ski resorts such as Courchevel and Megève. Every exuberant effort at a meaningful relationship between the two activities left me doing Mont Joly bumps on my posterior or a gimpy Travolta routine on the disco floor. I finally accepted what seemed to be the evident truth—some come for the skiing, others for the nightlife.

However, late one afternoon I sat contemplating, over a Pernod, yet another attempt at French après-ski when a case-hardened French ski veteran imparted his secret for mixing ski and après-ski in France, "I break the day into four parts—skiing, eating, nightlife and sleeping. First there is the skiing, which is done between ten in the morning and three in the afternoon." He glanced at me, asking with his eyes if I understood this basic premise. "Then I have a small glass of wine and talk with friends. I sleep from about five until nine in the evening. It is then time to eat, *n'est-ce pas?* Dinner is between ten and midnight. I visit the casino or discotheque from one until three, then sleep from three to nine in the morning." He returned his glass to the table with a flourish, and said, *"Voilà!* Is that so difficult?"

Never one to ignore advice from experts, I downed my milky concoction and headed home for a four-hour nap—the system works.

Courchevel, in the Trois Vallées, and traditional Megève are the late night jet-set capitals of French skiing. Val d'Isère is the most international with France's only crowded late afternoon après-ski bar scene and mercifully limited midnight to 3 a.m. activity. Tignes and Val Thorens are virtually devoid of nightlife, packed with skiers whose only interest is hurling themselves repeatedly down precipitous slopes, then heartily eating and soundly sleeping.

Italy

The Italians score with the best ski resort food anywhere in the world. Eating in this country is a religion. The Italians practice it with a fervor. It seems that the slopes empty for the minimum two-hour lunch. In the evening, after packing themselves into tiny bars for a bit of *chin-chin* with their friends and spirited discussions about the latest failures of the Italian soccer team, they once again make their sacred pilgrimage to the *tavola*. The evening meal takes another two to three hours. Discussions over an *espresso, frutta* and *formaggio* can easily prolong the meal by yet another hour. This only leaves an Italian reveler a window from about 11:30 p.m. to 2 a.m. to pack in nightlife. Yes, the discos do get packed, but the main activity is not dancing but talking—continuing where their group left off before dinner.

Spain

Here après-ski is very, very après. Nightlife here leaves the Swiss, Germans and Austrians in the dust. The Spanish dress to the hilt for their nightlife. You won't find any grunge groups. This is a land where the young want to look good and very fashionable.

The main action starts around midnight and might not really reach full steam until 1 or 2 a.m. Naturally, there is some spirited social "martini time" as the lifts close. Then a ski area version of the paseo and discussions over tapas take place about 7 p.m., but then everyone seems to disappear. They all reappear later for dinner. "Later" in Spain means about 8:30 p.m. in the Pyrenees and about 10 p.m. in the Sierra Nevada. Dinner ends about midnight and then the disco and dancing scene wakes up with flamenco, salsa or pumping European-techno music. Closing times stretch until 4 or 5 a.m.

So, what's my favorite? I career wherever there's a party. After too many hangovers and too many friends telling me what a great time I had, I'm sure that I'm no expert on how the party ends. I do know how it gets going. Austrians may start earlier than the French but don't have the same glitz, the Swiss may officially frown on wildness but secretly enjoy it, Germans still have a corner on the best beer, the Spanish show the most spirit and Italians claim the best food. Virtually every European dances, most speak English, smiles abound and, as always, the rest is up to you.

Charlie Leocha

To carry on with après-ski traditions check out the recipes in The World's Greatest Après-ski Drinks and Cocktails of the Florida Keys on the internet at http://www.cocktail.com.

When in the Alps...
A first-timer's guide to skiing in Europe

T-bar (tee-bar), n. 1. *Skiing.* A rolled metal bar or beam, with a cross-section resembling a T, used primarily to transport skiers up moderate slopes where constant contact with the ski surface can be kept at all times (not to be confused with definition 2).
    2. (*Alpine slang*) A European chair lift with unpadded seats.

Perhaps the first indication that things are done a little differently in Kitzbühel than in Killington comes when, instead of the constant *pull* of the T-bar, the uninitiated American begins to feel a *lift* in the seat of his or her long underwear. It's not enough that most T-bar rides in Europe are longer than the average American's commute to work in the morning, they also drag skiers up some very steep terrain.
    Welcome to Europe.
    Though the days of T-bars providing virtually all access to Alpine slopes has given way to more civilized chairlifts, almost every resort in Europe can still claims far more T-bars than found in all U.S. resorts combined. The good news these days is that you can spend your entire vacation on chairlifts using T-bars only to access the tucked-away trails.
    Try to remember that skiing is fundamentally a struggle of man against mountain, and anyone in the Alps for the first time carries something of a handicap. Here are a few pointers to help even the odds.

The mountains
    My first attempt at glacier skiing began ten-thousand-five-hundred-six feet, seven-and-one-half inches above Kaprun, Austria, on top of the Kitzsteinhorn peak. I was equipped with everything the resort brochure suggested I would need for summer skiing: brightly colored "jams," T-shirt, factor-infinity sunblock, sunglasses, and just for insurance, a blue jean jacket. Practically the only thing I hadn't packed was protection against freak blizzards with gale-force winds capable of dropping eight inches of snow in the 45 minutes it

takes to reach the summit of Kitzsteinhorn from the valley floor—a critical oversight.

Anyone who has ever skied powder in a blizzard wearing shorts and a blue jean jacket will not soon forget it, nor himself be soon forgotten. While Kapruners no doubt recall to this day the *Amerikaner Dummkopf* with the high, shrieking voice, for my part I will always remember that in Europe the weather in the valleys may have little bearing on the doings up top.

The drinking

Europeans don't encourage drinking on the slopes—they require it. I first learned this bit of skiing etiquette from a gentle Austrian giant named Hans, a friendly but persistent chalet owner in Mayrhofen who along with *Brötchen* and hot coffee served his own homemade schnapps from an unlabeled jug. Swilling straight gin at 7 a.m. is one European custom that takes some getting used to, and it was always teary-eyed and hoarse congratulations on a potent batch that I offered old Hansee.

While the drinks change depending on the area, nowhere in the Alps are skiers far from the pause that inebriates. That is especially true in Austria's Arlberg area, where skiing and drinking has been refined to something approaching high art. Thirsty skiers never even have to leave their slats at several ski-in, ski-out drinking stands such as the Ulmer Hütte above St. Anton, and at several ski-in bars above Lech. A favorite at such pit stops is *Jägertee,* a warm and delicious concoction of tea, spices and an all-purpose Austrian rum called Strohs (in a pinch, also useful for stripping old wax off your skis). In Bavaria they prefer *Glühwein,* hot red wine spiked with a local kicker, then heavily spiced with cloves and other goodies. The drink that sets the Swiss to yodeling is *Café Fertig,* strong, dark coffee with lots of sugar and kirsch (cherry) schnapps. *Obstler*—a fruit schnapps frequently combining apple, pear and plum—is a favored defroster throughout the Alps, while the mountain cafeterias of France and Italy often sport a larger wine selection than the restaurants back home that require reservations.

The eating

Speaking of reservations, don't expect to get served without them at La Marmite above St. Moritz, even though this gourmet restaurant is in the station atop Corviglia. As is rarely the case in restaurants that rate a mention in the Michelin Guide, however, the maître d'hôtel at La Marmite does not frown on ski boots.

While their devotion to the sport of skiing is undisputed, Europeans are generally not ones to allow their passions to clash. Rather, the spectacular views and exhiliration that so endear skiing to them are used as spice to enhance their love of good food. Though everyone who has skied Europe has his or her favorite moutaintop eatery, for sheer drama few can match the revolving Piz Gloria restaurant perched atop the Schilthorn in Switzerland's famed Jungfrau region. A set piece in the movie *On Her Majesty's Secret Service,* the Piz Gloria offers diners a 360-degree panorama unparalleled in the Alps, and a pitch-black run worthy of an 007. Just tell them the name is Bond. James Bond.

Other standouts include the mountain lodge restaurant in the Hotel Seegrube, which sits 5,700 feet above Innsbruck, Austria and is reached by the Hungerburg funicular railway; Switzerland's Top of Europe complex on the Jungfraujoch above Interlaken; and the rustic ambiance of La Datcha at Solaise, above the French resort of Val d'Isere.

The adventure

There exists in every adventure an element of uncertainty, and when in the Alps for the first time it is enhanced by your ignorance—other than in broad, continental terms—of where exactly you are. We're not talking here about minor factors as to which side of the mountain you're on, because let's face it, all the villages have funny, foreign-sounding names anyway. We're talking about not knowing which country you are in.

I embarked on one such adventure when I followed my skis down an inviting run just over the ridge of Testa Grigia, above Zermatt, Switzerland. When I hit the village below, I sensed that something was wrong. Somewhere between the top and the bottom of the run, the staid, clipped tones of Switzerland had been replaced by loose, wild-chatter Italian. So in true continental fashion, I invested my lunch money in a bottle of Chianti and quietly contemplated the strange ways of the Alps from a sidewalk *trattoria* in Cervinia, Italy.

Only when I returned to the lift, someone informed me that strong winds had closed the gondola, and the lift operators had thrown up their arms in true Italian fashion and gone home for the evening. Now, I had already heard the horror stories of French crevasses, German lift lines and Austrian schnapps. In fact, probably the only one I hadn't heard was the one about being stranded in a foreign country with no money for the four-hour bus ride back to Switzerland, no passport for the border and no embassy in sight. As an American novice in the Alps, however, you will find there's a first time for everything.

James Kitfield

Cross-country

All European resorts are not equal as far as cross-country skiing is concerned. Although this book focuses on downhill resorts, nearly all have excellent, well-developed cross-country facilities, easily accessible.

There are several areas in Europe which are considered the *crème de la crème* of cross-country regions, as follows:

Seefeld, Austria: Our top choice in all Europe is Seefeld, which hosted the 1964 and 1976 Olympic cross-country competitions. Nearly 100 miles of cross-country trails are maintained and most of the circuits lead from the Olympic Sport and Convention Center. Accommodations are outstanding and reasonably priced. In addition, an international atmosphere makes foreign visitors feel welcome. A challenging 18-mile circuit, with 15- and six-mile loops make up the heart of the trails.

For more information contact: Tourismusverband, A-6100 Seefeld, Austria; tel. 05212-2313.

St. Moritz, Switzerland: One of Europe's greatest. A paradise for the true cross-country fan. No one talks long about cross-country skiing without bringing up St. Moritz. This elegant resort has a remarkable network of 75 miles of trails in the immediate area, and there are about 200 miles of cross-country circuits on the valley floor and frozen lakes in the region. St. Moritz also has a mile-long lighted trail for night-skiing fans. The course of the famed Engadiner Ski Marathon race is nearby. St. Moritz is a great place to vacation for the skier who seeks cross-country only and demands great variety.

The Jura, France: Europe's greatest cross-country ski adventure is a 120-mile trek across the highlands of the French Jura region, which stretches from Belfort along the Swiss border toward Geneva. Nearly 40 percent of this mountain region is wooded, and the connecting trail, called the GTJ (Grand Traverse du Jura) is a superb run. The trail sections are difficult, ranging from 3 to 29 km. each, as you make your way from Maise, near Belfort, nearly 120 miles to La Pesse, south of St. Claude. There are inns all along the trail.

For details on the Jura trek, write GTJ: Office du Tourisme Regional, Place de l'Armée Française, F-25000 Besancon, France.

For general information on cross-country all-inclusive trips in the Jura, write Accueil Montagnard-Chapelle-de-Bois, F-25240 Mouthe, France; or A.G.A.D.-La Pesse, F-39370 Les Bouchoux, France.

Kaiserwinkl, Austria: This is a cross-country skier's paradise in the Austrian Tyrol a few miles off the autobahn between Munich and Innsbruck. The towns of Schwedt, Kössen and Walchsee have combined their trails for nearly 85 miles of Nordic runs. Each town has its own cross-country center and the interconnected circuits branch out from the centers. For information: Fremdenverkehrsverband, Postfach 127, A-6345 Kössen, Austria; tel. 05375-6287.

The Black Forest: Germany's best-known cross-country area. The best circuits are around Titisee and up to the slopes of the Feldberg, the highest mountain in the region. Altogether there are about 600 miles of trails in the Black Forest with nearly 75 miles of loops near Feldberg. Perhaps the most challenging runs are from Neustadt, where organized cross-country groups kick and glide for nearly 60 miles, with planned stops at hotels and guest houses along the way. We do not cover this region in detail —call the German tourist office for information.

Allgäu, Germany: An interesting network of cross-country trails is found in this region. The trails branch off from the ski towns of Oberstaufen and Immenstadt. Part of the network includes a great marathon-length, 26.2-mile loop. Contact the German tourist office for further information.

Kronplatz, Italy: Few resorts mix the pleasures of cross-country and downhill better than those in Italy's Pustertal. Here in the south Tyrolean region, Kronplatz resorts boast nearly 90 miles of cross-country trails branching out from the central town of Bruneck (Brunico, in Italian) below the Kronplatz plateau.

If you come in January, you can take part in the 35-mile cross-country race, which begins in Innichen (San Candido, in Italian) and ends in Antholz. The 24-mile race course ends at Olang. Downhill skiers can try out the slopes from the 7,462-foot Kronplatz summit.

For more information contact: Crontour, I-39031, Bruneck, Italy; tel. 0474-84544.

The following descriptions will let you compare cross-country possiblities. For more details about individual resorts—hotel, restaurant, nightlife and other information—see the resort chapters. We provide a ✔ rating from one ✔ to five ✔s.

Austria

✔✔ **The Arlberg:** If you are only looking for occasional cross-country skiing, this will provide limited alternatives to the downhill religion in this region. The St. Anton/St. Christoph side of the mountain offers the best cross-country with 40 km. of trails. Lech and Zürs are extremely limited with only 17 km. of trails.

✔✔✔✔ **Badgastein:** There's more than enough variety in the Gasteiner Valley for cross-country enthusiasts: The resorts have a total of 90 km. of trails. The six trails from Bad Hofgastein offer the most variety. There's an added incentive for cross-country here because anyone who completes 75 km. earns a bronze medal. The gold is awarded for 1,000 km., but clearly is beyond the reach of the one week-vacationer.

✓✓✓✓ **Innsbruck:** Perhaps the second or third greatest cross-country area in all Europe, with over 60 miles of trails in the immediate area of the city. Instruction is excellent. And as an added bonus, the marvelous resort of Seefeld is only a short bus ride away. Plus there is excellent cross-country skiing on 130 km. of trails in the Stubaital which is part of the overall regional ski pass.

✓✓ + **Ischgl and Pasnaun Valley:** An average network with 50 km. of trails in Ischgl and another 40 km. in Galtür.

✓✓✓✓ + **Kitzbühel/Kirchberg:** Some of the best cross-country trails in Austria. Great variety and some 200 km. of trails.

✓✓✓ **Mayrhofen/Zillertal:** Mayrhofen has 20 km. of tracked trails which connect with the connecting valleys. Zillertal has a good variety with over 60 km. of track.

✓✓✓ **Montafon:** When all 11 main resorts in the Montafon valley are considered, this is an excellent cross-country area. But you'll need a car to drive to the various areas—no single resort has enough variety for a vacation. Over a dozen trails total about 45 miles.

✓✓✓ **Saalbach-Hinterglemm:** Extensive cross-country in the Leogang sector with 40 km. of prepared trails. Saalbach itself has only 8 km. and Hinterglemm claims 10km. of cross-country trails.

✓✓✓✓ + **Schladming:** Excellent cross-country trails especially on the Ramsau side of the valley, where a wide-open plateau just below the Dachstein glacier offers perfect terrain. Plan to stay in Ramsau, because the other towns are a long trek away from the best cross-country areas.

✓✓✓ **Söll:** Average Austrian cross-country with some great connecting trails between Söll, Hapfgarten, Elmau and the Brixen Valley.

✓✓✓✓ **St. Johann in Tirol:** Excellent choice for cross-country vacation. Not as much variety as Innsbruck-Seefeld, but the nearly 100 km. of trails are maintained for the serious skier. Changing rooms, first aid and restaurant facilities are excellent on the loops. Also a great choice for the skier who wants to mix downhill with cross-country.

✓ **Oetztal:** Meager offerings. Less than 10 miles of trails.

✓✓✓✓✓ **Kaprun/Zell am See:** One of the best-kept secrets among cross-country devotees. A great network of hundreds of km. of trails and a connection to an additional 40 miles of trails in the neighboring valley. The ski school also has good courses.

France

✓✓ **Les Arcs:** Moderately interesting trails with only 20 km. up at the resort. More trails are in the valley with 40 km. at Peisey/Vallandry and 25 km. at Bourg-St-Maurice.

✓✓ **Chamonix:** Moderately interesting trails total about 43 km. in the valley. Best combined with downhill; not good cross-country on its own.

✓✓ **Les Clusaz:** Good cross-country possibilities with 42 km. of trails on Plateau des Confins ringing a frozen lake and another 19 km. on Plateau de Beauregard where kick-and-gliders share trails with downhillers. Trail fees are FFr25 a day for adults and FFr15 a day for children.

✔✔✔ **Megève:** Surprisingly good network of four main trails totaling nearly 100 km. in the Megève-Combloux area. The resort has excellent cross-country events such as night skiing. There is good variety and some good challenges on endurance. A long trail goes from the Mont d'Abois cable car to St.-Nicolas-de-Véroce.

✔✔✔ **Flaine and Le Grand Massif:** Flaine itself has not much to recommend it to cross country skiers, however the region is excellent. Virtually all trails are down in the valley between Samoëns and Sixt or at Les Carroz. Samoëons has a 50 km. loop, Les Carroz has 64 km. of trails with some limited night skiing.

✔✔✔ **La Plagne:** Champagny-le-Haut on the far side of the ski resort near the village of Champagny-en-Vanoise has excellent cross-country opportunities 79 km. of marked and groomed trails. Stay there rather than in one of the La Plagne purpose-built resorts. There are also 12 km. of trails between the main villages and an additional 32 km. of trails near Montchavin and Montalbert.

✔✔✔ **Morzine:** This resort has almost 100 km. of trails spread around fove different areas. You can find other cross-country in the Portes du Soleil region at Morgins with 20 km., and Chapelle d'Abondance with 22 km.

✔ **Tignes/Val d'Isère:** Poor choice for real cross-country skiers. Only short trails with a total of 15 km. of prepared track.

✔✔✔ **Les Trois Vallées:** Above-average network of trails by French resort standards. Nearly 100 km. of prepared loops spread over the rolling valley countryside. Méribel has almost 35 km. around the altiport sector, Les Menuires has about 30 km. between the village and St. Martin de Belleville. Courchevel has night skiing. Val Thorens sticks pretty much to downhill pursuits.

Germany

✔✔✔ **Garmisch-Partenkirchen:** You'll discover long, exceptionally scenic trails with nearly 200 km. of loops in the Garmisch-Partenkirchen area when linked with the Isartal and Loisachtal. Above Garmisch, in the Graswang Valley, there is beautiful cross-country skiing that takes you near Linderhof, perhaps the most beautiful of Ludwig's Bavarian castles.

Italy

Italy has developed an extensive cross-country system in the shadow of Mont-Blanc as well as in the Madonna di Campiglio area and in parts of the Dolomites.

✔ **Cervinia:** oOnly has a total of 15 km. of trails. If you want to kick and glide go somewhere else.

✔✔✔ **Courmayeur:** Good and scenic cross-country skiing beneath the towering Monte Bianco in the Val Ferret only minutes from the town. There are four major itineraries with 35 km. of prepared trails. The nearby resort of La Thuile has a 10 km. loop in its valley.

✔✔✔ **Pinzolo:** Only a few kilometers, or a 20-minute drive, from Madonna di Campiglio, Pinzolo was the site of one of cross-country's major 24-hour endurance races. The area near Campo Carlo Magno, in the **Madonna di Campiglio** area, has an expert cross-country course with a 30 km. trail.

✔✔✔ **Cortina d'Ampezzo:** Good cross-country area with more than 75 km. of prepared trails. A good place to mix downhill with cross-country. This resort was once the site of the Olympics. Cross-country itineraries take skiers into Austria and from village to village in the Dolomites.

✔✔✔✔ **Val Gardena:** Kick and glide along high mountain plateaus such as the Alpi di Siusi. The trails, though scenic, are short. There are over 1,000 km. of trails in the Dolomiti Superski region with 100 in this valley.

Switzerland

✔✔ **Arosa:** The cross-country trails are modest (about 30 km. of prepared trails) but well maintained, and from the beginning of December into April you can count on a variety of trails through the countryside.

✔✔✔ **Champéry and Portes du Soleil:** There are 150 km. of trails in the Swiss Portes du Soleil area. The best will be above Champéry linking Champoussin, Les Crosets and Morgins. Night skiing is in the Grand Paradis area of Champéry.

✔✔✔ **Crans-Montana:** There are three main trails with a total of about 45 km. Your best cross-country adventures will probably be on the nearly seven-mile loop on Plaine-Morte glacier. A long trails traverses the resort from Aminona to Plan Mayens.

✔✔✔✔ **Davos:** Excellent cross-country trails in classic Alpine scenery. Altogether there are nearly 75 km. of prepared trails with seven main loops kept in top condition. Good choice for cross-country. There is also a 7.5 km. loop that is lighted for night skiing. The Davos trails link with Klosters.

✔ **Engelberg:** Low-rated for the cross-country with less than 15 miles of prepared trails. Auto-free Melchsee-Frutt has nine miles of trails.

✔✔✔ **Flims/Laax:** Good cross-country area with a total of nearly 70 km. of double-tracked trails in Flims, Laax and Falera areas. Cross-country adventure treks with guides are offered in this region.

✔✔✔✔ **Gstaad and Weisses Hochland:** When considered with Saanen and other areas of the Weisse Hochland, cross-country is one of the best in Switzerland with nearly 100 km. of trails, guided adventure treks and very good instruction.

✔ **Jungfrau Region:** Grindelwald, with about 30 km. of trails, is the best in the area. They have good instruction. Wengen and Mürren are both very limited. The most beautiful trail is a 10 km. circuit in the Lauterbach valley near Lauterbrunnen. There is also nearby cross-country in Bonigen near Interlaken.

✔✔✔ **Klosters:** Moderately interesting, with nearly 60 km. of tracks split between four prepared trails. Combined with the next-door town of Davos, the area is quite extensive and beautiful.

✔✔✔✔ **St. Moritz:** See above(Pg. 42).

✔ **Saas-Fee:** Extremely limited with only an 8 km. trail.

✔✔✔ **Verbier:** The connecting network is not exceptional. The best cross-country facilities are at the base of the Châble cable car with about 30 km. of trails. There are short 4 km. loops at the village level and up on the glacier.

✔ **Zermatt:** Cross-country is only a side pursuit, with limited trails totaling only about 25 km. There is a lighted 3 km. course.

Resort-to-resort, valley-to-valley, and cross-border skiing in Europe

Resort to resort, valley to valley

Jagged peaks surround us towering starkly against a cobalt blue sky. Not a chair lift is in sight, not even another skier outside our small group. Here there are no children calling out to their friends, no ski instructors lining up their beginning classes, no clusters of skiers relaxing at mountain chalets, no lift lines, no droning grooming machines. All we can hear is the wind whistling across the crusty early-morning spring snow. The sun is just beginning its silent softening of the snow. Above us the peak of Le Cheval Noire seems to rear in anticipation.

Yesterday we arrived from the U.S., Canada, Sweden, Denmark and the U.K.—all English-speakers. Today, with fluent English-speaking guides, we test our "peeps" and prepare to cross over the divide from the lift-served, groomed and patrolled terrain of Valmorel into a parallel world of raw, natural, untamed pitches and ever changing snow. This is the best of all worlds—taking a resort's lifts to the ridge separating the untamed from the groomed, a chance to enjoy a touch of backcountry skiing without arduous hiking and climbing.

The "9 Vallées" guides call this adventure "soft." That means most reasonably fit skiers can manage the skiing, short climbs and traverses needed to reach virgin pitches and move with the sun.

Nothing is predictable in this world—not the pitches, not the snowpack, not the path. The world changes dramatically with passing clouds and every time one moves from sunshine to shadow. There is only one constant—the only way back to civilization is down through this uncertain, exhilarating backcountry.

Below us, almost 6,000 vertical feet of untouched snow drops across wide-open pitches, then curls around outcroppings disappearing into small valleys winding through tight trees and brush. At the base of the run is a small mountain hut in the dorf of Deux Nants, abandoned by farmers and herders during the winter. Here a band of mountain men who had hiked up narrow paths from the valley below waits with fresh bread, sausages, paté, cheese and wine.

This was a morning most skiers find only in their dreams. But it is an adventure virtually every skier from intermediate to expert can joyfully discover. Though backcountry-ish valley-to-valley skiing once was the exclusive province of the expert, deep-powder skier and boarder, with expert guides and today's new equipment (such as wider skis), more and more skiers can savor the solitude and get to know the intimate personality of the Alps.

In the United States, forest service permits, environmental restraints and poor trans-portation from remote valleys makes backcountry skiing a real test of endurance. You not only have to find your way to the skiable terrain, but you also have to hike miles to find your way back to your hotel or condo. In Europe, the out-of-bounds regulations are much looser, the resorts more closely knit and the transportation system along the valley floors allows backcountry adventurers easier movement between accommodations.

Even with a more favorable infrastructure, skiers in the backcountry need guides who know their way around the region and who understand the snow as it changes during the day. They also need a system of moving their belongings from town to town while they ski the untracked slopes between them.

 Our trip was organized by the Association 9 Vallées, a team of guides which has led skiers and snowboarders through the untracked valleys divid-ing many of the major Alpine resorts. They arrange hotel, pension or moun-tain hut half-board accommodation for each night; transport luggage between accommodations; purchase lift tickets for each resort the group traverses; and provide beepers and other safety equipment.

The Association 9 Vallées is based in Tignes in the French Alps. They offer these valley-to-valley, resort-to-resort backcountry experiences for skiers from basic interme-diates to super-experts. They also have programs for snowboarders who can free-ride and can handle all types of snow, terrain and traverses.

Their most popular tour is called the Tarentaise Ski Safari. It can be organized for every level of skier. Depending on conditions, skiers will visit Val d'Isère, Tignes, Les Arcs, La Plagne, Courchevel, Méribel, Les Menuires, St. Martin de Belleville and Valmorel. It is a trip avid skiers will never forget.

This Association 9 Vallées safari experience is virtually snow-safe. The Tarentaise mountains always have plenty of snow at upper altitudes. More importantly, backcountry routes for differing levels of skiers can be found at all times of the year. The guides all speak English and they work with competent local guides who add a native flavor to the tours. The entire experience becomes more than simply a ski trip—it is a life experience.

Association 9 Vallées also organizes tours to the Dauphiné region south of Grenoble connecting Alpe d'Huez, Les Deux Alpes, La Grave and Serre Chevalier; through the Dolomites of Italy to resorts such as Val Gardena, Sella, Canazei, and Arabba; to the Italian side of the Alps joining four major valleys with Zermatt in the shadow of the

Matterhorn; as well as Heliskiing in the Valgrisenche of Italy.

The bottom line is that every tour is customized for each group. As the guides get a feel for new skiers, they may break the group of ten into two of five. Both will enjoy the same Savoyard hospitality and cuisine in every new valley.

Prices for these tours range from about FFr6,500—6,900 for the Tarentaise Ski or Snowboard Safari to around FFr6,000 for programs to the Dolomites, Chamonix, the Dauphiné and Monte Rosa. Ski touring *with skins* costs FFr4,500 for the Haute Route from Chamonix to Zermatt. These rates include your guide, lift tickets for all resorts, half-board accommodation with breakfast and dinner based on double occupancy, luggage transportation from hotel to hotel, avalanche beepers and powder leashes. You are responsible for your own ski equipment, single supplements, drinks with meals, lunches, mountain rescue insurance and cancellation insurance.

For more information contact: Association 9 Vallées, Hameau Le Franchet, 73320 Tignes, France. Telephone: (033) 479.06.51.77 Fax: (033) 479.06.44.89. They speak English and German as well as French.

Cross-border skiing in Europe

Skiers experience an undefinable altered state when skiing from one country to another. When crossing borders at high altitudes, there's no one checking passports (but bring it along just in case) and few customs checkpoints. You just sense that you've changed worlds. In the first village, a new adventure begins. *Grüetzi* changes to *buon giorno*, lunch shifts from schnitzel to pasta, locals jingle lire rather than francs and the personalities of the border opposites are never the same.

Cross-border skiing is a unique European skiing experience. Though tales of cross-border ski adventures abound, interconnected areas along the borders are quite limited. After exploring the Alps for the past two decades I have discovered only five sections with lift-connected cross-border skiing.

By far the most extensive lift-connected area is the Portes du Soleil, straddling Switzerland and France just to the south of Lake Geneva. The Zermatt, Switzerland-Cervinia, Italy connection beneath the towering Matterhorn is perhaps the best-known. Ischgl in Austria connected with Samnaun in Switzerland is unknown to Americans but packed with Austrians, Germans and Scandinavians. Courmayeur, Italy lifts connect with Chamonix, France, but you need a bus or taxi for the return trip; and the small resorts of La Thuile in Italy and La Rosière in France were connected just two years ago. If you dream of skiing over borders, pack your passport. These are the places to do it.

Portes du Soleil

This area sprawls across the French-Swiss border from Lake Geneva southward almost to Italy. Portes du Soleil claims to be the largest interconnected ski area in Europe. Though the Trois Vallées make a similar claim, I didn't survey these areas to validate either claim, both areas are massive. The Portes du Soleil is more rugged and demanding than Trois Vallées.

The two main Portes du Soleil ski centers are Avoriaz in France and Champéry in Switzerland. There are also eleven smaller resorts, four on the Swiss side and seven in France, tucked into the mountain valleys in the area. Champéry is a tiny centuries-old Swiss village that still hasn't realized it's an international ski resort. Barn odors waft through the main street, occasionally a small goat rides by in the back of a station wagon, tractors tow loads of hay and in the unpretentious bars townsfolk discuss the latest village ice hockey scores. But change is evident—in the past two years hotels have been renovated and upgraded and a sports complex and a new cable car have been completed.

On the French side Avoriaz is as much of an opposite as one could imagine. A skier arriving from Switzerland is dazzled by the glitz. Where Champéry is traditional, Avoriaz is a modern purpose-built resort. In Champéry you look hard for a building with more than four stories, but in Avoriaz condos tower twice as high. Nightlife on the Swiss side consists of updated oom-pah bands in smoky bars, while the French resort rocks with neon discos and simmers in dimly-lit bistros. Champéry still has its cows . . . Avoriaz has never seen one.

Wide-open, expert skiing, though, is the common denominator. All the resorts in the Portes du Soleil share the marvelous terrain. Beginners can stick close to the resorts and intermediates won't have a problem if they stay on the trails, while experts will be stretched by both the extensive off-piste skiing and the exhausting expanse. For super-experts, the "Swiss Wall" along the Swiss-French border between Avoriaz and Champéry offers as steep a challenge as any trail in Europe.

Zermatt, Switzerland - Cervinia, Italy

This is the cross-border experience most American skiers have heard about. A series of three cable cars brings skiers from Zermatt to the top of the Kleine Matterhorn where they drop down to the Italian resort of Cervinia. It's wine, pasta and scaloppini, then the return trip to Zermatt. The once interminable lines in Cervinia have been tamed by the installation last year of a six-person gondola system .

The resorts, though connected, are as different as pizza and fondue. Zermatt is the picture-perfect Alpine village overflowing with chalets, Cervinia a collection of unimaginative concrete hotels. Zermatt offers some of the most challenging skiing in Europe, which humbles most experts; Cervinia, on the other hand, makes beginners feel like pros. Zermatt works with Swiss perfection, Cervinia thrives on Italian smiles and good nature.

The cross-border trip will take a full day, including a stop for lunch. The last lifts up to the top and back to Zermatt leave at about 3:15 p.m. Lift personnel will warn you if there is impending bad weather. Heed their advice. The lifts up to the border crossing have been known to close, owing to high winds or whiteout conditions, and strand scores of skiers on the wrong side of the border. The only recourse is an expensive overnight or a four-hour bus trip over the St. Bernard pass.

Ischgl, Austria - Samnaun, Switzerland

This is a strange marriage. Both partners are small villages deep in narrow mountain valleys. Ischgl is a pulsing world-class resort, Samnaun a tiny hideaway. Ischgl harbors hundreds of hotel rooms and thousands of apartments, Samnaun's hotels can be counted on one hand. Ischgl vibrates with après-ski; Samnaun sleeps.

Ischgl is a perfect ski resort. The town is packed with accommodations ranging from excellent to budget, but with no super-luxury establishments. The skiing is high above the town and reachable by three separate gondola lifts. Once on top, Ischgl's slopes seem endless. The wide-open skiing at the higher altitudes is shared by Switzerland and Austria. There is plenty of solid skiing to keep any enthusiast smiling from the opening of the lifts to closing time. And after the lifts shut down, Ischgl's après-ski is among the best in Europe.

The run from Austria down to Samnaun is a long intermediate trail. Samnaun is a duty-free shopping area with inexpensive whisky, perfume and cigarettes. Skiers regularly cruise back to Ischgl with backpacks bulging with contraband.

Courmayeur, Italy - Chamonix, France

This is a one-way, short-term springtime relationship. When the snows settle on the mountains surrounding Mont Blanc, the Vallée Blanche opens high above Chamonix. This is one of skiing's grand experiences and can be initiated from either Chamonix, France or Courmayeur, Italy. A series of cable cars takes groups of border-crossing skiers up from Italy. At the top they are met by guides who lead them over the glacier and down to Chamonix. The expedition by cable car cannot be made in the opposite direction, from France to Italy. At the end of the day buses are organized to take skiers from Chamonix through the Mont Blanc tunnel back to Courmayeur.

La Thuile, Italy - La Rosière, France

This is the newest of the interconnected international ski areas. It was linked only about ten years ago and is still undiscovered. La Thuile has been gaining popularity with the development of a giant resort complex, Planibel, featuring a luxury hotel and condominiums, with indoor pools, squash courts and ice skating. The main lifts leave directly from this hotel complex. The surrounding town has remained relatively unchanged. La Rosière is still a cluster of small hotels on the French side of the little Saint Bernard pass. Both resorts are frequented respectively by Italian and French skiers with little other international influence and very quiet nightlife.

Austria

If one were to ask any American, Canadian or Brit what they think of when the hear Austria, chances are, they will say skiing. Austria has marketed the concept of cozy Alpine villages and trails winding through forested mountains so well that many people imagine perpetual snow whenever they hear the name. Reality is as enchanting as the marketing images. For skiers, Austria is a wonderful mix of old-world chalet-studded villages, lift-linked ski areas, lively mountain huts, rustic wood-paneled restaurants and exceptional nightlife and après-ski.

For Americans making their first trip to Europe and finding their way into an Austrian village, there is a sense of *deja-vu*. When Americans and Canadians want to create the perfect ski resort, they send experts to study Austria. And when they build, they mimic Austria. Look at the town of Vail in Colorado, the Austrian-style condos throughout New England and the massive wooden chalet hotels constructed in Sun Valley. Though others may try to copy the Austrian style, the essence of Austria cannot be canned or crated and taken to new mountain. It needs to steep in deep valleys and evolve over centuries in hidden villages.

As important as atmosphere, mountains, chalets and skiing may be, Austria has another secret ingredient. This is a country where sincere hospitality is deemed as important as great skiing. Austrians seem to go out of their way to make visitors feel at home. From the ski instructors to the hotel managers to the restaurant owners, they seem to take genuine pleasure in knowing that you have enjoyed yourself in their country. Their word for this feeling of warmth and congeniality, *Gemütlichkeit*, sums up what they strive for as hosts.

Theories abound as to why certain Austrian resorts are touted by veteran skiers as the most friendly and fun in the Alps, and the simplest probably strikes closest to the truth—the locals are comparatively unspoiled by success. The chances are better in Austria than in any other Alpine country that your ski instructor or Bed & Breakfast hostess works on a farm in the summer, or did until recent years. Switzerland is more efficient, France is more sophisticated and Italy has a greater flair for food, but Austria is down-home friendly.

After countless visits to ski resorts around the world, every contributor to this ski guide can attest that no one knows how to have fun like the Austrians. In our Après-ski chapter we outline the traditions of schnapps on the slopes, tea time after skiing and late night partying.

Although Austria is one of the skiing capitals of the world, it is very affordable; this, with the hospitality you'll encounter, will help to ensure a fond memory of your trip.

Austria's Alps

The Austrian Alps have three major chains—the Northern Limestone Alps, the High Alps and the Southern Limestone Alps. The Northern Limestone Alps have many natural valleys and are home of resorts such as Lech, St. Anton, Ischgl and Kitzbühl. The High Alps are anchored by the Oetztal resorts of Sölden and Obergurgl and stretch to Innsbruck, Zell am See and Kaprun. These High Alps have few easy passes across them. Passes like the Brenner Pass and the Grossglockner are famous for their road, tunnel and bridge engineering which allows traffic to move north and south. The Southern Limestone Alps form the border with Italy and Slovenia.

The mountain elevation in Austria is lower than that found in Switzerland, France or Western Italy. But Austria gets plenty of snow in normal years since the winters get colder the further east one travels in the Alps. However, in the early winter and spring seasons, make sure to check the snow cover before planning a major skiing vacation.

Home of the Alberg Method

Austria's name has forever been linked with the development of modern skiing. It was in the Arlberg that a unified system of skiing was devised. Previously, skiers used a form of telemarking, but Hannes Schneider based his ski technique on the snowplow which allowed skiers to maintain control in all phases of skiing.

His methods were popularized through movies and then set up the first organized ski race, the Arlberg-Kandahar. Later Hannes Schneider would travel to the United States, after being released from Nazi prison for banking concessions, and start the first ski school in the Mt. Washington Valley, the Eastern Slope Ski School.

Driving in Austria

The Austrian highway system has just introduced a program of highway toll stickers somewhat similar to that used in Switzerland. Anyone driving on the Autobhnen must purchase this sticker. Drivers of automobiles can purchase the toll sticker at automobile associations before arriving in Austria or at a gas station near the border. Once inside Austria, additional stickers can be purchased for periods from one week to one year at post offices, tobacco shops and most gas stations throughout the country.

Most rental car companies have decided that they will be passing along the tolls to customers renting cars in Austria (see the rental car/Autobahn toll section page 23).

A note on prices

Most of the prices in this section reflect approximate current winter season rates and should be used as a guide only. They may change at any time. Where 1996/1997 prices were used, they have been clearly identified.

Prices are given in Austrian Schillings (Sch), and when last checked the exchange rate was about Sch13 to US$1; Sch20 to UK£; and Sch9 per Cdn$1.

When is high season?

High season: Christmas to New Year's, February through late March.

Low season: Before Christmas, January after New Year, and from late March through April closing.

For the exact high/low season weeks outside of holiday periods, check with the individual resorts: their dates may vary because of local school holidays.

☎ **Telephone country code for Austria is 0043.**

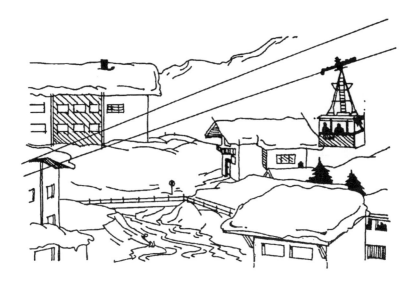

The Arlberg
Lech, Zürs, St. Anton, St. Christoph, Stuben

If you were to question a group of aficionados about the top Austrian ski destination, odds are they would say the Arlberg. This western region was, after all, where the country's skiing took its first faltering steps in 1907 and where legendary ski hall-of-famer Hannes Schneider perfected the technique which was brought to the U.S. in the thirties as the Arlberg Method.

So dense are the skiing opportunities there today, the area has been broken down in the collective skiing consciousness into the various town-resorts that compose the region. St. Anton, Zürs and Lech, even the smaller hubs St. Christoph and Stuben have become independent by-words in skiing circles. Separated by miles of snow fields, peaks and passes, they are all linked by a single Arlberg ski pass, by lifts and shuttlebuses to form a skiing wonderland for intermediate and expert skiers. Once remote—and inaccessible after heavy snow—the area is now only a three hour drive from Zürich Airport.

Strictly speaking, St. Anton and St. Christoph belong to the Austrian state of Tyrol, while Lech, Zürs and Stuben are part of Vorarlberg. Most skiers, however, skip such technicalities and simply call them the Arlberg slopes.

One of the allures of the region is that, while the individual resorts share the same snow, they all have a totally different flavor. Picking among them, you are sure to find your ideal.

St. Anton is a bustling resort, a party town. Straddling the main rail line and the major highway linking Innsbruck and Bregenz, it's the easiest to reach. The downside is that it fills up, especially on weekends. The upside is that the town has the most beds and the most varied accommodations in the region, ranging from low-cost pensions to ritzy hotels. A new quad chair has reduced the lift lines.

Stuben, a tiny and unpretentious village on the fringe of the Arlberg, is proportionately quieter, with more moderately priced hotels. Thanks to the Albona lift, which rises in two stages, the connection with the St. Christoph/St. Anton is easy. Because of its altitude it can be colder than the other resorts, but Stuben has an advantage in the spring: its snow is still good when Lech and Zürs are winding down.

St. Christoph is the highest Arlberg village at 5,400 feet, a smaller, more exclusive and more expensive version of St. Anton. It's a good place to get away from it all. St. Christoph's lift lines can be long on weekends, but the morning lift lines are shorter, and the lifts start from the hotel doors.

Only a few miles apart at the point where the Flexen Pass ends in a snow wall in winter, **Lech** and **Zürs** are often grouped together. Yet they are independent and, in many ways, opposite sides of the ski-resort coin. Lech is a bustling, full-fledged town with all the accompanying excitement. On the shoulder of the hill and accessible only by cable car, one of its satellites—Oberlech—is a small, contained group of hotels. The other, Zug, is a tiny village hidden away down a tree-lined lane and perfect for families with small children and those seeking peace after 9 o'clock. Zürs, only minutes away up the valley, is a compact cluster of only 35 buildings, most of them luxury hotels. When celebrities go skiing in Austria, this is where they often stay.

Thanks to their location at the end of the valley, Lech and Zürs have shorter lift lines and less crowded slopes than the St. Anton side of the Arlberg. From any hotel it's less than a few minutes amble to the nearest lift and from there you can tour the four resorts until you find one that suits the moment's mood.

The Arlberg resorts may be ranked, from most to least expensive: Zürs, Lech, St. Christoph, St. Anton and Stuben.

Mountain layout

The available ski area is significant. Over 50 grooming vehicles prowl the slopes covered under the Arlberg ski pass, creating 163 miles of piste and leaving 112 miles of deep snow. The area is served by 85 lifts and cable cars.

Perhaps the resort that best characterizes the Arlberg is **St. Anton** (or Stanton, as many Americans pronounce it). In mood it's an endearing mix of Alpine rusticity and the most modern elements of international ski high life.

Throughout the Arlberg you'll encounter guest houses, shops and perhaps a *Wurst* stand or two named for the Valluga, the 9,220-foot rocky pinnacle—the high point in St. Anton skiing.

It is from near the Valluga summit, reached by cable car, that one of the great intermediate skiing cruises in Europe begins. The slope from the Vallugagrat (8,692 feet) is filled with hundreds of turns as you work your way down for at least an hour to the valley floor.

Experts can take the final section of the cable car to the top of the Valluga. After a difficult climb—accompanied by a guide only—they can ski down to Zürs.

You'll find less nerve-rattling skiing further down. We recommend the massive mogul field off the Tanzboden lift, where you'll see the best skiers bouncing from bump to bump, throwing in the occasional 360-degree turn for flair. New covered quad chair lifts will be replacing T-bars on the Galzig Plateau under the Valluga lift. These new lifts will allow an expansion of the Galzig area and eliminate a dangerous spot where ski trails crossed the old T-bar tracks.

The village of **St. Christoph,** which sits along the crown of the Arlberg Pass at 5,904 feet, is the other ground station for skiing this side of St. Anton.

The blue and red runs are cruises that offer great enjoyment, and there's good skiing for beginners from the base at St. Christoph. Once served only by T-bars and a tram, St. Christoph will now have quad chairs taking skiers up to the Galzig area.

The other ski area on this side of St. Anton is the Kapall, a 7,629-foot summit where you'll enjoy the two blue runs to the Gampen midstation at 6,068 feet. From Gampen continue through the trees into town, or drop over the ridge into the Steissbachtal and take the last half of the Valluga run.

When the crowds are too much or the snow turns to mashed potatoes, head to St. Anton's third ski area, the Rendl (6,888 feet). It's less crowded because the single gondola that serves these slopes is a longer walk than the cable cars to the other areas.

The mountain is shaded in the morning, which means it can be icy, but by afternoon the snow is in better shape than in the rest of St. Anton, especially in the spring. The best intermediate run is from the Gampberg summit (7,895 feet) back into the village. Snowboarders will want to test their monoskiing skills on the newly created half-pipe.

The area is also the scene for après-ski activities. Sun worshippers flock to Rendl Beach to catch the afternoon rays and sip "Absolut Dream," a Rendl Beach concoction made of peach schnapps and vodka.

Zürs and **Lech** can be easily skied together, but there is no real connection between St. Anton and Zürs and between Stuben and Zürs. However, as noted, guides take experienced skiers—experts with guts—from the Valluga down the Lech/Zürs side. To get back you have to depend on your car or a free postbus.

Either Lech or Zürs would qualify for resort status by itself, even if their lift passes didn't cover the entire Arlberg. In Lech, skiing centers on the Oberlech region, reached by a cable car and two chair lifts from the center of the town. A system of 16 lifts takes skiers up to 7,799 feet. This area will keep an intermediate busy for two days, and off-slope skiing will challenge experts. Opposite Oberlech is the Rüfikopf area, reached by a high-speed cable car. From here experts—real experts—can drop straight down the face to Lech, while intermediates can loop around or cruise down to Zürs.

Zürs is a bit tougher as far as marked trails go. All the runs from the top of the Trittkopf (7,985 feet) are rated intermediate, but most would rate a black diamond in U.S. resorts. Once again, experts can make their own trails straight into town. The Madloch side of the valley has six long intermediate runs and three long beginner runs. However, after the area has been well skied, you can venture almost anywhere on this side.

One of the great runs of the area is known as the White Ring, a three-hour circuit that swings around both sides of the valley, connecting Lech, Zug, Oberlech and Zürs. Take the lifts to the 7,997-foot-high Madloch Joch and then ski the red Madloch run around the back into Lech. To complete the circle, take the cable car from the middle of town to Rüfikopf and ski down and across to the base of the Hexenboden lift and Zürs. For Zug, detour off the Madloch and then come back up on the Zugerberg lifts. From there, it's a red-rated cruise down into Oberlech.

Stuben is our favorite bargain village in the region, tiny with only a few lifts. The best run is intermediate—from the Albona Grat (7,872 feet). Stuben is connected with St. Anton/St. Christoph by the blue-rated trail from the Albona midstation to a crossover tow at Alpe Rauz. From there, take the chair lift to Pfannenkopf and work your way down into St. Anton.

Mountain rating

Intermediates run the show in the Arlberg region. St. Anton is overwhelmingly red and blue on the ski map, with some challenges that merit expert skills.

Although Lech and Zürs cover all the levels, prepared runs favor the intermediates on up. Experts will never get bored thanks to the wide-open expanses of off-trail powder, among the best in all Europe.

 ## Ski school (97/98 prices)

St. Anton advertises one of the largest ski schools in the world. There are 250 instructors registered here and a total of nearly 700 in the area. This is the home of the Arlberg Method, the standard for ski instruction throughout the world. The school classes form up in amazing numbers each morning at the base of the Kapall. Lech and Zürs also have 300 instructors, with classes forming at the base of the Schlegelkopf lift, in Oberlech and in Zürs. Another ski school, Skischule St. Anton, has 40 instructors and promises small, friendly classes. Ski school prices are approximately the same throughout the region.

If you can swing it, hire a private instructor for at least a day. One contributor noted, "In less than five minutes and without having to look back at me once, my instructor pinpointed my many bad habits. We spent the rest of the day hammering them out of my system. In the process, I easily skied slopes I'd have thought twice about before. And I lost my American-bred fear of mass mogul fields after I learned the right techniques for attacking them."

In addition, guides know where the best conditions are, and will give you an excellent overview of the extensive ski area. If the budget is slim, spread the costs out among several people.

Ski school prices for St. Anton/St. Christoph

Private lessons cost Sch2,050–2,220 per day and Sch1,850–1,990 a day after three days of lessons, with Sch160–170 per each additional person. Half-day private lessons cost Sch1,400–1,495.

Group lessons are Sch500–525 a day; Sch1,150–1,250 for three days; Sch1,470–1,525 for five days; and Sch1,520–1,580 for six days.

The cross-country ski school prices are the same as for Alpine lessons.

Ski school prices for Lech/Zürs

Private lessons cost Sch2,170, with Sch160 for each additional skier.

Group lessons cost Sch510 for a day; Sch1,140–1,050 for three days; and Sch1,750–1,570 for six days. Children receive additional discounts for multiday lessons.

 ## Lift tickets (97/98 prices)

The bargain is the Arlberg pass. Note: Arlberg region guests get about 7 percent discount for six days or more.

High Season Rates	Adults	Children
half day (from noon)	Sch350	Sch210
one day	Sch465	Sch280
two days	Sch890	Sch530
six days	Sch2,310	Sch1,390
seven days	Sch2,610	Sch1,570
fourteen days	Sch4,230	Sch2,540

There are discounts of around 20 percent for seniors (men over 65 and women over 60). Children 6–15 get a reduced rate. There is also a 15 percent discount (approx) in low season (until December 23, most of January, late March and April).

Accommodations   (97/98 prices)

The first price below is for the special one-week Pulverschnee packages offered in January (similar packages are offered throughout the year priced within 20 percent or so of each other). The packages include seven days room with half board, and six-day ski pass. The daily rate is the per-person price in high season for a double room. Rates are 15–20 percent less in low season.

St. Anton (telephone prefix 05446)

Hotel Schwarzer Adler (tel. 2244, fax 224462) from Sch9,870–11,020. Great atmosphere in a place doing business since 1570. Daily: Sch1,390–2,240 (half pension).

St. Antoner Hof (tel. 2910; fax 3551) Sch11,370–13,120. Hotel is away from the main downtown street and a three-minute walk away from the action and five minutes to the lifts. Daily rate: Sch1,860–2,390 (half pension).

Sporthotel (tel. 3111; fax 311170) Sch10,180–11,020. In the pedestrian zone. Here you can arrange a week's lodging, dance in the nightclub, and enjoy a steak in the restaurant. Daily rate: Sch1,620–2,100.

Hotel Mooserkreuz (tel. 2230; fax 3306) Sch9,270. On the edge of town. Sauna and indoor swimming pool, plus at the end of the day, ski back to the hotel. Daily rate: Sch1,360–1,480 (half pension).

Grieshof (tel. 2331; fax 202417) Sch11,580. Located across the street from the Mossmer, this four-star hotel boasts an indoor swimming pool and friendly service. Daily rate: Sch1,780–1,980 (half pension).

Montjola (tel. 2302; fax 23029) Sch9,340–9,970. The recent addition of rooms has not detracted from its cozy lodge feeling. About a three-minute walk (uphill) from the center of town. Daily rate: Sch1,100–1,750 (half pension).

Kertess (tel. 2005; fax 200556) Sch7,900-9,550. It's away from the center of town and quiet. Excellent cooking; friendly service. Daily rate: Sch1,780 (half pension).

Hotel Pension Rendlhof (tel 2951; fax 310050) Sch7,660–8,360. This hotel has received rave reviews from readers. It is only minutes from the center of St. Anton and out of the range of the late-night singing as revelers stagger home. Daily rate: Sch1,150–1,400.

Hotel Mossmer (tel. 2727; fax 272750) Off the pedestrian zone in an area that's quiet and close to the action. Ask for a room in the recently added wing, and pay due homage to the Mossmers' guard dog, Daisy. Daily rate: Sch650–800 (B&B only).

Ehrenreich (tel. 2353; fax 23538). from Sch7,800. Just minutes away from the lifts but away from the crowd, this quaint lodge looks over a mountain stream and the Ferienpark. Daily rate: Sch1,150–1,300 (half pension).

Ski Chalets: Inghams/Bladon, Chalet World, Ski Mark Warner, First Choice (see page 27 for phone, fax and internet addresses).

St. Christoph (telephone prefix 05446)

Arlberg-Hospiz (tel. 2611; fax 3545) Sch13,800–15,100 (without ski pass). The most exclusive spot on this side of the Arlberg. The restaurant is one of Austria's best. Daily rate: Sch3,400 (half pension).

Maiensee (tel. 2804; fax 280456) from Sch7,990–8,990. Next to lifts with all amenities. Daily rate: Sch1,090–1,790 (half pension).

Lech (telephone prefix 05583)

Hotel Post (tel. 2206; fax 2206–23) Attracts a slightly older upscale crowd, but is a beautiful and cozy hotel. Daily rate: Sch1,980–5,050 (half pension).

Almhof Schneider (tel. 3500; fax 3500–33) Sch25,910 Together with the Post, considered the best in town. It is cozy, not as formal as the Post, and more modern. Daily rate: Sch1,980–4,590(half pension).

Angela (tel. 2407; fax 240715) Sch14,220. This beautifully-appointed and ideally-positioned hotel is a real ski-in/ski-out spot with plenty of solitude in Lech. Daily rate: Sch1,580.

Arlberg (tel. 2134; fax 2134–25) Old elegance, slightly worn. Daily rate: Sch2,080–3,740 (half pension).

Berghof (tel. 2635; fax. 26355) Sch10,840—13,030. Top quality with sauna, whirlpool and tennis, but no pool. Daily rate: Sch1,300–2,500 (half pension).

Kristiania (tel. 2561; fax 3550) Sch15,410 A bit out of the mainstream but nice. Daily rate: Sch1,780–3,680 (half pension).

Krone (tel. 2551; fax 255181) Sch17,390 A hotel with every modern amenity and with an award-winning restaurant. Half board doesn't get much better. Sch1,025–1,940.

Sonnenburg (tel. 2147; fax 2147-36) Sch10,500–12,750 (half pension). In Oberlech above Lech, a car-free zone reachable only by cable car. Daily rate: Sch1,200–2,400 (half pension).

Haldenhof (tel. 2444; fax. 2444-21) Sch9,790–11,980 (half pension). A small family-owned hotel. It is the perfect Austrian inn. Daily: Sch1,080–1,980 (half pension).

Hotel Lech (tel. 2289; fax 22898) Sch8,040–10,790 (half pension). Daily rate: Sch900—1,600 (half pension).

Kristall (tel. 2422; fax 2422-3) Sch8,040–8,550. Central location and friendly service. Daily rate: Sch900–1,100 (half pension).

Pension Sursilva (tel. 2970; fax 2970-22) Sch8,040–10,090 (half pension). Good value and modern facilities. Daily rate: Sch870–1,300.

Hotel Central (tel. 2263; fax 226349) Sch8,040–10,090 This B&B has a terrific location and view as well as a nice bar. It allows you to sample the restaurants around town. Sch480-640.

Just outside Lech, in Zug, **Gasthof Rote Wand** (tel. 3435 ; fax 343540) Sch12,200—15,370 (half pension) is really special and has an indoor pool, health club, sauna and so on. Daily rate: Sch1,410–2,320 (half-pension).

Ski Chalets: Inghams/Bladon (see page 27 for phone, fax and internet addresses).

Zürs (telephone prefix 05583)

The packages in Zürs include ski school as well as accommodations and meals.

Zürserhof (tel. 2513; fax 3165) Sch15,350—17.680 (full pension). This is one of the most luxurious hotels in the Alps, in a class with the Palace in St. Moritz. Suites and mini-apartments cost Sch17,540—23,840 during the ski weeks in low season. Daily: Sch3,020–3,320 (full pension).

The other hotels in Zürs are all quite good. Try the **Albona Nova** (tel. 2341; fax 234112) Sch12,200—15,370 (half pension). Tucked round the back, away from the road and right by a lift, this splendid hotel has carved-wood ceilings, an intimate appeal. Daily rate: Sch1,850—2,400.

Arlberghaus (tel. 2258; fax 225855) Sch9,400–14,180 for the ski week or Sch1,280–1,930 daily rate with half board. The **Schweizerhaus** (tel.2463; fax 246327) is one of the least expensive: Sch8,490—8,580 for the ski week and Sch780 for the daily rate (Bed & Breakfast only).

Stuben (telephone prefix 05582)

Post Hotel (tel. 761; fax 7626) Sch9,200–10,080. A good choice for uncomplicated skiing with on-site ski rental, ski school and a bank. Daily rate: Sch780.

Haus Erzberg (tel. 729; fax 7294) Sch6,000—6,200. Small hotel (13 beds), includes breakfast only. Daily rate: Sch420–450.

Hotel Mondschein (tel. 511; fax 736) Sch8,400—10,500. Excellent hotel in historic 1739 building. Indoor pool, friendly atmosphere. Daily rate: Sch950–1,320.

Apartments

If you want to rent a vacation apartment, ask for the apartment listing brochure from each of the tourist offices in the Arlberg. They maintain a complete list of hundreds of apartments and chalets available in season.

In Lech, apartments can be rented with four beds for about Sch1,800 a day, high season. In Zürs, expect to pay around Sch1,950 a day. In St. Anton, a four-bed apartment can be rented for about Sch2,000 a day. These prices are about average; you'll also find them much more—and somewhat less—expensive.

 ## Dining

Our tip in St. Anton is the dining room in the **Hotel Kertess**. If food plays a big part in your ski vacation plans, book your room here too.

The **Schwarzer Adler** (tel. 2244) sets a table that brims with Austrian specialties. Prices start at Sch150.

To demolish your budget, we recommend the **Arlberg Hospiz** at St. Christoph where you can dine on sumptuous noodles, creamed mushrooms, roast duck and so on. Don't count on seeing Prince Charles on the day you've reserved, although he's numbered among its star-studded clientele.

Reasonably priced meals are always on the menu at the **Aquila Cafe** and **Grieswirt**. And don't leave St. Anton without a pizza from the **Pomodoro**—it's cheap and friendly, and you may see your ski instructor there.

On the mountain, the most popular spot is the cafeteria at the Valluga cable car's second station. Or head to the sit-down restaurant at the Galzig (2,050m).

In Lech, many restaurants have instituted a children's menu with a fixed price of Sch100. For good food try the restaurants in **Hotel Montana** (tel. 2460), which has the best wine cellar in town. The **Arlberg** (tel. 2134) is highly recommended with an Austrian-influenced gourmet menu. **Hotel Salome** (tel. 2306) gets good recommendations. **Hotel Krone** (tel. 2551) is a shrine of local cooking with exceptional use of local ingredients.

For nouvelle Austrian cuisine, try the **Goldener Berg** (tel. 2205) or **Brunnenhof** (tel. 2349). The **Hotel Post** (tel. 2206) and the **Schneider** (tel. 3500) serve excellent traditional recipes. **Restaurant Ambrosius** (tel. 2621; not expensive) has the best Italian in town with a fabulus anti-pasta buffet. Plus, it's bar downstairs is quite a scene after 10 p.m.

Just outside Lech, in Zug, the restaurants **Alphorn** (tel. 2750) and **Rote Wand** (tel. 3435) offer excellent food in the best of Austrian tradition.

For cheaper eats, try **Pizza Charly** (tel. 2339) for good Italian food and head up to **Gasthof Omesberg** (tel. 2212) for great traditional Austrian fare.

In Zürs, the best dining is in the **Zürserhof** or **Edelweiss** (tel. 26620) with a menu that changes weekly. Try the **Lorünser** (tel. 2254) and **Hirlanda** (tel. 2262), for excellent meals.

Après-ski/nightlife

In St. Anton's pedestrian zone, you'll be able to find something that suits your night tastes by simply taking a stroll. There are dozens of small bars and gasthofs.

Just to say you partied with the party animals, stop by the **Krazy Kanguruh,** with its reputation as the region's wildest watering hole. We can't praise it wholeheartedly: it's wild, but away from the center of town, and Bo don't know crowded till he gets there. Since you can't get there by foot, spare time on your last run down the mountain and pay your respects when the joint isn't as jammed.

Closing in on the Kanguruh for bad-boy status is the **Mooserwirt.** Its happy hour has skiers bouncing off the walls and the outside terrace, and there's often live music, unless out-of-control patrons force the town fathers to take away the bar's license until things cool down. This is another one that's tough to get to on foot; partyers who can't stand on their own two skis have been known to take the tops of the picnic tables and sled back into town.

Closer to town and somewhat more sedate are the hangouts at the **Post Hotel.** On the outside terrace, you can sip Glühwein and watch the last of the sun's rays climb up the peaks, or sweat it out in the two basement bars. Both feature live music, but one attracts the heavy drinking, heavy smoking young crowd, while in the other a slightly older group disco and polka ski kinks away.

If peace is what you're after, try the cozy **Valluga Bar** in town or the **Underground,** a popular British pub that rocks through the late afternoon into the wee morning hours.

Late night discos and karaoke bars abound—try your best off-slope maneuvers in the **Picadilly, Disco DropIn, Hacienda** or the **Kartouche.**

In Lech, many skiers spend the early evening hours in the **Pfefferkornd'l** before heading out to such discos as the **Hotel Almhof-Schneider.** A more chic after-hours address is the bar and disco at the **Tannenberghof,** or head to the **Hotel Krone** where there is disco and a good local crowd.

Anywhere you go to drink, expect to pay between Sch60 and Sch100 for a drink and a coat check fee of about Sch20.

Zürs has discos in the **Hotel Edelweiss** and **Hotel Zürserhof**. The most upscale is the Zürserhof. The **piano bar** in the Hotel Alpenhof is pleasant and **Ambiente** fills up for tea time and après-ski in the Sporthotel Zürsersee.

Child care

Ski courses for kids from age 4 are offered, as are a ski kindergarten, and babysitting services (from 2 1/2 upward). The ski school includes lunch with a drink and there are reductions if parents are also enrolled in the ski school. Hours are 9 a.m. – 4:30 p.m.

Ski school rates	St. Anton	Lech/Zürs	Stuben
one day	Sch710	Sch510	Sch490
three days	Sch1,750	Sch1,040	Sch1,300
six days	Sch2,400	Sch1,440-1,600	Sch1,620

Kindergartens, for children 2 1/2 and older, are available in all the resorts. In St. Anton you'll pay Sch525 a day and Sch1,580 for six days with lunch. Prices in Lech and Ober-lech are Sch500 a day and Sch1,330–1,420 for six days. Lunch is Sch80 extra. Open from 9 a.m.–4 p.m. Babysitting on a weekly, daily or hourly basis can be arranged through the tourist office.

In Lech, Hotels Austria, goldener Berg, Rote Wand and Sonnenburg all have private kindergartens.

Other activities

If you're an insatiable skier, other ski areas within close proximity are Ischgl and Innsbruck in the Austrian Tyrol and Malbun in Liechtenstein.

In addition to downhill, there's rodeling, cross-country skiing, snowboarding, paragliding, walking and skating. Heliskiing is available in Lech and Zürs.

St. Anton (tel. 2538) and Lech offer horse-drawn sleigh rides through the forest. The price for up to five people is around Sch800 for about an hour. Other activities include swimming, tennis and sightseeing. Shopping in the resorts is limited to ski wear and souvenirs.

Getting there

You'll probably fly into Zurich, although the trip can be just as easy from Munich or Innsbruck.

Driving from Zurich, take the autobahn to St. Gallen, then to Feldkirch and the Arlberg Pass (tunnel toll each way is Sch130). From Munich and Stuttgart, it is easiest to drive to Bregenz, then to Feldkirch and the Arlberg. From Zurich, it's a little over three hours by car, or take the train directly to St. Anton or Langen.

Lech and Zürs lie further up the Flexen Pass. Get off the train in Langen and take a bus up the hill, or get off the train in St. Anton and take a different bus.

Direct trains connect Langen with Cologne, Dortmund, Munich, Innsbruck, Salzburg, Zurich, Paris, Brussels and Calais. The Orient Express (800-237-1236) also makes a stop in St. Anton beginning in late March.

More convenient than the train is direct ski bus service from Zurich Airport to all the Arlberg resorts that runs on Friday, Saturday and Sunday. On Fridays departure is at leaving at 12:30 p.m. On Saturday buses leave at 10 a.m., 12:30 and 6:30 p.m. On Sunday two buses leave at 12:30 and 6:30 p.m. Fares are Sch500 one way and Sch800 round trip. The trip takes about three hours and at times can be quicker than driving since the bus drivers know how to avoid the weekend traffic jams. Make reservations through Arlberg Express (tel. 05582-226, fax 05582-580).

There is a Saturday bus connecting the Munich airport with St. Anton. Call Tiroler Landesreiseburo at 0512-43315 or 491626, fax 0512-392854.

Tourist information

St. Anton: Tourismusverband, A-6580 St. Anton am Arlberg; tel. 05446-22690, fax 2532. **Stuben:** Verkehrsverein, A-6762 Stuben; tel. 05582-399, fax 3994. **Lech:** Tourist Office, A-6764 Lech; tel. 05583-2161, fax 3155. **Zürs:** Zürs Tourism, A-6763 Zürs; tel. 05583-2245, fax 2982.

☎ **Telephone prefixes**
St. Anton: 05446; Stuben: 05582; Lech and Zürs: 05583.

Bad Gastein

Skiing may be the number-one pastime in the Gasteiner valley, but the area's popularity as a meeting place for European vacationers keeps it lively the year round. Austrians from all parts of the country head up the valley in winter. The area is a group of four ski systems: Bad Gastein, Sportgastein, Bad Hofgastein and Dorfgastein.

Curiously, skiing was not the original reason for the arrival of tourists; Bad Gastein first gained fame as a thermal spa. It is still Austria's top spa and one of the best-known in Europe. The therapy is based on submersion in radon-laced water. A curious hot spring-fed pool has been carved into rock for this therapy. Another form of the treatment takes place in the nearby town of Heilstollen. Here small trains carry those seeking the cure deep into abandoned mines where different chambers with high radon content and differing temperatures above 100 degrees F are visited according to doctor's orders.

Because of the spas, the resort attracted the upper crust of society and a rather etiquette-conscious clientele. The formality that developed over the years, especially in the grand hotels—many of which still have private thermal pools—continues today. The winter coat of preference will probably be fur, and the lineup of shiny automobiles in front of the casino often makes it look like a Mercedes or BMW showroom. Although spa visitors still cling to protocol, the modern skiing tourist has softened the stiff rules of decorum. This is a town where you can live elegantly, complete with black tie, or casually, never changing from your ski jacket.

Mountain layout

The best skiing is from the top station on the Stubnerkogel at 7,373 feet, where an exceptional intermediate run stretches nearly seven miles. This run, the Angertal, drops 4,264 feet. From the ground there is a lift connection to the Schlossalm area above Bad Hofgastein.

There's a challenging World Cup run from the sides of the Graukogel opposite the Stubner. The lift takes you up to 6,556 feet, and the black run takes you down (a side trail accommodates intermediates).

Also try Sportgastein, about six miles away and easily accessible by bus. The best of the runs is from the top of the Kreuzkogel. The new eight-seater Goldberg-Bahn gondola takes you to the top in 14 minutes.

At the top, a choice of four different trails awaits you. The best of them is the north trail, which is left unprepared and provides great powder skiing, given the right conditions. The nearly five-mile run covers a vertical drop of almost 4,950 feet.

Mountain rating

The valley, particularly Bad Gastein, is intermediate country, with the most notable exception being the World Cup course. It is a good place to tune up one's ski legs, leaving some spring in them for partying later. Solid experts, will enjoy the approximately dozen black runs, but once finished with them they'll be ready to move on. Experts should check out an off-trail group or a guide for a morning. Both will offer little-known runs down unprepared sections of the resort, and these should provide most of the challenge.

Lift tickets (97/98 prices)

The best choice is the Gastein Super Ski Schein, a combined ticket for the area resorts, linking 60 lifts and a network of buses and trains. These are high-season prices. Children are kids up to age 15.

	Adults	Children
one day	Sch400	Sch250
two days	Sch790	Sch480
three days	Sch1,120	Sch670
six days	Sch1,990	Sch1,190
seven days	Sch2,250	Sch1,390

Low-season prices are about 15 percent less.

Ski school

Six ski schools have a total of 130 instructors in the valley. In Dorfgastein, call 06433-7538; in Bad Hofgastein, call 06432-8485; and in Bad Gastein, call 06434-2260 or 4440. Average instruction price for one hour of private lessons is Sch450 an hour. Group lessons will cost: One day, Sch590; three days, Sch1,360; and six days, Sch1,650. Three-day cross-country lessons are Sch850.

Accommodations

Choose from a great selection of hotels in Bad Gastein and Bad Hofgastein. There is less variety in Dorfgastein nearer the entrance to the valley. Of the three, Bad Gastein probably offers the most European ski atmosphere, including a healthy helping of nightlife.

Our favorites in town are **Elisabethpark** (tel. 2551) and **Hoteldorf Grüner Baum** (tel. 25160), which remain excellent choices for accom-modations outside the town center. The Elisabethpark is the most expensive with daily rates from Sch1,250–1,850 for half pension. In the Grüner Baum, rooms are Sch1,150–1,850 with half pension.

Das Weismayr is a centrally located, 135-bed hotel (tel. 2594) offering traditional accommodations with sturdy old-style European furniture, thick carpets and tapestries. Rates are Sch846–1596 with half pension.

Hotel Mozart (tel. 2686) has rooms with breakfast from Sch425 a day, or Sch525 a day with half pension. Another budget choice is the **Hotel Stubnerhof** (tel. 29910); half-pension rates start at Sch320 a day, or Sch260 for B&B only.

In Bad Hofgastein try the **Osterreichischer Hof** (tel. 06432-62160, fax 06432-676051). This hotel in the center of the town has a country manor atmosphere. Rooms are Sch375–1,060 for half board or Sch340–930 for B&B only.

Ski Chalets: Inghams/Bladon (see page 27 for phone, fax and internet addresses).

Apartments

Most visitors stay in hotels and pensions or a few private homes in the Gastein valley. But vacation chalets are also available, with the largest number in Bad Hofgastein. Details on chalet and apartment rentals are available through the tourist offices in any of the resorts.

Dining

Galt Millau recommends some of Bad Gastein's top restaurants. The **Hoteldorf Grüner Baum** (tel. 25160), virtually a private village tucked in a nearby side valley, serves excellent Austrian mainstays amidst wonderful scenery. **Villa Solitude** (tel. 51015) owned by the same family as the Grüner Baum provides a French bistro atmosphere and a notable collection of beers.

For a traditional, inexpensive Austrian meal, try the **Orania Stuben**.

Après-ski/nightlife

After a day on the slopes, the elite choose the tables at the **Casino** in Bad Gastein or retire immediately to the bar near the playing tables.

After 11 p.m. the evening grows progressively wilder at the **Salzburger Hof,** the **Blockhäusl** and the **Pilsquell** in Bad Gastein. The **Glocknerkeller** in Bad Hofgastein is a typical Austrian pub with music and dancing each night.

Child care

Child care is offered for children three years and above in Bad Gastein and Bad Hofgastein. The minimum age in Dorfgastein is four. Individual babysitting service is also offered. Get more information through the tourist office.

Getting there

The best international airport connections are through Salzburg or Munich. The best way to get to the resorts is by car, driving south, along the magnificent Tauernautobahn to Bischofshofen and on to the

Gastein valley. Expect about an hour's drive. Train connections from Europe are also excellent.

Other activities

The three towns have a great variety of outdoor recreation. A day trip to Salzburg with a tour down the salt mines is one of the preferred outings. Bad Gastein and Bad Hofgastein are famed thermal spring resorts. Take time to enjoy the hot springs during your visit.

For non-skiers, the view from the Schlossalm at 7,000 feet is worth the ride up from Bad Hofgastein. In Bad Gastein, visit the Nikolauskirche built in the 15th century. This church, now not in use, has an unusual star-shaped vaulted nave, several interesting murals and is built around a central pillar.

In Badhofgastein the Gothic church with its high vaulted ceiling is worth a visit. The town of Dorfgastein also has an interesting parish church dating back to the 14th century.

Tourist information

Kur- und Tourismusverband, Kaiser-Franz-Josef-Strasse 27, A-5640 Bad Gastein; (tel. 06434-25310 or 3666; fax 253137; e-mail fvv.badgastein@aon.at. Kurverwaltung, A-5630 Bad Hofgastein; (tel. 06432-7110).

Verkehrsverein, A-5632 Dorfgastein; (tel. 06433-277).

☎ *Telephone prefix for Bad Gastein is 06434; for Bad Hofgastein the prefix is 06432; for Dorfgastein it is 06433.*

Innsbruck

Innsbruck, Austria's most famous ski city, has twice hosted the Winter Olympic Games (1964 and 1976), but Innsbruck, capital of the Austrian Tyrol, is no quaint ski village. This city of 128,000 residents in the valley of the emerald-green Inn River has such a collection of cultural attractions that skiing is not the dominant factor. This bustling city just happens to be surrounded by a group of small resorts with good skiing.

If you stay herein the city you have a longish ride to the lifts, but you can ski six nearby areas, and can also strike out for a day in St. Anton, Ischgl or Kitzbühel. Europe's best cross-country resort, Seefeld, is right next door. Innsbruck is a great place to try out a lot of Austria's skiing to get an idea of where to spend more time next season.

With a major university and lots of cultural history—castles, cathedrals and the like—Innsbruck has many sightseeing opportunities as well. It also has a great deal of beauty and charm, with the Inn River flowing through the city and good walking areas in the old city center, up and down the riverbanks and parks. Virtually all sightseeing is within a ten-minute walk of the city center. There is a good tram and bus system up to Igls, Hungerburgbahn and the hiking trails.

The city is also a good family environment, with lots of affordable restaurants, and activities for kids like the zoo and gondolas and trains going up into the mountains.

No slopes or cross-country trails are accessible from the hotels directly, but an excellent ski shuttlebus system connects downtown with the five surrouding areas as well as several other major resorts.

Igls

This village on the south side of the Inn Valley, is quieter, more sedate, and a little more upscale than Innsbruck, and only a 20-minute bus ride (or 30-minute tram ride) from the city. Commercialism hasn't taken over—attractive walking paths through meadows leading to nearby villages add to the relaxed charm and genuine sense of retreat. Not prohibitively expensive, it attracts a slightly more moneyed and older crowd. Restaurants are generally 20 to 25 percent higher in price and quality than in Innsbruck. There are a few local nightspots, but this is more a place for a fine dinner with drinks afterward than for a rocking party night of disco and barhopping.

Seefeld

In the shadow of the Solstein to the north of Innsbruck, Seefeld has an abundance of restaurants, pensions, ski services and shops laid out in classic Austrian mountain style. It doesn't offer a wild time at night, but is a good place to spend a relaxing evening and intimate dinner after a day on the trails.

A half-hour train ride from Innsbruck, Seefeld is also easily accessible from the city, and convenient for an overnight stay for those wanting to escape to the country. Many of the cross-country trails begin within walking distance of the train station.

Mountain layout

The six major ski areas ringing Innsbruck are—in descending order of difficulty—Hungerburg-Seegrube, Axamer-Lizum, Patscherkofel, Tulfes, Igls, Mutters, and the Stubai glacier. Altogether, nearly 124 miles of trails are prepared for downhill skiers.

Experts should strike out for Hungerburg, north across the Inn River: this is the gateway to the great black trails of the Hafelekar. Wend your way down the mogul-studded steep black run from the 7,657-foot-high summit. It's one of the most challenging in Austria and a good test of expert status.

Of the Olympic slopes, the Axamer-Lizum is best known. The slopes of Axams, a village about six miles outside Innsbruck, start at the 5,249-foot level. Here you can find every major resort amenity short of lodging.

Heresy to say, but we liked three other runs better than the famous Olympic course, the Hoadl (7,677 feet). The first two, from the nearby 7,336-foot Pleisen and slightly lower Kögele, take you all the way back to the valley floor. The Kögele is the better of the two, with a great four miles of skiing. The demanding run down the Birgitzköpfl on the opposite side of the valley was the most difficult in the area. The moguls pound your thighs and the steep slopes test an intermediate's courage.

Tulfes, nearly eight miles from Innsbruck, has skiing from the 8,783-foot level. For powder and off-trail skiing, we highly recommend the area around the Glungezer summit (but you have to climb half an hour to enjoy the best off-trail variations).

Igls, at 2,952 feet, is in the shadow of the Patscherkofel, the 7,372-foot summit for the men's downhill run. You can ski the same 2.4-mile course traveled by Franz Klammer to win a gold medal at the 1976 games and you have the added advantage of new snow-making equip-ment that will keep the entire descent white, no matter what the weather. The bobsled run is also at Igls, and visitors are allowed try bobsledding on the course for Sch300 per person.

The Mutters ski area, around the mountain from the Axamer-Lizum (or over the Birgitzköpfl and down the mountain), is good intermediate territory. The runs branch out from the Pfriemesköpfl (5,904 feet).

Stubaital, home of one of Europe's top summer skiing areas, guarantees Innsbruck skiable terrain throughout the ski season. This area, about an hour from downtown Innsbruck, offers relatively mild skiing, but offers a chance to experience some of Austria's most beautiful countryside.

Mountain rating

As a twice-Olympic city, Innsbruck offers plenty for the expert. Each of the major ski areas will give the intermediate countless tests.

And beginners need have no fear: all those Austrians had to learn how to ski too, and the beginner and training rope tows and J-bars are usually right at the bottom of the longer chair lifts. The moment you're ready, so is the mountain.

Lift tickets (97/98 prices)

Day tickets for the individual areas of the Innsbruck region cost Sch295–420. The best bargain is the regional pass, good for a minimum of three days and includes the Stubai glacier. These are the Club Innsbruck (see Accommodations) reduced prices:

With Glacier	Adult	Child (6–15)
three days	Sch1,010	Sch610
six days	Sch1,830	Sch1,100
thee of four days	Sch1,050	Sch630
three of six days	Sch1,120	Sch670

Buses run daily from Innsbruck to the main slopes and to the Stubai glacier. For information, call 59850. Buses also take skiers to the area's best cross-country circuits.

Ski school (97/98 prices)

Each area has organized instruction with a total of approximately 200 teachers working in the region daily. Private and group lessons for downhill and cross-country are given. Call the Innsbruck ski school (0512-582310) for details.

	Innsbruck	Igls
1 hour private lesson	Sch500	Sch400
4-hour private lesson	Sch2,300	Sch1,950
one day group lesson	Sch500	Sch450
three day group lesson	Sch1,200	Sch1,050
five day group lesson	Sch1,500	Sch1,250

School courses meet on the slopes, which you can reach by shuttlebus.

Cross-country

Lusens

This area is about 45 minutes from Innsbruck in a high mountain pass, with only about 12 km. of trails, groomed in two basic loops, one loop encircles a lake (8 km.) and passes through woods, and the second (4 km.) begins at the nearby downhill ski area. Both offer beautiful high mountain scenery but no real backcountry or wilderness travel. It is also hard to lose the crowd. A couple of good pensions make a handy lunch stop. Trails are well-groomed, and the lake loop can offer some thrills for advanced beginners and intermediates.

Seefeld

This cross-country paradise, with 320 km. of trails offers lots of possibilities on beginner and intermediate runs extending into backcountry woods, deep forest and meadows; skating lanes are possible too. It's generally rolling terrain, but with enough turns, dips and downhill runs to keep it interesting for most skinny-skiers. There are a few restaurants and inns along the way for rest stops and lunch. The ski bus isn't supposed to stop at Seefeld, but most drivers will, if you ask.

Trails are extremely well laid out and groomed. In complicated backcountry areas a map would be handy because many trails intersect and directions are not always well marked. Here, as elsewhere in Austria, trails tend to be overrated for difficulty, at least by American standards. An intermediate trail is usually just a little beyond beginner level, and an intermediate can easily handle one marked difficult.

Accommodations

While it may be more romantic to stay in one of the neighboring villages, the attraction of Innsbruck is that you can enjoy the benefits of a major city and one of Europe's cultural capitals.

The city tourist office advertises accommodations ranging from a sleeping bag to a king's bed. The best budget lodgings are offered through the tourist office-sponsored Club Innsbruck plan. This is for half board. (Telephone are*a code is 0512)*

Europa-Tyrol (5931, fax 587800) Sch1,250–1,950. On Südtiroler Platz, this is the quality choice for Innsbruck. It is only a short distance from the old city and near the top attractions.

Hotel Holiday Inn (5935, fax 5935220) Sch845–1,470. Innsbruck's other top hotel, next to the new casino and close to the ski shuttlebus stop.

Hotel Greif (587401, fax 579577) Sch730–1,060. An old Innsbruck standby, with a shuttlebus stop at the door. Once upon a time it was charming but with remodeling it is more convenient with less charm. One visitor described it as a slightly worn Austrian HoJos.

Central Hotel (5920, fax 580310) Sch860–1,110. Another Innsbruck tradition on the Sparkassenplatz. Modernized lobby with classically Austrian rooms.

Goldener Adler (586334, fax 584409) Sch970–1,670. is a four-star hotel in the city center. Good Tyrolean restaurant on the ground floor.

Golden Krone (586160, fax 5801896) Sch680–890. Traditional Austrian hotel in good location at the arch; rooms are a little more contemporary but hotel is also an old Innsbruck mainstay.

Maria Theresia (5933 fax 575619) Sch950–1,600. Now a Best Western on the main drag, right in front of the tram stop.

Weisses Kreuz (59479, fax 5647990) Sch675–865. A good deal: has nice single rates for comfortable rooms and a good location, right in the old center. Known for possibly the best breakfast buffet in Innsbruck; restaurant on the ground floor.

Weisses Rossl (583057, fax 5830575) Sch750–900. Good value in the Altstadt.

Hotel Innsbruck (59868, fax 572280) Sch870–970. A more modern hotel on the Inn. Not much character or charm, but central location and a good view of the river and mountains across the way.

Igls

This village in the hills above Innsbruck is the closest thing to a mountain resort in the area. In fact it makes a very pleasant destination in itself, with Innsbruck available for occasional forays.

Sporthotel in the center, directly across from the bus stop (377241, fax 378679).

Five-star hotel and the top place in Igls. Bright outdoor terrace for drinks and lunch and another terrace at night for drinks and dancing. Restaurant is upscale Austrian, with prices to be expected in a five-star hotel.

Batzenhäusl Lanserstrasse 16 (38618, fax 386187). Four-star hotel just outside the center. Traditional rural Austrian flavor with a restaurant almost equal to the Sporthotel's.

Schlosshotel Villersteig (377217, fax 378679). Another five-star with the ambiance of a retreat surrounded by woods and lawns on the edge of town, but still a ten-minute walk, at most, from the center.

Although Igls may lack restaurants and nightspots, it has hotels and pensions in abundance. After the four and five-star hotels, they break down roughly as follows:

For middle-of-the-road hotels, try the **Astoria** or the **Bon-Alpina** for Sch740–840 per person per night. **Gruberhof** is a good low-priced establishment where you can get good half board for Sch500–750 per person a day.

Two very nice Bed & Breakfast places are **Hotel-Garni Leitgebhof** and **Pension Tyrol** with rates about Sch430–480 per person a day. **Pension Oswald** is another good basic B&B with a rate of Sch300.

Some of the smaller pensions aren't all that small in Igls, though they still offer more local color than the several-star hotels. There's not much variation in quality, spaciousness and so forth; you can count on all to offer a reasonable, comfortable place to stay.

For picturesque small pensions try: **Haus Maria, Haus Kaserer, Pension Isabella, Pension Oswald,** and **Villa Juliana.**

Apartments

Lodging in Innsbruck is primarily in hotels and pensions. For information on chalet and apartment rentals nearer the slopes, contact the Innsbruck tourist office.

There are more apartments in Igls. Send your requirements to the tourist office and it will send back a list of available apartments in addition to those below:

Bellevue Appartments Patscherstrasse 7. Large modern three-star complex that would offer a lot of creature comforts but not much local color or charm.

Tirolerhof Lanserstrasse 15. Another large complex less obviously modern than the Bellevue.

Private rooms in Igls will end up costing, with breakfast, Sch200–250 per person a night.

 ## Dining

Restaurants listed below are in the heart of the city, where you'll also find the best lodging. In the individual towns there are countless dining establishments and mountain restaurants.

Sweet Basil is a European chain, but its location in the arcade part of old town and its international selection of food, including a great vegetarian selection, make for a good break from its heavier Austrian competitors. It's also seems the "in" spot for locals; you'll be seated next to smartly dressed Austrians chatting on their cell phones over a plate of Thai Noodles or Lemon Pepper Yellow Fin Tuna. Expect to pay about Sch130–240 for main dishes; their fine selection of Austrian wines begins at Sch290.

An excellent combination for eating and overnight lodging is **Weisses Rössl** (583057) at Kiebachgasse 8 in the old city. The menu is Sch60–125. The staff prepares excellent typical Tyrolean dishes.

Visit the **Goldener Adler** (586334) in the old city if you have a craving for good beef, especially grilled T-bone. An excellent traditional restaurant. Expect to pay $40 for two. Another great Austrian restaurant is the **K&K Restaurant** in the Hotel Schwarzer Adler (587109). For pizza with great atmosphere head to the **Pizzeria Romantica** in the old town.

We agree with a Tyrolean friend who took us to the **Altstadtstüberl** (582347), promising that it was one of the most reasonably priced restaurants in the old city. The menu begins at Sch70. The **Restaurant Kapeller** (343106) is considered the best restaurant in town by many.

If you need a hometown fix there are the ubiquitous **McDonalds** and a **Chili's** with beef from the good old USA. Chili's almost always requires reservations. But even though the names are American, the prices are not, and seem to be a little high, even for Austrians. On our last trip, the family in front of us plopped down almost $40 for a meal for two adults and two medium kids. Chili's is more reasonable for what you get: Fajitas for two (with directions on how to eat them) run about $25.

Canton China (Maria-Theresien-Strasse 37) is a good Chinese spot, with Sch63 midweek specials (Monday–Thursday, not holidays). This has attractive upscale decor, but prices are quite reasonable. It is not at all your run-of-the-mill Chinese food. This may be the best Chinese in town.

La Mamma Churrasco (Innrain 2) is a bright family place right on the riverbank just outside the old city center. Enjoy pizzas and interesting pasta dishes.

Papa Joe's (Saillergasse 12) serves Americanized buffalo wings and burgers, just inside the Altstadt. Enjoy a Tex-Mex mixture in a younger, single, sports bar spot.

Pizzeria Romantica (Kiebachqasse 11) is a typical pizzeria with a bit of rustic Italian ambiance character.

Lotos Chinese (Saillergasse 5) in the Altstadt has basic Chinese in a very pleasant setting.

Don Camillo (Marketgrabben 3) in the city center is a typical pizzeria but with a bright, cozy and quaint interior with clean charm.

Chili's (Boznerplatz) serves acceptable Tex-Mex food even if somewhat Austrian style in a fairly good cantina decor. It is frequented by a younger crowd, and is popular with locals and tourists. You can enjoy the usual nachos, fajitas and burritos.

Al Dente (Meranerstrasse 7) has very interesting creative pasta dishes with lots of variations. It is quite affordable, with a good salad bar as well.

Panini (Herzog-Friedrich-Strasse 17) is a good lunch stop, in the Altestadt, near the Goldenes Dachl. It's a step above Au Bon Pain. You'll find good pizza squares, sandwiches, soups and desserts.

Country Life (Maria-Theresien-Strasse 9) is a good cozy vegetarian spot with an earthy character. This is the place to go for ratatouille, good soups and salads.

Philippine Vegetarian (Müllerstrasse 9) is an excellent vegetarian place a short walk from the center. The cooking is not at all Philippine, or even oriental. They have an intersting menu with creative dishes. The wild rice risotto and the Greek potatoes are both excellent.

Igls—Nightspots/restaurants

Club Igls is bar/cafe and a pleasant place for after dinner coffee, dessert or drinks with a semi-bohemian ambiance and a good stock of newspapers and magazines. It earns its nickname—the Reading Room.

Pub Ala (Hilberstrasse 16) is a pleasant casual bar that also serves up light meals right in the center of town.

La Fontana is an attractive Italian restaurant with a very homey rural flavor tucked away in the woods.

Dorfstube (Hilberstrasse 8) is another pleasant bar in the village center. It is a bit livelier than the Pub Ala.

Tanzpalast Igls (Hilberstrasse 2) is Igls' hot spot for music and dancing; the crowd still tends toward the young side. This is the place for action in sedate Igls.

Imbisstube Lebersmittel (Lanzerstrasse 5) is traditional in decor with basic Austrian food and a large outdoor garden terrace that catches bright afternoon sun.

 ## Après-ski/nightlife

We recommend you walk the Maria-Theresien-Strasse and the central old city for just about all the nightlife you could ever desire. The view is beautiful and you'll find small pubs and bars hidden in alleys and under archways.

Check with the tourist office for a list of concerts taking place around town—tickets are also sold at the information office. You never know who's touring Europe while you're on vacation.

Innsbruck's casino, the largest in Austria. near the Hotel Scandic Crown at Salurner Strasse 15, is open for elegant gaming. Jackets are required.

Innsbruck has a bit of something for everyone. Here's the lowdown:

Dom Cafe/Bar (Pfargasse 3) with a well-done antique interior. is an après-ski place for a younger set, that stays lively late at night. It draws a few more tourists than the Buro or La Copa/La Cabana.

Piano Cafe/Bar (Herzog-Friedrich-Strasse 5) is definitely for an older (40s and up) upscale crowd, and probably the best nightspot in the center. It is relaxed and comfortable with an antique interior with paintings filling the walls. Look carefully—it's easy to miss.

Cafe Club Filou (Siftgasse 12) is a large Victorian bar with high ceilings and a smoking club atmosphere. Ring the bell to enter. The club has a large and spacious interior with seating in loft over the main floor, and a quieter, more intimate bar to the side. The crowd is mixed, and leans toward the older side.

Treibhaus tucked in a back alley behind China Restaurant, just outside the Altstadt, is Innsbruck's real bohemian hangout for all ages and types, tourists and locals alike. A spacious upstairs has a kitchen serving mediocre pizza and the basement is known for hot local jazz on most nights and Sunday mornings.

Irish Pub and Testarosa get rave reviews from the 20s crowd. The former is packed with English-speakers, the latter with German-speakers. Both are across from the Hotel Greif.

Another bar called Jimmy's also gets good reviews from the younger crowd.

Piccolo Bar (Seilergasse 2) is rather small and cozy, with gaudy Victorian parlor design heavy on the velvet and gilt gold. Buzz to enter. This is Innsbruck's (probably) only gay bar. It is low-key and discreet.

Altstadtstuberl (Riesergasse 11) is a bright, pleasant arty cafe frequented primarily by locals, serving coffee, desserts and some meals. A good find right in the center that the tourists don't seem to hit.

Charley's Friend's Billiards (Burggrabben 31) with an English club interior is a casual, relaxed local poolhall with about six tables. It offers a good diversion from skiing, eating and barhopping, and a chance to kick back with the locals.

Just Outside the Center

Cafe Central (Central Hotel/Boznerplatz) is a true Viennese music café offering live piano music Sunday evenings (8–11 p.m.). It also has a meal menu with elaborate pastries and desserts. Eat amidst a semi-grand interior and enjoy a large collection of international newspapers. This is the traditional coffeehouse of Innsbruck.

Club 29 (Leopoldstrasse 29) is a local hangout for the younger set. It doesn't get lively until late.

New American Bar is a shiny disco for the young rocking set. Buzz to enter. It's open 10 p.m.-4 a.m.

Zoo Cafe (Maria-Theresien-Strasse 10) is a mellower disco than the New American. High-tech decor dominates but music volume is toned down a bit. Jazz on tape played by a disc jockey.

 ## Child care

Child care and ski kindergarten courses (age four and up) are available in Innsbruck's ski areas. Contact the Schikindergarten (582310) for details or the Children's Day Care Centre, Pradler Platz 6 (345282). Igls has a free kindergarten in the Kurpark (378908). Call for hours and restrictions.

 ## Other activities

Innsbruck shares with Grenoble the distinction of being a town in the Alps with more than 100,000 residents; as noted, it's a provincial capital and has a wealth of art and historical treasures. It is also on the way to the Brenner Pass, gateway to the Italian Lakes and Venice.

Innsbruck is accustomed to visitors in ski outfits, whether inside a museum or at a fine restaurant. Visitors always head for the heart of town along the Maria-Theresien-Strasse for the outstanding view of the Karwendel mountain range.

The best way to see Innsbruck is to walk through the old town. Allow about two hours. The most photographed house in the old city is Goldenes Dachl, a former royal building from the 16th century, with gold-plated copper shingles on the roof.

Visit the Hofburg Palace, St. Jakob's cathedral and the Tyrolean folklore museum. The city boasts dozens of other attractions listed by the tourist office.

The money-saving Innsbruck Card costs Sch200 for 24 hours or Sch280 for 48 hours and Sch350 for 72 hours. These passes are discounted by 50 percent for children 6–15. The card provides unlimited access to all public transportation and entrance to 21 major sightseeing attractions in and near the city. These include the Imperial Palace, the Museum of Tyrolean Folk Art, the Provincial Museum, Ambras Castle, the Alpine Zoo, the Railway Museum and the multi-media displays at the Swarovski Crystal Worlds.

A good selection of classical music concerts takes place at the Concert House and the Konservatoriumsaal (music school), Museumstrasse 17a.

Husky Winter in Innsbruck is offering dog sled rides on Wednesday and Friday for Sch100 per adult and Sch50 for kids 6-16. Younger kids are free. Call the tourist office for reservations and information.

Cinematograph (Museumstrasse 31) is a good art cinema offering relatively contemporary and classic films in original language, not dubbed. The only cinema in Innsbruck for this and something of a rarity in Austria.

Just outside Innsbruck is a dazzling new multimedia museum dedicated to Swarovski crystals, one of Austria's most famous collectibles. Swarovski Crystal Worlds (05224-51080) features a spectacular array of the colorful glass, from the world's largest crystal (alas, at 300,000 carats, it is a bit large for Elizabeth Taylor's neck), collections of costumes and artifacts made with innumerous pieces of crystal and a 122-meter long wall filled with 12 tons of brilliant crystal.

Getting there

Innsbruck airport has daily jet service throughout Europe. Munich is the international airport most often used by travelers from the United States, but traffic through Innsbruck airport is increasing. Tyrolean Airways, Innsbruck's hometown airline, has scheduled service from Amsterdam, Frankfurt, Zürich, Vienna and Paris, offering a perfect alternative to trains, buses, or a long drive by car.

By car from Munich, take the autobahn to the Inntal autobahn and then to Innsbruck— no more than three hours. A more scenic drive is from Munich to Garmisch-Partenkirchen, scene of the 1932 and 1936 Winter Olympic Games, and then about 70 minutes over the mountains to Innsbruck (add at least two hours for sightseeing in Garmisch).

Shuttlebuses connect Munich Airport with Innsbruck and Seefeld with departures every Saturday from Munich at 11:30 a.m. Contact Menardi Bus at 0512-574949, fax 0512-571347 or Lueftner-Reisen at 0512-589371. Bus fare is approximately $36 each way. Limousines are also available through Four Seasons Travel (0512-584157, fax 0512-585767) but require advance reservations. They leave Munich Airport daily every two hours. The fare is about $44 one way and $75 round trip.

Tourist information

Tourismusverband Innsbruck-Igls und Umgebung, A-6021 Innsbruck, Austria; 0512-59850, fax 0512-598507.
Internet: www.tis.co.at/tirol/innsbruck

☎ *Telephone prefix for Innsbruck is 0512.*

Ischgl, Galtür
and the Paznaun Valley

After a few short days, Ischgl (pronounced Ish-gull) became one of our favorite Austrian resorts. Yet this ski center in the Paznaun Valley—high in the Alps (4,592 feet), hard on the border with Switzerland—remains untapped by non-European skiers.

The town itself is a small Alpine resort built on a knoll in a deep valley. No modern hotels seriously mar the effect. The ski area is far above and out of sight from the road, the base stations and the town. Eleven smaller hamlets complete the region.

Ischgl is a resort that has it all—41 lifts, 125 miles of wide-open trails, cross-border skiing into Switzerland, extensive off-trail areas, cross-country, small Alpine village atmosphere, and some of the wildest après-ski and nightlife in Austria. With 90 percent of its ski area over 6,600 feet, snow is virtually assured until the beginning of May.

From the slopes above Ischgl, you can cross into Switzerland and visit duty-free Samnaun.

Galtür

Twenty minutes higher up the valley is Galtür, a picturesque little village of only 700 inhabitants and 20 restaurants spread out around a late-baroque church. Although connected to Ischgl by bus (and the Silvretta ski pass), it's much smaller and quieter with a correspondingly smaller ski area (25 miles of runs). It is particularly known for its cross-country and ski-touring opportunities. The highest village in the Silvretta-Paznaun region, it has a long snow season (November to May).

The ski school is well-organized, with good English-speaking instructors and a popular ski kindergarten. Drawn by its quiet charms and unhurried pace, families return to Galtür generation after generation.

Mountain layout

Ischgl's slopes are the most extensive in the valley, with neighboring See, Kappl and Galtür servicing smaller areas. Across the mountains to the south, in Switzerland, Samnaun is connected by lift with Ischgl.

From Ischgl three gondola lifts rise to the main skiing area 3,280 feet above the town. The Silvrettabahn and the Fimbabahn take skiers from opposite ends of town to the Idalp area (7,582 feet). The Pardatschgratbahn goes from the eastern section of town to Pardatschgrat at 8,609 feet. Although the lift lines at the Silvrettabahn look daunting, the wait even on the busiest days is not excessive. Uphill capacity is 5,500 skiers an hour.

From the Idalp sector, lifts fan out to all corners of the resort. Skiers choosing to go directly to the higher Pardatschgrat still have to pass through the Idalp area. The immediate Idalp area serves as the nursery runs, offering a long, very easy swath with excellent lift support.

From Idalp, intermediates and experts take the chair lift up to Idjoch. Here, drop down into the Swiss Alp Trida section for long intermediate runs, or continue up to the Greitspitz for more challenging skiing in the Austrian section beneath the Palinkopf into the Hölltal or over another ridge to the Taja Alp.

At the end of the day, take one of the runs from the Idalp or down the Velilltal for beautiful, wide-open, intermediate cruising. Or if you want to end the day with a challenge, drop from the Pardatschgrat. If you are staying near the Silvrettabahn, you will want to head left toward the middle station, then follow the No. 1 trail into town. For those closer to the Fimba or Pardatschgratbahn stations, keep going straight down into town. Where the trail forks, ski to the right.

Determined off-trail skiers can arrange for a snowcat to take them to the Piz Val Gronda or the Heidelberger-hütte with a guide for a day of skiing across untracked snow. This area is scheduled for lift development, but it still seems to be few years away. The Swiss must first construct an additional lift from Samnaun before the Austrian lift-builders can raise a wrench.

Down to Samnaun

Swiss Samnaun is the target of many Ischgl skiers because they are either determined to experience skiing over the border to a Swiss town, or they are hot on the trail of duty-free cigarettes, perfume or whisky. In any case, the run from the back side of the Palinkopf is relatively tame and the town itself hardly more interesting than the nearest airport duty-free store.

Duty-free here is big business. If one smokes or wants to fill up the hot toddy cabinet, Samnaun is wonderful, but once is more than enough for the run from Palinkopf. A new cable car takes skiers from the center of Samnaun-Dorf back to the slopes above Ischgl. There is normally about a half-hour wait for the tiny, slower Ravaisch cable car that, up until this season, was the only way to return.

There is another trail from Alp Trida down to Compatsch. This trail is rather difficult and often closed owing to avalanches (too much snow) or rocks (too little). If you do get down, a postbus will carry you back up to the Ravaisch cable car.

Galtür

A ten-minute shuttlebus ride takes you from the village to Wirl, a collection of on-piste hotels and the gateway to the slopes. The skiing here is mellow-to-intermediate, better than Ischgl for beginners and families who want to ski together.

A quad-chair carries skiers up from the base at Wirl to Birkhahnkopf. From there, take the Ballunspitz lift to a choice of three easy expert runs or a good intermediate trail. A couple of log-cabin restaurants dot the surrounding slopes. From there you can ski down to the frozen reservoir, the Kopssee, or traverse round the back of the mountain to the Innere Kopsalpe, which offers the toughest runs. On a sunny day, this back bowl offers an advanced intermediate fun for an entire morning or afternoon.

Mountain rating

Intermediates and experts will have a wonderful time in Ischgl. The area offers wide-ranging, well-prepared trails and 50 miles of off-trail challenges. Experts looking for super-steep terrain will be disappointed. The resort is perfect for a mixed intermediate and expert group.

Ischgl is not recommended for absolute beginners. English at the ski school is limited to technical ski jargon, and the nursery slopes are far above the town. Galtür, with its wide-open slopes and relaxed atmosphere, makes more sense for younger skiers and beginners to intermediate.

Ski school (97/98 prices)

Ischgl has the largest ski school but probably only as many good English-speakers as Galtür. Both teach the Austrian method.

Group lessons are approximately 10 percent less expensive in middle season. For participants in the week-long January ski program there is an additional 10 percent discount.

The ski school operates on a high/low season. High season is Christmas/New Years and February to mid-April. Low season is early December, mid-January, and late April.

Ischgl ski school prices:

Private lessons	High Season	Low Season
two hours	Sch1,150	Sch1,150
each additional person	Sch150	Sch150
one day (4 hours)	Sch2,100	Sch2,100
each additional person	Sch200	Sch200
Group lessons		
one day	Sch500	Sch500
two days	Sch950	Sch950
three days	Sch1,200	Sch1,200
five days	Sch1,400	Sch1,350
six days	Sch1,500	Sch1,430
five half days	Sch1,200	Sch1,200

Galtür ski school prices:

Private lessons

one hours	Sch550
each additional person	Sch200
one day (4 hours)	Sch2,000
each additional person	Sch200
two days	Sch2,000

Group lessons

one day	Sch480
two days	Sch850
three days	Sch1,100
five days	Sch1,350
six days	Sch1,450

Lift tickets (97/98 prices)

All skiers except beginners should buy the Silvretta ski pass, good for all area lifts (Ischgl, Galtür, Samnaun and the entire valley), plus shuttlebus transport. These are prices for those staying in hotels in the valley.

	High Season	LowSeason
three days	Sch1,350	Sch1,160
six days	Sch2,470	Sch2,105
seven days	Sch2,785	Sch2,370
ten days	Sch3,615	Sch3,100
thirteen days	Sch4,305	Sch3,655

Individual area day tickets in Ischgl cost Sch460 in high season and Sch400 for low season. In Galtür prices are about Sch350 for high season and Sch315 for low season. These are prices with the guess card for Galtür/Ischgl guests.

Seniors over 60 and children 7–15 get about a 40 percent discount.

Silvretta half-day passes valid after 11:30 a.m. are Sch350 for adults, Sch190 for children and Sch240 for seniors. Five half days out of seven days will cost Sch1,885 for adults in high season, Sch1,720 in low season, Sch1,170 for children and Sch1,430 for seniors.

Accommodations

Prices noted are approximate for half board. HS: high season; LS: low season.

Ischgl

For the best in town, head for **Hotel Elisabeth** (5411) Sch2,100–3,000 HS; Sch1,700–2,500 LS. Located at the base stations of the Fimbabahn and the Pardatschgratbahn. A perfect location. Good English, pool, sauna and solarium.

Madlein (5226) Daily price is Sch1,600–2,380 HS; Sch1,350–2,100 LS. Central location. Features one of the best discos in town. Pool, sauna and solarium.

The aging **Hotel Post** (5233) has all amenities, including a swimming pool. Staff at the **Sonne** (5302) and **Trofana** (5150) are good with English. Prices are around Sch1,600

HS and Sch1,200 LS. The Sonne also has excellent après-ski.

Gasthöfe Goldener Adler (5217) boasts one of the best kitchens in town, a sauna and steambath. Sch1,140–1,620 HS; Sch920–1,370 LS.

Moderate

Olympia (5432) Sch1,250 HS; Sch950 LS. Near Fimba and Pardatschgrat lifts.

Yscla (tel.5275) Sch870–1,750 HS; Sch690–1,400 LS. Near the Silvretta lift. Convenient to everything, with one of the best restaurants in town.

Charly (5434) Sch1,000 HS; Sch800 LS.

Bed and Breakfast

The best in town is **Christine** (tel.5346) Sch750–1,100 HS; Sch500–800 LS.

A moderate B&B is **Edi** (5351) Sch590–680 HS; Sch490-550 LS. A bit out of the way, but a good haven for English speakers, and it has reasonable rates.

The recommended lower-priced B&Bs—**Palin** (5445) Sch640–700 HS; Sch500–600 LS. **Lasalt** (5121) Sch650–700 HS; Sch450–550 LS. **Erna** (5262) Sch600–700 HS; Sch400–500 LS.

Galtür

Prices in Galtür are considerably lower than those in Ischgl. Be sure to ask about the guest card when you arrive. It confers several considerable discounts in the town. The hotel prices noted here are the HS-LS range with half board and bath. Telephone prefix is 05443. Many of the hotels have special prices for children. Let the tourist office know you are bringing children and they will direct you to hotels that cater to little ones.

The best lodging here may be the **Gasthof Zum Rössle** right on the center square. It has got a fine, traditional restaurant and spa facilities (8232). Sch1,350-840. Also in the center, the Post has one of the few discos in the village (8422). Sch1,470–930.

The **Alpenhotel Tirol** (8206) is another four-star. Sch1,250-890.

Fluchthorn (8202) Central village location. Sch1,120–750.

Zum Silbertaler (8256) A three-star near the tennis center and pool. Sch890–590.

Gampeler hof (8307) Sch850–520.

Bergfried (8208) Sch720–550.

Luggl (8386) Sch810–665.

Bed & Breakfast

Alpenhaus Salner (8288) Sch410–350.

Dr. Köck (8226) Sch395–375.

Belvedere (8219) Sch412–345.

Apartments

The rental apartment business is well organized and bookings can be arranged through the tourist information office. When writing, provide details about when you plan to arrive, how many people will be sharing the apartment and what facilities you desire. In return you will receive a list with several choices.

Make your selection and notify the tourist office or the individual owner, depending on the instructions you get.

Normally, linens and kitchen utensils are included in every apartment. Heat, taxes, electricity and cleaning services may be extra. Expect to pay Sch180–270 per person a night, depending on how many are sharing the apartment, where it's located and its relative position on the luxury scale.

Dining

In Ischgl perhaps the best restaurant is the traditional kitchen of the Goldener Adler. Locals also recommend highly the **Trofana** for good international cooking. Try the **Kitzloch** for fondue and grilled steaks. Yscla has a good French and local menu.

In Galtür, be sure to eat once at the **Rössle** (ask for the local schnapps), **Landle** and at **Zum Silbertaler**. The **Fluchthorn** also serves hearty fare at reasonable prices.

In Samnaun, try a meal at the **Hotel Post**. It's pricey but one of the best in town.

Après-ski/nightlife

Here Ischgl shines. It has one of the best après-ski scenes from 3–7 p.m., then excellent nightlife from 10 p.m.–2 a.m.

The best après-ski spots are **Kuhstall**, just up from the Silvrettabahn and across from the Post and Goldener Adler, and the **Kitzloch** at the opposite end of town near Hotel Elisabeth and the Fimba and Pardatschgratbahn. Both spots rock from about 4–7 p.m., with a disc jockey spinning music, the bar serving half-liter beers and the crowd singing and dancing in ski suits and ski boots. The **Sonne** also has a lively crowd, but no dancing.

The three major discos begin to crank at about 10 or 11 p.m. The **Tenne** in the basement of Hotel Trofana offers the most crowded venue, with dancing and wild contests alternately competing for attention. The **Club Madlein** in Hotel Madlein and **S'Lobli** in the basement of Hotel Post offer the best dancing, but you'll find yourself wanting to shift with the crowd, depending on which club has the best live band. Club Madlein has a Sch50 cover charge.

Galtür

Try **Almhof, Alpkogel** and **Wirlerhof** for après-ski at the bottom of the lifts. After dinner the "in" place for action is the **Weiberhimmel** or try the **Post**. The Wirlerhof's disco is relatively quiet, good news if you're staying near the lifts and trying to sleep. You might also enjoy the traditional zither evenings at **Zum Silbertaler** Tuesdays and Thursdays and at **Hotel Almhof** on Fridays.

Child care

Child care services are available. Contact the Ischgl Tourist Office (05444-5266) for assistance.

There is a guest kindergarten without ski school at Idalp. The price, including lunch, is Sch250 a day, and without lunch, Sch170; or half-days (10 a.m.–12:30 p.m.) are Sch100.

The Ischgl ski school (5257 or 5404) runs a children's program for kids four and up. Prices include a lunchtime snack.

	High Season	Low Season
one day	Sch580	Sch580
three days	Sch1,340	Sch1,340
five days	Sch1,750	Sch1,700
six days	Sch1,930	Sch1,860

In Galtür the ski school is open for children 4 and above. It's near the Birkhahn chair lift in Wirl. Children attending ski school can get lunch and after-class supervision for an additional charge. Kindergarten for non-skiing children under four runs from 9:30 a.m.– noon, 1:30–4:30 p.m. Prices per child with Galtür guest card are Sch120 for a full day without lunch, Sch95 for a half day, Sch195 with lunch for a full day, and six full days without lunch cost Sch530.

The Galtür ski school has a special children's ski school for skiers from 4 years. Lessons last four hours a day from 10 a.m.—noon and 1:30–3:30 p.m.

one day	Sch450
three days	Sch1,050
five days	Sch1,350
six days	Sch1,450

Getting there

The nearest international airport is in Munich. From there, the easiest highway route is Garmisch, Fern Pass to Landeck or Innsbruck, and on to Ischgl. The train stops in Landeck, where there is regular bus service to Ischgl and Galtür.

Other activities

Winter merely enhances rather than disguises the beauty of Galtür, a mountain village some 5,197 feet high. Galtür is the gateway to the Silvretta Alpine Highway, open in warm-weather months. If taking photographs of beautiful buildings is one of your hobbies, visit the spired parish church Maria Geburt in Galtür. Everyone buried there seems to have had Wattes as a last name.

In Galtür the Tennishalle is open from 10 a.m.–4 p.m. with charges of Sch220 per hour and then from 4 p.m.–midnight court time costs Sch250 per hour. The swimming pool is open from 11 a.m.–9 p.m. and costs Sch70 for adults and Sch50 for children (7–16). A booklet of seven pool tickets is Sch340 for adults and Sch210 for children. Galtür also has Kegelbahnen, an Austrian version of bowling.

Landeck, an Alpine crossroads near the entrance to the valley, is a regional shopping center and is distin-guished by the towering Fortress Landeck.

As additional excursions from the Paznaun Valley, you can travel to Innsbruck and Munich.

Tourist information

Tourismusverband, Postfach 9, A-6561 Ischgl, Austria; 05444-5266; fax 05444-5636.

Tourismusverband, A-6563 Galtür/Tirol, Austria; 05443-8521, fax 05443-852176.

☎ *Prefix for Ischgl is 05444; for Galtür, 05443.*

Kitzbühel
and Kirchberg

Framed by rugged mountains, Kitzbühel dates back to the ninth century, when it landed on the map as a copper mining and trading town. With storybook snow-covered scenery, it's hard to believe that skiing is relatively new here—it wasn't until 1892 that skis were first introduced. But the sport rapidly gained popularity, and two years later a large consignment of skis arrived from Norway, paving the slopes for Kitzbühel's first ski championship.

The rest, you might say, was all downhill. Today Kitzbühel is the undisputed king of Austrian ski resorts. It's also the most commercial, glamorous and expensive. This is a resort where booking your ski vacation with a package tour can save a bundle.

Kitzbühel has always been known as one of the most beautiful Alpine towns in Austria, as one of the hot spots for après-ski and for excellent intermediate skiing. It lives up to its reputation.

If possible arrive in Kitzbühel before nightfall, when the wrought-iron entranceway lamps and flickering candles in the restaurant windows lend a special charm to the streets. You'll hear the jingle of bells on a horse-drawn sleigh, and in the distance someone in a gasthaus will let out a hearty laugh that rises above the sound of a piano or zither. The exterior of Kitzbühel is old and lovely and quite romantic. The atmosphere is bright, boisterous and never dull. In Kitzbühel the skiing day is long enough to tire you out, and it's followed by nightlife that can last forever. This is Austria's winter entertainment capital, with top European performers appearing throughout the season.

In January, during the famed Hahnenkamm Downhill World Cup (usually the middle weekend), Kitzbühel vibrates with action. The streets are filled even at midnight with music and laughter that ripple through the narrow alleyways. This is the perfect time to be in Kitzbühel.

Kitzbühel is a resort a vacationer with plenty of pecuniary resources should consider. As at Aspen or Vail, you'll rub shoulders with the rich and famous and be treated like royalty.

Kirchberg, a smaller town 3 miles to the west, shares much of the same mountain and has become a major player in the area. Filled with a younger crowd, attracting families and more dedicated skiers, Kirchberg has a more limited nightlife and significantly lower prices than its flashier neighbor. Where information differs, we describe Kirchberg separately below.

Mountain layout

If you ski well, Kitzbühel is close to unbeatable. You can spend all day on its slopes and not use the same lift or ski on the same run twice. There are 55 prepared runs across an amazing 160 km. of mountain. This is the site of the legendary ski safari, where skiers travel 15 km. by lift and descend 35 km. between Kitzbühel and Pass Thurn. Get an early start: the trip takes a full day.

To avoid long lift lines from town, drive or take the shuttlebus toward neighboring Kirchberg and take the Fleckalmbahn to the Ehrenbachhöhe above the Hahnenkamm race circuit. On the way down, ski the Streif Run, then begin working your way around the Ski Safari. It's marked by round signs with an elephant on skis pointing the way. Don't pass up the red runs on either side of Pengelstein. The trail to Kirchberg off the top is the better of the two.

The best runs are a closely guarded secret. Guides are tight-lipped about where to find good powder and empty runs. For a long uninterrupted slope try the Niedere Fleckalm, which in the morning is uncrowded and offers a very fast gondola. In the afternoon stick to the Ehrenbachhöhe, which provides a variety of terrain from intermediate to challenging.

Mountain rating

Trail skiing in Kitzbühel and Kirchberg is strictly intermediate. There are enough blues for the beginner and lower intermediate to keep harmony in any mixed-skill group.

Experts, except those concentrating on their times down the Hahnenkamm run or the Gaisberg course above Kirchberg, should wedel on something more challenging than the prepared runs. Guides can take serious skiers on off-trail expeditions from Kitzbühel or Kirchberg that will delight even the most hardened experts.

Ski school (97/98 prices)

Group Lessons

Joining a ski group generally costs about Sch500 per day and is a good way to sharpen your skills if you're out of practice, and a good way to get to know the mountain.

Four ski schools compete for the Kitzbühel vacationer. Ski School Total (72011), Kitzbühler Horn (4454), Egger Hahnenkamm (3177), and Rote Teufel (Red Devils) (2500) all charge Sch500 for one day of lessons. Three days are Sch1,150. Six days will set you back Sch1,300.

Total also offers special ski clinics with a private instructor. A one-day ticket for any group (5–7 skiers) costs Sch2,500. Contact Ernst Hinterseer at Total (72011).

Rote Teufel teaches special group and racing schools. One day of racing school is Sch500 and three days Sch1,250. Call Rudi Sailer (2500).

Kirchberg has three ski schools. The two largest are Skischule Kirchberg (2209) and Skischule Total (3726). Prices are more or less the same, with full day lessons costing about Sch550, three-day lessons about Sch1,250, and five-day lessons about Sch1,350.

Private lessons

One of the best ways to discover the beauty of these mountains while improving your technique is to hire a private guide. Costs vary: most instructors for one to two people cost Sch1,950–2,200 per day; Sch1,400 for a half day.

A little known benefit of hiring a private guide is that it gives you instant access to the overcrowded Hahnenkamm gondola, which is the only nonstop lift from Kitzbühel to the action. Private groups get special passes that allow them to cut ahead of the lines, which can be as long as 1 1/2 hours on weekends and peak season.

Snowboarding

A half-pipe was recently constructed near the Brunellenfeld on the Kitzbühler Horn to give shredders a place to practice their technical skills, but snowboarders still generally prefer weaving alongside skiers at high speeds.

Heinz Snowboard Center at the Kitzbühler Horn rents boards at a daily rate of Sch280, while three days cost Sch760. Call Gabi Mueller at 2701. Snow Fun Centre Hochbrunn at the Hahnenkamm rents boards at a daily rate of Sch200, and also offers Eagel monoskis at Sch60 per hour. Rote Teufel holds special all-inclusive courses in snowboarding, starting at Sch600 per day. Three days amount to Sch1,400.

Kirchberg ski schools have three-day snowboarding lessons for Sch1,150 and a snowboard weekly lesson for Sch1,750.

Cross-country skiing

There are four primary trails ranging from easy to difficult and stretching some 36 km. around Kitzbühel. But a short ride on the free ski bus gives you access to 120 km. of other trails in the region, with breathtaking Alpine views far removed from the frenetic pace of the downhill slopes.

Three ski schools offer cross-country lessons. Rote Teufel at Maurachfeld 25 in Kitzbühel (71374) offers a half-day lesson at Sch400, while three half days amounts to Sch900. The Kirchberg Ski School charges Sch950 for three half-day lessons. At ski school Total (72011, fax 72012) cross-country rates are available on request.

Lift tickets (97/98 prices)

Kitzbühel offers a variety of lift tickets, including senior citizens' and children's discounts. All passes allow unlimited access to all 64 Kitzbühel area ski lifts, free shuttlebus service between ski areas and swimming in Kitzbühel's Aquarena (even if you're staying in Kirchberg). No credit cards are accepted for the purchase of lift tickets.

High season includes Christmas and New Year weeks and February 1 to mid-March. Before Christmas, January after New Year, and late March on are low seasons.

	High Season	**Low Season**
one day	Sch410	Sch385
two days	Sch780	Sch700
three days	Sch1,100	Sch990
six days	Sch1,890	Sch1,700
seven days	Sch2,180	Sch1,960

Seniors (60 and over) get approximately 15 percent discount. Children's daily tickets (born after September 1, 1982) are always half of the high season price.

Accommodations

At first blush, Kitzbühel's hotels might easily be mistaken for well-kept farmhouses, with their sloping roofs and white façades. On the inside, however, they are as efficient as they are clean. Approximate prices (low season per person, per day, half-board unless marked B&B only) are noted as follow—$$$=Sch1,000–1,200; $$=Sch700–1,000; $=less than Sch700. High season prices are approximately 10–15 percent higher.

The **Hotel Goldener Greif** (4311) bills itself as an ancient Tyrolean inn dating back to 1271. However, the property was completely redesigned in 1954 and now features such modern amenities as a casino, sauna, swimming pool, solarium and Turkish steam bath. $$$

With its sliding glass doors and wide-open lobby, the **Sporthotel Reich** (3366) is by far the brightest of the Kitzbühel hotels. Also offered is a spa where trained therapists provide massages, facials, treatments and relaxation programs. $$$

At the **Schweizerhof** (2735), one of the few ski-in/ski-out inns, guests can also enjoy a full-service spa. Live après-ski entertainment is the order of the day in high season. Minimalist design, sparse decor. $$$

The **Hotel Zur Tenne** (4444) leaves the guest with the impression of living inside a giant ark, with heavy wood walls and ceilings. Right in the middle of the town, it features some of the nicest antiques, plus a fireplace, sauna and steam rooms. $$$

The stained-glass windows and mounted antlers in the **Tiefenbrunner Hotel** (2141) tell a story of its Tyrolean heritage. Paintings and carvings lining the lobby wall narrate the history of this part of Austria. $$$

Schloss Lebenberg (4301) A converted castle just on the outskirts of the town. All the amenities you could ask for. $$$

The **Kitzbühler Hof** (71300) is a quiet Bed & Breakfast inn with an attentive staff. The spacious rooms offer cable television and minibars with plain but functional furniture. $$ B&B only.

Alpen-Golfhotel Am Lutzenberg (3279) An excellent middle-range ho$$

Montana (2526) Next to the Hahnenkamm lifts. Pool, sauna and kindergarten. $$

Edelweiss (2587) $

Klausner (2136) $$

Eggerwirt (2455) A find. Our favorite, with a great restaurant. You'll love it. $$

Haus Toni Sailer (3041) $

Pension Foidl (2189) Sch350-380 $ B&B only. Small, with 31 beds.

Kitzbühel has scores of very affordable B&Bs that are perfect for anyone traveling on a budget. Contact the tourist office for reservations and information.

Ski Chalets: Crystal, Inghams/Bladon, First Choice (see page 27 for phone, fax and internet addresses).

Kirchberg

The accommodations here are not as luxurious as those in Kitzbühel nor as expensive. You can expect the prices to be about 20 percent less than in Kitzbühel. If traveling with your family, Kirchberg is a perfect place to stay.

Hotel Alexander (2222, fax 3407) the top spot in Kirchberg in the town center. $$

Hotel Sonnalp (2741) A four-star hotel with sauna and pool. Great for families. $$

Parkhotel Kirchberg (2383) No pool. Three-star ho$$

Residenzhotel Cordial (2842) Good four-star hotel with heated outdoor pool, sauna and kindergarten. $$

Hotel Seehof (2228) Beautifully redone rooms in a three-star hotel, great location with skating on the lake by the hotel. A real bargain. $

Gasthof Kirchenwirt (2852) Newly renovated and in town center with good food. $

There are scores of B&Bs in Kirchberg with prices in the Sch250–350 per night range. Contact the Kirchberg tourist office for more information and for reservations.

Ski Chalets: Crystal, Inghams/Bladon, First Choice (see page 27 for phone, fax and internet addresses).

Apartments

An annual directory of apartments is available from both the Kitzbühel and the Kirchberg tourist office.

A number of pensions allow visitors to rent rooms with kitchens in ski season, but as always, it's best to check with the tourist office.

Read the directory carefully and ask the property for a *Prospekt* or brochure, before deciding where to stay.

Prices per night per person for four people sharing an apartment range from farmhouse inexpensive—about Sch175 a night in high season—to downtown expensive, Sch500 a night in the same time period. Apartment prices in Kitzbühel and Kirchberg are about the same.

Remember, in Austria you're charged by the person, not by the room. Something else to keep in mind is that in most apartments in Europe you will be charged for various services. Meals, cleaning, linen and often utilities can all add up. Ask about what is and isn't included.

Dining

For one of the best meals in the area try the Gault Millau two-toque rated **Schwedenkapelle** (5870). This restaurant is exceptional and has dinner served on Wednesday and Saturday with musical accompaniment. Expect to pay Sch250–700 for a full meal.

The **Landhäusl** (4007) serves the largest portions in the area. Make reservations! Most tables seat six to eight people, and the staff won't hesitate to seat you next to someone else—not a good idea if you want a romantic dinner for two. Worth recommending: the Wienerschnitzel and Kaiserschmarren, a pancake-style dish. Dinner for two costs about

Sch500. Credit cards accepted.

Locals gravitate toward the **Huberbrau** (5677), for Tyrolean specialties as well as standard Austrian fare. Eat early or late to avoid a wait. Dinner for two costs around Sch450. No reservations and no credit cards are taken.

If you're pining for American food, your best bet is probably **McDonald's**, not the **American Pub** near the main square, which serves U.S.-themed sandwiches. Decorated with American license plates and neon signs, the American Pub is the kind of place you visit for the decor and company rather than the dining. A quick bite will set you back about Sch250. No credit cards.

Looking for Mexican cuisine? You're in luck; there are two restaurants that dish out tacos and cold Coronas. The most popular is **La Fonda** (73673). Service is slow, but you'll eventually get your chimichangas. Dinner for two costs about Sch350. Credit cards aren't taken, but there's an automatic teller machine around the corner.

In Kitzbühel, it's pizza, not schnitzel, that seems to be everywhere. Most bars serve small single size pizzas, but they're not what you might expect—an Austrian pizza has a thinner crust and less topping than its American cousin.

The **Restaurant Pizza and Pasta** (2166) serves an excellent selection of spaghetti dishes, as does **Il Gusto** (72790). Dinner for two runs around Sch400.

Insomniacs should drop by **Zum Zinnkrug** (2613) which is the closest thing to an all-night diner. Open all the time, it serves a great Kaiserschmarren and accepts credit cards. Dinner for two costs roughly Sch400.

In Kirchberg, most arrangements are for full pension. If you want to go out on the town, the best restaurant is the one attached to the **Sporthotel Alexander**. For excellent wild game, try the **Kirchenwirt**.

On the slopes, head for the **Gasthof Schroll** for *Kaiserschmarren aus der Pfanne*.

 ## Après-ski/nightlife

What you do in Kitzbühel after skiing is as important as the skiing itself; for some it's even more important. The nightlife should be renamed morning life, because things don't really get underway until 2 a.m. or so. That's when you can hear the whoops, yells, laughter and song of bar-crawling skiers as they slide down the sidewalks.

Amazingly, there are only a few bars that cater to the after-hours crowd. Jet-laggers searching for a cold brew and a warm pizza should follow the stairs in the cellar of **Praxmeier** (01143 5355/2646) open 10 p.m.–2 a.m., "but we really don't close until five or so," says the bartender. Watch out for the darts!

British expatriates can rely on their instincts to find the **Londoner** (71427) and **Big Ben** (71100), two almost authentic pubs. The Londoner is across from McDonald's. You'll find Big Ben if you wander along the town square in the *Fussgängerzone* (pedestrian zone) .

In the mood for a little sing-along? Head down to the **Happy Horse** on the outskirts of town at Ehrenbachgasse, the only karaoke in Kitzbühel (73716).

There are four discos in the town square area. **Club Take 5** at Hinterstadt 22 (713006), **Olympia** at Hinterstadt 6 (72271), **Royal** at Hinterstadt 9 (51094) featuring the only English-speaking disk jockey, and **K&K** on Bichlstrasse 3 (3425). Generally, discos don't open until 9 p.m., and often close at dawn.

Gambling guests can spin the roulette wheel at Hotel Goldener Grief's **Casino**

Kitzbühel open 7 p.m.–2 a.m. daily during the regular ski season. Visitors may try their luck at baccarat, blackjack, wheel of fortune, red dog, poker and slot machines. Call 2300.

Although we said earlier that Kirchberg is quieter than its somewhat fancier neighbor, it does claim perhaps the wildest après-ski bar in Europe, **The Londoner.** This bar has been copied in other towns, but none is as exciting as the original. It's dance-til-you-melt time from about 4–8 p.m., when most head off to dine in their hotels. This is the wild après-ski party you've dreamed of.

Later, head to the **Fuchslöchl** or **Arena** for dancing. The party seems to shift locations each night, but Kirchberg is small enough to make it easy to check out the action and then head back to where everyone's hanging out.

Child care

The Kitzbühel tourist office (2155-0 or 2272) keeps a list of licensed, multilingual babysitters. Ski schools also offer full-day lessons for ski kindergarten for kids from ages two-and-a-half to five.

In Kitzbühel, the kindergarten for children one to three is handled by Silvia Egert (74891) for Sch400 a day including lunch and snacks. Anita Halder (55852), a nurse, also watches children for an hourly charge.

In Kirchberg there is the **Krabbelstube** (4255), a kindergarten for children from infant to six years, open Monday through Friday, 7:15 a.m.–6 p.m. and Saturdays from 7:15 a.m.–noon. Prices are Sch220 for a half day and Sch440 for a full day. **Happy Kinderland** in Residenzhotel Cordial (2842) is open daily, except Saturdays, 8:30 a.m.–5 p.m. Cost is Sch150 a day, which includes lunch. Babysitting service is available through the tourist office. The ski school in Kirchberg also has special children's programs; rates are the same as for the normal ski school, with an additional Sch85–90 for lunch. The **Children's Mini Club Total** has care for Sch250 per half day and Sch450 for a full day.

Other activities

The Aquarena (4385) is the indoor sports area, with a swimming pool, sauna, steamroom and solarium. Admission is Sch80 for adults, Sch50 for children.

Kitz-Tandem-Flights at Winklernfeld 1, (3143) offers parasailing flights. Basic courses run from Sch5,500–5,900. Clinics cost Sch1,000 per day. Or contact Hermanns Flugschule (3097) and Flugschule Kitzbühel (05334-68680); both operate courses and testflights.

Balloon trips are available through Balloning Tyrol in St. Johann (05352/5666). Other activities include ice skating at the Center Court, which charges Sch70 for adults, Sch35 for children for a 2 1/2 hour session.

Sleigh rides are available through Henntalhof at Unterbrunnweg 21, (4624). They cost Sch500 per hour, and one sleigh can seat up to five people. Rides are also offered by Eberl Hubert at Innerstaudach 58 (37242). Carriages seat up to five people and cost Sch500.

Getting there

The most common route to Kitzbühel is via Munich. Innsbruck and Salzburg are also popular arrival points. Although train service is available, many prefer the 3 1/2 hour drive from Munich in a rental car. Express trains shave about an hour off your travel time and leave twice a day. Round-trip tickets are about Sch500 from Munich, Sch456 from Salzburg, and Sch312 from Innsbruck. A ski bus connects Kitzbühel and St. Johann with the Munich Airport twice each Saturday leaving the airport at noon and 3 p.m. for the two-and-a-half-hour trip. The fare is approximately $40. Call Busreisen Tirol at 0512-2455511, fax 0512-266460.

Tourist information

The Tousimusverband Kitzbühel (Kitzbühel Tourism) is reachable at A-6370 Kitzbühel, Austria; 05356/2155-0 or 05356/2272, fax 05356/2307.

Toursimusverband Kirchberg, Postfach 28, A-6365 Kirchberg, Austria; (05357-2309, fax 05357-3732).

For snow reports in English, 05356-182.

☎ *The local prefix for Kitzbühel is 05356;*
   for Kirchberg the prefix is 05357.

Mayrhofen
Zillertal and Tuxertal

The three ski regions around Mayrhofen—Penken, Ahorn and Horberg/Gerent—keep their snow longer than most Austrian resorts because of their altitude (about 1,800 to 2,250 meters). Its geographic location in the mountains to the southeast of Innsbruck ensures an extended season with better-than-average conditions.

There are 99 km. of runs in the Mayrhofen area for a total of 1,370 meters of vertical drop. Like a fortress protected on all sides by steep cliffs, its slopes are inaccessible except by gondola in winter and a winding one-lane road in summer.

English is spoken by most natives, but most visitors to Mayrhofen originate from Germany and the Netherlands, with a strong contingent of Britons and Australians and an occasional American.

In February, Austria is Mayrhofen's biggest customer, offering a steady flow of visitors on one-week holiday. It's best to check before making vacation plans so you don't hit a busy week.

A smaller town that makes resort noises is Zell am Ziller at the head of the valley. Hintertux is far up in the Tuxertal Valley at the base of one of the best glaciers for summer skiing. (Hintertux makes no pretense of being anything but a glacier ski resort: if it had sidewalks, they would be rolled up when the lifts close.)

Mountain layout

The Ahorn ski area provides beginners with a good place to start. But with only six runs, intermediates will soon lose interest and look longingly across the valley to the Penken region.

The recent refurbishing of the Penken gondola lets skiers zip to the base station of the ski area in virtually no time. Once at the top it takes two more lifts to reach the summit. Trails tend to be steep and well-worn, regardless of where you descend.

If you want more of an opportunity for powder, try the Horberg/Gerent area, one ridge over from the Lärchwald Express lift. Slopes leading directly to Mayrhofen are usually closed, but most skiers ignore the signs and ski as far down as they can.

Elsewhere in the valley, we recommend Hochfügen, only a short distance from the autobahn exit. Drive to the town from Fügen along an eight-mile mountain highway. From there, lifts ascend to 7,226 feet.

Take the Spieljoch cable car directly to the 6,562 foot level above Fügen. From the top, at the Onkeljoch, there is a four-mile run back into the valley, the Zillertal's longest downhill run.

Skiers need not be concerned about missing a trail marker and ending up at the bottom of the wrong mountain, because the trails are very well marked.

Zell am Ziller is a beautiful town, the most important in the lower part of the valley, but the skiing was too far from town to suit us. You can drive the steep 2.5-mile road up to the Gerlosstein lifts, but if you are not used to driving with chains, take the bus or try another resort.

Hintertux and the Tuxertal

The glacier opens at the end of the valley, and from the ground station you can see most of the nearly 50 miles of trails above. The best run is the trail from the Grosser Kaserer (10,700 feet) down over a great steep field of bumps to the gondola. A nice intermediate run leads from the top of the Gefrorene Wand to the Spannagel house, a cozy Alpine hut serving excellent food.

Opposite the glacier is the Sommerbergalm, with skiing from the 7,544-foot level.

Mountain rating

This valley is glowing intermediate, linked with some of the best beginner terrain in Austria and made even more desirable thanks to Mayrhofen's excellent ski schools.

For snow reports, call 62373.

Ski School (97/98 prices)

There are five ski schools in Mayrhofen with more than 150 qualified instructors to teach all grades of skiers. The Austrian ski method is used on all courses. The Hintertux ski school (tel. 63363) has 20 instructors.

Group Lessons

Prices are uniform, and competition for the skier is tight.

Regardless of the school you select, you'll pay Sch600–630 for one day of lessons, Sch1,250–1,300 for three days. Six days will amount to Sch1,450.

Children's lessons are slightly less and include lunch. The schools are: Ski School Uli Spiess, owned by World Cup winner Uli Spiess (tel. 62795), Ski School Manfred Gager (tel. 63800), Ski School Mayrhofen Total (tel. 63939), and Peter Habeler Ski and Alpine School (tel. 62829). Most ski schools offer rentals.

Snowboarding

Again, prices seem to vary little from school to school. Classes cost Sch380. A great way to learn and save money is with friends. Most private lessons include one to three people at a daily charge of Sch2,000 (one person) to Sch2,800 (three people). Your choices: snowboarding school Yeti-Club Mayrhofen (tel. 62795), Mayrhofen Total (tel. 63939) and Peter Habeler Ski & Alpine School (tel. 62829) and Manfred Gager (tel.63800).

Private Lessons

Mayrhofen's private groups can include up to three people, and as with snowboarding, the more in your group, the more you save. A private lesson for one person, for instance, costs Sch2,000. But for three people, the total charge is Sch2,800—a far more reasonable expense if you're skiing with family or friends and want to improve your style.

Cross-country

If you left your cross-country equipment at home, don't worry. Rentals are less expensive than downhill equipment—Sch80 to Sch110 per day, depending on the store. Weekly discounts are always available.

Mayrhofen offers nine trails with a total of 20 km. All trails are rated easy, making this an ideal place to learn. Overall, cross-country opportunities are not really outstanding, though, especially for the more advanced.

Cross-country lessons generally cost the same as downhill instruction, and are usually offered privately. Your choices: Ski School Uli Spiess, owned by World Cup winner Uli Spiess (tel. 62795), Ski School Manfred Gager (tel. 63800), Ski School Mayrhofen Total (tel. 63939), and Peter Habeler Ski and Alpine School (tel. 62829).

Lift tickets (97/98 prices)

Buying a lift ticket can be a perplexing task. Mayrhofen sells a variety of passes with a complex price structure. Want to ski exclusively at Mayrhofen, or at all 154 Ziller Valley lifts? Tickets for each individual resort are available, as well as for the regional Zillertaler-Superskipass. We recommend buying the Superskipass.

Mayrhofen area lifts

half day (starting at 11 a.m.)	Sch310
one day	Sch350
two days	Sch650
three days	Sch915

Zillertaler–Superskipass

	With Glacierlift	No Glacierlift
four days	Sch1,410	Sch1,210
six days	Sch1,965	Sch1,650
seven days	Sch2,225	Sch1,860

Youths (14–18) get a 20% discount. Childern under 14 get a 40% discount.

Accommodations

When considering an appropriate hotel or apartment in Mayrhofen, keep a few points in mind. First, the number of stars on a property only means you'll pay more, and not always get more. Second, price is dictated less by proximity to lifts than by which bank of the Ziller river it sits on. Cross the bridge to the west bank and you'll pay less—not just for lodging but food and drink as well. Prices here are per person, half-board, based on double occupancy.

American visitors usually prefer the **Hotel Neuhaus** (tel. 6703). Guests are treated to authentic Alpine motif lobbies, with sparsely furnished rooms and an indoor pool. Visitors may watch a movie, go bowling, shoot pool or get a massage in the spa. Prices range from Sch750 to Sch1,200. Credit cards are accepted.

The **Hotel Zillertaler Hof** (tel. 62265), a quiet and modern property, also features an indoor pool. With its venerable antiques and wood carvings on display, this inn emanates style. Rates don't reflect the impressive list of amenities. Prices are Sch690–890.

For a little extra room, try the **Hotel Neue Post** (tel. 62131), with its airy, tastefully decorated lobby and generous-sized rooms. One of Mayrhofen's earliest guest houses, it was recently remodeled and now includes sauna, whirlpools, solarium, extensive restaurants and dining rooms. Rates are Sch700–780.

Want lots of antiques? The **Hotel Strass** (tel. 6705) prides itself in its historic furniture and decorations. But its prices are very up-to-date. Three other properties are also owned by the same family: **Sporthotel Strass, Villa/Aparthotel Strass** and **Hotel Garni Strass**. Prices are Sch730–940.

Across the Ziller River is the **Gasthof Brücke** (tel. 62232), which is also a big après-ski attraction. It has a nice lobby, medium-size rooms with antique furniture and beautiful tiled floors. The Gasthof plays host to a decidedly younger crowd. Many skiers take a short stroll from here to the town's only outdoor watering hole, Nikki Shirmbar. Guests should expect to pay Sch650 to Sch750 depending on the time of year.

Hintertux has several hotels right at the base of the glacier. If you're intent on skiing and little else, they're a good choice.

Hotel Rindererhof (tel. 05287-501, fax 50210). Excellent location right at the gondola going up to the glacier. Superb for the enthusiastic skier.

Hotel Neu Hintertux (tel. 05287-318, fax 318409). Almost as close to the lifts as the Rindererhof.

Badhotel Kirchler (tel. 05287-312). Large, beautiful, expensive and comfortable.

Hotel Kirchlerhof (tel. 05287-431). A comfortable, medium-priced hotel in Lanersbach catering to families. Excellent breakfast buffet.

Zell am Ziller is a picturesque village tucked in a secluded section of the valley. The family-run **Hotel Theresa** (tel. 05282-2286, fax 05282-4235) has been described as four-star with five-star amenities. The English-speaking family does everything it can to make your visit enjoyable. The ski shuttlebus comes to the door and credit cards are accepted.

There are 23 different mountain huts spread across the valley. These offer inexpensive, rustic accommodations in dorm-like rooms. The tourist office will provide a list of these huts. A quick glance at the column listing beds is enlightening when the listing reads 8 beds/26 mattresses.

Apartments

As elsewhere, the quality of apartments varies in Mayrhofen. Some double as hotels in peak season and offer a long list of amenities; others are simple rooms, with little else. Usually, the farther from town they are, the less you'll pay, though you'll find exceptions.

The Ziller River remains an important natural boundary—on the west bank the cost of a room drops.

Prices vary dramatically. Some properties will charge Sch200 in peak season for a no-frills room, while others ask for Sch710 per night.

A directory of apartments is available from the Mayrhofen tourist office.

Dining

A cursory survey of restaurants in the Mayrhofen area suggests that there's a dining cartel setting menu prices. But a careful survey will reveal that some restaurants are trying their hardest to stay competitive. (Again, cross the river to find the best prices.)

At the **Fleishhauerei** (literally: The Butcher Shop), just across the river along the Ahornstrasse, patrons may order a decent Spätzle, an Austrian pasta specialty with cheese, or any number of native meat dishes. During the evening, witness locals wagering their Schillings on card games, which can be more entertaining to watch than play. No credit cards. Dinner for two costs about Sch250.

The **Grillküchl** (36126) is a small, cozy restaurant with prices that certainly don't match the rich and intricate wood decor. Show up early to get a table and enjoy an outstanding steak sandwich. No credit cards. Dinner for two costs roughly Sch250.

If you're looking for a romantic dining spot with real Austrian cuisine try the **Hotel Neuhaus Restaurant** (6703). Be sure to make early reservations to get into one of the small Stube, a dining area with wonderful ambiance. Servings are small, so several courses are a must. Credit cards accepted. Dinner for two costs at least Sch500.

The most controversial and garish building in town, where pronounced pastels decorate the circular edifice, is home to the **Cafe Rundum** (63737). It serves light meals and desserts. No credit cards. Pizza costs around Sch75.

The **Singapore Restaurant** (63912) dishes out authentic hot and sour soup and flavorful main courses that will jump-start your taste buds. Credit cards welcome. Dinner for two costs Sch450, but lunch is a bargain at about Sch220.

On the slopes Mayrhofen has excellent restaurants as well. There are two on the Ahorn side of the valley and more than a half-dozen on the Penken.

 Après-ski/nightlife

Most bars get hopping about an hour before the lifts close and stay open until 1 a.m. or shortly thereafter. Discos, the most common nightlife outlets, usually close at 4 a.m. on the dot.

There are six discos in town. The two most popular are the **Sports Arena Disco** (6705) and **Papageno** (6700. Other dance spots include **Schlüsselalm** (62232) **Post Tenne** (62131) **Andreas Keller** (62615) and **Fuchslöchl** (62519). Cover charges can vary from Sch50 to Sch100.

Across from the **Café Rundum** is **Scotland Yard** (62339), a British-style pub complete with an operating British phone booth. The selection of on-tap beers is extensive.

At **Nikki's Shirmbar**, an outdoor watering hole with loud music, expect to see skiers dancing on tables in their boots. At Nikki's, just across the river along Ahorn strasse, the fun starts around 3:30 p.m. If you're looking for a specialty drink, avoid the main bar (under the umbrella) and head to the side bar where Schnapps Shots (say that three times fast) in edible wafer shot-glasses are prepared for around Sch50. Don't forget the napkin!

Sporthotel Strass (6705) serves more reasonably priced drinks and features excellent après-ski entertainment. The crowd packs the inside and outdoor bars. It's a madhouse. After 9:30 p.m. it gets unbelievably crowded, even on weekdays.

In Hintertux, try the **Batzenkeller**, the **Almbar**, the **Nostalschi Bar** in the Hotel Berghof, or the **Papperla-Pub**.

Child care

This is an area of resort expertise where Mayrhofen excels. Ski schools provide day care and ski instruction for children. **Riki's Skikindergarten and Kinderskischool** was Austria's first children's ski school, its organizers told us, and its program provides instruction, meals and entertainment for the children during non-skiing time.

Rates with lunch are for one day Sch730, for two days Sch1,290, for three days Sch1,610, and for six days, Sch2,170.

Ski school without lunch is Sch600 for one day; for two days, Sch630; for three days, Sch1,050; and for six days, Sch1,250.

Mayrhofen's Guest Kindergarten, called **Wuppy's Kinderland,** takes children from three months to two years of age. It is open Monday–Friday from 8 a.m.–6 p.m. Price for a full day of supervision is Sch320, for a half day Sch180 and for five consecutive days, Sch1,500. Lunch costs Sch50 per day. The kindergarten also hires out strollers, prams, and cots for children. It has a swimming pool, nursery school facilities and other activities. Private baby-sitters are also available.

The Mayrhofen Tourist Office (6760) provides a babysitting referral service. They also publish a directory of services, which includes information about child care.

Getting there

Mayrhofen is nestled in the Ziller valley, about 190 km. from Munich and 170 km. from Salzburg. Rail connections are available, but the most popular way of getting to Mayrhofen is by bus or car, since the train operates on a single small track, and direct rail service is not available from either airport; passengers must switch to a train or bus at Jenbach. For more information on rail or bus connections, call the Mayrhofen train station at 2362.

Other activities

Tobogganing is the extracurricular activity of choice here, perhaps because it includes heavy drinking. Sledders hitch a ride to the Tuxer Valley in a motorcoach and ascend to the top of a 6-km. run at the Höllenstein Hütte (which appropriately means the hut built on hell's stone). There they imbibe mulled wine before zipping down the mountain. For more information, call Action Club Zillertal at 62977. Cost is Sch270 per person.

Snowbobbing is another enjoyable alternative to skiing. Again, drinking is recommended for adults. You bounce down the slope on inner tubes. Call Action Club Zillertal or Happy Bobbing at 62977. Cost is Sch80 per hour.

Skiers who feel a little lebensmüde (tired of life) can try heart-stopping flights over the Zillertal. About Sch700 will get you airborne. Three operators provide the tours.

Tourist information

The Mayrhofen Tourism is located at the Europahaus in Mayrhofen, Dursterstrasse 225, Postfach 21, A-6290 Mayrhofen, Austria; (05285) 5285 or 2305, fax (05285) 411633.

E-mail: mayrhofen@zillertal.tirol.at

Web site: http://tiscover.com/mayrhofen

☎ *Telephone prefix for Mayrhofen is 05285.*

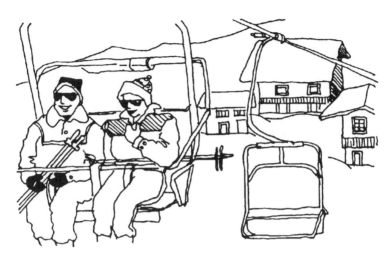

Oetztal
Sölden, Hochsölden, Obergurgl, Hochgurgl

If it's great skiing you want with unforgettable scenery, the Oetztal is in a class with only a handful of European ski valleys. The tall jagged mountains are an effective barrier to severe weather, and help preserve good snow conditions during the end of the year. To the south, across a road passable only in summer, lies Italy. To the north a winding road spills out of the Oetz Valley after numerous tunnels and bridges.

With the possible exception of a few warm weeks in August and September, these mountains are always skiable. When the snow disappears in the lower elevations, vacationers ascend to the glacier and ride its eternally frozen runs.

Once upon a time, all the resorts worked together with a valley ski pass that included the Sölden/Hochsölden areas together with the higher Obergurgl/Hochgurgl areas. This no longer seems to be the case with each section of the Oetztal going its own way. Since the lift systems were not interconnected, the only people who suffer are the skiers with less options for skiing. The Sölden region and the Gurgls are covered separately in each section below.

The two main resorts in respective valleys are Sölden and Obergurgl. Hochsölden is a suburb of Sölden, huddled above the larger town, and Hochgurgl is merely a cluster of six hotels up the mountain from Obergurgl.

Sölden is stretched along the main road that traverses the valley. If only the road could go around the town, this would be an even more fantastic resort. Unfortunately, visitors will have to dodge the constant traffic cutting through the town. Hochsölden is perched on a small plateau above the main town.

Obergurgl and Hochgurgl are both a further fifteen-minute drive back into the mountains from Sölden. Obergurgl is a picture-perfect Alpine town tucked into the mountains, complete with old church steeple and picturesque hotels. Another village, Untergurgl, is even smaller and less expensive with its own rural charm, but not within walking distance of lifts; however, it is adjacent to one of the main cross-country systems.

Obergurgl is, unlike Sölden, virtually traffic-free. It has a tradition of serving British clientele. You will quickly realize you are in a true Austrian village where time-tested tradition reigns. The smaller dorf of Hochgurgl is a clutch of remote, excellent hotels clinging to the side of steep slopes.

Mountain layout

Sölden

Let's look first at the ski slopes above Sölden. They are split into two areas—the Giggijoch-Hochsölden and the Gaislachkogl. The skiing overall is wide open. Though there are trails marked on the map, with good snow, you can ski virtually anywhere, which makes Sölden a favorite of powderhounds and means plenty of skiing above the treeline. The skiing is basically various levels of intermediate with some expert off-piste runs thrown in for good measure. In fact, an adventurous expert will have no trouble keeping busy above Sölden and in the Obergurgl/ Hochgurgl areas. Beginners will be limited in their choice of trails.

Access to the slopes is either by cable car starting from the upper end of Sölden or by gondola from the lower end. The gondola drops skiers in the middle of the Giggijoch-Hochsölden sector. Take either the chair or surface lift up to Rotkoglhütte, or traverse over to the restaurant and take the chair up to Haimbachjoch. The Haimbachjoch side of the mountain is by far the more difficult of the two.

Regardless of your ability, don't miss a trip up the Gaislachkogel gondola, an ultra-modern high-speed lift that whisks skiers to one of the highest summits. You can reach the lift from either the bottom, at the Mittelwindau, or via its middle station along Trail No. 1. On a clear day you can see the highest peak in Italy and, just a few kilometers from where you're staying, the famous site where the 5,000-year-old frozen body of Oetzi, known to some as the Iceman, was discovered just a few years ago.

The trails from the top of the Gaislachkogel are challenging for advanced intermediates and above.

To avoid crowds on the Hainbachjoch quad, take the two other nearby chairs that deliver downhillers to equally good or superior spots on the mountain with far less wait.

Snowboarding is extremely popular in the Oetztal. A formidable half-pipe is cut above the Langegg chair lift allowing shredders to practice their stunts. A new snowboard park has been created to international standards at the Giggijoch.

Obergurgl and Hochgurgl

The skiing above Obergurgl and Hochgurgl is more extensive than Sölden, but served by fewer lifts, with plenty of off-piste action. For years skiers could cruise down from Hochgurgl to Obergurgl but there was no lift to bring them back up the Hochgurgl trails— this year a new lift connects the two areas. The slopes are not particularly difficult, but more challenging than those in Sölden. Above Obergurgl, the Festkogl lift opens to a wide face with unlimited intermediate skiing. Experts can drop to the right-hand side of the lift and take the unprepared run through the Ferwaltal back to the lower lift station. This area is high (6,369 to 10,015 feet) with good, crisp snow. For a change, traverse over to the

Hohe Mut area, which has a good unprepared run from the Hohe Mut restaurant and a group of shorter lifts and runs.

Hochgurgl is reached by bus, if you aren't staying there. This town has developed into a relatively upscale community anchored by one of the best luxury Alpine hotels in Europe, the Hotel Hochgurgl. Lifts peak out at 10,170 feet, where a mountain restaurant provides spectacular views. The skiing for experts is down the Königstal, for beginners in the center of the area, and for intermediates under the Kirchenkarlift. Like Obergurgl, this area is perfect for continuous off-piste cruising.

Both Obergurgl and Hochgurgl have good beginner slopes.

This region, with glacier skiing above 6,270 feet, has excellent summer skiing.

If you want to concentrate on cross-country skiing, choose another area. Some trails exist, but not the network you'll need to ensure variety.

One last hot tip: ski on Saturday. German visitors, like clockwork, consistently and predictably use Saturday as a travel day and leave the slopes practically abandoned.

Mountain rating

With a few exceptions, particularly from the Gaislachkogl, these runs are for intermediates. Some contributors have rated every marked run some variation of intermediate.

There are enough training areas at the bottom for ski schools. The beginner has plenty of terrain, especially in the center of the Giggijoch/Hochsölden sector, to ski. Overgurgl and Hochgurgl would be the best choice for absolute beginners or those on their second trip to the slopes.

Experts looking for wild steeps will find the Oetztal only moderately interesting, but those seeking unlimited off-piste will find a dream come true. In summer, when skiing is a real luxury, this is one of Europe's finest areas.

Slopes are well-marked and considerably wider than at other Austrian resorts.

The Gurgls offer wonderful above-treeline skiing where if you see it, you can ski it mountainsides. There is skiing for every level of skier. Beginners have plenty of room and experts can look for wide open spaces but without much extreme challenge.

Ski school (97/98 prices)

There are three ski schools in the region with about 250 instructors.
Group Lessons

A day of lessons is Sch700, Sch1,500 for three days. The weekly charge is about Sch2,500. Children's lessons are slightly less but include lunch. The schools are Sölden-HochSölden Ski School (tel. 2364), Oetztal 2000 (tel. 2203-500) and Total Vacancia (tel. 3100).

Snowboarding

Classes cost Sch600–700 for a day and Sch1,990–2,040 for six days. Private lessons (one to three people) cost Sch 1,400 for two hours or Sch2,200 for four hours.

Private Lessons

One of the best ways to tour the Oetztal is to hire a private ski guide.

Instructors are also more knowledgeable of the best off-piste skiing, which can only mean one thing, powder, powder, powder!

As elsewhere, the more people to join your private group, the less you'll end up paying. A private lesson for one person, for instance, costs Sch2,300, but for three people the total charge is Sch 2,900.

Above in the **Gurgls**, the two main schools are associated with the two main towns. The Obergurgl Skischule (tel. 05256-305) has about 85 instructors and is considered on of Austria's best. **Group lessons** cost Sch560 for a full day, Sch1,200 for three days, and Sch1,480 for five days. There is no significant reduction for children. **Private lessons** for one or two skiers are provided by half day (two hours) or full day (four hours). Expect to pay approximately Sch2,300 per day when signing up for three days of lessons and then discounts start to kick in of about Sch100 per day. Additional skiers will add Sch250 per day to the rates. Half-day rates are set at Sch1,400 per two-hour session.

Obergurgl snowboard lessons cost Sch350 for an afternoon, Sch990 for three afternoon lessons or Sch1,850 for six afternoon sessions. Cross-country lessons are Sch350 per half day for groups of at least five skiers.

The Hochgurgl Skischule (tel. 05256-26599) is much smaller with just over a dozen instructors. Its reputation is not as polished nor its courses as organized. Group lessons cost Sch590 for a full day, Sch1,250 for three days, and Sch1,490 for five days.

Cross-country skiing

There is a 19.5-km. loop around the Sölden region. However, 50 km. of tracks are accessible via the cross-country ski bus to Langenfeld (or a 20 minute hike). Rentals are available at all sport shops in the area. The daily charge for rentals is Sch 100–150 per day, depending on the store. Weekly discounts are always available.

The Sölden-Hochsölden Ski School (2364) offers cross-country and telemark instruction for about the same prices as downhill lessons.

Obergurgl, Hochgurgl and Untergurgl have limited cross-country tracks near each village. Hochgurgl is pretty much for downhillers and snowboarders.

Lift tickets (97/98)

Sölden/Hochsölden

Because the Sölden is a year-round ski area, a variety of passes and tickets are sold. The rate schedule can seem even more confusing than a lift map. High season includes the Christmas/New Year period and February through early April. Middle season is for the last three weeks of January. If you want to ski more than three days, bring a photograph for identification purposes in both the Söldens and the Gurgles. Children are generally 8-14 years. These are Solden's high-season rates; low-season rates are about 10 percent less.

	Adults	Children (8–14)	Youth (15-19)
one day	Sch450	Sch280	Sch320
three days	Sch1,170	Sch690	Sch830
six days	Sch2,100	Sch1,170	Sch1,470
14 days	Sch3,610	Sch1,810	Sch2,610

Seniors (men over 65 and women over 60) pay about Sch100 less per lift ticket than normal adults. Children under 8 ski free. A special family rate allows certain kids to ski free, but the formula is complicated and should probably be figured out on the spot.

Skiers may also buy a Rettungskarte (mountain patrol card) for about Sch40. If you get lost and require assistance from the patrol, or if you're injured in an accident, the card acts as insurance. Without the card, the charge is Sch1,500 or more.

The Gurgls

	Adults	Children (8-16)
half-day (from noon)	Sch330	Sch210
one day	Sch420	Sch280
three days	Sch1,170	Sch740
six days	Sch2,090	Sch1,280
14 days	Sch3,530	Sch2,160

Seniors over 60 years of age are charged the same rate as children.

Accommodations

The prices are half board, based on double occupancy. The first price is the low end of the middle season, normally most of January and the first week of February; the second price is the top price during high season (Christmas, New Year and Feburary).

The most lavish and beautifully decorated hotel in Sölden is the **Central Hotel** (22600; fax 2260511)—a true five-star in every sense of the word. Even its pool is a cut above anything else in Austria. With Roman architecture, tall ceilings and classic paintings, it is unlike any winter resort on earth. Its prices are Sch1,234–2,374.

One of the newer hotels in town is the **Hotel Tamara** (5040; fax 50415) which offers what may be the friendliest concierge service in Sölden. The furniture is new but the antiques are real. Its prices Sch784–1,104.

At the **Liebe Sonne** (22030; fax 2423) modern mixes with the old. A large rock fountain, marble floors and modern art combine with minimalist furniture. Rates are Sch900 –2,100; apartments are available. They have their own ski school.

Hotel Erhart (2020; fax 20205) A four-star with great restaurant. Frans, the owner and generous host features ski safari and dinner/toboggan Ride to entertain guests. The ski safari starts with schnapps and then skiing. Guests are grouped by skiing ability. On Thursday nights Frans takes the guests up the mountain to a hut for dinner and a toboggan ridedown. Offers both vegetarian and children's menu, beautiful wine cellar, sauna, and ski room. This newly renovated hotel is a 5-10 minute walk to the Gaislachkoglbahn Talstation. Rates are Sch774–1,354

Hotel am Hof (2241; fax 2121111) This hotel has rustic post and beam construction, with wooden floors, fitness and massage room, suana and steam bath, parking garage and ski room. It is off of the main road and central to town. Rates are Sch790–1,130

Hotel Sölderhof (5030; fax 50350) Some rooms have showers and some have baths— if you have a preference, please request. Most rooms have a balcony. Hotel hosts weekly activites for guests from a ski safari to curling instructions and games. Suana, whirlpool, solarium and ski room round out the ammenities. The restaurant also serves the public. Rates are Sch694–1,254

Hotel Hochsölden (2229; fax 225951) Halfway up the mountain, in Hochsölden, this is a ski-in/ski-out property for most of the season. There are few extras, but the location is unbeatable. Rates are Sch780–1,600. They have their own ski school.

Montana (2327; fax 232750) A B&B with apartments, suana, tanning bed, T.V. and radio in rooms. It is at the base of the Giggijochbahn cable car. Apartment accomodates two to six people and has a living room, bedroom, T.V., snd kitchen All rooms and apartments are Sch330–550, and the rooms include a buffet breakfast.

Arnold Andre (2269; fax 2954) A B&B owned and operated by World Cup ski racer

Andre Arnold and his wife. Rates are Sch390–500.

Gastehaus Larchenpark (2386; fax 2386) This B&B with its stained glass and crystal displays is near the Giggijoch lift. All 22 rooms have either a shower or bath and toilet. The cost is Sch300–500.

Obergurgl and Hochgurgl

The Special Week price is for the January package, which includes seven days half pension and six days of lifts. The last price is per person for half board based on double occupancy during the main season; high-season rates are 10–15 percent higher.

Hotel Hochgurgl (05256-265; fax 26510) Perhaps one of the best hotels in the Alps, by any measure. It matches elegance with the Zürserhof in Zürs and the Palace in St. Moritz. Special Week: Sch15,770–17,240. Daily rate: Sch1,690–1,990.

Hotel Edelweiss and Gurgl (05256-223; fax 449) Very close to the lifts. Special Week: Sch8,070–9,680. Daily rate: Sch890–1,200.

Hotel Madeleine (05256-3540; fax 354355) Special Week: Sch6,568–7,768. Daily rate: Sch718–1,056.

Pensione Wiesental (05256-263; fax 3583) Very convenient to the lifts in the old town. Special Week: Sch6,670–6,950. Daily rate: Sch610–790.

Hotel Gamper (05256-5450; fax 31760) In the center of the town with an excellent kitchen. Special Week: Sch7,090–8,140. Daily rate: Sch650–950.

Hotel Ideal (05256-2900; fax 302) The bargain of Hochgurgl with all the amenities—sauna, fitness room, and garage. Special Week: Sch7,195. Daily rate: Sch750–810.

The **Hotel Wurmkogel** and the **Hotel Laurin** in Hochgurgl are also recommended.

 ## Dining

Solden has over fifty different restaurants, plus the hotels offer excellent meals as part of their full- and half-board options. These are some or our suggestions.

At **Sölderhof** (2317), two four-course meals with a salad bar are offered daily for hotel guests. The menu changes daily and the food is consistently good. Some credit cards taken. Reservations are recommended. Dinner for two is Sch500.

Cafe Heiner (2467) is the closest thing to a diner in Sölden, serving a lighter fare, like personal pizzas, and drinks. Lunch runs about Sch350 for two.

Restaurant Dominic (2646), connected to the après-ski bar Bla-Bla, provides a religious experience, with stained glass ceilings, ornate wood carvings and pew-like chairs. Be prepared to donate for food and scenery about Sch250, and bring your credit card.

The **Parkhotel** restaurant (2250) specializes in grilled food such as steaks and lamb chops at reasonable prices. Dinner for two is about Sch450. No credit cards.

The **Stefan Restaurant** (tel. 2237) opened in 1351; some of the furniture appears to go back at least that far. It is as typically Austrian as you will find. Specialties are game dishes from Tyrol. No credit cards. Dinner is Sch600 for two.

Freizeit Arena Restaurant (tel: 5254) has great steak and pasta. Lego toys are available to entertain the kids. Moderate.

In Hochgurgl, the **Hotel Hochgurgl** has a wonderful **Tiroler Stuben. The Hotel Ideal, Hotel Laurin** and the **Wurmkogl** all serve good basic cooking as well.

In Obergurgl head to the **Romantik** and **Belmonte** for Italian food. Try the **Gamper** and then the **Grüner** for good Tyrolean cooking. The **Josl** is known for its wild game.

Hubertushof has good fondue, raclette and tyrolean specialties. The **Wiesental** also serves excellent meals in the center of town.

Après-ski/nightlife

Apres-ski activites in Solden start after 3:00 p.m. and last until promptly at 7:00 when all bars empty of guests who head home to ready for dinner and nights filled withdancing, drinking, and smoking. Expect to pay a cover charge of $5.00 to get into most bars for the later night life.

On the way down the mountain make a stop at **Philipps** in Innerwald. This is a favorite outdoor bar on the main trail back into town.

Cafe Haus Heiners' outdoor bar is wild, with its D.J. dance music blasting in the streets. For coffee and conversation head inside. North end of Solden.

Joker — Da ist die Hölle los (We're raising hell here) is decked out in an infernal motif, with flames, goblins and demons. Old chair lifts converted into restaurant chairs are suspended from the ceiling. The early crowd is teenage and the later clients are older. They offer a selection of specialty drinks, and a climbable cliff leads to the **Bierhimmel** (Beer Heaven) similarly decorated with angels and clouds. Loud music and pizza are served up. Closed on Sundays. Some credit cards are accepted at both establishments.

Climb down to the **Oetzi Keller** (2234), decorated in tribute of the famous 5,000-year-old frozen body found in the nearby glacier. This is the late-night hot spot in town.

Dancers should go to **Centro Club CC** (2401-730) but not before 10 p.m. This cavernous disco and laser-light show is packed until 3 a.m. Beer is cheap, so let's party.

Another hot spot is the glass-enclosed **Bla-Bla Eisbar** at the Hotel Dominic (2646) which opens at 3 p.m. in time for the first après-skier. This is a young snowboarder crowd. Fun if you can squeeze in. **Madeus Dancing Bar** has a dance floor and a D.J. playing '70s dance music. **Lawine** blasts live rock'n'roll music. If you want a break from the rocking crowd, play pool if you get a table. **Stamperl Bar** has a Hawaiian motif. It is hopping after 2 a.m. The American-friendly owner lived in Hawaii and speaks excellent English. **Nanu Pub Cafe and Bar** is a good place in the evening after dinner for ice cream specialties, coffee drinks and conversation.

Crave mixed drinks with music for ballroom dancing? The upscale **Alibi Bar** at the Central Hotel (22600) is home to the Sch140 margarita—not for the faint of wallet. Credit cards accepted. At **Jacob's Weinfassl** (23170) you can taste a variety of Austrian and Italian wines in a quieter atmosphere.

In Obergurgl, the **Nederhütte** rocks with accordian and guitar for aprés-ski which should lubricate you for the final run down to the hotels. A stop at the **Edelweiss** Bar at the base of the Gaisberg lift is then in order. Later head to the **Joslkeller** with country music then discover the **Hexenkuch'l** in the Hotel Jenewein, the Krumpn's Stadl at Pension Schöne Aussicht, and the **Austria Keller** in the Hotel Austria with umm-pa-pa music and mugs of beer.

In Hochgurgl the place to be seen is the either the African Bar in the Hotel Hochgurgl or **Toni's Almhutte** at Sporthotel Olymp.

Child care
Sölden Region
The tourist information center in Sölden keeps a list of qualified babysitters and care providers, which is available upon request.

The ski kindergarten in Sölden (tel. 2364) accepts children three to eight years old and is open Sunday through Friday, 9 a.m.–4 p.m. Meals are Sch90 per day. A full day costs Sch480; three days are Sch1,110; and six days will be Sch1,600.

Ski School Total Vacancia for children includes child care during lunch, a terrain garden and children's racing school. The school is open 9:30 a.m. to noon and 1–3:30 p.m. Lunch is Sch110 per day. A full day costs Sch470; three days are Sch1,200; and six days will be Sch1,500.

Ski Kindergarten Oetztal 2000 is open from 10 a.m. to noon and from 1–3:30 p.m. Lunch is Sch50 per day. A full day costs Sch800; three days are Sch1,700; and six days will be Sch2,300.

Nursery services are offered. For information, contact the Sporthotel Schöne Aussicht in Hochsolden (tel. 2403).

The Gurgls

In Obergurgl the ski school runs a special course and a special course for nonskiing children. The cost for supervised lunch in the Gurgls is Sch180 per day.

Children's snow costs the same as ski school (basically the normal adult rate). Children 3–5 are accepted. It is open from 9:30 a.m.–12:30 p.m. and 1:30–4:30 p.m.

Getting there

Train service is not available to the Sölden area, making the bus and car the fastest way to get there. Located 225 km. from Munich (a 3 1/2 hour drive in good conditions) and 266 km. from Salzburg, this remote Alpine region along the Italian border offers a scenic, but at times difficult to traverse, 20-minute stretch of winding roads from the Autobahn. Bus service is also available every hour from Innsbruck. Prices start at about Sch200, but phone the train station at 05266-88225-34 before buying a ticket.

Other activities

Tobogganing tops the list of extracurricular activities in Sölden. Tradition calls for lots of drinks beforehand. Call Hotel Alpenland at 2365 or Gasthof Silbertal at 2987.

At the Freizeit Arena, a hot spot on cold and snowy days, visitors can swim; soak in a steambath; bake in a sauna, tan in the solarium, work out on an indoor tennis court or play volleyball, badminton or bowl. For more information call 2514.

Tandem flying provides a birds-eye view of the entire mountain range. Jump off a cliff in a parachute and hang for hours on thermal currents. Call Happy Flying at 2079. One trip costs roughly Sch 1,400.

Tourist information

Tourismus Oeztal, A-6450 Sölden, Austria; 05254-22120, fax 05254-3131.
Tourismus Gurgl, A-6456 Obergurgl, Austria; 05256-466, fax 05256-353.
Tourismusverband, A-6458 Vent, Austria; tel. 05254-8193.

☎ *Telephone prefix for Sölden, Hochsölden and Vent is 05254; for Hochgurgl and Obergurgl the prefix is 05256.*

Saalbach-Hinterglemm

You may have heard Saalbach's reputation as an après-ski "Animal House," but nothing can prepare you for the reality: you have stopped to enter the dark, woodsy Hinterhagalm tea bar on the last run down, having worked up a thirst on the nearly two-mile Asterabfahrt trail into Saalbach. By the time the first beer arrives, the waitress has to swing her tray to adjust to the unspoken rhythm of the overflow crowd, the clumping of ski boots keeping time to the beat of traditional Austrian folksongs from the live band.

Even before the T-bar outside the door closes for the day, the entire chalet is transformed into a dance floor. Legs dangling over the upstairs balcony jig to the two-step. By the time you're ready to locate your skis for the final 300-yard glide into the village, the way out is blocked by a swaying mass of bodies. You have to literally get down on your hands and knees and make a crawl for it. No one seems to notice. Then, just before you make it between the last set of legs separating you from the door outside, you hit your head on something. Looking up, you see you've bumped heads with someone crawling in. Welcome to the Saalbach-Hinterglemm Ski Circus, Austria's season-long version of Mardi Gras—one of the premier areas in Austria, strictly on the strength of its ski slopes and extensive lift circuit. There's no denying that this area attracts more than its share of the fun-loving.

The village of Saalbach forms the epicenter of the activity. Nestled in the narrow throat of the valley, with mountains crowding in as a backdrop for the chalet-style hotels and their carved wood balconies, the village is as quaint as any you could hope for in the Alps. The custard-yellow steeple of an old church dominates the packed rooftops, and a mountain stream rushes soothingly through the center of town.

The valley floor broadens considerably just a mile up the road at Hinterglemm, and the Saalach river, which runs the length of the valley, divides the town in two. Here hotels are larger and the village fans out over a wider area. While it is as central to the main ski crossroads of the valley as Saalbach and has more mid- to upper-level hotels with full amenities, Hinterglemm loses some of the coziness that you find along the streets of Saalbach. While Hinterglemm has the look and feel of a resort, everything about Saalbach says that it was an Alpine village in its own right before the ski rush began.

Mountain layout

Sallbach-Hinterglemm offers what may be the best interconnected lift system in Austria. Even an expert skier determined to put as many miles under his skis as possible would find himself hard pressed to cover the area from one end to the other in a single day—never mind stopping along the way to enjoy the skiing. Because resorts seem to use different measurements for charting how many miles of prepared ski runs they have, it's almost useless to compare numbers. Let's just say that there are 60 separate ski lifts in this area, as well as Austria's largest cable car. Alas, Saalbach also confirms that Austria remains more fond of the T-bar than any other country in the Alps.

The linear layout of the resort, with lifts covering both sides of a long valley, also argues for staying in its most central spot: Saalbach. That way you can head up the valley for one day's ski excursion and down the next. Anyone staying in Leogang on the other side of the mountain, for instance, will find it hard to even reach the area above Hinterglemm without having to immediately turn around to catch the last lift home. (While there's excellent bus service up and down the length of the valley serving both Saalbach and Hinterglemm, Leogang actually rests in another valley.)

Experts should head directly for Austria's largest cableway, the 100-person Schattberg. The black run directly beneath the cable car is a good example of why U.S. expert skiers keep coming back. It has good grade, it's bumpy, it's long, and there's a single ride back up for those with enough stamina to do it again.

For another uniquely European experience, head left at the top of the Schattberg cable car down the Limberg-Jausern trail. Though a relatively easy intermediate run, this is the longest trail in the area and worth taking just for the sake of adventure. Vorderglemm at the bottom of this run represents the southern boundary of the area, and you can cross up to the other side of the valley on the Schönleiten cable car.

Experts who turn right at the top of Schattberg (Schattberg-East) and up the short Westgipfel DSB III lift to Schattberg-West can enjoy a whole mountainside of advanced intermediate trails leading down into Hinterglemm. There's plenty of tree skiing on this broad swath of mountain, and the run all the way down is worthy indeed. Rather than heading back up the two lifts to Schattberg-West, cross over to the Zwölfer, let the new cable cars take you quickly back to the summit; you can ski down and continue up-valley to the next peak.

The runs down to the midstation from the top of Zwölfer (6,509 feet) are nice and very bumpy, and there are lots of fine cutovers into untouched sugar for powder monkeys (snow permitting, of course). From the top you can also cut over to the Seekar T-bar, which has advanced intermediate runs from the top and an excellent powder bowl off to the right. The adventurous can skirt the ridge heading left off the top of Seekar, then head through the trees.

Intermediates and advanced intermediates will discover that they truly have the ringside seats for the Ski Circus. The entire north side of the valley is one intermediate run after another down an open mountainside. Spend a day in the Hasenauer Köpfl and

Reiterkogel area just above Hinterglemm. If you head further to the left up the valley toward Spieleckkogel, you will stand about as high as you can in the valley (6,522 feet). The advanced intermediate run all the way down to the valley floor is long and excellent with a double chair lift back up.

Advanced intermediates will also enjoy taking the long Kohlmaisberg cable car, which begins in Saalbach near the old church. From the top, there's a long 3-km. advanced run down into Saalbach. This is one of the nicest sections of mountain in the entire area. Because of the relatively low height (5,886 feet from the top) of this area, all the runs seem to skirt or cut through beautiful forests. And at every juncture, there's the obligatory hut where you can enjoy a drink and a spectacular view from a balcony.

For a top-to-bottom basher, cut over to the Bergeralm chair lift, and from the top enjoy the challenging 7-km. Bergeralm-Schönleiten run (Nos. 57 and 67 on the trail map) down to the valley floor to the Schönleiten cable car. The eight-person cable cars will whisk you all the way to the top of Schonleiten, where from the restaurant you can enjoy the most spectacular view in the entire valley, and one of the truly memorable panoramas in the Alps. If you care to digest your lunch over some bumps, round the ridge toward Leogang and ski the three T-bar lifts. They're short but sweet.

Beginners should take the Bernkogelalm chair lift from Saalbach and change lifts to make it all the way to the top of Bernkogel. The run from the top to the midstation is gentle, wide and very confidence inspiring. In fact, this is where the Austrian ski instructors take their classes of first-timers. The adventurous will find manageable, broad runs down from the top of both the Kohlmaiskopf and Bründkopf lifts.

Mountain rating

There are only a few runs that are strictly for experts, but there's plenty of challenging terrain in the Ski Circus to keep excellent skiers occupied. The fact that the area occupies so much of a broad valley means there always seems to be a tree glade beckoning somewhere.

Intermediates have discovered Nirvana. The whole north side of the valley is a canvas of intermediate runs waiting only for the intermediate skier to choose his or her favorite brushstroke. There is really no part of the Ski Circus that is off-limits to the intermediate (with the exception of the run under the Schattberg cable car). You can enjoy all the pleasures of exploring the entire circuit without hitting a dead end.

Beginners and advanced beginners will find Saalbach-Hinterglemm much to their liking. There are plenty of broad slopes, even from the top, that lead them on a gentle curve miles down into the valley.

Ski school

There are nine major ski schools in both Saalbach and Hinterglemm. Combined, there are over 200 instructors in the area.

Group lessons (four hours, 10 a.m.–noon and 2–4 p.m.) are Sch520 for a full day, Sch1,350 for three days, and Sch1,550 for six days.

Children's classes run from 10 a.m. to 4 p.m. A week (including lunch) costs Sch1,550.

Cross-country ski lessons are also available, and there are 10 km. of cross-country trails in the area.

Lift tickets (97/98 prices)

Saalbach-Hinterglemm Ski Circus (high season is about December 20–January 6 and January 24–March 13).

	High Season	Low Season
half day	Sch310	Sch300
one day	Sch400	Sch380
three days	Sch1,095	Sch970
six days	Sch1,960	Sch1,700
12 days	Sch3,030	Sch2,680

There are reduced lift prices for children 15–18 and further reductions for those younger than 15. Children get 15 percent reductions Christmas week. There are special reductions for Family Weeks during the second and third weeks of January.

Accommodations

Where prices are noted they are for January low season per person based on double occupancy. Hotel and pension prices noted below are with half board; B&B prices include breakfast.

Very Expensive

Alpenhotel (tel. 66660) Every resort has its flagship hotel, and this is Saalbach's. The big red arch dominates the entrance of the village, and it announces that the Alpenhotel caters to all whims—sauna, solarium, massage, exercise room, indoor swimming pool, whirlpool and so on. The hotel also houses the most exclusive disco in Saalbach, the **Arena**. Sch1,400.

Expensive

Haider (tel. 6228) Not as fancy or as large as the Alpenhotel, the Haider is quaint in the traditional Austrian mold, with carved wood headboards on the beds and shutters. There's a sauna, solarium and a hot whirlpool, as well a hideaway lounge with fireplace. Besides an excellent restaurant serving traditional Austrian fare, there's also an informal pizzeria—always a plus for carbo-hungry skiers. Sch800.

Sporthotel Ellmau (tel. 672260) and Glemmtalerhof (tel. 7135) Both of these hotels in Hinterglemm are excellent and offer full amenities, such as sauna, solarium and indoor swimming pool. There's also babysitting on the premises. Sch1,070.

Moderate

Mitterer (tel. 6219) This inn in Saalbach is a good choice for those who want most of the trappings of a top hotel (including sauna and whirlpool), but in a quaint and more personable package. Sch800.

Zwölfer (tel. 6317) Count this inn in Hinterglemm as a good value. It's strategically near the Zwölfer cable car. Sch670.

Bed & Breakfast

Scharnagl (tel. 6284) It's too new to rate as quaint. This pension scores high because of its location next to the old church and across the street from both the Kohlmais chair lift and the Schi-Alm, perhaps the best après-ski bar in town. The rooms are clean and airy, and the proprietress, Frau Brudermann, is always willing to help. Sch500.

Other recommended pensions in Saalbach are the **Montana** (tel. 6283) Sch430–510 and the **Berger** (tel. 7140) Sch420–470. In Hinterglemm, try the **Flora** (tel. 7100) Sch420.

Ski Chalets: Crystal, Inghams/Bladon (see page 27 for phone, fax and internet addresses).

Apartments

Saalbach has hundreds of apartments for rental with two major agencies handling the procedure. Contact either of the two agencies or the tourist office for apartment information. Give them your arrival and departure dates and level of luxury you desire.

Dining

Austrian cooking mirrors the country and its people—hearty, simple and unpretentious. Few sights are more welcome after a full day's skiing than a generous pork filet with mushroom gravy and a heaping portion of *Spätzle*, Austria's unbeatable doughy noodles. For a sweet treat on the mountain, try *Germknödel* (a sweet doughy bread filled with jam and covered with warm vanilla sauce).

The **Hinterhagalm** just at the top of the Turm T-bar is something of a local legend. Its 5 p.m. tea bar is one of the most notable après-ski events in the valley, yet at night this beautiful old lodge serves traditional Austrian dishes with old-world atmosphere. This restaurant was the backdrop for "The Sound of Music."

Nearly all the major hotels in both Saalbach and Hinterglemm feature good restaurants, and you'll find menus with prices conveniently posted outside. Those with man-sized appetites should try the restaurant in the Hotel **Sonne** (tel. 67202), featuring more than 20 different steak dinners. Highly recommended is Chateaubriand for two at the **Hotel Reiterhof** (tel. 6682).

No ski resort is complete unless it has an informal pizzeria with good food and reasonable prices, and in Saalbach the pizzeria in the Hotel Haider (tel. 6228) gets our vote.

No less than 40 mountain chalets serve food, and each lift seems to have one of these either at the top or bottom—or both. Two mountain huts deserve special mention—the **Wildenkarhütte** at the top of the Schönleiten cable car for its spectacular panoramic view, and the rustic **Thurneralm** (on the trail midway up the Reiteralm T-bar) for its hunting lodge flavor and ski-up bar.

Après-ski/nightlife

Saalbach-Hinterglemm's reputation for great nightlife has more to do with the atmosphere and attitude of the area than the number of discos (officially only five). Along with the wild-and-crazy Austrians you're bound to meet, there's also a healthy contingent of Scandinavians (especially Swedes) and British.

The **Arena** disco in the Alpenhotel is the upscale nightspot. The action inside doesn't start until after 11 p.m. Expect to pay a cover (it varies depending on the entertainment) and about Sch110 for a mixed drink. There are two bars, a live band and plenty of overstuffed couches and tucked-away alcoves for a break from the dancing.

The disco in the Sporthotel, just up the main street from the centrally located Alpenhotel, is where the young and adventurous let their collective hair down. There's a circular balcony that overlooks the dance floor, and you need only pick out the partner of your choice from this vantage point and then leap merrily into the crowded fray.

Cross the stream just off the main street and walk uphill to the **Backstatt Stall**. The upstairs disco is on two levels, with another balcony for scoping the dance action. The atmosphere is a little more woodsy and mellower than the spots mentioned above, and it's easier to find room on the dance floor.

Après-ski has to be witnessed to be understood. Where else, except inside the **Schi-Alm** at the bottom of the Turm T-bar (across from the old church), can you see Austrians dancing the cancan to "New York, New York," stacked three on top of one another and swaying like demented totem poles? The bedlam at the **Hinterhagalm** tea bar just up the slope is a rival for honors as Après-Ski Madhouse of the Mountain.

The new Harley Davidson and Bikers' **Pub**, in the basement of the Hotel Zur Dorfschmiede, features a shiny selection of fullsize Harleys and motorcycle memorabilia, lots of leather and studs, and an owner who dishes "hog" talk with the best of them. Hokey, but a lot of fun.

Child care

There are several hotels that offer all-day nursery services and kindergarten for children 1 and older. You have to call ahead, however, and make reservations to be sure they have enough help on hand.

Skischule Wolf (tel. 634640) is one provider taking kids from two years of age. The **Hotel Theresia** in Hinterglemm (tel. 674140) has child care, and the **Partnerhotel** in Hinterglemm (tel. 67135) has a miniclub. **Hotel Lengauerhof** (tel. 672550) has nursery service from Sunday through Friday 9:30 a.m.–4 p.m.

Getting there

By train

There are direct trains to nearby Zell am See from both Munich and Salzburg. You can either take a cab the remaining 18 km. to Saalbach or wait for the regularly scheduled bus, which makes the trip to Saalbach nine times a day from the train station.

By car

The drive from the Munich airport to Saalbach takes about two and a half hours. From the Salzburg autobahn take the Siegsdorf exit, then follow signs to Lofer-Maishofen, then signs to Saalbach-Hinterglemm.

Some hotels offer parking, and you can also park in the multideck garage on the outskirts of town. Once in Saalbach you won't need a car.

Other activities

Try an afternoon excursion by horse-drawn sleigh. Lindlingalm offers tours that include a stop for a traditional Austrian lunch (tel. 06541-7190). Sleigh rides are also offered by Taxi Schmidhofel (tel. 06541-7163) and Lengauerwirt (tel. 06541-7255).

Tourist information

Contact the Informationscenter, A-5753 Saalbach, Austria; tel. (06541) 680068; fax (06541) 680069. The snow phone is 680040.

E-mail: tvb@saalbach,co,at Internet: www.saalbach.co.at/saalbach

☎ *Telephone prefix for Saalbach-Hinterglemm is 06541.*

Schladming/Ramsau
with Dachstein-Tauern Region

This is the area in Europe where Arnold Schwarzenegger comes to ski, but more on that later. Whether you are looking for the challenge of the fastest World Cup downhill or wide beginner and intermediate runs through thick pine forests, whether you seek the excitement of skiing on the Dachstein Glacier or the serenity of one of the most extensive cross-country areas in Austria, it's all in Schladming.

Schladming, in the center of Austria about an hour's drive from Salzburg, hosts thousands of Austrian, German, Swedish, Danish, British and Dutch tourists. Already one of the leading vacation centers for the Austrians, the region has completed an extensive series of developments that have turned the valley into a world-class resort. The local term for this area is *Skiparadies*.

Schladming, the hub of the area, is nestled around a traditional town center, with shopping, nightlife and restaurants—all within a five-minute walk from the main lifts.

Rohrmoos, about a five-minute drive up the mountain, features more hotel rooms than Schladming, and guests can step out their door, put on their skis and set off down the mountain. But Rohrmoos is spread out and a long walk from the Schladming village.

Ramsau lies on the opposite side of the valley, with a southern exposure. It is settled on a long plateau that features some of the most interesting cross-country skiing in Austria: the 1999 Nordic World Championships will be held here. Accommodations are extensive but dispersed. At the top of the Ramsau cable car (elevation 2,700 meters) you overlook the entire Tauern region mountain range and the Enns River Valley. Haus im Ennstal, a short drive along the valley from Schladming, is perhaps the most picturesque of the main villages in the region, Haus has not succumbed to modern hotels and kitschy shops or loud discos. It remains traditional, anchoring the Hauser Kaibling ski area. It is connected with the other villages by frequent shuttlebuses.

Mountain layout

The *Skiparadies* ski pass opens more than 75 miles of prepared runs at the eight ski areas along the Dachstein-Tauern valley. The major areas are Planai (6,214 feet) above Schladming; Hauser Kaibling (6,610 feet) above Haus; Hochwurzen (6,069 feet) above Rohrmoos; and the Reiteralm (6,102 feet) above Pichl. Currently, only the Planai and Hochwurzen areas are connected by lifts. Other areas are connected by shuttlebuses that ply the valley continuously in skiing hours. Each area offers plenty of skiing for a day.

The **Planai** is served by an efficient gondola—waiting time in the valley is minimal even on Sundays. A new quad chair lift adds to the lift capacity in this region. T-bars open the back bowls of the Planai area; the valley face of the mountain is crisscrossed by beginner and intermediate runs. The No. 1 run, from the top of the cable car to the bottom station, is the longest on the mountain and an absolutely joyful experience. Intermediates can cruise, and beginners can handle the entire run—the steep sections (short ones) are wide, for an easy traverse.

The **Hochwurzen** area is reached through a series of T-bars and chair lifts. The lifts can take almost an hour if you start from the connecting chair with the Planai area. For people staying in Rohrmoos or coming by shuttlebus, a gondola whisks skiers to the top or take the double chair lift. The upper areas are intermediate and the lower ones, around Rohrmoos, a beginner's paradise.

Hauser Kaibling, rising above Haus, is normally not so crowded as Schladming. At times you'll find yourself alone on a beautiful mountain with some of the best intermediate slopes under your skis. Intermediate is the main focus of this mountain. Take the bus or drive to the base of the Hauser Kaibling cable car just outside town. (The cable car rising directly from the upper reaches of Haus looks great on the ski map but may be skipped unless your hotel is nearby—it takes only eight skiers, about every 15 minutes.)

Reiteralm, above the towns of Pichl and Gleiming, provides a good day's worth of skiing for intermediates. Beginners have too limited an area to make the half-hour series of lifts worthwhile unless they are staying in one of the base towns.

Overall, the area uses up a week of skiing without repeating a section. Even good skiers will be hard-pressed to cover every trail in six days of all-out skiing.

Mountain rating

The area is an intermediate's paradise. Beginners should center their efforts on Rohrmoos, although all sections have beginner runs. After three days of lessons, beginners can make their way all the way down each of the mountains with their instructors.

Experts should keep an eye out for good powder and test themselves high up on Hauser Kaibling or on the lower sections of the World Cup downhill runs both in Haus and Schladming. The real experts should hire a guide to take them off trail for a great day or week of skiing.

Ski school (97/98 prices)

Private lessons

two-and-a-half hour lesson	Sch1,000
additional person	Sch150
one hour lesson	Sch500
additional person	Sch150

Group lessons

one day	Sch500
three days	Sch1,200
five days	Sch1,400

Lift tickets (97/98 prices)

The regional lift tickets cover seven cable cars, 13 chair lifts, and 58 T-bars. Each town in the region offers single-day limited-lift tickets. These rates are for the entire eight-mountain area.

The lift rates are based on high and low season. High season is Christmas/New Year (to early January) and early February to mid March. Discount season is early December 3 to Christmas week, January 8th or so to February 1st or so, and late March. Special family rates are also available.

High season	Adult	Children
half day (from noon)	Sch300	Sch145
one day	Sch385	Sch205
six days	Sch1,890	Sch1,040
seven days	Sch2,035	Sch1,120

Low season	Adult	Children
half day (from noon)	Sch300	Sch145
one day	Sch365	Sch205
six days	Sch1,760	Sch1,040
seven days	Sch1,890	Sch1,120

Accommodations

The Dachstein-Tauern Region has a series of lodging deals that include seven nights lodging, half pension or breakfast only, six days of lifts and pool per person based on double ocupancy during mid January.

	Adults 14 and older	Half-board	B&B
★★★★ hotel	Sch7,295	Sch6,595	
★★–★★★ hotel	Sch5,580	Sch4,670	
Gasthöfe	Sch5,370	Sch4,460	
Pension	Sch4,850	Sch3,940	
Private room	Sch4,390	Sch3,480	
Room with no private bath	Sch4,040	Sch3,130	

Here is our list of recommended hotels with their normal daily rates based on double occupancy with half board during low and high seasons.

Sporthotel Royer (tel. 23240) The only five-star hotel in Schladming. This is a modern hotel with pool, indoor tennis and squash courts, sauna and pony rides. This is the favorite of Arnold Schwarzenegger, who grew up in a small village not far away. The hotel lounge and bar feature thick leather chairs around a fireplace. Guest rooms have plenty of closet space, CNN on the television, hair dryers and showers over the tub. Daily rate half pension Sch1,220, high season Sch1,420.

Romantik-Hotel Alte Post (tel. 22571) In Schladming—the oldest, most traditional hotel on the main square. Daily rates: half pension Sch950; high season Sch1,200.

Hotel Zum Stadttor (tel. 24525) In Schladming. Whirlpool and sauna. Daily half board: Sch710 –980.

Hotel Pichlmayrgut (tel. 06454-305) If you want to stay in an old Austrian estate, this fills the bill. Amenities include pool, sauna and steambath. Pichl lifts start a five-minute walk from the hotel, or catch the ski bus to Haus or Schladming. Daily half board: Sch810–1,300.

Moderate to Budget

There are many hotels and pensions for Sch430–500 a day, including half pension. One recommendation in the center of Schladming is **Gasthof Tritscher** (tel. 22435).

In the center of the charming town of Haus you'll find the **Hotel Hauser Kaibling** (tel. 03686-2378) with pool and sauna. Rates are Sch790–850 a day with half pension.

The adventurous can stay near the top of the Hauser Kaibling in the **Krummholzhütte**, where you have to share a bathroom and shower, for Sch280 a day, half pension. You get a room near the summit and about a 10-minute schuss down the mountain right out the door.

Contact the tourist office and describe what you want and how much you will pay. The office has a computer system that tracks all bookings in the area.

Dining

The best restaurants in town are the **Alte Post, Sporthotel Royer** and the restaurant in the **Stadttor**. The place to spend the least money and still eat well is **Restaurant Tritscher**.

For great ski-slope meals on the Planai, stop in at **Onkel Willi's Hütte** (yes, Uncle Willi's Hut), only a few ski glides from the top of the main Planai lift. On the Hauser Kaibling, the **Krummholzhütte** at the top, and the **Stöcklhütte** where the three lifts meet, are good. Try **Gasthof Steger** in Haus/Ennstal.

At the base of Schladming's Planai, host of the 1982 FIS Alpine World Championships and known for its ultra-fast downhill, is a small inn called **Charly's Treff** owned by Charly Kahr, the Austrian who coached the national team at the 1960 Squaw Valley Olympics and the British women's team in the early 1970s. He also coached Olympic and World Cup champion Franz Klammer, a local hero. In his restaurant, savoring a schnapps, Charly regales visitors with stories of the skiers he has trained.

Many visit Charly's Treff to sample hearty dishes Aus Oma's Kochbuch (From Grandmother's Cookbook). The Geschnetzeltes (pork and noodles, Sch125) was very good, and you don't leave hungry. Salzburger Käsnock (cheese and spätzle noodles) at Sch95 is another favorite.

Charly retired from coaching in 1985 and now spends his time overseeing his restaurant, visiting with friends like Schwarzenegger, and skiing. "I like the tree skiing and village atmosphere of Schladming," says Kahr. He also runs a ski rental shop, The Downhill Club.

The **Brand Alm**, a classic mountain hut about halfway down from the base of the Ramsau glacier cable car, is the quintessential Alpine hut. At outside tables framed by the majestic mountains, you'll see customers in lederhosen, since many people hike up from Ramsau for lunch. The Teller Erbsensuppen (split pea soup) is hearty and the Krainer sausage, served with the best sauerkraut I've ever eaten, should not be missed. You can try a Radler, a mixture of lemonade and beer that Austrians find thirst-quenching. Be sure to have your camera full of film.

Outside Ramsau, the **Grahstub'n** (tel. 81072) is a tiny inn serving tasty food. One of the famed mountain men of the region was Jorg Steiner, an army deserter during WW II who lived in the mountains as a poacher and is said to have had 27 wives housed in various mountain huts. One of his daughters, Gretl Steiner, sings Austrian folk songs in the restaurant with her companion, Helmut Gebauer, himself a famous, if aging, mountain climber.

Après-ski/nightlife

For wine and quiet talk, try the **Talbachschenke** in three small rooms, each built around a toasty ceramic stove. The best dancing is at the **Sonderbar** under the Hotel Rössl. Other cozy meeting places include **The Pub** and **The Beisl**, both just off the main square. The Beisl is in the passageway at 12 Main Square and is a good place to meet people. Check out **La Porta**, near the town's old gateway.

The two main discos outside town, and also the best spots for meeting European skiers, are the **Sport Alm** in Ramsau and the **Erlebniswelt** in Rohrmoos. In Haus/Ennstal, stop into the new **Pub Remise** in the old castle.

Child care

There is a ski kindergarten for children without lunch costing Sch550 for a full day and Sch1,200 for three days.

Children four and over can sign up for ski school, which takes children for the entire day, at the same prices as adults. Add Sch70 a day for lunches.

Getting there

There are good train connections from Munich and Salzburg. Both have international airports. Salzburg is a 58 mile drive from Schladming. Take the Ennstal exit.

Other activities

Visit Salzburg and its neighboring salt mines.

The Loden fabric factory gives tours—arrange them in advance by calling 06454-203. The factory and outlet are in Mandling, only about 10 minutes from Schladming.

Some of Austria's most famous caves are in this region. Kappenbrullenhöhle, the Ice Cave and Mammoth Cave and are open for visits. Call 06134-362.

Horse-drawn sleigh rides are available, ice skating rinks are open in Rohrmoos and Haus/Ennstal, and there are public swimming pools in Schladming and Ramsau.

Tourist information

The central tourist office for the region is Gebietsverband Dachstein-Tauern, Kuschargasse 202, A-8970 Schladming, Austria; tel. 03687-23310, fax 23232. It handles reservation requests for any town in the area. There are also local tourist offices in Schladming, Pichl, Haus, Rohrmoos and Ramsau.

☎ *Telephone prefix for Schladming is 03687.*

Söll

The village of Söll in the Wilder Kaiser area of Austria is a tremendous favorite with English skiers and young people. The wide expanse of slopes with the backdrop of the rocky Wilder Kaiser boasts more than 90 lifts spread above nine villages, earning the title of the largest connected ski area in Austria.

The entire ski area is perhaps the most accessible in Austria to skiers coming in from Germany. It's only 20 minutes from the Kufstein border crossing, which is about an hour from Munich.

Söll carefully cultivates its small-town image with little shops whose operators are overwhelmingly friendly and strike up a conversation in English at the first opportunity. The main street is full of visitors at almost any hour of the day or night. While traffic is heavy, pedestrians have taken priority, causing motorists to wait, sometimes impatiently, as the shoppers stroll across the roadway to browse.

It's quite clear from the heavy traffic in the local grocery stores that not everyone takes full pension. Full shopping bags mean a lot of picnic lunches and breakfasts prepared back in the room. Everywhere you encounter young couples strolling hand in hand, a change from the more elegant and expensive European resorts where the crowd is older and not always so affectionate.

Mountain layout

The best skiing is concentrated in the valley headed by Söll, pronounced "Zull." Up the valley are Scheffau, Ellmau and finally Going. Around the mountains in another valley are Itter, Hopfgarten, Kelchsau, Westendorf and Brixen Thale. Each has lifts, and all but Westendorf and Kelchsau are on an interconnected circuit. Free bus service is provided from Westendorf, providing skiers with a two-valley network of lifts and hundreds of trails.

The most convenient access is from Söll, where an eight-passenger gondola carries skiers up the mountain. From the top of the Hohe Salve (5,670 feet) at Söll you can appreciate the massive dimensions of the Wilder Kaiser area which the English and Austrians know from brochures as Ski World. Your view includes the 5,115-foot Brandstadl summit at Sheffau, the 4,820-foot Hartkaiser at Ellmau-Going and further to your right the town of Kirchberg, gateway to Kitzbühel.

On the skyline you see ski slopes as far as Pass Thurn, and the famed Grossglockner is on the distant skyline.

Good parallel skiers should do the Ski World tour, which begins and ends in Söll. Skiers work their way up and down the ridges, visiting Itter, Hopfgarten, the outskirts of Brixen, then back up to Zinsberg, and finally back to Brandstadl and over to Hartkaiser, stopping along the way in Sheffau, Ellmau and perhaps Going.

The black run from the summit of Hohe Salve above Söll will challenge a good skier. It's a 4 km. trail with a vertical drop of about 2,200 feet. The best intermediate run is the Rigi along the back side and then around the Hohe Salve, all the way down to the Gasthof Kraftalm where they serve a *Jägertee* (Hunter's Tea) that will blast your ski boots off. The recipe, according to the Gasthof owner, is tea, some rum, red wine, plenty of schnapps, a goodly amount of sugar and some herbs for aroma. He adds, "Don't light a match near it while it's hot."

Mountain rating

The Wilder Kaiser is intermediate country with a capital "I." You can head down any slope without hesitation and enjoy moderately challenging, well-groomed runs. A fine place to hone your skiing skills. Not recommended for the demanding skier craving black-trail thrills.

Ski school (95/96 prices)

Söll has two ski schools. The largest of them, Schischule Söll/Hochsöll (tel. 5454), has 90 instructors. The other is Ski School Söll-Hohe Salve (tel. 5005). Both are noted for their English-speaking instructors, a strength in the Wilder Kaiser region.

Lessons are offered daily. Week-long lessons begin on Sundays and Mondays. Instruction is 10 a.m. to noon and 2 to 4 p.m.

Private lessons are also offered through the ski school office for Sch460 per hour, with another Sch150 for each additional student. The telephone information number is 5454 or 5484. Beginner lessons are given directly across from the ski center on the beginner slope. Advanced skiers and experts are taken up the mountain immediately. Even beginners go up after a couple of days.

A private instructor for a day costs Sch1,840, with additional persons costing Sch300.

Group lessons: A full day session will cost Sch570, three days runs Sch1,160, five days is Sch1,260; and six days costs Sch1,200. A special half-day (two hours a day) course for intermediate skiers and above is available one day for Sch400, three days Sch780, five days Sch830.

Lift tickets (97/98 prices)

The individual towns sell tickets good only for the local lifts, but the regional Ski Welt ticket is a better bargain and makes sense for the active skier.

Söll area only	Adults	Children
half day (noon)	Sch250	Sch150
one day	Sch340	Sch190
three days	Sch825	Sch455
six days	Sch1,455	Sch825
Grossraum all areas	Adults	Children
half day	Sch280	Sch165
one day	Sch360	Sch210
three days	Sch990	Sch580
six days	Sch1,745	Sch970

Check also the special ticket which allows some variation on ski days. A choice of five our of seven ski days is Sch1,600 for adults and Sch910 for children. A choice of seven out of ten ski days is Sch2,005 for adults. A choice of ten of 14 ski days is Sch2,520 for adults and Sch1,420 for children. *Note: A photo is required for all ski passes of eight days or longer.*

Accommodations (97/98 prices)

Söll is the first of the seven towns you come to in the Wilder Kaiser and the one we liked best. These are low to high season prices.

Gasthof Greil, a ten-minute walk from the center of town is quiet, the food tasty and filling and the staff friendly. About Sch650–890 per person daily, half pension (tel. 5289).

The best hotel in town is **Postwirt**, a renovated, beautiful building near the local tourist office. Room and breakfast is Sch690 daily, half pension is Sch890. Low-season rates are slightly reduced (tel. 5221).

Equally attractive and historic is **Feldwebel**, just down the street. This 85-bed hotel has rooms from Sch460 in high season (Sch580, half pension). Tel. 5224.

Hotel Tyrol, about halfway between the Greil and the center of town, is Sch580–830 daily, with breakfast and about Sch680–950, half pension (tel. 5273).

On the mountain we liked the **Salvenmoos**, where bed and breakfast was Sch350–400 and half pension was Sch480–530. This is for skiers who want to hit the slopes immediately and don't need to go into town often (tel. 5351).

There are over two dozen hotels in the Söll area proper. Private rooms and Bed & Breakfasts are numerous. The tourist office, next to the Postwirt Hotel, can arrange rooms in all price ranges (tel. 5216).

Soll: Crystal (see to page 21–22 for phone, fax and internet addresses).

Dining

The best meal we had was in the **Greil**. The **Stube** of the Postwirt has the most atmosphere, given the group of old timers at the big front table who puff on their pipes and argue loudly about everything from Austrian politics to the merits of retired Formula One driver Niki Lauda and current ace Gerhard Berger (both Austrian, naturally). The food is good and filling. The Stube came in second for best apple strudel in town. It was good but not quite as fine as **Cafe Mirabel's**, up the street past the Thomson Tours office.

Après-ski/nightlife

The ski instructors and longtime visitors gather after skiing in the small bar of the **Postbierstube**. Just keep going past the Stube and you'll find the bar tucked away on the left. For laughter, some sing-along action and live entertainment, the **Pub 15**, a British place despite the name, is the place to visit. When we dropped in, the singer was American and the songs were English and American favorites. A good place to meet new friends is the **Dorfstadl** in the cellar of the Hotel Tyrol. There's a younger crowd and louder music at the **Whiskey Muhle** and **Western Saloon: Buffalo** at the Pizzeria Venezia.

Child care

The ski kindergarten is across the street from the ski school building. Prices are reduced for children from five to 14 who have at least one parent in the adult ski school.

Five-day children's ski school costs Sch1,220 and a three-day program will cost Sch1,120.

For an additional Sch100 daily the ski kindergarten includes care and instruction from 9:30 a.m. to 4:15 p.m. For information call 5454 or 5005.

A new Mini-Club has opened next to the gondola station for non-skiing kids. A full day of care including lunch will cost Sch300; a half day (9:30 a.m. to 1:30 p.m.) including lunch is Sch240.

Getting there

The main arrival airport is Munich, about 70 minutes by bus from Söll and other towns in the area. If you're driving, take the Salzburg autobahn out of Munich and then the Rosenheim cutoff (called the Inntal autobahn). You cross the border near Kufstein and take the second exit, Kufstein Sud. Söll will be marked on the autobahn exit sign. From the turnoff, it's about 15 minutes on a two-lane highway over one slight uphill grade to Söll.

Other activities

Söll has a well-developed recreation complex with a network of cross-country trails. The recreation center has a beautiful indoor pool with a heated outdoor extension.

Both Salzburg and Innsbruck, with a wide range of museums and scenic outdoor attractions, are within an hour's drive.

In addition, it is not unusual for the visitor with a car to visit Innsbruck and then venture down the Brenner motorway for a short excursion into Italy. The same is true for a visit to Munich for those who arrive from Innsbruck or Milan.

Tourist Information

You'll find the tourist office in all the villages of the Wilder Kaiser helpful, particularly so in Söll. Tourismusverband Söll, Postfach 21, A-6306 Söll am Wilden Kaiser, Austria. Call 05333-5216; fax 05333-6180.

☎ *Telephone prefix for Söll is 05333.*

St. Johann in Tirol

St. Johann in winter is a Tyrolean resort town just far enough from the lifts to keep locals aware of the need to welcome visitors with a smile. The town is afloat in a sea of snow, lending a special atmosphere to a place that can't decide whether it is a resort village or a valley town.

Although St. Johann is only 2,297 feet above sea level, the snowfall here is certain and heavy from Christmas to March. That alone should please serious skiers. The setting is picturesque, with the familiar outline of the Kitzbüheler Horn forming part of the panorama. Kitzbühel is about 6 miles away.

The typical Tyrolean hotels here are large and have a deserved reputation for hospitality sometimes missing in bigger, better known resorts. At night you'll know immediately from the lower decibel levels that this is not Kitzbühel. The streets don't exactly fold up at 8 p.m., but the nightlife is quieter. (The tempo picks up a bit for the cross-country races in February.)

The town has an excellent shuttlebus system that links hotels and apartments with the town and the lifts.

Like Igls, St. Johann is a little more sedate and on the quiet side. Not at all a rowdy or happening place, but it still offers plenty of activity at the end of the skiing day. Nicer shops and restaurants show it clearly caters to a higher-class clientele, though not necessarily a chic set. Being a little more off the beaten track than Innsbruck or other resorts, it offers more of the feel of genuine, rural and conservative Austria—with ski resort attached.

One of the year's biggest events is the Koasalauf, an international cross-country championship staged in late February. It begins at the Koasa Stadium cross-country center on the edge of town. St. Johann offers more than 40 miles of cross-country runs.

Mountain Layout

The trails run along the flanks of the Kitzbüheler Horn. You can reach them from neighboring Oberndorf by chair lift or cable car from St. Johann. The top station is Harschbichl at 5,577 feet. From there you have a choice of blue and red runs and one black trail.

We liked the black run, which really begins from Penzing at 4,799 feet and swings down through mogul fields to the parking lot above Oberndorf.

Intermediates take the run to the Eichenhof lift on the far side of St. Johann for a good downhill cruise. From the Jodlalm, just below the Harschbichl, you can follow the lines of a dozen different trails cut into the mountain.

Beginner slopes are at the bottom of the mountain.

Mountain rating

St. Johann is for intermediates—primarily for lower intermediates. The slopes are rarely challenging, and only beginners and the lowest intermediates will find the skiing interesting enough for a week. However, with the regional ski pass you can try a number of challenging slopes in the area, in particular those on the Steinplatte above Waidring, about 10 miles from St. Johann.

Cross-country

Well-laid-out, groomed trails extend in two opposite directions from town. The ski touring center toward one end of town provides good maps, rentals and a base to start from, though it does close relatively early (4 p.m.). The trails here, as at Innsbruck, tend to be overrated for difficulty, though they offer pleasant rolling terrain, a taste of backcountry woods, if not all that extensive, and a couple of traditional inns along the way for lunch, rest and refreshment.

Lift tickets (97/98 prices)

The St. Johann pass includes 18 lifts serving 37 miles of prepared trails on the north side of the Kitzbüheler Horn. Lift include two gondolas, a quad chair, one triple chair, two double chairs, two single chairs and 10 surface lifts. Lift capacity is 20,100 skiers per hour.

These are high-season prices. There is a small discount in low season, and children pay approximately 50 percent less with those under six skiing for free.

half day	Sch270
one day	Sch345
three days	Sch945
five days	Sch1,400
six days	Sch1,620
seven days	Sch1,830
13 days	Sch2,775

A combination ski and pool pass for six days in high season costs Sch1,770; for 13 days, Sch3,065.

From early March through the end of the season, children 4–15 ski free with a lift ticket-purchasing adult at St. Johann.

Ski school (97/98 prices)

St. Johann has approximately 130 instructors available for the winter season.

Private lessons (for 1 to 2 persons)

half-day	Sch1,200–1,400
one day	Sch 1,650–2,000

Group lessons

one day	Sch500–590
three days	Sch1,120–1,180
five days	Sch1,280–1,390
six days	Sch1,350–1,390

Cross-country lessons

one day	Sch500
three days	Sch1,050–1,120
six days	Sch1,290–1,350

Accommodations

St. Johann has one of the best organized accommodation services in Austria. In fact, using the St. Johann hotel-apartment list with an accompanying reservation form, available free from the tourist office, you can arrange for any type of accommodation—from simple B&B to apartment rental.

We recommend that you come in January or March when the maximum price reductions are offered. Two sport packages are outstanding. Variation A includes a six-day ski pass for St. Johann, and six days of the pool with one sauna visit. Variation B includes a six-day ski pass for St. Johann, and six days of ski lessons with one sauna visit and six days of ski school.

Variation A costs Sch1,520 for adults and Sch825 for children. Variation B costs Sch2,600 for adults and Sch1,905 for children.

Our favorite deluxe hotels are the **Hotel Crystal** (tel. 62630) and **Gasthof Dorfschmiede** (tel. 62323).

The sport package price for a first-class hotel or guesthouse is about what you'd pay just for accommodations at some resorts. St. Johann hotels and guesthouses offer the mid-range all-inclusive package. We recommend these three:

Hotel Schöne Aussicht (tel. 62270) with an excellent location on the slopes.

Gasthof Hinterkaiser (tel. 63325) is a cross-country skier's paradise in the heart of the trail circuit, but isolated for Alpine skiing.

St. Johann has a multitude of excellent accommodations; we've never been disappointed. The tourist office can provide a full list and help with reservations.

Apartments

Apartment rental is as easy as finding hotel or pension lodging in St. Johann. Contact the tourist office and tell them your arrival date. They will send a list of available apartments. You then contact the apartment owner directly. Apartments that sleep four range in price from Sch500–1,100 a night.

Dining

The **Lemberg** (tel. 63542), **Fischerstüberl** (tel. 62332 or 62653) and **Post** (tel. 62230) serve Austrian specialties. **Chez Paul** (tel. 64419) has good French fare.

Café Platzl Very good ice cream bar and family restaurant upstairs, lively but not too rowdy bar for the twenties generation down. Easy to find right on the main plaza in the center of town.

Café Rainer Informal family restaurant with live local (but not Tyrolean) music on the main street. It even fills up for lunch during the day with locals who munch on treats from the impressive pastry shop attached.

Hotel Bruckenwirt/Restaurant Ambiente Quite the upscale place in St Johann. The restaurant is top of the line and an elegant piano lounge offers an authentic English tea service. A smaller bar is attached to the lounge. One would be expected to dress up a little for dinner in the restaurant, but things can be a more casual in the lounge and bar.

Park Hotel Also offering Tyrolean and Austrian specialties in a not-so-formal atmosphere.

Pizzeria Masiano Affordable pizzeria serving Italian basics and some Mexican additions to the menu (the Austrians have their own approach to Mexican food).

Café Eulenspiegel A semi-elegant bar-cafe near the Chez Paul on the edge of town for the slightly older crowd.

Pizzeria Rialto (tel. 64168). The usual. Pizza and the rest right at the station in what could have been the old station house. Pleasant and charming with northern Italian/Tyrolean decor. The **Pub Treff** is attached.

La Rustica (tel. 62843) serves meals from pizza to pasta to scallopini.

A fairly adequate Chinese restaurant is located between the Bunny Pub and the Hotel Crystal.

Eateries with great views include **Gasthof Hochfeld** (tel. 62985) at an altitude of 1,000 meters, which also organizes sledding evenings, and **Schöne Aussicht** (tel. 62270). The **Hinterkaiser** (tel. 63325) organizes horse-drawn sleigh rides with fondues and dinner, but call for reservations. **Gasthof Rummlerhof** (tel. 63650) is a perfect spot for lunch or dinner if you are on the cross-country trails. For great pastries, head to the **Café-Konditorei Vötter** at Kaiserstrasse 26.

Après-ski/nightlife

We liked the **Café Rainer** where the après-ski atmosphere was excellent from 5 o'clock tea onwards.

For a change of pace, visit the **Café Klausner's** traditional Tyrolean evenings with dancers and music.

Cafe Passage is a bright and cheerful bar-café with an older, mellow local crowd. Polished wood tables with attractive greenery lend it a bit of elegance. Tucked in a passage off the main street, it has a short meal menu.

Bunny Pub, one of the livelier places to go, is easygoing and casual, good for après-ski with a happy hour, karaoke and live music later in the night.

Max Pub is fairly lively. An open air tent at the foot of the slopes. Frequented by a young and middle-aged (but lively) crowd, some of the older folks are attracted to the younger set. Also has karaoke and live music at night.

Hotel Crystal, just a short walk down from the Max Pub, is almost at the foot of the slopes. For the most part a middle-of-the-road family restaurant with live Tyrolean music. Free entry.

Chez Paul Bar and Café serves small meals just a short walk from the town center. Pleasant and informal, though slightly yuppified. More for a thirty-something crowd than a disco set.

Scala is a hopping disco/dance hall near the Cafe Passage, the younger hangout for those who like the music turned UP.

Tirolerkeller is the absolute flip side of Scala. Live Tyrolean music for an older crowd. An Austrian equivalent of the VFW hall or Moose Lodge.

Pub Treff generally attracts younger groups and families. At night it turns into a local young hangout, but not rocking and rolling. Bored kids would hang out here since they don't have a McDonald's.

Bar Tropical, right beneath the Rialto and the Treff is where kids looking for a little more action after they tire of the lack of it upstairs gravitate.

Child care

Ski instruction for children and a ski kindergarten are offered (tel. 64777 or 65930). The ski instruction prices are the same as for adults.

For details on babysitting services, call the St. Johann tourist office (tel. 62218 and 63335).

Getting there

St. Johann is about 68 miles from Munich and 59 miles from Innsbruck; most visitors arrive from Munich. Take the Inntal autobahn and exit at Felbertauern/St. Johann in Tirol. Train service connects St. Johann with Innsbruck and Munich.

Other activities

In recent years St. Johann has pushed hard to expand its recreational activities. Tennis (tel. 63377 or 62625) is now a popular activity. Horse-drawn sleigh rides cost Sch190 for two and a half hours at both the St. Johanner Hof (tel. 62207) and the Hinterkaiser (tel. 63325). There are Kegelbahns in the Hotel Goldener Löwe (tel. 62251) and in the Tennis Center (tel. 63377).

For Hot-air balloon rides call Balloning Tyrol GmbH, Flugplatz (tel. 65666). They cost Sch3,800 per person.

Sightseeing flights leave at 9 a.m. and 2 p.m. Call 62711.

The town itself is beautiful to look at, with one Tyrolean house after another presenting traditional Austrian scenes and motifs painted on the exterior walls.

Tourist information

Tourismusverband St. Johann, A-6380 St. Johann in Tirol, Austria; tel. 05352-62218 or 63335, fax 05352-65200.

For snow conditions call 05352-4358.

Internet: http://www.tiscover.com/st.johann

E-mail: tvb@st.johann.tirol.at

☎ *Telephone prefix for St. Johann is 05352.*

Zell am See-Kaprun

Here is an Alpine combination as compatible as beer and pretzels. Yes, these two neighboring resorts fit together hand in glove, like a finely tuned dance team where both partners have learned to subtly complement each other for the best possible performance. Above the low-key village of Kaprun, the Kitzsteinhorn glacier guarantees wide-open bowl skiing the year round, while the majority of Zell am See's Schmittenhöhe slopes sweep down through the trees, more reminiscent of Colorado's Breckenridge or classic New Hampshire trails.

Together they comprise the Europa Sports Region, a land rich with winter and summer outdoor activities. In the spring, high-energy types can ski in the morning and windsurf the lake in the afternoon. Austrian and European skiers have long known the Europa Sports Region as an ideal location for skiing. The area was one of the first resorts in Austria with descents recorded as far back as 1893.

Lake Zell serves as the region's focal point. This long narrow body of water sprawls 13 kms. along a picturesque valley shadowed by the Hohentauern, Austria's highest mountain range. When the lake freezes in winter, townspeople fish through the ice, go ice-boating, or skate across Zell's surface to the village of Thumersbach on the other side.

Zell am See sits on a flat semicircular piece of land that juts into the lake, squeezed from the mountains ringing the shore. Cream-colored buildings huddle around the well-preserved 13th century church of St. Hippolyt, and the Vogtturm (city tower) which dominate Zell's skyline, giving it the air of a medieval mountain town rather than a bustling ski village. One could wander for hours through the town's winding streets and have no trouble envisioning merchants and traders from bygone days going about their business.

Today the streets are still lined with unpretentious shops—sport stores, well-stocked markets, intriguing crafts shops. You'll also find cozy cafés, gasthauses and restaurants filled with locals and tourists alike. Zell am See, with a year-round population of almost 10,000, has honed the fine art of balancing the fantasy sought by tourists with the real needs of its citizens.

On the surface, Kaprun puts on a quieter face than does Zell am See, partly because it is much smaller in scale. But its laid-back atmosphere sets a more relaxing pace, and the village common gives it the air of a small New England college town. The Kitsteinhorn was Austria's first glacial ski area.

 ## Mountian layout

There are two major areas: Zell am See's Schmittenhöhe lifts take skiers to the 2,000-meter level, while Kaprun is famed as a year-round ski area with runs on the glacier beneath the peak of the 10,506-foot Kitzsteinhorn.

To ski the Schmittenhöhe, avoid the main cable car from town and take either the Sonnenalmbahn or better still, the newly-extended Areit gondola from neighboring Schüttdorf direct to the Breiteck peak. You can also take the Zeller Bergbahn and work your way up the left side of the mountain.

The runs are good for intermediates and there are some expert challenges too, particularly the two runs used in the World Cup and regional downhill races. Our favorite is the trail from the Kapellenlift summit to Breiteckalm and then down a wonderful turning slope parallel to the woods. From there, it's black to the bottom. Locals call this run the Trass. Intermediate skiers may enjoy the Standard—it drops from the top to Breiteck but then breaks back to the right over the Hirschkögel trail.

Kaprun is about six miles from Zell am See and it's another three and a half miles to the base of the area's lifts. Take the two-stage cable car up to the glacier, or take the Standseilbahn, which climbs the mountain inside a tunnel—both go to Alpincenter. A third section of the aerial cable car continues to the top of the Kitzsteinhorn at 9,935 feet.

Kaprun's skiing is for the most part intermediate. Experts will want to tackle the final part of the run from the top of the Gletscherbahn to the Langwied midstation, runs 31 and 32 from the Sonnenkarbahn, or run 36 on the left side of the glacier. While up at the peak of the Kitzsheinhorn, take your skis off and walk the 360-meter-long tunnel for a 360-degree panorama view of the Hohe Tauern National Park and the Grossglockner, a 3,798-meter-high giant of a mountain.

Finally, for the area's ultimate in off-piste expert skiing hire a guide (contact any ski school) and leave the back side of the Kitzsteinhorn glacier and ski to the valley of Neidersill.

Snowboarding

Competitive Snowboarders should head to the Gipfelbahn area to find the "boarder cross," a gnarly race coarse made up of gates, bumps, gaps and a 360 degree ramp. Access the halfpipe and quarterpipes on the Kitzsteinhorn glacier via the Keeslift. Intermediate and Alpine Snowboarders will be happiest riding down the wide cruisers of the Schmittenhohe and riding the aerial lifts, rather than riding T-bars to the relatively flat terrain of the glacier. Expert boarders should hire a guide from any ski school and ride off-piste both at the Kitzsteinhorn and Schmittenhohe.

Mountain rating

Zell am See is outstanding for intermediates; its network of trails and connecting lifts offers new challenges and different aspects to the slopes as you work your way across the area. For the beginner there are training slopes and plenty of room to take a fall or two without serious suffering. Experts will head for the glacier at Kaprun, where there are also challenging intermediate runs, The combined ski region offers 55 lifts and 126 km. (78 miles) of trails. A very efficient bus system, included with your Europa Sport Region ski pass, serves both areas.

The Kitzsteinhorn glacier is an easy intermediate area. Though there are ultra wide, gradual runs, the vast number of skiers and the altitude make it an intimidating experience for the beginner. Experts will have to search for ravines (*renne*) or gullies (*wassarkar*) to the sides of the groomed pistes for bumps and steeps filled with powder.

Lift tickets (97/98 prices)

Tickets for the Europa Sports Region Pass:

	High Season	Low Season
two days	Sch780	Sch710
three days	Sch1,110	Sch1,010
four days	Sch1,420	Sch1,310
five days	Sch1,710	Sch1,570
six days	Sch1,970	Sch1,820

Children get approximately a 40 percent discount. Daily rates at the separate sections of the Europa Sports Region are Sch410. Zell am See Schmittenhöhe daily rates are Sch410 during high season and Sch380 in low season.

Shuttlebuses and local transport between Kaprun and Zell am See are free if you buy the regional ski pass.

Ski school (97/98 prices)

Zell am See/Kaprun ski school has approximately 260 instructors. Courses range from beginner through competition racing techniques. Beginner classes start at 9 a.m. and advanced classes begin at 10 a.m. Information is available through the ski school office in the valley station of the Sonnenalmbahn (tel. 3207 or 2324).

Private lessons cost Sch2,000 for one day (four hours) or Sch500 per hour, Sch100 per additional persons.

Group lessons for a day (four hours) are Sch500; three days cost Sch1,300; and for four to six days run Sch1,500

Accommodations

Zell am See (telephone prefix is 06542)

Many of Zell's hotels and pensions are near the lifts. In addition, for those who want to be closer to the Kaprun glacier, there are accommodations in Kaprun.

Thumersbach, across the lake, is separated from the best skiing but quite scenic. Check with the tourist office in Zell for further information.

Zell also offers 24-hour service to individuals who come without reservations. Visitors can use an information board similar to those used at airports: push a button next to the hotel name, and its location is illuminated on the map. You can then telephone the hotel directly and check on room availability.

The all-in package is called Schnee-Okay, and is available in low and middle season. First-class half-board is available from about Sch6,940 a week. Schnee-Okay includes seven days accommodation, a six-day regional pass, unlimited use of the ski shuttlebus and six days' admittance to swimming pools in Zell and Kaprun. At the other end of the price scale is the simple B&B starting at Sch2,845 a week.

Lodges are plentiful in Zell am See. One of the most romantic is the Grand Hotel, at Esplanade 4 (tel. 723880) on the shores of Lake Zell. This stylish beauty was built to be enjoyed from bottom to top. Dine in its casually elegant restaurant, then head upstairs to the glass-domed Wunderbar for a nightcap.

The Hotel Salzburgerhof, Auerspergstrasse 11 (tel. 728280) is Zell am See's only five-star hotel. Lodging at this large, chalet-style hotel includes a whirlpool, sauna, swimming pool, solarium and massage facilities.

A very nice four-star hotel is the **Hotel Neue Post**, Schlossplatz 2 (tel. 73773). Well located and handy to shops and restaurants, this family-owned condominium property features an outdoor hot tub, sauna, massage, fitness room, and television in all rooms. The lobby bar is a good place to meet friends. Friendly desk clerks will have your laundry done for a very reasonable price.

Closer to the slopes, the **Hotel Berner**, at Nikolaus-Gassner-Promenade 1 (tel. 72557) sits just a block or so off the main thoroughfares, a short walk from the Zeller Bergbahn gondolas. The warm friendly personalities of the Berner family will make you feel very much at home.

Other recommended four-star hotels are:
Hotel Zum Hirschen, Dreifaltigkeitgasse (tel. 72447).
Hotel St. Georg Schillerstrasse (tel. 73533).
Hotel Metzgerwirt Sebastian Horl Str. 11 (tel. 72520).
Hotel Alpenblick Alte Landstrasse (tel. 75433).

Three-star recommendations:
The Sporthotel Lebzelter, Dreifaltigkeitgasse 7 (tel. 06542/ 724110) is one of Zell am See's most conveniently located lodges, right in the heart of town and just a few steps away from prime shopping.
Hotel Krone Kitzsteinhornstrasse 16 (tel. 757421).
An excellent two-star choice is **Gasthof Steinerwirt**, Schlossplatz 1 (tel. 72502).
For B&Bs or Fruhstuckspension try the Alpenrose (tel. 2570), the **Landhaus Buchner** (tel. 2062), the **Hubertus** (tel. 2427), or the **Klothilde** (tel. 2660), all of which have English-speaking employees, who are quite interested in interaction with tourists.

Kaprun (telephone prefix is 06547)
For its size, **Kaprun** boasts an array of accommodations you would expect to find at much larger resorts, and the Kaprun/Zell am See transportation system has so many pickup spots that location isn't really an issue.

Sporthotel Kaprun (tel. 8625) is one of the better full service lodges. At the south end of town, it offers a panoramic view of the village from its north-facing side and a dazzling look at the Kitzsteinhorn from the other. Sit on the terrace in early morning and watch the sun dance off the Kitzsteinhorn's peaks. Hearty buffet breakfasts are served each morning. Lunch and dinner are also served in the hotel's spacious dining room.

One of the best four-star "downtown" hotels is the **Orgler** (tel. 8312). You'll want to tiptoe over the fine oriental rugs scattered about its light pine-paneled lobby.

Other recommended four-star hotels: **Steigenberger Advance**, Schlossstrasse 751 (tel. 76470, fax 7680). **Hotel Antonius**, Schlossstrasse 744, (tel. 76700, fax 76700). **The Hotel Zur Burgruine** (tel. 83060, fax 830660) is near the Kaprun fortress ruins. The hotel's cheerful dining room is excellent for dinner whether you stay here or not. **The Hotel Sonnblick** (tel. 83010, fax 830166), just off town central, is another outstanding spot if only for its wide balconies made for enjoying the views.

Other three- & two-star recommendations are: **Katharinehof** (tel. 8866), **Alpenrose** (tel. 7240,8238), **Eschenhof** (tel. 8674), **Alpenblick** (tel. 8477), **Jaga-Hias** (tel. 8345) and **Heidi**, near town center (tel. 8223).

Ski Chalets: Inghams/Bladon (see page 27 for phone, fax and internet addresses).

Apartments

The tourist office will provide a list of available apartments and chalets in the area. In addition, you can book directly through agencies in the area. For more information, call the Prodinger Travel Agency (tel. 2170) and Apartmentservice (tel. 80480). Apartments large enough to sleep four will range in price from Sch800–1,200 per night.

Dining

Ampere (tel. 2363) is a chic bistro with a horseshoe bar complete with electric generator and the main dining room upstairs. Recommended by Gault Millau. Schmittenstr. 12, Zell am See.

For the best combination of fine dining in a comfortable atmosphere (lots of wood carvings and unusual wall lights), try the **Steinerwirt** in Zell am See. It specializes in sirloin steak Vienna style (with onions and small dumplings), and the Salzburger Nockerl (a tasty soufflé) is not to be missed for dessert.

Delicious cordon bleu and pepper steak top the fare at **Traubenstube**. The **Landhotel Erlhof** (tel. 66370) is highly rated by Gault Millau for gourmet cuisine. For a light meal, sample **Pizzeria Giuseppe**.

The **Café Konditorei Mosshammer** and **Café Feinschmeck** are your best bets for a late afternoon snack, especially if your taste buds crave mouth-watering pastries and chocolates.

The **Guggengbichl** hut features Kasnocken (noodles, cheese and butter) baked and served in a huge skillet. Scraping out the bottom of the pan for the crusted delicacy is fun for the whole table. The inn rises above Kaprun and diners are allowed to climb a mile above and slide down to the entrance in sleds provided for the thrill. It's a good way to work up an appetite . . . or work off the huge dinner.

The **Steinerwirt** provides good moderately-priced meals. **Vanini** on Banhofstrasse has the best and largest variety of Austrian and other pastries. For pizza try **Zum Casar** (747257).

Crazy Restaurant, located upstairs from the Crazy Daisy Pub is a Scandinavian-owned Mexican restaurant with an inexpensive menu, featuring among other items "breath killer" garlic bread.

On the mountain, at the top of the Schmittenhohe, **Brettlachhutte** is the lunch choice. Here Peter Radcher, owner, chef, waiter, bartender and perfect Austrian host, serves a hearty traditional Austrian fare.

In Kaprun, dining is good at the large hotels. Two favorites: Sport**hotel Kaprun** and **Hotel Zur Burgruine.**

Jagawirt (tel. 8737) near Kaprun is a charming inn, owned and operated by Hans and Theresia Nindl, which provides an outstanding dining experience. We enjoyed wild goat (Gamsgebraten) in mushroom sauce with black bread dumplings (Schwartzbrotknodel) and cranberries (Pieiselbeer); a venison filet (Hirschrunckenfilet) is cooked medium (Rosabebraten) with mushrooms (Steinpilen) in Burgundy sauce, Sch265. Nindl is an avid hunter and he takes some of the local game (venison, antelope, goat) for the restaurant. Two delicious desserts are blueberries heated with flour and eggs with vanilla ice cream (Moosbeernocking) for Sch78, and Mandelecken, a light almond cake floating in blueberry and kiwi sauce for Sch78. The inn is also a popular après-ski stop for skiers coming down from the Kitzsteinhorn glacier. Jagawirt is only open September through May. African art and artifacts decorate the walls of the restaurant, attesting to the Nindls' living in Rhodesia part time.

Saustall (Pork Bar), just outside Zell am See, serves rich fried pork, veal and beef steaks on wooden planks. Tropfen Amelner, about 90 proof, is a perfect *digestif.*

Gletchenmuhle on the glacier is a good luncheon spot with its Tyrolean fare, spectacular views, huge deck and sun chairs for rent.

Dorfstadl is the locals' favorite restaurant in the region. The setting is hand-hewn post and beam and the food is spectacular not only in taste but in presentation. Try the garlic soup for an appetizer and apple strudle for desert. For a main course any selection will please.

Head to the Cafe Konditorei for wonderful pastries in Kaprun.

 ## Après-ski/nightlife

Come evening, intimate taverns and rollicking discos open their doors. Those looking for quieter entertainment might head for the **Wunderbar** on the top floor of the Mövenpick Grand Hotel overlooking Lake Zell.

The Felsenkeller, in the Hotel Lebzelter, is an après-ski bar built in the 1700s, with bartenders in lederhosen. It is open 4 p.m.–4 a.m. and offers an atmosphere where locals and tourists gather for a cold beer or a hot Jägertee. Here townsfolk sometimes challenge each other at *Stocknagaln,* a game where the object is to hit a thin nail imbedded in a block of wood with the sharp blade of an ax.

The **Jagawirt** mentioned in the dining section is one of the most picturesque après-ski gathering spots for locals and tourists alike.

Curiously, the largest (and the most lively) night haunt in the region lies on the outskirts of tiny Kaprun, not in Zell am See: **The Baum Bar** burned to the ground a few years ago, and when it was rebuilt it bounded back better than ever. A huge dance floor is usually packed by midnight. Partygoers boogie till the 6 a.m. closing time.

Entertainment is harder to find in Kaprun, but it is there. The **Idefix Pub** and the **Austrian Pub** are perfect for whiling away the hours. Another good disco is the **Nindl-Dancing. Charly's Kneippe, Kitsch & Bitter** and **Zum Schnellen Bier** are three popular drinking spots.

In Zell am See, one of the most popular stops for vacationing Europeans is the **Crazy**

Daisy Pub, 10 Brucker Bundesstrasse, full of Brits, Dutch, Swedes and other party-hardy types. Bands play seven nights a week. Order drinks like "No Thanks I'm Fine," "Against the Wall," "Orgasm" and "Slippery Nipples." The Pinzgauer Diele has great après-ski 'till 7 p.m., then after 11 p.m. it's considered the top disco—loud with ski movies. The Bierstadl features 33 different kinds of beer. **Evergreen** features live music, but can be a bit smoky. **Hirschenkeller** is a blues, rock and reggae bar across the street from the post office under Hotel Zum Herfeken . . . **Viva Club** disco heats up after 1 a.m. at 4 Kirchengasse. The locals will be drinking at the Bierstadl. Après-ski can be enjoyed at the outside bar atop **Schmittenhohe**, overlooking the church and at **Ampere** near the Seller Bergbahn.

Child care

The kindergarten is at Schuttdorf-Areitalm (tel. 56020). Rates are Sch500 for full day, Sch1,100 for three days, and Sch1,650 for six days.

Ursula Zink (tel. 56343) also sits for children from one year of age. Rates: one day, Sch450; three days, Sch1,000; six days, Sch1,500.

Fesienolorf Hagleituer (tel. 57935) for one year old and up, Monday-Friday, 10 a.m. to 4 p.m.; Sch350 for one day, including lunch.

The children's ski school is open daily from 10 a.m. to 4 p.m., except Sunday. Lunch is included, and children four to ten are accepted for Sch1,390 for three days and Sch1,650 for four to six days.

In Kaprun, call 82380 for children's ski school information; in Zell the number is 3207 or 56020.

Getting there

Zell is about 56 miles from Salzburg, which has jet service from other European airports. The usual airport for international arrivals is Munich, about 143 miles away. Vienna is about 240 miles distant.

Zell has regular national and international train service and bus service to Kaprun.

By automobile from Munich, drive to Salzburg by autobahn, and head toward Bischofshofen. Rental cars are available in Salzburg or Munich.

Other activities

A visit to nearby Salzburg (see Gateways to the Alps Chapter), made famous a generation ago by the movie *The Sound of Music* and always famous as Mozart's home, attracts hundreds of thousands of tourists each year.

Both Zell am See and Kaprun deserve exploration. The Zell skyline is distinguished by the outlines of the St. Hippolyt church and the Vogtturm (city tower).

Even nonskiers will enjoy the Schmittenhöhe on a clear day when you can see at least thirty 3,000-meter (9,843-foot) or higher peaks in the region.

On Sunday evenings in Kaprun, the tourist office stages folk entertainment and story telling around a bonfire within the ruins of an old fortress. You'll enjoy the music, though the stories are in German.

At Kaprun, visit the Gothic Pfarrkirche in the middle of town and the castle ruins, even if you're not there for the storytelling and music.

The Kaprun Optimum with an indoor and outdoor swimming pool and fitness center is packed with fitness-minded Europeans and a great place to meet other skiers. The pool is open from 11 a.m.–10 p.m. Entrance is Sch85 for adults or Sch450 for seven tickets. The sauna at the pool costs Sch145 per session or Sch810 for seven tickets.

Castles are located in Prielau and Kaprun.

For Alpine sightseeing flights call 757937. Try **bowling** at Schlossstrasse (tel. 8222). For **horse-drawn sleigh rides** check out Endtalbauer (tel. 7210 or 86430) or Pichlbauer (tel. 7322 or 8430).

There is an illuminated **tobaggan** run from Jausenstation Guggenbichl, Kaprun. There are also runs from Schaufelberg and Lechnerberg.

For **ice-skating** head to the Sports and Leisure Center (tel. 733880)

For a fine selection of Austrian crafts and ceramics stop in at Hierner & Co. Stadtplatz 6, ZellamSee. For Austrian souvenirs there are a multitude of choices throughout the village.

Tourist information

Check with the Kurverwaltung, A-5700 Zell am See, Austria; tel. 06542-770, fax 06542-72037, and Verkehrs-verein Kaprun, A-5710 Kaprun, Austria; tel. 06547-86430, fax 06547-8192.

☎ *Telephone prefix for Zell am See is 06542;*
for Kaprun the prefix is 06547.

France

Thanks to the Winter Olympics, France is now a well-known skiing region. Albertville, the largest town in the area—one without any skiing, ironically—anchored the events, but the real scene was at the resorts of Courchevel, Méribel, Val d'Isère, Tignes, Les Arc and La Plagne.

While the 1992 Olympic Games focused world attention on French ski areas, surprising many viewers that French skiing was so well established, the French have been on the slopes for a long time; resorts like Chamonix, Megève and Val d'Isère shared in the initial development of Alpine skiing half a century ago. But many of the modern French resorts have been purpose-built for skiing: this means entire villages, such as Avoriaz, Tignes, Courchevel, Flaine, La Plagne and Les Arcs, have been created with skiing uppermost in the designers' minds. The result has been thousands of apartments and hotels that give you the convenience of walking out your door, stepping into your skis and skiing some of the most extensive slopes in the world. In addition, the après-ski life is great and the food and wine reflect France at its best.

France is home of the most extensive skiing found anywhere in the world. The Trois Vallées region, the Portes du Soleil region (shared with Switzerland) and the Espace Killy region of Val d'Isère and Tignes are unparalleled in the skiing universe for wide open spaces and dramatic skiing.

The French skiers that vacationers will meet in the mountains are also some of the friendliest people one can meet. The abrupt manner some tourists associate with French locals just won't be found here. In the mountains, everyone comes to enjoy life and share the wonderful beauty of the mountains.

From breakfast with croissants and café au lait, to a lunch *picnique* on a sunny terrace, to sumptuous dinners, no one will forget the love affair the French have with cusine and the passion with which they enjoy the culinary life. Don't feel that to get the most out of French cooking, one has to spend for gourmet haute cuisine. Here in the French Alps, some of the best local meals in France can be found. Meats from cattle grazing in mountain pastures, fish from sparkling unspoiled streams and lakes, cheese aged in hidden caves, and liquors fermented in local barrels, all make up a cuisine that is hard to beat. Start with *Kir*; test the charcuterie—paté,sausage, dried ham; enjoy the local cheeses—Beaufort, Rublechon, Chêvre; savor crêpes with Grand Marnier; and drink local wines—Gamay and Crépys.

The French add a bit of drama and love to having Fondue Savoyarde—when a woman loses her bread in the fondue cheese pot, she must kiss her neighbor to her right (imagine the jockeying for places at some fondue tables); when the man loses his bread, he must buy a round of drinks.

Getting Apartments in France

Apartments are the way to go in France. They are inexpensive and often right on the slopes . . . but they are small from an American's point of view. If you want space, get the next larger sized apartment than you would normally reserve. Studios are one large room. *Deux pièces* means two rooms or one bedroom with a living room that can sleep two more people; *trois pièces* is three rooms, usually two bedrooms plus a living room.

A note on prices

The prices in this section are valid for the 1997/1998 winter season unless otherwise noted. You can expect prices to increase 3 to 5 percent a year for the following winter seasons. Use these prices only as a guide.

All prices are given in French francs (FFr). Information for the book was gathered when the franc was at an exchange rate of approximately FFr6 to US$1; FFr9.9 to UK£1; and FFr4.4 to Cdn$1. Any subsequent shift in the exchange rate will be the biggest factor affecting prices.

The seasons

High season: Christmas and New Years, then all of February to mid-April .
Low season: January after the New Year holiday, then late April.

Use these as general guidelines, because some resorts may have slightly adjusted seasons owing to local school holidays. Check with your destination resort to get the exact dates if you are planning your trip on a season borderline.

Telephone notes

There are no area codes or prefixes in France for cities and towns, except for Paris. The area code is part of the normal eight-digit telephone number.

The country code for France is 0033.

Les Arcs
Bourg-St. Maurice

Les Arcs is not a town or village: it is a group of modern complexes high above the Savoy transportation hub of Bourg St. Maurice. It was designed expressly as a ski resort; a purpose-built collection of large sprawling hillside buildings with an unusual swooping roof design.

Les Arcs displays a remarkable unity, not only in its architecture but also in its infrastructure and support systems. You have the sense of being inside a smoothly running machine rather than a village of competing shops, restaurants and owners. It's not a bad feeling—just curiously different.

Many of the rooms are reached by ramps, giving the appearance that no two rooms are on the same level. Of the three high-altitude complexes that comprise Les Arcs (each named for its altitude in meters), Arcs 1600 was the first, a family-oriented area with four hotels, shops and a nursery that takes children from four months old. Rooms tend to be functional and more moderately priced, and the nightlife is minimal. Arcs 1800 is the largest complex, with the biggest selection of restaurants and shops. Arcs 2000 was constructed last, as the lift system expanded to reach the higher elevations. It offers easy access to the glacier and surrounding expert terrain, and is known as a shrine for serious skiers.

Overall, the resort is decidedly international, more than half its clientele arriving from outside France. You'll have no difficulty finding someone who speaks English if you need help, nor will it be a problem striking up conversations in bars or on the lifts.

Included in the ski pass for the area (see Lift Tickets) are lifts originating in the lower-elevation villages of Peisey-Nancroix, Vallandry and Villaroger. These hamlets are centuries-old settlements that offer a strong contrast to the stylized angular atmosphere of Les Arcs.

For visitors who want to combine a bit of local flavor with their high-tech ski adventure, a seven-minute funicular ride down the steep slope from Arcs 1600 to Bourg St. Maurice offers a chance to spend a few hours in the shops, museums and restaurants of a typical Savoyard town. A bustling open-air market on Saturdays offers Savoy specialties such as mountain ham, wine and the rich and creamy rebluchon cheese.

Mountain layout

Les Arcs is glorious for the ski-till-you-drop-and-then-do-it-some-more crowd. Snowboarders come from all over the northern hemisphere because, as one American enthusiast was heard to say, "In France you have the right to die." This doesn't detract from France's excellent safety records, but the French are not saddled with the onerous liability problems faced by American resorts. Trails are marked but this is generally seen as a formality or as a handy guide in white-out conditions. Otherwise, ski at your own risk.

Les Arcs is has two large sections and two smaller ones. The first major area is the face above Arc 1800 and 1600, with 28 lifts servicing six expert trails, 15 intermediate runs and 19 beginner slopes.

The second major area is a massive valley above and beyond Arc 2000 bounded by the 10,484-foot peak and ridge formed by the Col du Grand Renard and the Arpette. This area has 15 lifts and 10 expert, 10 intermediate and 11 beginner trails, as well as plenty of off-piste possibilities.

The connected area of Peisey-Nancroix Vallandry is part of the overall ski area, but does not have a particularly easy connection to the Arc 1800/1600 sector. This area has one expert trail, a baker's dozen of mellow intermediate runs and 10 beginner runs. In cloudy or windy weather, the tree-lined slopes of Peisey-Vallandry offer good visibility.

Finally, there is the Villaroger sector, at the end of the two long Aiguille Rouge runs. It has only two direct lifts back to the crest above Arc 2000. Another lift allows those who have skied below Arc 2000 to reach Villaroger without returning to the top of the Aiguille Rouge.

Mountain rating

This is one of the best compact areas, featuring something for everyone from beginner to expert. There is great intermediate skiing all across the face above Arc 1800 descending from Arpette, Col des Frettes and Col du Grand Renard. Advanced intermediates will love the runs from the Aiguille Rouge across the glacier and down the Piste du Grand Col. Beginners and intermediates will have plenty of area at the bottom of the valley between Aiguille Rouge and Arpette. Experts face some exhilarating runs from the Aiguille Rouge across the glacier, then can drop down the massive face above Arc 2000.

Above Peisey-Nancroix Vallandry are relatively gentle intermediate and beginner runs. The drop along the ridge to Villaroger is for strong intermediates and experts.

Experts should sign up with a guide to tackle the off-trail tours circling behind the Aiguille Grive and the Aiguille Rousse or for an itinerary off the backside of the Aiguille Rouge looping around to Villaroger.

Ski school

There are two Les Arcs ski school groups—the French Ski School and the International Ski School. The French Ski School has offices in all Arc villages and the International Ski School is based in Arc 1800 and Arc 2000. Hours are 9 a.m. to 12 noon and 2 to 5:30 p.m. All prices are approximate.

Group lessons

The standard rate for three hours a day for six days is FFr800. A reduced rate of FFr700 is available for children.

Private lessons

These are offered based on the availability of instructors. The price per hour is FFr180 for most of the season for one to two skiers. January has reduced prices.

Lift tickets (97/98 prices)

Your ski pass is valid for the entire Les Arcs, Peisey-Nancroix and Villaroger area; it also allows you to ski La Plagne, Val d'Isère-Tignes l'Espace Killy, and the French-Italian area of La Rosiere-La Thuile for one day per resort while your pass is valid. For La Plagne, Val d'Isère and Tignes, present your pass at the main ticket window of the resort. For La Rosiere-La Thuile, you must pick up your pass in Les Arcs at a STAR ski pass office.

Normal lift ticket rates: full day, FFr212; six days, FFr995; seven days, FFr1,125.

Parents staying at Les Arcs and buying a lift pass for themselves can obtain a free lift pass for each of their children younger than seven. Identification is required.

Accommodations

Clone architecture has created a group of hotels that are very similar, so far as size of rooms and layout are concerned. All hotels noted here are exceptionally good and are similar in quality. Rates are for one week double ocupancy with half board. Low season prices are January 9–23, and high season February 13–March 6.

Hotel du Golf*** (479 41 43 43) was the first constructed in Arc 1800 and is still the flagship hoIt features one of the best restaurants in the region. Rooms are simple, functional, and comfortable with exceptional views from either side. The hotel has an extensive fitness and health center. FFr3,430–5,075.

Hotel Latitudes*** (479 07 49 79) in Arc 1800 is an easy five-minute walk from the main commercial center of Le Charvet. The rooms are modern and sparsely decorated. There is a small fitness center. Evening meals include two theme dinners each week and an entertainment evening. FFr3,570–5,470.

Hotel Les Melèzes*** at Arc 2000 (470 07 50 50). You won't have to worry about whether the person next to you has a better room; they're all just alike. Watch out for the solo rooms sold to singles "with no supplement!" Signing up for this arrangement means that you will be sharing a toilet and bath with a stranger in another solo room. FFr1,820 –3,680 (full board).

Hotel de l'Aiguille Rouge** (479 07 57 07) a notch below Les Melèzes and across the skating rink from it. Our inspection showed it to be every bit as comfortable. Rooms here are offered in a special package with half board (drinks included), six-day lift tickets. Rates per person are FFr2,785–4,185.

La Hotel Mercure*** (479 07 65 00) a new 80-room hoSix days half board FFr3,380–6,095.

Apartments

Les Arcs is oriented more toward apartments than hotels; there are thousands more apartments than hotel rooms. An apartment is a better bargain if you're willing to do without the amenities of hotels, and despite some horror stories about tiny French apartments there *is* enough room, unless you insist on fitting four people into a studio. January low-season and the February high-season prices are noted here. There are two other price ranges between these extremes.

In Arc 2000, a studio apartment for two in January low season will cost FFr1,470 a week; in February high season it is FFr3,675. A two-room apartment for four people in January low season will cost FFr2,400 a week; in February expect to pay FFr6,600 .

Arc 1800 studios cost FFr1,645 a week in January low season; the same room costs FFr4,130 in February high season. Two-room apartments for four run FFr2,555 in January low season and FFr7,100 in February.

Contact the tourist office for reservations.

 ## Dining

Here the focus is on the functional—just like the architecture. When we asked locals about the restaurants the response was usually a puzzled look and a smile, after ponderous thought.

Here are Les Arcs' best, it seems:

Arc 1800

The **Hotel du Golf** main restaurant (479 41 43 43) is the best restaurant in Les Arcs. The atmosphere is modern elegance and the menu costs around FFr250 a person before considering wine.

Le Choucas (479 07 42 25) serves local Savoyard specialties in two simple rooms with fake wooden beams and sparse country decor. Expect to spend FFr180–200.

L'Equipe (479 07 41 76) may be the most popular restaurant in Les Arcs. Heaping portions are served under heavy rafters with a wide picture-window view of the valley. Dinner is FFr150–180 with wine.

L'Auberge Rouge (479 07 44 68) has the most character of any restaurant in Les Arcs, exuding a happy spirit. It only serves light fare, such as crêpes, pizzas and salads. The figure of a pirate pulling a sled with a cask of wine stands next to the stairs. Upstairs ten red tables are tucked under the sloping roof. Crêpes cost FFr20–40.

For pizza, try **Casa Mia** in Arc 1800 Le Charvet with its wood-fired oven. Pizza costs FFr45–60. In Arc 1800 Les Villard, try the pizzeria **Gargantus.**

In Arc 1600 try the fondue and other specialties served with gusto by the owner of **Chez Maryse** (479 07 78 14) .

Arc 2000

Le St. Jacques (479 07 29 45) serves fine fondue and raclette. Little else can be heartily recommended.

For a special lunch on the mountain don't miss Belliou **La Fumée** (479 07 29 13) named after a Jack London story, in the valley of Arc 2000. This unique family-run restaurant was built in the 15th century by King Victor Emmanuel of Italy as a bear-hunting lodge. Omelets cooked over an open fire are served in the pan, and other regional specialties are prepared and served with care. Or after a long ski down to the bottom of the Villaroger lift, visit La Ferme, a small restaurant serving excellent mountainside food.

Since many of the best restauants are in far-flung places surrounding Les Arcs, consider a visit to L'Ancolie (479 07 93 20), reported to be a beautiful little restaurant in Peisey, or take a sled to dine at Le Boid de Lune (479 07 17 92) in Montevenix.

Après-ski/nightlife

In Arc 1800, the ski instructors head to **Bar Le Gabotte** in the center of Le Charvet, as does the majority of the English-speaking crowd when the lifts shut down. The overflow congregates in **Bar le Thuria** across the square.

In the Les Villards section of Arc 1800, the best après-ski is in **Bar Russel,** a very British-looking pub with dark wooden tables and bar and 40 different bottled beers. The lounge of the Hotel Du Golf has live jazz before and after dinner in front of a flickering fire.

At Arc 1600, an older crowd (meaning over 25 or so) gathers at the small chalet of L'Arcelle that offers music after dinner.

There are discos in Arc 2000, 1600, and 1800, and all follow the French disco formula: drinks in the FFr80 range and opening times around midnight, closing about four in the morning. If you have insomnia, try **Le Fairway** in the basement of Hotel du Golf in Arc 1800. **Le Rock Hill** disco is packed with teenagers. **Apokalypse** is the spot in the Arc 1800 Les Villards section. If you are staying in Arc 2000, disco **K.L.92** normally is the place of choice for visitors of all ages.

Child care

All three villages—Arc 1600, 1800 and 2000—have nurseries and programs for children 1–6. The nursery at Arc 1600 takes children from four months.

The ski school organizes a special miniclub for children four to eight, to allow them time to play and learn the fundamentals of skiing. Children four to eleven who have the basics down can join a special ski school course.

The nursery, for children 1–3, costs FFr940 for six full days during most of the season and only FFr825 in January. Six half days, either mornings or afternoons, will cost FFr595, or in January low season, FFr515. Lunch for children costs FFr385 a week.

Kindergarten for kids 3–6 costs FFr910 a week for full days in normal season and only FFr825 in January low season. Six half days, either mornings or afternoons, will cost FFr495 in regular season and FFr455 in low season. Meals cost FFr385 a week.

The miniclub for a week costs FFr1,625, with FFr385 additional for lunch.

Other activities

Three squash courts are available in Arc 1800 on the upper square of Les Villards. They are open daily 5 to 10 p.m. There are skating rinks in the Arc 1800 and 2000 villages. Hang-gliding lessons and accompanied flights can be arranged by calling 479 07 41 28. Horseback riding is available at the La Cavale Equestrian Center (479 07 72 13) at Arc 1600.

Getting there

Les Arcs is directly above Bourg-St. Maurice, which is now linked to Paris by TGV speed train service.

The nearest airport is Geneva Cointrin. It is connected with Les Arcs by four scheduled buses each day.

By car, take the Albertville exit on the autoroute, then follow the signs to Bourg-St. Maurice.

A funicular runs from Bourg-St. Maurice about every 20 minutes 7:40 a.m.–7:20 p.m.

Tourist information

There are tourist information offices in all three villages. They are open daily, 9 a.m. to 7 p.m. There you can also send faxes and buy photocopies, bus tickets to Bourg-St. Maurice and telephone cards.

For information call 479 07 12 57 or fax 479 07 45 96.

Avoriaz/Morzine
Portes du Soleil, France

Situated about an hour from Geneva, just south of the lake, these contrasting resorts anchor the French side of Portes du Soleil.

Traditional Morzine is the largest settlement of Les Portes du Soleil, with 3,000 residents, 70 hotels, 45 restaurants and 20 ski shops. Although Morzine is at a relatively low 3,000 feet, a network of lifts reaches the panoramic Chamossière at 6,006 feet. And Avoriaz, at 7,080 feet, is a mere cable car ride away.

Morzine attracts an English-speaking crowd, so rudimentary English is widely spoken, a plus for Americans who don't want to grapple with French.

The old part of town, going back to the 16th century, rises to a 19th-century church and the tumbling Dranse River. With its own Gallic identity, the town is a pleasant place for walking and relaxing. Although nightlife lacks the glamour of Megève or Courchevel, there is plenty to do, with three discos, two cinemas, many bars and an ice skating arena that has hosted the world's top skaters.

Avoriaz

More than just a lodge or restaurant at the top of the cable car, car-free Avoriaz sits perched above steep rock cliffs at 5,400 feet with a racy angular modern outline that the French call "integrated architecture." By any name, it's a visual spectacular. Jazzy music fills the streets, and a casual, colorful atmosphere prevails with sleighs whooshing through the streets and skiers nonchalantly modeling fashions at café tables.

Jean Vuarnet, the sunglass king, returned to France with a gold medal from the 1960 Olympics at Squaw Valley and persuaded a big real estate agency to invest up above. The original structures of 1966 have now grown to a cluster of 42 modern condos, a Club Med, two hotels and 30 restaurants.

Avoriaz is gaining attention with its World Professional Snowboard Championships held late February through early March. Its Children's Village, managed by Olympic medal-ist Annie Famose and a staff of 120 instructors, is acclaimed for teaching youngsters three to 16 to ski.

Avoriaz is at the center of Les Portes Du Soleil wheel, the main link between France and Switzerland. The question becomes, "Do you just go there to ski, for a meal, for a drink and a look around," or "Do you stay?" In the old days getting there meant climbing into a cable car and then taking a reindeer-drawn sled to your accommodations; today a road climbs up from Morzine, 14 km. and a half-hour drive away. The cable car runs every 15 minutes to Les Prodains, which has a bus connection to Morzine. Ski runs also plunge down from Avoriaz to Les Prodains, although with light snow cover they can be treacherous.

 ## Mountain layout

If you have come to really ski, Avoriaz is perhaps the best base from which to explore the Portes du Soleil area. As well as easy access to the Les Crosets/Champoussin sector via the Swiss Wall, Avoriaz has easy access to Plaine Dranse with perhaps the most enjoyable and varied skiing of the region. The slopes directly above Avoriaz will challenge skiers of every level.

Beginners go to Le Pleney, which is a one-stop ascent by tram or cable car. Nyon has a nice mix of black, red and blue descents, and Chamossière has outstanding views, good long black runs and some fine cruising through the Col de Joux Plane. Some of the best tough skiing of the entire Portes du Soleil is nearby—from Pointe de Nyon to Col du Forney in France and, in Switzerland, from Planachaux to Grand Paradis and Champéry. Plan to go with a guide, however. The Wall of Death between Avoriaz and Switzerland can be skied by an intermediate when the snow cover is good, because there are broad segments for traverses and turns. Fearful skiers can take the chair lift down.

Mountain Rating

A good mixed bag of skiing opportunities awaits, and most of them can be enjoyed by an intermediate. Morzine is also a very good place for beginners, relaxed and wide-open. The variety of lifts, terrain and passages makes sometimes less than challenging runs interesting.

Avoriaz has some of the best beginner facilities in the Portes du Soleil region. Experts: this is what locals call *sauvage*—wide open all-terrain, all-condition descents. For intermediates—you'll never have to ski the same run twice. (*See Mountain Rating in the Swiss Portes du Soleil chapter.*)

 ## Ski school (97/98 prices)

The Morzine ski school (tel. 450 79 13 13, fax 450 75 94 59) has 140 instructors and a strong following—fully one-quarter of Morzine's visi-tors take lessons. The rates for downhill and cross-country ski lessons are the same.

The Ski School of Avoriaz meeting place is the Place du Téléphérique. You can sign up for lessons in the Tourist Office and in the Cap-Neige building near Fontaines Blanches. Ski passes are not included in the lesson prices.

Group lessons: six days, 10 a.m. to noon and 2–5 p.m., FFr800. One day lesson is FFr195 for adults.

Private lessons: one hour, FFr170.

Monoski, snowboarding and competition lessons cost FFr175 for a half day; FFr830 for six half days; and FFr1,150 for six full days.

Lift tickets (97/98 prices)

A ski pass for the entire Portes du Soleil costs: one day, FFr203; two days, FFr388; three days, FFr542; five days, FFr814; six days, FFr928.

The pass for only the Avoriaz section of the Portes du Soleil costs: one day, FFr160; two days, FFr287.

Children under 16 receive about a 20 percent discount. Those under five ski free.

Accommodations

Morzine has seven three-star hotels, which include:

Les Airelles (450 74 71 21) is modern, well-designed, and centrally located, with a big swimming pool, a toilet and phone in each its 45 rooms. Rates are FFr550–790, full board; FFr486–750, half board.

Le Champs Fleuris (50 79 14 44) has a pool, tennis and sauna for FFr380–550 for full pension, or FFr300–570 for half pension. **Le Dahu** (50 75 92 92) has similar amenities for just a bit less per night.

Le Tremplin (450 79 12 31; fax 450 75 94 11) has a friendly atmosphere and a pleasant sitting area and bar, and is located next to the slopes. Its rooms, irregular in size, cost FFr500–850 with full pension and FFr400–750 with half pension.

La Bergerie (450 79 13 69) is an attractive residence hotel. It doesn't have a dining room, but has kitchen facilities in the rooms, telephone, television, a parking garage and sauna. Cost is FFr400–800.

Morzine has 18 two-star hotels, which include:

Le Carlina (450 79 01 03; fax 450 79 17 49) is FFr400–630 with full pension; FFr320–550 with half pension.

Le Samoyede (450 79 00 79) has 27 rooms, FFr380–468 with full pension and FFr340–428 with half pension.

Le Sporting (450 79 15 03) has 28 rooms and costs FFr360–495 with full pension, FFr390–385 with half pension.

Avoriaz:

This is primarily a resort of condos. The two hotels do not take groups. High season, when rooms are toughest to get and prices are highest, is Christmas, Easter and February.

Hotel les Dromonts (450 74 08 11, fax 450 74 02 79) has 38 rooms. Approximate rate with breakfast is FFr406–800; half pension, FFr600–950; full pension, FFr880–1,340.

Ski Chalets: Crystal, First Choice, Thomas Cook/Neilson (see page 27 for phone, fax and internet addresses).

Apartments

This is what Avoriaz is all about. The tourist board will send you a list of rental agencies who will make arrangements.

Approximate prices (one week) with contact agency:

Avoriaz Location (450 74 04 53): studio for four, FFr1,700–4,500; two-room for five, FFr2,250.

Immobiliere Des Hauts-Forts (450 74 16 08): studio for four, FFr1900–4,740; two-room for five, FFr2,650–6,250.

Pierre et Vacances (54, Avenue Marceau, 75008 Paris; (1) 47 23 32 22): studio for four, FFr1,680–3,990; two-room for four to five, FFr2,100–5,565.

Maeva (30, Rue D'Orleans, 92200 Neuilly-Sur-Seine; (1) 47 45 17 21): studio for four, FFr2,500–5,950; two-room for four to five, FFr2,840–6,300.

To contact the Office of Tourism, write F-74110 Avoriaz, France; (450 74 02 11, fax 450 74 18 25).

Dining

In Morzine, head to La Chamade's where the owner, Thierry Thorens, trained with celebrated chef Paul Bocuse near Lyon. Grilled food, local dishes and traditional French cuisine are served in one area. In a larger room, gourmet service is about FFr300 minimum per person.

More typical of the regional and traditional food, with raclette and fondue, is L'Etale, where a meal will run FFr80–110. There is a disco downstairs.

Les Sapins has an excellent view of Lake Montriond and is known for its home cooking. Roger Muffat, father of the owner, prepares the dried meats, ham, and everything else himself. A five-course meal is FFr110–180.

Avoriaz has a good collections of retaurants but book in advance. The four-star restaurant in Hotel Dromonts charges about FFr350 for a meal; La Grignotte, at the base of the cable car, costs FFr100–120; Crepy runs FFr100–150. Petit Vatel specializes in trout; Bistrots prepares mountain specialties that with a bottle of wine will cost FFr150. Sample Marmottes, L'Eau Vive and Braize. For late-night fare, try Mama's Pizza or Lapon.

Since Avoriaz is on the mountain, its restaurants certainly qualify. However the dorf of Les Lindarets, on the other side of the ridge, has a wonderful collection of small restaurants. They are all good but Les Marmottes, Pomme de Pin and Cremaillerie stand out.

Après-ski/nightlife

Generally low-keyed and relaxed, Morzine is no jet-set town crammed with sports cars. It is, however, good for pleasant wandering and window shopping, with several opportunities to stop for a hot chocolate or beer. Opéra Rock disco attracts locals and young people. Dixie Bar is a nicely decorated piano bar near the church. Le Café Chaud attracts young swingers. Le Pacha starts pulsing later at night.

Avoriaz has plenty of action—The Place and Le Chouca are fun, and The Midnight Express—begins filling up after midnight.

Child care

In Morzine, kindergarten l'Outa welcomes children and infants from two months to four years. The chalet is in the center of the resort, near the slopes and ski school. There is a large playroom for indoor activities, a nursery and a very large yard where instructors give first lessons to the youngest. Parents can bring a meal or take advantage of the special menu. Ski lessons are available for children over four years at the ski school. Instructors speak English. Phone is 450 79 26 00.

The children's supervised play school and nursery (450 79 26 00) for ages two months to twelve years, may include skiing. Costs are FFr99–129 for a half day (four hours), and

FFr173–203 a full day with ski lessons. Six half-days cost FFr495–675; six consecutive days cost FFr865–1,225 with ski lessons. Infants are charged a slightly lower rate.

Avoriaz child care takes care of children and teaches them to ski. The Children's Village, in the center of Avoriaz, is open 9 a.m.–5:30 p.m., and accepts youngsters three to 16 (450 74 04 46). Children not taking lessons can play in the snow playground. Half days are FFr114; full days, FFr226 (FFr200 without lunch); six half days, FFr525; six days, FFr1,095 (FFr950 without lunch).

For baby sitters, call the tourist office at 450 74 72 78.

The town also has a nursery, Les Pe'tits Loups (450 74 00 38; fax 450 74 18 25). Rates are FFr130 for a half day up to four hours, and FFr230 for a full day. Six consecutive days cost FFr1,100 and six consecutive half days cost FFr625. Lunch costs an additional FFr30 per day.

Other activities

The arena complex at Morzine offers curling, skating, ice hockey, table tennis, a weight room, dancing and gymnastics. Painting exhibits, figure skating, ice dancing, hockey games and movies are also scheduled there. For information in Morzine, call 450 74 72 72.

At Avoriaz, all in a small radius and easy to find, there are para-sailing; ultra-lights; squash courts; a fitness center with exercise machines, weights, squash courts, sauna and Jacuzzis; and a cinema and bowling alley. The Avoriaz tourist office also publishes a regular schedule of movies.

Getting there

The nearest airport is in Geneva. From the airport a bus runs daily. The tourist office at the airport has the latest schedule.

Avoriaz and Morzine can be reached by a train/bus combination. The train from Paris and Geneva arrives several times a day, and a bus makes the 40-km. climb.

Driving, take the Geneva-Mont Blanc autoroute and exit at Morzine/Avoriaz. Morzine is 60 km. from Geneva and Avoriaz only 15 km. further.

Open-air parking in Avoriaz costs FFr240 for a week; covered parking for a week is FFr480. Transfers, available 24 hours a day from the parking lots in the town center, cost FFr38–60 for three to four people with luggage.

Parking in the Morzine lot at the bottom of the cable car is free. Avoriaz is a 20-minute drive from Morzine. Cable cars leave every 15 minutes, 7 a.m.–9 p.m.; on Friday and Saturday it closes at 1 a.m. Those with lift passes ride free 9 a.m.–5 p.m.; otherwise the charge is FFr35.

Tourist information

L'Office du Tourisme, Place Crusaz, 74110 Morzine, France; tel. 450 74 72 72; fax 450 79 03 48.

L'Office du Tourisme d'Avoriaz, Place Centrale, 74110 Avoriaz-Morzine, France; tel. 450 74 02 11; fax 450 74 18 25.

Chamonix Mont-Blanc

Chamonix is the most famous ski town in France. It also breaks every normal European rule for a resort. None of the trails drops directly into town; instead, the ski areas are spread along a valley almost 10 miles long. Only two of the areas are interconnected. Some lift lines can be long, especially for the Grand Montet. Shuttlebuses are crowded and erratic but eventually come. The weather can change in a matter of hours from sunshine to a stormy whiteout. But what Chamonix does offer is perhaps the world's best expert and advanced skiing on spectacular mountains rising more than 12,500 feet above the valley. And Chamonix itself has a strong Alpine flair. You won't find the space-age structures that set the tone for so many of France's other resorts. The world's best expert skiing and one of the world's most picturesque settings, in the shadow of 15,767-foot Mont Blanc, creates an experience that is hard to beat.

Small-town coziness is the rule, with plenty of restaurants, narrow streets for shopping and good hotels. This atmosphere can make one forget about the logistics of getting on the trails. But remember, to fully enjoy Chamonix, you'll need a car or a bus to get to its slopes, spread out for miles along the valley floor. There is an erratic shuttlebus service from Chamonix center to the outlying areas; some hotels provide bus service.

In Chamonix you can ski hard all day long, then sit at a café in a small square and sip a kir, wine or beer. The bars are crowded with an international group, and you are surrounded with other skiers who are here not for the ritz and the glitz but for the challenge and the exhilaration of testing themselves against Europe's most spectacular slopes.

 ## Mountain layout

From the slopes of Les Houches to Chamonix and on to Argentière and Le Tour, a string of lifts takes skiers up both sides of the valley. On the Mont Blanc side you ascend above outcroppings and slopes of this magnificent peak, while on the opposite side you enjoy the Mont Blanc panorama as the lifts take you to outstanding runs.

In Chamonix, most skiers choose the challenges of **Le Brévent** at 8,288 feet. The cable car rises from the town to Planpraz, where the skiing really begins. The second section of the cable car takes experts and hardy intermediates to the top of Le Brévent, and a chair lift carries the less than advanced intermediates to the Les Vioz area. Try the black run from the back of Le Brévent with another skier. If after the first few hundred feet you're not confident of your turns, you can branch to the left and take an advanced intermediate trail.

Intermediates may prefer the midstation slopes at Plan Praz, especially the chair lifts that reach the 6,560-foot level. In addition, work your way to the right and take the chair up to the Col Cornu's 7,488-foot level for a good intermediate run and off-trail skiing.

Ten minutes away by car is **Les Praz,** ground station for the cable car to La Flégère midstation. From here, a gondola takes you to L'Index at 7,822 feet, where the skiing is outstanding for intermediates. There are off-trail challenges to the right and the left of the upper gondola.

The intermediate run from L'Index to Les Praz ground station will take 30 minutes, a challenging, advanced intermediate romp. However, in high season you can wait as long as 45 minutes at the bottom to get back on the cable car. You'll want to stay on the upper mountain unless you're moving to another slope or making the last run of the day.

For our money, the best skiing in the valley is reached by driving ten minutes up the valley to Argentière. The wait at the cable car base station at **Argentière** should not be more than a half hour, even in high season. From the midstation there are only three main lifts. But these lifts open up excellent skiing. As one instructor observes, "Why ride lifts when you can ski?" Here, you can really ski. A gondola and a chair lift offer excellent intermediate terrain and plenty of off-trail skiing for experts.

Advanced and expert skiers should head up the second stage of the cable car. You'll have to pay an additional FFr25 to take the second car—it is not included on the Mont Blanc pass. For experts, the skiing is definitely worth the extra cost. At the top of Les Grands Montets take time to ascend the observation deck for one of the most spectacular views in the Alps. When you are ready to ski you have two basic choices—both offer 4,200 feet of vertical skiing, as good as it gets. This part of the mountain has never seen a grooming machine. You can drop down a black trail across the Argentière glacier to Croix de Lognan, or go around the other side of Les Grands Montets and ski under the cable car. There are wide-open off-trail opportunities for any skier willing to go for it. In fact, the "trails" offer only a general direction to the midstation. The red-rated trail branches off from the glacier route and then drops beneath the cable car to the midstation. It is often almost as much of a challenge as the expert-rated runs.

At **Le Tour** there is a system comprising one gondola and five other lifts at the end of the valley. This area is perfect for beginners and intermediates and families who are looking for comfortable cruising in the sun.

The most talked-about adventure in Chamonix—not necessarily the most challenging in terms of simple skiing—is the 13 mile-long glacier run from the Aiguille du Midi (12,601 feet) back into Chamonix (3,363 feet). The scenery is magnificent, and the memory of the Vallée Blanche and the Mer de Glace will remain forever.

The **Vallée Blanche** expedition could be more appropriately called ski mountaineering than simple skiing. Go prepared for changing weather and changing terrain: the weather in town may be balmy, with a howling wind at the top of the Aiguille du Midi and zero visibility. Be ready for freezing, windy weather—goggles or mountaineering glasses, good gloves, a warm jacket with a hood if possible, and your ski hat.

You start by climbing—roped to your guide and with your skis tied together—down a narrow windy ridge. At the end of the ridge, you break the tether with the guide and, sheltered from the wind, step into your skis. (For this trip ski straps are recommended because snow brakes often don't work on ice.) Groups are separated from one another by several hundred meters. You may be skiing on trails for a time, then turn off for powder if your guide finds it. Sometimes the the trail simply ends, which means climbing over rocks with your skis on your shoulder or balancing over a snowbridge spanning a deep crevasse.

The mountains surrounding you are all famous in the annals of climbing. The Vallée Blanche starts on the upper, smooth portion of the glacier; as it begins to break up and crevasses block the route, skiers sideslip down narrow chutes in a region called the Seracs. At the end of the Seracs and after almost two hours descending on skis, there is often a stop at the Refuge du Requin for a warm drink. From the refuge the run enters a wide-open area called the Salle à Manger (dining room).

The needlelike Aiguille de Dru, with Europe's longest climbing vertical, towers above the glacier. From this point the Mer de Glace begins its drop into the valley. Above and to the left, the Hotel Montenvers stands stately guard over the glacier; below the hotel workers dig a tunnel into the ice, which will be visited by hundreds of thousands of people during the coming summer. In late spring your guide may take you down to see the work in progress. As the glacier ends, another refuge, Les Mottets, offers snacks and drinks. Then it's back into the town, the entire trip having taken about four hours.

The Vallée Blanche run is usually not open until February. Although guides are not required, they are strongly recommended. In fact, unless you are an expert mountaineer, you'd be crazy to attempt this adventure without one. If the clouds close in, the guides bring you down by compass and you're assured of having someone to belay you when crossing over crevasses and during the initial windy climb down the ridge. As an extra precaution, each participant receives a beeper. Guides cost about FFr1,220 for one to four skiers. Add FFr100 for each additional person. If traveling alone, check with the guide office in town to register for a group.

What level of skier can handle the Vallée Blanche? A solid intermediate, comfortable on skis, who can sideslip easily and make quick turns can make the trip. You need to be in good enough condition to tour more than four hours at high altitudes.

An additional feature of Chamonix is the chance to travel through the Mont Blanc tunnel into Courmayeur, Italy, on the opposite side of the massif, where skiing is very good. There's often good weather here when Chamonix is clouded over.

Mountain rating

Beginners should stick to Le Tour, Le Brevant and Les Houches. Though experts rave about the resort, thousands learn to ski here every year. But realize that this is not a walk-to-your-lesson resort.

Intermediates choose Chamonix year after year as an ideal area to increase their skills on challenging terrain.

Experts need never worry that there may not be a bigger challenge over the mountain: here, there always is.

Chamonix can best be enjoyed by all skiers with a guide to take them to their most suitable level. Chamonix Ski Fun Tours, part of the French Ski School, has weekly packages that include a guide for small groups.

Ski school (97/98 prices)

A total of 300 instructors offer courses in Chamonix (450 53 22 57) and Argentière (450 54 00 12).

Private lessons (one to five people) cost FFr195 an hour. A day of private instruction runs approximately FFr1,390.

Group lessons for a half day (two hours) cost FFr105. A six-day course, consisting of daily morning and afternoon instruction (four hours a day), is FFr800.

Out-of-bounds ski guides for groups of up to six skiers can be hired for FFr1,480 (full day) or FFr800 (half day).

Lift tickets (97/98   prices)

The normal Chamonix lift ticket, called Cham'Ski, covers lifts in the immediate valley, shuttlebus service, two trips to the top of Les GHrands Montets cable-car if you purchase six to twelve days and four trips with a lift ticket of twelve days of longer, plus one day of skiing in Courmayeur, Italy with passes of six days of more. These tickets are for consecutive days.

	Adults	Children (4-11)	Seniors (60+) Juniors (12–15)
one day	FFr230	FFr161	FFr196
two days	FFr410	FFr287	FFr349
three days	FFr560	FFr392	FFr476
six days	FFr930	FFr651	FFr791
thirteen days	FFr1,640	FFr1,148	FFr1,394

The Mont Blanc Skipass is valid for the entire Chamonix valley and Argentière, with Megève, St. Gervais, Combloux, Cordon, Praz-sur-Arly, Passy, St. Nicolas de Véroce, Les Houches and Vallorcine, for a total of 500 km.of trails served by 180 lifts. Four days of skiing in Courmayeur, Italy is included as well. This pass is available for six days only. The price is FFr1,080 for adults; FFr756 for children (4–11); and FFr918 for seniors 60+.

You also need a photo taken without sunglasses or ski hat for the Mont Blanc Skipass. Your pass must be shown at each resort for a ski pass outside the Chamonix valley.

Day tickets are also available for the separate areas in the valley. For example (96/97 prices): Brévent will cost FFr130 a day and FFr96 for a half day. Les Planards costs FFr80 for a full day anmd FFr43 for a half day. The lifts at Argentière (excluding the upper part of Les Grands Montets cable car) cost FFr185 for a full day; FFr172 from 11 a.m.; and FFr146 from 1 p.m. to closing time. A ride up the spectacular Aiguille du Midi cable car will cost FFr180 round trip, or FFr158 if you're skiing back down.

Accommodations

The Chamonix reservation service (which also has listings for Argentière and Les Houches) is provided by the tourist office, which you can contact at Place de L'Eglise (450 53 23 33). Nearly 90 hotels provide a range of accommodation from luxury suites to dormitory-like rooms. Because of the many restaurants and snack bars, don't hesitate to book a hotel without a half-pension plan. $$$$=FFr600–1,200 a day, double occupancy, half pension; $$$=FFr330–700; $$=FFr260–425; $=FFr200–260.

Mont Blanc (450 53 05 64) A grand old hotel that is being renovated by its owners. Most of the updated rooms are being recreated as suites, which offer roomy, upscale accommodations not found elsewhere in the town. The restaurant is considered one of the best in the region. $$$$

Auberge du Bois-Prin (450 53 33 51) A Chateau and Relais Hotel, this is best in town for quiet and coziness, but is a long walk uphill from the center of town. Rooms are decorated in dark wood and fixtures are brass and gold. The views of Mont Blanc from most rooms are spectacular, with Chamonix spread out below. $$$$

Hôtel du Jeu de Paume (450 54 03 76) Above the village of Le Lavancher, this hotel is understated quiet luxury, built in the wooden chalet style. It has an indoor/outdoor pool and well appointed rooms. $$$$

Le Prieuré (450 53 20 72) This is an excellent functional hotel with some Alpine touches. It is large, short on quaintness, and long on convenience. It also has a private shuttle to the ski areas, as well as covered parking, should you be driving. $$$

Hotel Savoyard (450 53 00 77) This small hotel is created with a French country motif. It oozes charm and the management is very helpful. It is next to Le Brévant gondola at the top of a steep climb from the town. Its location is great for skiing Le Brévant and a climb down for virtually everything else. $$$

Hotel des Aiglons (450 55 90 93) A modern hotel with a beautiful soaring lobby and great views of Mont Blanc. It is near the popular Restaurant Impossible. $$$

Alpina (450 53 47 77) Alpina makes no attempt at Alpine or regional decor. It could just as easily be a high-rise hotel at Denver's Stapleton Airport, but the views from the rooms across the valley to Mont Blanc are spectacularly different. Its location in the center of town can't be beat, and the rooms are among the largest in town. $$$

Sapinière Montana (450 53 07 63) This hotel is only a five-minute walk from the center of town. A shuttlebus takes skiers to the different ski areas. Rooms are basic and slightly aging. $$$

de la Croix Blanche (450 53 00 11) Centrally, this property has decades-old interiors that are nonetheless well maintained and pleasant. $$$ (B&B only)

La Vallée Blanche (450 53 04 50) Run by Patricia Byrne, a delightful Irish lady with big renovation plans, this small two-star hotel is next to the river running through town and steps from Chamonix's center. Rooms feature beautiful locally-made Alpine furniture. Breakfasts are an Irish feast. $$$

Ski Chalets: Crystal, Inghams/Bladon (see page 27 for phone, fax and internet addresses).

Apartments

Chamonix has hundreds of furnished chalets and apartments offered through several agencies. Prices for a studio with sleeping arrangements for two to four: FFr2,850 in high season, FFr1,900 during low season. A two-room apartment housing four to five people will cost FFr3,800 in high season; FFr2,650 in low season. The tourist office provides direct booking. Call 450 53 23 33.

Dining

Chamonix's excellent dining is augmented by the fact that it's a real town, not a resort, so prices are generally very reasonable. And it has its share of excellent, top-quality restaurants. Prices are all approximate and vary depending on beverage and meal.

Albert Ist et Milan (450 53 05 09) is Chamonix's best, where the chef mixes nouvelle cuisine with local mountain cooking. The giant dining room features expansive views of Mont Blanc. The food is praised equally by France's top critics and the locals, who are most pleased by the size of the portions. The menu is an exceptional value—expect to pay about FFr400.

Le Matafan (450 53 05 64) in the Mont Blanc Hotel, is laid out around a large fireplace. Try the foie gras and the veal with figs. The wine cellar is one of the best in the region, with more than 14,000 bottles ranging in price from FFr80–4,400. The normal gourmet dinner menu is FFr 400.

Auberge du Bois-Prin (450 53 33 51) is intimate in an old home. Dinner is served by waitresses in local costume. The restaurant is noted for taking the normal and making it special. Meals cost FFr220–280, with a gourmet menu at about FFr4000.

Eden Restaurant (450 53 06 40) in the hotel is a bit out of the center of Chamonix in the suburb of La Praz. The views of Mont Blanc and the Drus are spectacular. Specialties are fish, with trout amandine and lobster au gratin. The menu costs FFr150–350.

La Cabana (450 53 23 27) next to the golf course, a few minutes' drive outside town, is a rustic chalet. The accent is regional meat and potatoes. Expect to pay about FFr290 for a full dinner.

Restaurant L'Impossible (450 53 20 36) This eatery is built in an ancient barn and is as rustic as it gets. The place gets packed so reservations are recommended. Expect to pay FFr130–160 for a meal.

Atmosphere (450 55 97 97) is a very elegant restaurant decorated in subdued tones. Try to get a table in the sunroom overlooking the river for a most romantic spot. The evening menu will cost FFr140 without wine.

Calèche (450 55 94 68) is an elegant regional restaurant with the traditional mountain wood tastefully mixed with flowered fabrics and stuffed chairs. They serve everything from fondue and raclette to full dinners. A very reasonable FFr145 evening menu offers choices of nine appetizers, five main courses and six desserts.

Chaudron (450 53 40 34), also on Rue des Moulins, is very rustic. A heavy stone wall lines the small restaurant, you dine under rustic wooden beams, and farm tools and a giant wagon wheel add a country flavor. Specialties are regional dishes, grilled meats and brochettes. Fixed-price menu for dinner will run FFr130.

Boccalatte (450 53 52 14) This new restaurant serves Savoyard meals in a blond wood setting. Prices are reasonable. Fondues cost FFr85 and the Alsace Choucroute, FFr75.

L'M is a brasserie serving low-ticket crêpes, galletes and meals in the middle of town. In the spring a large terrace opens, which makes snacking and nursing a long drink most enjoyable. Most selections with a drink will range between FFr50–95.

Grillandin, just off Rue Joseph Vallon, is the self-service cafeteria in town. The food is quite good and very reasonable. Enjoy a filling meal here for FFr75.

 ## Après-ski/nightlife

The immediate après-ski usually consists of having drinks in one of the bars in the center of town. Try the **Chamouny**, the **Brasserie du Rond Point** and the **Irish Coffee**. In spring the outdoor tables fill up with skiers. **La Cabolée** fills up with skiers coming down **Le Brévant**.

Nightlife devotees have plenty of choices here besides gambling. The **Blue** is excellent, with live acts **Le Pèle** disco is large, loud and packed with teenagers. One of the main meeting spots for English-speakers is the **Choucas Video Bar**, which is normally packed, dark and smoky. For the hard-partying crowd head out to **The Jeckl** between Hotel Des Aiglons and Restaurant Impossible.

Child care

The **Chamonix Ski School** (450 53 22 57) takes children 4–12 years. Lessons and lunch are included for FFr270 a day or for FFr1,350 for six consecutive days.

Child-care services are available at the larger hotels, and babysitting services are available for around FFr85 (half day) or FFr150 (full day). For information, contact the tourist office.

Maison Pour Tous kindergarten on Place du Mont Blanc (450 53 12 24), takes children 18 months to 6 years. It's open 7:45 a.m. to 6:30 p.m. Monday to Friday. Rates: half day, FFr150; one hour, FFr50. Pick up kids for lunch noon–2 p.m.

The Panda Club has kindergarten with ski instruction in both downtown Chamonix and in Argentière at the cable car station (450 54 04 76). The Panda Club Chamonix is on Clos du Savoy (450 55 86 12). Children six months to three years are admitted to the downtown center, and Panda Ski at the Argentière station takes kids 3–12 years. These child care centers have games, crafts, ski lessons with videos and outdoor snow games. Rates (with meals): Infants six months to 3 years, half day FFr245; full day, FFr285; six half days with meals, FFr1,225; six full days, FFr1,425. Older children up to 12 can receive care and supervision for FFr180 for a half day, FFr270 for a full day, FFr925 for six half days, and FFr1,375 for six full days.

Getting there

Nearly everyone arrives by the autoroute or by train from Geneva. However, Chamonix—with Courmayeur on the other side of Mont Blanc—is ideal for visitors who have skied in Italy and who want to work their way up through Switzerland and France.

The TGV leaves Paris at around 8 a.m. and arrives in Sallanches at about 1 p.m. There is also a special train/bus combination, with the train departing from Paris just after 7 a.m., a change to bus in Annecy and arrival in Chamonix before 1 p.m.

Taxi from the Geneva airport will cost about FFr660, and a bus from the airport to the resort costs FFr165.

Other activities

More than any other area you may visit, this merits an aerial tour. The Mont Blanc massif and the stunning series of surrounding peaks are best seen from the air. Choose from four different trips ranging from FFr160–590 per person. Call Air Mont Blanc at 450 58 13 31.

The swimming center has three pools, all heated, plus sauna and turkish baths. There is also an ice rink, indoor tennis, bowling and a casino.

Tourist information

Tourist Office, Place du Triangle de l'Amitié, F-74400 Chamonix, France; 450 53 00 24; fax 450 53 58 90.

La Clusaz

The center of town is easy to find in La Clusaz. The church on the central square can be seen for miles around, its sturdy-looking tower topped by a distinctive clock and a graduated wedding-cake steeple reaching high above the surrounding wood-shingled rooftops. Newly restored and modernized, with excellent acoustic properties, it doubles as a concert and lecture hall for visiting dignitaries and perfomers.

La Clusaz has been a bustling village since the 16th century, but today its 1,800 year-round inhabitants open their doors and hearts to as many as 19,500 visitors at one time, in the peak winter season. The first ski lift here was built in 1935, but La Clusaz was a village long before it became a ski destination, and it has succeeded in keeping its lived-in, workaday atmosphere. Here visitors are initiated into the traditions and customs of *"Les Cluses,"* as they call themselves, rather than the other way around. In winter on Mondays, farmers turned innkeepers and local merchants put on humorous welcome night races that end in convivial silliness on the village green (now white), accompanied by hot wine. This large snow play area adjacent to the skating rink and cable car is flanked by restaurants and outdoor tables, and provides a safe playground and sledding slope for children. It also serves as the viewing area for the World Cup mogul and ski jumping competitions. La Clusaz is a center for freestyle skiing, boasting three world champions and an Olympic champion.

The compactness of the village, its wrap-around views of ski runs, forests and peaks, its old winding side streets and leisurely pace make La Clusaz a winner for skiers who wish to get away from the hustle of modern life. Children are welcomed and families will find this resort easier to manage than most. Don't expect to find noisy, swinging nightlife: here the emphasis is on lingering over dinner with family and friends, and the traditional French Alpine atmosphere makes it hard to believe that Geneva is only a 40-minute drive away. (On weekends it becomes much easier to believe, as the city-dwellers stream in.)

 ## Mountain layout

This area has five different areas to ski. Visitors can ski a different section each day. Just a tram ride above La Clusaz, intermediate and beginner terrain allow wide-open cruising. Here Beauregard Mountain rises to 1,690 meters and true to its name, offers beautiful views and cruising trails through magical forest terrain. On the right side of Beauregard (looking down the mountain) is a good expert trail. Beyond Beauregard, Massif de Manigod offers a network of 15 lifts serving mostly beginner and intermediate trails. Moving around the valley to Massif de L'Etale, the runs become steeper and longer. Massif de L'Aiguille has excellent advanced terrain and a long plunge through Combe du Fernuy for strong skiers.

Massif de Balme offers good bump skiing and usually has the best snow. Here skiers will find some of the best expert stuff. La Clusaz has good bump skiing as well as freestyle. The return to the village is a 4km.-long trail along a mountain road through the woods.

Mountain rating

Beginners and intermediates will have a swell time here. This is a wonderful place for a romantic getaway for a mixed-ability couple—many lifts offer side-by-side beginner and intermediate trails meeting at the bottom, perfect for families or friends of differing abilities.

Experts who know the area or who ski with a guide will find some toothy terrain, but this is a mellow adventure—with patches of difficulty—rather than an endurance test.

There is excellent cross-country here with 70 km. of prepared trails in the valleys.

Ski school (97/98 prices)

The school (450 02 40 83) is in the village and beneath the tram.

Private lessons: A one-hour lesson for one to three people costs FFr180; for four to five people, FFr235. A guide for the full day costs FFr1,500 in high season and FFr1,100 in low season; for 4 hours, FFr930 in high season and FFr770 in low season; for 3 hours, FFr710 in high season and FFr580 in low season.

Group lessons: One session for adults costs FFr108; for children under twelve, FFr93. One week of half-day sessions costs FFr465 for adults and FFr380 for children; for a week of full-day sessions, FFr770 for adults and FFr615 for children.

Lift tickets (97/98 prices)

	Adults	Child/Senior
half day from noon	FFr115	FFr98
one day	FFr149	FFr120
four days (high season)	FFR520	FFr370
six days (high season)	FFr750	FFr560
fourteen days (high season)	FFr1,750	FFr990

Children are those less than 15 years. Seniors are those 60 and over. High season is Christmas/New Year period and February through mid March. Low season is early December, most of January, late March and April. Adult rates are about 15% less.

Accommodations

La Clusaz has seven three-star hotels and 15 two-star lodgings. For information or reservations see the tourist office. All rates presented here are based on double occupancy. When visitors purchase the weekly package, the seven-day lift ticket costs only FFr70.

The best hotel is the **Beauregard** (450 32 68 00; fax 450 02 59 00) with half-board for FFr615–650 in low season and FFr735–780 during high season. Weekly rates with half board range from FFr4,080–5,815.

Next on the list is **Hotel Alpen Roc** (450 02 58 96; fax 450 02 57 49) with half-board for FFr467 in low season and FFr650 during high season. Weekly rates with half-board range from FFr4,080–4,915.

Alp'Hotel (450 02 40 06; fax 450 02 60 16) a three-star oozing with traditional wooden charm, in the middle of town with parking and indoor pool. It costs FFr405 in low season and FFr570 during high season. Weekly rates with half-board range from FFr3,055–4,400.

Les Chalets de la Serraz (450 02 48 29; fax 450 02 64 12) is a typical mountain chalet a bit above the town with a wonderful restaurant. Half-board rates are FFr395 in low season and FFr575 in high season. Weekly rates with half-board are FFr3,055–4,425.

Hotel Carlina (450 02 43 48; fax 450 02 66 02) a three-star with great south-facing balconies. It costs FFr300-380 in low season and FFr440-550 during high season. Weekly rates with half-board range from FFr3,055–4,600.

Christiana (450 02 60 60; fax 450 32 66 98) is a two-star hotel. Rates with half-board are FFr280-340 in low season and FFr395-425 during high season. Weekly rates with half-board range from FFr2,755–3,305 (not available during Christmas).

The **Telepherique Hotel** (450 02 44 00; fax 450 02 54 75) at the top of the cable car is a unique experience. If you miss the last cable car, there is no access. Rates are FFr260–330 for half-board.

Hotel La Ferme (450 02 50 50 ; fax 450 32 63 16) without meals runs FFr250–350 a night per person based on two people in a room. Weekly rates with breakfast range from FFr1,800–2,050.

Apartments

La Clusaz has 1,500 chalets and apartments. Contact La Clusaz Tour (450 32 65 06) for reservations and package rates.

For two to four, expect to pay FFr1,365–1,835 a week in January, FFr3,150–4,725 in February, and FFr2,100–2,700 in March or April.

For four to six, rates run FFr2,100–2,520 in January, FFr5,000–5,880 in February, and FFr2,940–3,360 in March or April.

For six to eight people, you'll pay FFr2,625–3,150 in January, FFr6,090–7,140 in February, and FFr3,465–4,095 in March or April.

 ## Dining

Try some of the local specialties—Reblochon cheese; La Pela, a pan of potatoes, onions and ham; *Le Matafan, Le Forçon* or *Farcent, Les Doits* and *Les Atriaux*. you'll love these discoveries. If you feel adventurous, go ahead—as the locals say, "You cannot get a bad meal in La Clusaz."

Le Symphonie, in the Hotel Beauregard, is one of the best classic French and nouvelle restaurants. L'Ourson, next to the Tourist Office, is also one of the best spots to eat. **Le Foly** has wonderful Savoyard regional cooking, but it is 4 km. out of town. **Le Chalet du Lac,** also a bit outside of town, may require a short walk to reach, but the regional home cooking and the charming setting make it worth the trip.

La Bercail on the Massif de l'Aguile is accessible by skis and at night by sleigh or snowcat. Dinners are typical Savoyard served in a most rustic setting.

La Crêperie, a charming crêperie in the village with amiable owners offers a FFr70 menu. Also try **L'Ecuelle** for a good inexpensive meal.

Eat inexpensively but well, by having your big meal at lunch. At this time of day many restaurants offer a daily special for about FFr40. For a lunch menu with appetizer, soup or salad, entrée, cheese or dessert, the price is typically FFr70–80.

 ## Après-ski/nightlife

Two bars are **Le Tex-Mex and Bali-Bar** with have pool, darts and videos, and **Le Pressoir,** popular with British skiers and locals, offers a big selection of beers, videos and a rugged atmosphere.

An ice skating rink at the bottom of the ski area stays open until 11 p.m. Cost is FFr17 for admission and FFr18 for skate rental. Curling is offered at the rink, and there are ice hockey, curling and skating competitions. Call 450 02 48 45.

Even if you don't dance and hate discos, plan to visit **L'Ecluse,** a glass-bottomed disco that shows off the town's river flowing beneath. A wide picture window also frames the frothy water. The FFr80 admission includes a drink.

Club 18 is a small disco and piano bar where French songs are sung and you dance in close quarters. Admission is FFr80 except Mondays, when tourists are admitted free.

 ## Child care

Le Club Des Mouflets (450 32 65 37) at the ski resort above the tourist office, takes children eight months to 4 1/2 years. Its rooms are adapted to the ages of the children. Kids are kept entertained by indoor activities, including musical games, collage-making and crafts.

Le Club des Champions (450 32 65 00) accepts children 3 1/2–6 who can ski. One-hour ski lessons are given to children 3 1/2–4 years old; 2 1/2-hour lessons are offered for children 5 and above. There are other outdoor activities as well, such as snow games and sledding, plus indoor activities.

Rates for both clubs are as follows: half day, FFr80; full day, FFr120; six half days, FFr420; six full days, FFr630. Lunch is included for an extra FFr60 a day.

 ## Getting there

From Geneva airport, a daytime taxi ride costs FFr450 (FFr620 at night). The bus to Annecy costs FFr50. A bus to Geneva is FFr250.

The train (TGV) from Paris to Annecy takes 3 1/2 hours and costs about FFr600 round trip. From there, La Clusaz is reached by bus or taxi (a taxi from Annecy costs about FFr280).

 ## Other activities

One open-air heated swimming pool is open throughout the season (during the 97/98 season it will be closed for renovation). There's a fitness center, hang-gliding, and ski paragliding, as well as snowshoe walks, snowmobiling, ice skating and horse-drawn cart drives.

 ## Tourist information

Maison du Tourisme, Place de L'Eglise, 74220 La Clusaz, France; 450 31 65 00, fax 450 32 65 01.

For ski/snowboard packages call La Clusaz Tour; 450 32 65 06.

Flaine

Flaine is an all-or-nothing proposition: either you take to this purpose-built concrete and steel French resort in the Haute Savoie, or you search deeper into the Alps for quaint chalets and sleighs as backdrop to your downhill adventures. You may or may not like Flaine's exterior appearance, but its skiing, which is overwhelmingly intermediate, is bountiful and good. And this is a car-free resort which makes it great for families.

Let's face it: to anyone expecting an Alpine village, Flaine is an odd sight. The rectangular flat-topped buildings, reputedly designed by Marcel Breuer, clinging to the slopes of this narrow valley appear to have all been poured from the same grey cement in an effort to spare time and expense. However, in terms of practicality, they seem to serve the purpose: cars are unnecessary, and housing and services are clustered to provide maximum convenience for skiers. There is also a cluster of chalets, Le Hameau de Flaine, only a kilometer from the base area and served by a regular free shuttlebus.

Everything here is designed with winter sports in mind, and at 1,580 meters (almost a mile high), snow is practically guaranteed from December to May. Flaine is connected by a system of lifts to the more traditional lower-altitude towns of Les Carroz, Morillon and Samoens, and by bus to Sixt. Together they form a wide-ranging ski circus of 77 lifts and more than a hundred marked trails totalling 160 miles of downhill adventure. Marked runs are predominantly intermediate and upper intermediate, but adventurous experts will find numerous possibilities just off-piste.

Mountain layout

First, all but beginners should take the cable car to the top of Les Grandes Platières to drink in the magnificent views of Mont Blanc and the jagged-toothed range running north (to your left) from the Aguille du Midi. Here on the treeless top of the world you can get a feel for the distances and a variety of terrain spreading out in three directions. Behind you, down the cable car route, are a black run and several alternate intermediate routes running directly back into

Flaine or connecting with the chair and surface lifts in this section.

To your right is the Lindars section, reached by another cable system from Flaine, "The Eggs," and a chair to the top.

To your left stretches another whole system of lifts and trails that drop down, on the near side to the gentle beginner area near Flaine center, on the far side to the Gers expert terrain, and further left to the long winding trails down to Samoens, Morillon or Les Carroz. Each of these villages is at the bottom of its own system of trails and lifts, so plan one or two all-day excursions on this side when you have time to explore, stop for lunch and still wend your way back to Flaine before the lifts close.

Les Carroz, Morillon, and the valley town, Samoens, are Flaine's supporting cast, but their attraction for thousands of skiers each year lies in their more traditional Alpine accommodations.

Of the runs above these towns, we liked the blue-rated trail from Cupoire summit (6,166 feet) to the chair near the parking lot in Morillon. With easy turns, a few moguls, and trees for orientation, it's a fine cruise. The runs on this side are almost invariably intermediate. One exception to try is the black trail from Plateau des Saix summit to the Vereland lift station.

Mountain rating

Beginners will like Flaine because of its training slopes and the quality of the ski instruction.

Intermediates are in the majority here, and the slopes are laid out with that in mind. Les Grandes Platières is an intermediate's mountain, offering at least 15 different red-rated variations.

Experts will find plenty of challenges, particularly if they enjoy off-trail skiing.

Ski school (97/98 prices)

Flaine excels in ski instruction. There are two schools here: the French Ski School (450 90 81 00) and the International Ski School (450 90 84 41).

Private lessons for up to four people at one time will cost FFr360–370 for two hours, and a full day costs FFr960–1,290.

Group lessons are a good bargain when class size is limited. The ESF guarantees a limit of not more than 10 people. Group lesson prices for six half days of instruction are FFr665–700 (adults) and FFr515-550 (children).

An extended ski school with four hours a day for six days costs FFr695 for adults and FFr565 for children.

Snowboard lessons will cost FFr695 for six days of three-hour lessons for adults or FFr545 for children.

Lift tickets (97/98 prices)

A half day (Flaine only) costs FFr135; a full day FFr155 (Flaine only). Passes for more than a day are sold for the entire Grand Massif area— two days, FFr335; four days, FFr640; six days, FFr860; seven days, FFr965; 13 days, FFr1,630.

Juniors/Seniors (12–15 and 60+) ski for two days, FFr260; four days, FFr490; six days, FFr640; seven days, FFr710; 13 days, FFr1,210.

Children (5–11) pay two days, FFr225; four days, FFr440; six days, FFr580; seven days, FFr640; 13 days, FFr1,100.

Kids under age 5 ski free.

 ## Accommodations

Flaine primarily offers apartment accommodations, although you can also choose from the hotels listed below near the Forum square.

Hotel Totem*** (450 90 80 64; fax: 450 90 88 47) daily rate with half board is FFr515 during low January season, and FFr730 during high season.

Hotel Le Flaine*** (450 90 80 64; fax: 450 90 88 47) daily rate with half board is FFr350 during low January season, and FFr510 during high season.

The Aujon** (450 90 80 10; fax: 450 90 88 21) rate for B&B only is FFr205 during low January season, and FFr350 during high season.

Chalet La Cascade (450 50 90 87 66; fax 450 90 85 20) up on the slopes costs FFr280 in a double with half board during January low season and FFR400 during high season.

Le Hameau de Flaine is a village of Scandinavian chalets. Weekly ates are from FFr3,950 for a two-room apartment that sleeps four or six in a squeeze during January low season to FFr6,230 during the high season. A four-room chalet, for eight to ten, costs FFr5,850 during January low season and FFr8,600.

If you stay at Flaine booking six or seven nights you receive a Grand Massif ski pass for five or six days, plus rental equipment (skis or snowboard and boots) *or* six two-hour lessons.

Apartments

Apartment complexes in Flaine have been built on three levels. Above the Forum on the hillside are the units of Flaine Forêt. These are the better apartments, many privately owned. Apartment buildings are also clustered around the main Forum square and there are more below the Forum level at Front de Neige. The most convenient are those in the Forum area.

The least expensive studio apartment on the Forum level in middle season (first two weeks of February) costs about FFr1,350 a week, and in high season (end of February and holidays) about FFr3,050.

For rental bookings there are four agencies: Pierre et Vacances (450 90 87 99); Agence Renand (450 90 81 40); Agence Home International (450 90 82 93); Agence Astrid Bichon (450 90 83 91).

 ## Dining

Choice of where to eat is limited because most hotel guests are on full-pension plans and apartment guests cook in their own kitchens. We recommend the fixed-price menu at the Totem, which is rated as the best restaurant in town by both Michelin and Gault Millau.

Dine in a rustic chalet atmosphere in the restaurant Les Chalets du Michet (450 90 80 08) serves good food in a converted cow shed, or try La Perdrix Noire (450 90 81 81) for excellent basic French food. At Chez Daniel (450 90 81 87) try raclette or fondue, or sizzling your meat on hot rocks. One night a week, with reservations, you will be treated to the *descente aux flambeaux*, a torchlit ski home after dinner at **Blanchot** (450 90 82 44). The restaurant in the **Aujon Hotel** (450 90 80 10) serves basic daily fare. Pizza can be found at **Mario** (450 90 42 51) or at **La Pizzeria** (450 90 84 56).

On the mountains lunchtime offerings are pretty much standardized; you pay less on the Samoëns-Morillon side. Halfway down the Morillon side, **L'Beu** (450 90 17 89) serves simple, good regional specialties. In Flaine, get a quick, tasty snack at **Trattoria** (450 90 80 49) and if Madame takes to you, she'll dish up a stream of insults with your meal—in French, of course.

Après-ski/nightlife

Plan on staying in Flaine, because the road down the mountain can become treacherous, particularly after the sun goes down. Hotel bars are good meeting spots. Try the very British (and nice) **White Grouse Pub** or strike out for **La Bodega** if you are looking for more disco action. **Cime Rock Café** has live music every night.

Child care

A ski kindergarten, the Green Mouse Club, is conducted Sunday to Friday from 9 a.m. until 5 p.m. The fee for a half day without lunch is FFr140; half day with lunch is FFr180; six half days cost FFr640 without lunch or FFr880 with lunch. Full-day ski kindergarten runs FFr210 (FFr260 with meals), or FFr930 for a week of full days (FFr1,200 including meals).

The Rabbit Club ski school is another children's program, which last season cost about FFr1,220 for six days with lunch (FFr930 without lunch) and FFr225 for one day with lunch (FFr180 without lunch).

Other activities

There is an ice-driving school (450 90 82 59) with one- to three-day lessons. Helicopter rides (450 90 80 01), a climbing wall (450 90 80 74), paragliding (450 90 81 00, 450 90 01 80 or 450 03 33 46) and a cinema are available. The swimming pool (450 90 84 99) is open three mornings a week and every afternoon; entry is FFr30 for adults for six swims and FFr18 for children for six swims.

Getting there

Geneva airport, about 45 miles away by the Geneva-Chamonix autoroute, is the closest. Take the Cluses exit.

There are five shuttles to Flaine daily from the Geneva airport or the downtown Geneva bus station. Tickets are FFr180–250.

You can also take the train to Cluses and then a Transport Alpbus (450 03 70 09) to Flaine. The bus costs FFr64.

Tourist information

Office du Tourisme Flaine, F-74300 Flaine, France; 450 90 80 01, fax 450 90 86 26.

Internet: www.skifrance.fr/~flaine

La Plagne

La Plagne translates to the plains—much of the higher elevation terrain is a treeless plateau surrounded by modest-looking snow-covered peaks. This is the largest single ski resort in Europe, if you base such a superlative on the number of lifts and lift capacity. Other ski regions may be larger, but they are formed by combining several independent resorts such as the Trois Vallées, the Dolomites or the Portes du Soleil.

La Plagne claims a vertical of 6,500 feet. The lower 1,700 feet of that is through trees and along winding roads. Still, when the snow is good a skier can start out from Roche de Mio at 8,775 feet and drop to Montchavin at 4,062 feet, which means more than 4,700 feet of working vertical. Another vertical drop across the western face of Bellecote down to Les Bauches provides almost 4,000 feet of nonstop vertical that will challenge any skier.

Even in the modest upper ranges of the resort, the working vertical is about 2,500 feet—more than Aspen's. Since it is one of the highest resorts on the continent, La Plagne can't be beat for certainty of snow; there will be snow here even in the middle of August.

La Plagne revolves around apartment life. It offers more than 40,000 beds in small apartments, and only about 1,500 beds in the eleven hotels in the region. The purpose-built sections of La Plagne consist of the six high-altitude modern clusters, connected by a creative series of public conveyances called telemetro, telebus, and telecabine, and traditional shuttlebuses. Each complex has apartments, with stores and ski shops all interconnected by tunnels and walkways. These underground passages, while extremely practical in snow country, give several of the areas an oddly urban feel, reminiscent of a subway shopping mall. Four lower villages are also connected to the lift system.

Plagne Centre at 6,463 feet is the original, constructed 30 years ago as one of France's first built-for-skiing villages. What the buildings lack in charm they make up for in convenience—two hotels, dozens of restaurants, scores of shops, a cinema and apartments, all connected by underground passages with 20 lifts fanning out from it.

Plagne Villages at 6,726 feet is a cluster of small apartment houses and Alpine-style buildings with wooden features and peaked roofs. There are no hotels, only apartments and shops.

Plagne 1800 is a consistently designed neo-Savoyard mountain village with wooden chalets and peaked roofs. This grouping contains squash courts and a good fitness center. The village clings to a mountainside somewhat removed from the main ski areas, making it less accessible than the other centers, and the return to your room après-ski could include a steep hike uphill.

Aime La Plagne, also sometimes called Aime 2000, is a newer purpose-built complex above Plagne Centre. Many consider it the most convenient, with many of the best apartments in the resort. There are a cinema and a good collection of shops and restaurants. A cable car connects Aime La Plagne with Plagne Centre.

Plagne Bellecote is a group of massive interconnected high-rise buildings over an underground shopping mall. There are no hotels in this group, but it has La Plagne's only heated outdoor swimming pool and is the starting point of the gondola to the glacier at 8,858 feet.

Belle Plagne is the newest of La Plagne's centers, built in the Savoyard chalet style. An underground garage system allows one to reach each of the chalet groups. A multilevel shopping arcade with covered walkways provides a touch of Alpine charm. There is also a fitness center, complete with sauna and Jacuzzis.

Villages that are part of the complex have their own ski sectors. All have ski schools and ski kindergartens for children plus ski rentals.

Plagne Montalbert at 1,350 meters with a couple of two-star hotels, a selection of apartments and eleven restaurants has its own lift system that connects with the rest of the La Plagne region.

Montchavin and Les Coches are at 1,250 meters and 1,450 meters respectively. These villages have a separate lift system that may be purchased separately as well as a two-star hotel some chalets and apartments and 14 restaurants.

Champagny-en-Vanoise at the top of a valley separating La Plagne from the Trois Vallées area ios a picturesque town clinging to the mountain walls. A cable car takes skiers up to giant snowfields that connect with Plagne Centre, Plagne Bellecote and Belle Plagne. During the past two years, new lifts have made the connections between Champagny and BellePlagne very easy. Skiers staying in Champagny-en-Vanoise can ski into town down two challenging intermediate trails with plenty of off-piste possibilities.

This region also has 90 km. of excellent cross-country trails that criss-cross the region. There is good cross-country in the Champagny area.

Mountain layout

There are 123 trails, including six black and 34 red, covering 210 km. of ski area with 110 ski lifts, eight of which are gondolas, and one that connects Bellecote and Belle Plagne with the glaciers. The remainder of the lift network comprises 33 chair lifts and 68 surface lifts.

What you see, you can ski. Just to take off and explore different sections of the resort on different days. No intermediate will get into any trouble here if they stick to the upper slopes and stay off the glacier.

Adventurous skiers can find plenty of challenge along the fringes of the resort. Experts will want to drop behind the ridge above Aime La Plagne basically following the Morbleu and Les Etroits trails looping around to the Des Coqs lift and then challenge the Les Coqs and the Emile Alais trails.

Another expert adventure is to take the Bellecote cable car from the peak of Roche dy Mio to the Glacier of Bellecote at 3,000 meters. This spectacular ride takes skiers down 150 meters before rising almost 500 meters. From the glacier advanced skiers in tip-top shape can follow the hazy Bellecote or Le Rochu runs down more than 2,000 feet of vertical to the Chalet de Bellecote lift. Skiers with guides will take the Traversé lift and set off across the face of Bellecote and drop towards Les Bauches some 1,200 meters (3,900 feet) of vertical below. It is a daunting ski afternoon or morning. The restaurant at Les Bauches certainly seems welcoming after that descent. From here lifts reconnect skiers with the network.

A similarly challenging descent can be made from the Bellecote Glacier to Champagny-le-Haut along the Col du Cou du Nant with a guide. A shuttlebus takes skiers back to the cable car at Champagny-en-Vanoise.

Experts can drop alongside the bobsled run for some good skiing through trees and across pastures down toward Plagne Montalbert. Snow is fine during most of the season, but in the spring ask about coverage.

Mountain rating

La Plagne is an intermediate and beginner mountain, at least as far as the prepared trails go in the Bellecote, Belle Plagne, Grand Rochette, Montchavin, Les Coches, Plagne Montalbert and Champagny sectors go.

Intermediates will think they have died and gone to skier heaven. The rolling mountains offer acceptable steeps where intermediates can play, and mellow off-trail areas for developing deep-snow skills. The Champagny section is pretty tame but the run into the town and return ride makes a great outing.

Beginners and lower intermediates are in one of the best European resorts for learning to ski. Here beginners can have the experience of taking a lift to the highest point, with all the thrill of the spectacular views, and still be able to get back down the mountain safely.

Advanced skiers will find challenging skiing on the back of the Biolley sector. There are plenty of spots for creative experts to go off trail and find more than enough to keep them busy for a week. Any expert will be challenged by the runs down the glacier. The more skill you have, the further off the basic trails you can venture. With good snow this glacier area is fantastic for even the best skiers.

Ski school (97/98 prices)

The La Plagne ski schools has 550 instructors available throughout the various village complexes. Prices vary depending on which program and village you select for lessons.

Private lessons are available for full days, 9:15 a.m. to 4:45 p.m., for FFr1,290. Half-day private lessons cost FFr700. Hourly lessons are about FFr200 on Sundays. Private lessons are limited to ten persons or fewer.

Group lessons Six full days cost about FFr900; six half days cost from FFr700. *Nouvelle glisse* courses, alternating between skiing, monoskiing and snowboarding are available, as well as competition courses.

Lift tickets (97/98 prices)

The La Plagne region has a lift ticket system that is made up of four sectors. Lift passes may be purchased for only the villages of Montchavin/Les Coches, Plagne Montalbert or Champagny. The La Plagne overall pass prices are below. They have some limitations, however together with an inter-resort shuttle pass will allow skiers to go virtually anywhere in the region.

	Adults	Children/Seniors
		(7-16 and 60+)
Half day	FFr158	FFr119
Full day	FFr216	FFr163
Three days	FFr555	FFr420
Six days	FFr1,005	FFr755
14 days	FFr1,850	FFr1,390

Lift tickets bought for six days or more permit one day a week skiing in Val d'Isère, Tignes, Les Trois Vallées or Les Arcs.

Accommodations

Prices here are daily rates for half-board based on double occupancy, unless otherwise indicated. The low price is normally for January low season or pre-Christmas and the high price is for high season.

Hotel Eldorador (479 09 12 09; fax 479 09 12 09) Overall the atmosphere in Belle Plagne makes the Eldorador's location desirable, but what one gains in atmosphere one loses in choice of restaurants and shops. Expect to pay FFr350-650. If you are a single and someone tells you that there will be no supplement, beware. These "half rooms" for singles with no supplement mean you will be sharing a shower and toilet with another unfortunate half-roomer.

Hotel Graciosa (479 09 00 18; fax 479 09 04 08) is high above Plagne Center, which makes reaching its shops or those of Aime La Plagne inconvenient. The restaurant here is one of the best in the resort, so arranging for full pension is a good bet. The rooms are relatively small but have cable TV. Rates are FFr510–580.

Hotel Les Alpes in Aime (479 09 70 24) has one price of FFr190 for single or double occupancy. This small hotel only has 15 rooms.

The new **Chalet/Hotel Les Montagnettes** (479 55 12 00; fax 479 55 12 19) in Belle Plagne has some wonderful and new apartments with more space than older apartments in Plagne Centre. This is an upscale choice in the region. Weekly rates for an apartment for six to eight are FFr6,900 in January low season and FFr12,000 during high season.

In the villages there are two-star hotels. **Hotel l'Ancolie** (479 55 05 00; fax 479 55 04 42) in Champagny has a great location right at the base of the cable car. Rates are FFr340–460. **Hotel La Tourmaline** (479 55 62 93; fax 479 55 52 48) also in Champagny costs FFr365–428. **Hotel Bellecote** (479 07 83 30; fax 479 07 80 63) in Montchavin has rooms by the week for FFr1,995–3,290. **Hotel l'Aigle Rouge** (479 55 51 05; fax 479 55 51 14) in Plagne Montalbert charges FFr245–390. Children normally get a thirty to fifty percent discount in most of these hotels.

Ski Chalets: Crystal, Simply Ski, Chalet World, First Choice (see page 27 for phone, fax and internet addresses).

Apartments

Apartments are by far the most popular form of accommodation in La Plagne. There are more than 20 times the number of apartment beds than hotel beds. Accommodations range from tiny 17-square-meter rooms to spacious. Two can make it without any trouble in a normal two-person French apartment, but will be much more comfortable if they can afford to rent a place advertised for four. In Belle Plagne, a studio or one-bedroom apartment with plenty of room for two will run FFr1,500–2,000 a week in January. There are also bargain weekly rates of only FFr1,300 per person, including ski lifts, lessons and equipment rental discounts (if more people share) in January. Such rates are hard to beat.

Dining

Most of the restaurants listed below are in Plagne Center. Since Plagne Center is connected with both Aime La Plagne and Plagne Villages by cable car and telebus, it serves as a center for these three complexes. The restaurants here prove that even in modern surroundings small cozy eating spots can be created with all the atmosphere and charm one might expect to find in a traditional town bistro. Although La Plagne is considered an economical resort by French standards, meals can still cost a bundle. Top restaurants here will run about FFr210 for a full meal, excluding wine. The moderate restaurant meals run about FFr115–160, including wine, and the inexpensive ones will have a fixed-price menu at about FFr90 without wine. For those looking for less expensive meals, try one of the crêperies or a pizzeria where a meal can end up costing as little as FFr60, with a beer.

Plagne Center

The restaurant in the Hotel Le Graciosa, **L'Etoile d'Or** (479 09 00 18) is one of the best in La Plagne—the view is certainly tops. Meals are about FFr170–190 with wine.

Le Bec Fin (479 09 10 86) offers excellent French cooking for a fixed-price menu of FFr180. The decor looks best in the dark by candlelight. English is spoken by almost all the staff.

Le Chaudron (479 09 23 33), in the open field in the middle of Plagne Center, presents excellent grilled specialties cooked over an open fire in the middle of the dining room. Expect your meal to cost FFr120–180.

Le Refuge (479 09 00 13) is the oldest in the resort. Photographs of bobsled champions cover the walls in the very local, very French bar out front. In the dining room each table is centered under a telescoping copper hood, which vents smoke while guests barbecue their own steaks at the table. Expect to spend about FFr120–140.

Le Mille Pates (479 09 12 15) offers an elegant dinner, typical regional foods, and pasta dishes; FFr120 menu.

Le Crêpe (479 09 04 82), is the most popular crêperie in Plagne Center. On weekends and holidays expect to wait in line for a seat. Crêpes cost FFr16 for a butter crêpe to FFr70 for a smoked salmon crêpe with salad. They also serves raclette and fondue.

Across the hall from Le Crêpe are three moderate to inexpensive restaurants: **L'Estaminet** (479 09 12 69) serves Alsatian specialties in huge portions; **La Metairie** (479 09 11 08) has Savoyard specialties on wooden tables with a fixed-priced menu of FFr83; and **Le Bistroquet** (479 09 22 11) has great atmosphere, lace curtains, and red tablecloths.

For simple pizza and an exuberant welcome by the owner-cook, head to **Pizzeria**

Rolando (479 09 05 36) where you can get away for as little as FFr60 for a pizza and beer. Or walk to the end of the hall and pick up—would you believe, a pizza to go—at **Pizzeria Domino.**

Aime La Plagne

Here, our favorite is **l'Arlequin** (479 09 05 29) After winding down a circular staircase you will have the chance to sample pizza if you insist, but with a difference. They make a pizza *quattro formaggio* with four French cheeses; its owners also have created a smoked salmon pizza. One unique creation you've probably never tasted—*tagliatelli foie gras.* Try the normal raclette and fondue or the special rouergat, a duck fondue where the duck is cooked in liver oil. Or order the "royal stone," which is a superheated rock upon which you grill an assortment of mixed meat and foie gras. For the atmosphere, unique food and good service you'll end up spending FFr120–170 and leave stuffed.

La Soupe aux Schuss (479 09 06 44) is a tiny place with space for less than 30 diners. The atmosphere is pure French country, with wooden tables, lace tablecloths, wine in baskets, and pine cupboards. The food is excellent but on the expensive side—expect to walk out spending at least FFr220 without wine.

Au Bon Vieux Temps (479 09 20 57) on the slopes above Aime 2000 in a charming old chalet, offers specialties from FFr80 for lunch, or dinner with reservations starting at about FFr100. Le Saint Louis also offers a special with regional dishes.

Belle Plagne

The most popular restaurant is **Le Matafan** (479 09 09 19), which is normally packed. Tables fan out around an open fire, country cupboards stand against the wall and lace curtains drape the windows. A series of eleven different luncheon plates are offered, including mountain ham, paté and cheese for FFr62, or an omelet with bacon, salad and fries for FFr70. Dinner portions are mountain-sized.

Chez Moustache and **La Cloche** serve up good food in a less formal atmosphere. **Winform,** which offers a meal plan for the Résidence Carene, has a FFr90 menu for good regional specialties.

Head to **The Cheyenne Café** for a taste of Tex/Mex at affordable prices.

Plagne 1800

La Bartavelle (479 09 07 75) is perhaps the best gourmet-type restaurant, with the average meal in the FFr210 range before you add in wine. The elegant dining room with open fireplace and beamed ceiling goes with the upscale meals and price. **Loup Garou** (479 09 20 17) (better than Loup Blanc) also offers tasty dinners.

Plagne Bellecote

Le Cairn (479 09 03 07) presents a cozy woodsy atmosphere. Each evening live music adds to the atmosphere. Lunch runs about FFr80, dinner FFr160–210. **La Perre** (479 09 29 32) has good local food with fish specialties.

On the slopes

There are 22 different mountain restaurants, not including the restaurants in the complexes themselves, which offer excellent midday dining. Included are **Vega, La Galerne** and **Le Chaudron** in Plagne Center. Most of the mountain restaurants are self-service. **Le Biollet,** above Aime La Plagne, gets the most sun. For sitdown meals, try **Le Val Sante** at the far left edge of the resort area and be ready to ski home slowly, stuffed with lots of great food. **L'Arpette**, just above Belle Plagne and recognizable by the motorbike hanging from the rafters, serves up good mountain food. **La Bergerie** above Plagne Bellecote has a rustic atmosphere and pricey mid-mountain dining. **La Grande Rochette**, at the top of the gondola from Plagne Center, offers spectacular views at lunch and dinners on Thursday.

Après-ski/nightlife

The showtime Cafe in Plagne Bellecote has live music some nights and kareoke on others.

The Must in Plagne Centre offers disco fare from 10:30 p.m. Prices are the standard FFr90–100 per drink. **The King Cafe** in Plagne Center is a coffee house offering concerts and a gathering place for the young crowd.

Tom's Bar at Plagne 1800 has bar service from 4–10 p.m. and disco from 10 p.m., when all drink prices increase. Tom's is run by a Brit, but the prices would make anyone back on the island turn a whiter shade of pale. Free bus back to your room after 2 a.m.

Child care

Each complex in La Plagne has a nursery for children two to six. These facilities offer indoor activities, as well as outdoor snowgarden play depending on the age of the child.

Nursery Marie-Christine in Plagne Center (479 09 11 81) takes children above two years for FFr170 a day, without meals, or FFr95 for a half day. Belle Plagne nursery (479 09 06 68) accepts children eighteen months to six years.

Daily rates are FFr195, plus FFr45 for lunch; half days are FFr125. Six days with lessons but no lunch cost FFr825; six half days of lessons in the ski garden, FFr625; six days with lunch, lessons and nursery, FFr1,260.

For older children, the ski school organizes special programs designed for young skiers. Absolute beginners can take a course that includes lifts and classes for six days for FFr1,070. Six normal lessons will cost FFr825 for full days, and six half days cost FFr625.

Getting there

Local transport

Plagne Centre to Aime La Plagne is served by a telemetro 8–1 a.m.

Plagne Center and Plagne Village has a telebus from 8–1 a.m.

Plagne Center and Plagne 1800/Bellecote are connected by shuttlebus on the hour and half hour, 8:30–12:30 a.m.

Bellecote–Belle Plagne cable car links Belle Plagne from 8 –1 a.m.

Bellecote–Plagne 1800–Plagne Center are connected by a shuttlebus at quarter past and quarter to the hour, 8:45 a.m.–12:45 a.m.

Telemetro and telebus are FFr14 for two trips. The shuttlebus is free.

Taxi: Christian Bouzon (479 09 03 41); or Taxi Silvestre (479 09 70 58).

Other activities

The heated pool in Plagne Bellecote is open from 3:30 p.m. to 7 p.m. The ice rinks, in Plagne Bellecote, Aime la Plagne and Les Coches are open from 2:30 p.m. to 7 p.m.; on Wednesdays and Fridays they're open to 10:30 p.m. Adults pay FFr40 and children pay FFr32, including skates.

Rent squash courts in Plagne 1800 at Maeva reception.

In 1989, La Plagne constructed an Olympic bobsled run for the 1992 games, making it the official bobsled capital of the Alps. Visitors may arrange a hair-raising 80-kph plunge down the 19 curves of the track in a special (safe) sled when the track is not being used for competition.

There are English-speaking doctors in the Plagne Centre medical center. It is open 8:30 a.m.—7 p.m.

Tourist information

Reservations: Call 479 09 79 79, fax 479 09 70 10.

The tourist information office is in Plagne Center. Send mail to Bureau de Tourisme de La Plagne, BP 36, 73210 La Plagne, France. 479 09 02 01.

Internet: www.skifrance.fr/~laplagne

Megève

Megève exudes old-fashioned charm. The small village is huddled around the old church, a medieval tower and the town hall, with narrow streets, small squares, trendy boutiques, quality antique shops, crowded bistros and dozens of small hotels. The upper crust of Europe and especially France make Megève their winter home when cold weather forces them to abandon the Riviera. Furs are the coats of choice for strolling past shop windows, and the latest fashions are found on the slopes during the day and in expensive gourmet restaurants and some of France's best discos and nightclubs after dark. You can spend your nights bouncing to the beat in packed jazz clubs or wandering the romantic streets listening to the jingle of bells and the clip-clop of horses.

Like Zermatt, Megève has a look that Walt Disney might have imagined had he created a ski resort, from its Old World town buildings to its narrow streets, from its art deco deluxe hotels to its perfect French country inns, and from its gourmet restaurants to its pulsing late-night casinos and discos. Megève hits all the notes between hedonistic excess and traditional ski village delight.

For skiers, Megève's own ski area is relatively uninspiring, but the town has leveraged its ambiance with the slopes of neighboring towns, creating an area with exceptional variety of terrain. It links the slopes of neighboring Saint-Gervais-les-Bains, St. Nicolas de Véroce and Combloux, creating an overall skiing domain of almost 200 miles of trails with something for every level of skier.

Mountain layout

Although Megève's slopes are not of the caliber of Val d'Isère, nor as extensive as Les Trois Vallées, when the snow cooperates the region has some of the most varied skiing you can find in Europe. Megève does suffer from a low elevation, which can be a serious drawback in winters with meagre snow, but this is also a blessing, because it offers more comfortable skiing for the entire winter without the chilling cold found in higher resorts.

Priority areas on any expert's list should be Mont Joly and Mont Joux. Both peaks are actually in the St. Gervais area, but the St. Gervais and the Megève ski runs are so well integrated that the connection is virtually seamless. The two peaks separating Megève from St. Gervais are lined with black- and red-rated runs, as well as excellent off-trail drops down toward Le Gouet in St. Nicolas de Véroce. A favorite from the top of Mont Joly is the chair lift run, which starts from the 7,637-foot summit of the lift and drops precipitously to the base at 6,107 feet. You have one real choice coming down, and it's black all the way. Nearby, a shorter run that descends from the Epaule lift is also rated black. To the right and left of both runs are wide-open steeps with off-trail action.

From atop the Mont Joux lift there are a half dozen runs down to St. Nicolas that shift from steep to mellow, starting from wide-open snowfields and ending in tree-lined trails. You can also descend the other side of Mont Joux and back into Megève.

The Mont d'Arbois summit offers a mix of black, red and blue runs. The summit is served by four lifts on the Megève side and by another four climbing up from St. Gervais. From this point long cruises for beginners or intermediates are the order of the day; they can drop back into Megève or down to Le Bettex, or when the snow is good continue back into St. Gervais.

Across the plateau from Mont d'Arbois rising above Megève are three peaks—Rochebrune, Alpette and Cote 2000. This series of peaks offers another varied system of runs. The best is a descent from the Rochebrune summit through the trees and back to the valley station. Experts can test themselves skiing from Cote 2000 down to the altiport on black and red runs. Beginners and basic intermediates can enjoy a field day with the swooping runs from the Alpette peak.

The third area served by the Megève pass is Le Jaillet. This lift system is half owned by the town of Combloux. It is best suited to beginners and lower intermediates who are gaining confidence or for experienced skiers who want to spend some time playing and cruising down mellow slopes. Advanced beginners and lower intermediates will find Le Jaillet, at 5,576 feet, ideal. There are also four black-rated runs; as skills (and courage) increase, you won't have to look far to find something more challenging.

Most scenic of the black runs is the mile-long trail (6,133 feet) from Christomet. Our favorite on this side is the run through the woods along the Creve Coeur lifts just below Le Jaillet summit.

Mountain rating

Taken together, Megève's mountains offer several challenges and make the area an acceptable destination for the expert skier who realizes that this is no Chamonix or Val d'Isère. (Although if you're skiing on a Mont Blanc ski pass, Chamonix is a possibility any day of the week.) Intermediates and those trying to push to advanced level should find this a great place to improve and test their skills.

Beginners should go to Megève without hesitation. There's enough good skiing at the lower ability level to keep them going until the improvements come. Then it's on up the mountain with the big boys.

Ski school (97/98 prices)

About 200 teachers are registered in the Megève area. Large ski classes are conducted by schools in Megève, notably the French Ski School (450 21 00 97), Ski School International (450 58 71 75), St. Gervais (450 47 76 08) and Combloux (450 58 60 49). Note: English-speaking instructors are a limited commodity—if you need one, make sure he speaks English well.

Group lessons Ten hours of morning lessons will cost FFr450.

Snowboarding: Special one-week twelve-hour afternoon courses cost FFr680–910.

Private lessons cost FFr190–200 for one hour; for a full day, FFr1,500–1,550.

Cross-country skiing instruction is available, and the amount of prepared trails—more than 75 km.—attests to the sport's popularity here.

Lift tickets (97/98 prices)

Mont Blanc's ski pass also includes the Megève area. It is by far the best lift-ticket bargain. In addition to Megève, it covers Chamonix, St. Gervais, St. Nicolas, and Les Contamines, plus eight other resorts around Mont Blanc. It comprises 201 lifts and more than 700 km. of prepared runs. Six-day rates are for consecutive days. Children are those younger than 12. Seniors are 60+.

	Adults	Children/Seniors
two days	FFr342	FFr273
three days	FFr432	FFr394
six days	FFr9871	FFr657
seven days	FFr975	FFr780
13 days	FFr1,470	FFr1,176

Local tickets are available for 300 km. of trails served by 81 lifts in the areas of Megève, St. Gervais, Saint Nicolas and Combloux.

	Adults	Children/Seniors
one day	FFr170	FFr136
two days	FFr326	FFr261
three days	FFr470	FFr376
six days	FFr832	FFr665
seven days	FFr931	FFr745

The Megève local pass offers discounts of about 15 percent during the middle two weeks of January and late March/early April.

Accommodations

Megève has the best collection of upscale, beautiful elegant hotels of any ski resort in Europe—in the world, for that matter. In style they range from avant-garde and art deco palaces to gilt and velvet luxury to rustic French provincial.

Lodge Parc (450 93 05 03, fax 450 93 09 52) This introverted oasis of art deco creates its own environment. Halls are lined with chrome columns set against white walls on either side of black runners lined in royal blue, all highlighted by splashy modern canvases. Many feel this hotel hideously ignores its Alpine surroundings; others revel in its luxury. Rooms with every amenity are dominated by the same colors and chrome.

The bar claims to have the best liqueur selection in the French Alps and serves them over a 1920s bar inlaid with mother of pearl. The main hotel restaurant, La Rotonde, serves gourmet dinners. Rooms and suites run FFr680–1,580 per person half board.

Chalet du Mont d'Arbois (450 21 25 03, fax 450 21 24 79) is a small super-luxurious chalet hotel owned by the Baron and Baroness Rothschild. Arrivals are treated like personal guests rather than hotel residents—an atmosphere that prevails for the entire stay. If you can imagine yourself moving into your own mountain chalet, you'll enjoy the decor, which features a lot of mountain wood, giant fireplaces and priceless antiques. Room and half board: FFr1,105–1,380.

Les Fermes de Marie (450 93 03 10, fax 450 93 09 84) is not just a hotel: it is a phenomenon. Jocelyne (a painter and designer) and Jean-Louis Sibuet (a builder) have created a private hamlet just minutes from the center of Megève. Farmhouses from all over France were painstakingly taken apart and reassembled here with a combination of warmth, tradition and good taste. There are 69 bedrooms, three restaurants, living rooms, a library and bar, and a spa with an indoor pool and a wide range of beauty and health treatments. The food is excellent, and one restaurant specializes in cheese dishes, with the hearty local tartiflette and fondue always on the menu. The rooms and suites are tastefully decorated, often with paintings by Jocelyn Sibuet. A double room with half-board costs FFr750–1,800.

In addition to the main hotel complex, the owners, who also operate Au Coin du Feu, have opened two large luxury residences just outside of town called **Les Fermes du Grand Champ** (450 93 03 10, fax 450 93 09 84), that can each be rented by one or more families. These are spacious, decorated with antiques, and include saunas, swimming pool, garage, private meal service, and other amenities. The larger chalet sleeps eight to ten people and includes an office, covered swimming pool and fitness room. It rents for US$9,000 to US$16,700 per week, depending on the season.

Hotel le Fer à Cheval (450 21 30 39, fax 450 93 07 60) is like staying in a French country cottage. Every highlight is rendered in wood, the furniture is rustic, with walls covered in country patterned fabrics and stencils, and hand-painted doors. Double room, half board: FFr600–905.

Au Coin du Feu (450 21 04 94, fax 450 21 20 15) is another country-perfect setting, owned by the brother of the Fer à Cheval's proprietor, with similar French country touches. In the restaurant wooden cupboards line the walls, alternating with stone arches around a fireplace. The hotel has 23 rooms, with many converted into minisuites. Rates for the normal double rooms with half board, based on double occupancy: FFr600–850 per day .

Hotel Alpina (450 21 54 77, fax 450 21 53 79) in the center of town on Place du Casino. The rooms, recently remodeled in the woodsy mountain style, all come with TV. Breakfast only. Rates for double occupancy in high season—Christmas, February and Easter—FFr525–710.

Hotel La Prairie (450 21 48 55, fax 450 21 42 13) is an excellent three-star hotel in Megève. The chalet-style building is bright and spacious, the rooms are simple with heavy wooden doors and pine highlights. Every room has a TV, and you are an easy five-minute walk from the center of town. This hotel is breakfast only, with a snack served 7-8:30 p.m. Double occupancy rates: FFr450-690.

Week-End Hotel (450 21 26 49, fax 450 58 90 40) is next door to Coin du Feu, about a five-minute walk up a relatively steep hill from the town center. The rooms have been redone and almost every room has an extra bed for a child or third person. Perhaps something as simple as getting rid of the chenille bedspreads would make the Week-End look more up-scale, as it should be. The owner speaks excellent English. The hotel has breakfast only. Rates for double occupancy: FFr490–570.

La Chaumine (450 21 37 05, fax 450 21 37 21) just a short walk from the center of town, near the cable car of Chamois, is an inexpensive newly renovated two-star hoThis old restored farm B&B is cozy and charming. Rate for two runs about FFr530–600.

Les Sapin (450 21 02 79, fax 450 93 07 54) five minutes from Rochebrun, offers excellent cooking, presented in a lovely dining room, and prepared with pride by the owner. Full pension is FFr555 each. A floodlit heated outdoor swimming pool has an unusual swim-out entrance, so you need not walk outside to dive in during the winter.

The **Saint Jean Hotel** (450 21 24 45, fax 450 58 78 50) offers B&B for FFr500–550. The husband/owner cooks, the wife welcomes the guests in this small hotel near La Chamois lift.

Other excellent possibilities for rooms in newer, very attractive Alpine hotels include **La Grange d'Arly** (450 58 77 88, fax 450 93 07 13) and **Le Manege** (450 21 21 08, fax 450 58 95 32).

Megève Reservation books rooms, apartments or chalets (450 21 29 52, fax 450 91 85 67). Altogether there are 48 hotels and pensions in town, although not all are open year-round. The wealth of restaurants and the liveliness of Megève's night scene may suggest the choice of a hotel without half board. Accommodation is available starting at the weekly prices below. These are low-season prices available for most of January. They include seven full consecutive days with half board, taxes and services (per person) in a double room occupied by two people, with bath or shower and a six-day lift ticket for the Megève area.

Four	★★★★	FFr5,610
Three	★★★	FFr4,490
Two	★★	FFr2,740

Apartments

Write to the Megève tourist office (see Tourist Information), which will contact the major rental organizations in town. You will hear from several—make your pick and let the agencies know your decision. Mid-January, expect to pay about FFr2,500–4,500 a week for a two-room apartment for four persons. In February the price will be FFr4,800–7,500 a week. In the Christmas holiday apartments are rented for two-week periods and will cost FFr7,500–12,000. Linen is an additional FFr140 a week.

 ## Dining

You won't have any problem getting excellent food—there are six Michelin-rated and twelve Gault Millau-listed restaurants.

Lodge Park (450 93 26 61) Surrounded by glass, you'll be able to look outside into the woods for an effect that, augmented by the tiny ceiling lights and the candles, is magical. Expect to pay between FFr200 and FFr300 for dinner, without wine.

Chalet du Mont d'Arbois (450 21 25 03), This chalet belongs to Baron Rothschild. Enjoy Michelin one-star meals in a country atmosphere created by heavy beams and soaring, stuccoed arches. The chalet claims one of the best wine cellars in Megève. A meal will cost FFr275-400.

Michel Gaudin (450 21 02) is a gourmet restaurant awarded two toques by Gault Millau. It serves a combination between traditional mountain cuisine and light Mediterranean cooking.

Le Prieure (450 21 01 79) Nestled between the church and the priory on the main square, this spot is as cozy as meals get.

Les Fermes de Marie (450 93 03 10) serves fine French meals and cheese specialties in a French country atmosphere.

Le Cintra (450 21 02 60) has a seafood bar in a lively ambiance.

St. Nicolas (450 21 04 94) is a restaurant in the basement of the Hotel Au Coin du Feu. Its country atmosphere is set by giant wooden cupboards, armoires and stone basement arches. The chef serves up Savoyard country specialties. Expect to pay FFr230-280.

Fer à Cheval Restaurant (450 21 30 39) in the hotel of the same name also has a very rustic country feel. Country cooking with a Savoyard gourmet flair will cost about FFr230-275 per person for dinner.

Auberge du Grenand (450 21 30 30), about 3 km. outside of town on the road to Leutaz Very, is worth the trip. This restaurant is set in a rustic chalet with plenty of mountain atmosphere and a roaring fireplace. Meals will cost about FFr210, including wine.

Les Drets (450 21 31 78), better known as "Chez Lou," gets a lot of repeat customers who claim they return because of the owners. Driving there is easiest: it's on the road to Cote 2000 just before you get to the altiport, but you can also get there for a skier's lunch by a short walk. Chez Lou is open only for lunch, which can cost as little as FFr110.

For local mountain specialties of fondue, raclette and *pela* (a regional country dish of pan-fried potatoes and bacon covered with melted cheese and served in the pan with a selection of mountain-dried beef and sausages), make sure to visit three small restaurants all within a one-minute walk of each other:

Le Chamois (450 21 25 01), next to the church and old town tower, specializes in cheese fondue at FFr90 per person. Unlike most restaurants, Le Chamois will serve a single guest who arrives with a fondue craving.

Les Marronniers (450 21 22 01) is a tiny rustic cafe at the opposite end of the same building that houses Le Chamois. The wooden walls are lined with hundreds of colorful old pastel coffee pots. Raclette is served the old-fashioned way—scraped off with a knife—for about FFr110. They also serve crêpes, galletes (like thick pancakes), and omelets.

Le Savoyard (450 58 71 72) under the Hotel Alpina opposite the casino, has revived the art of creating *pela*. A rich and hearty plateful costs FFr95 per person. With the recommended local white wine and coffee you can walk away with paying just over FFr220 for two.

Pizzeria del Marc offers creative pizzas on the cheap.

For eating on the mountain we have recommendations for each area. The best overall is **L'Alpette** between Rochebrune and Cote 2000 (450 21 03 69). **La Petite Coterie** in Le Bettex (450 93 11 74) is also excellent. Both will be crowded in high season, so you should make reservations. On the top of Mont d'Arbois, choose from refined dining at **Ideal Sports** with its south-facing terrace or try the **Igloo** self-service (450 93 05 84) next to the upper station of the Princesse lift. On top of Mont Joux, the new **Espace Mont Joux** has great views of Mont Blanc. The best mountain eatery on the Rochebrune sector of the resort is **La Cote 2000** (450 21 31 84) near the Altiport or try the spot at the top of

Rochebrune with a 360-degree view. Across the valley in Le Jaillet, try **Le Jaillet Supérieur** (450 21 06 51) at the top of the gondola.

La Ferme de Chateluy (609 30 54 15), a restored historic farm where the toilet is literally in the woodshed, and the salads and desserts are top-notch. It is off the Chateluy blue run from the top of the Bettex gondola. Follow the little sign to the left of the blue run—a tiny path leads directly to the restaurant. The view of Mont Blanc is worth the small detour.

Also notable for its straight-on view of Mont Blanc, **Au Petit Montagnard** (450 93 25 09) offers a tomato fondue specialty and can be found on L'Olympic piste, just above St. Nicholas village.

Near the bottom of the ladies' Olympic downhill course and on the cross-country route, the **Cote 2000** (450 21 31 84) offers delicious regional specialties, and the sun terrace attracts numerous loungers.

Après-ski/nightlife

La nuit, c'est Megève! roughly translates as "the night is Megève." Despite the rustic atmosphere, Megève is modern in all aspects. Discos pulse and lights flash, keeping beat with the thumping music. The live entertainment ranges from France's top singers and entertainers to transvestite revues. It all continues until at least 4 a.m.

Don't plan to tackle Megève's nightlife after an eight o'clock dinner. There isn't any to speak of, not until much later. Discos don't get rolling until after midnight, and even then they seem deserted.

The village sparkles for as long as you let it. About 10 p.m., head to the **Jazz Club Les 5 Rues** in the tiny back streets of Megève and vibrating with great jazz in very rustic surroundings. The **Cave de Megève** also has jazz.

The recently redecorated casino opens at 5 p.m., but doesn't really get rolling until about midnight. The discos are packed by 1:30 a.m. Squeeze into **Pallas** across from the ice rink. The young crowd packs the **Village Rock Café**. Expect to pay FF90–100 for a drink or if you are planning to stay, a bottle of whiskey runs FF900–1,000.

Child care

Meg' Loisirs (450 58 77 84) kindergarten near the Jaillet runs is for children 12 months to 6 years and costs FFr240 with lunch.

Other day care facilities are available for children from ages 3–6 that include beginning ski lessons. L'Alpage (450 21 10 97) is on Mont l'Arbois. La Princesse (450 93 00 86) is near the Princesse lift. La Caboche (450 58 97 65), on the Rochebrune slope next to the Caboche cable car, takes kids 3–10. Meg' Loisirs (450 58 77 84) is near the sport center. Prices range from FFr240–395 for a full day with lunch and FFr120–230 for a half day without lunch. For details, call the tourist office at 450 21 27 28.

The tourist office maintains a list of multilingual babysitting services.

Getting there

Geneva is the main arrival airport; from there it is about an hour by car to Megève. There is also a scheduled bus service from the Geneva airport.

Trains run to Sallanches, 13 km. away, where bus and taxi services are available. The TGV makes the run from Paris in only five hours. A bus from the Sallanches train station to Megève will cost about FFr35.

Other activities

Megève and the neighboring villages draw many nonskiers who walk throughout the area. Walkways are better kept than most you'll encounter at other Alpine resorts. Stores are perfect for window shopping—prices can destroy budgets. Day outings to Chamonix and Geneva are popular as is the easy trip through the Mont Blanc tunnel to Italy for shopping.

Megève has an excellent sports center with skating, swimming with two covered pools, saunas, fitness rooms, covered tennis and golf practice ranges. Rates for the Sports Center are normally FFr25 for skating or swimming. Tennis courts can be reserved by calling 450 21 15 71 and will cost FFr100 per court-hour or FFr500 for six coupons, good for six hours of court time.

Tourist information

Office du Tourisme, rue de la Poste, F-74120 Megève; 450 21 27 28, fax 450 93 03 09.

Office du Tourisme, F-74920 Combloux; 450 58 60 49, fax 450 93 33 55.

Office du Tourisme, F-74190 Le Fayet; 450 93 64 64.

Office du Tourisme de St. Gervais, F-74170 St. Gervais; 450 47 76 08; fax 450 47 75 69.

Internet: www.skifrance.fr/~Megeve

Les Trois Vallées

Courchevel, Méribel, Les Menuires, Val Thorens

All skiers dream of virtually endless slopes and trails at ;any resort where they plan to vacation. The Trois Vallées is about as close as anyone can come to that dream of a chance to wake up each morning and choose a different village to explore, mountain to schuss, or scenic vista to capture. If it is the call of an endless ski safari that you hear, then the epicenter of that siren song is France's Trois Vallées region.

The four main villages comprising Les Trois Vallées, all purpose-built for skiing, are Courchevel, Méribel, Les Menuires and Val Thorens. On paper the area is overwhelming; in person it is mind-expanding. Two hundred ski lifts on a single pass, 525 km. of ski runs, 132 km. of cross-country trails, 1,296 snow cannons, 280 ski patrollers, 1,160 lift attendants. It is as if some ingenious Frenchmen had decided that the preferred method of getting from one place to another may be the car and autoroute on the flatlands to the north, or the gondola and canal in the wetlands of Venice, but here in the Alps it is a cable car and a pair of trusty boards. Some executives in the area even admit to skiing to meetings in neighboring villages, so efficient is the interconnecting lift system.

The same irreverence that has led to what must be the most efficient—and most obtrusive—lift systems in the world, also explains the atmosphere of the area. There is little that is quaint or Old-World about Les Trois Vallées. Where the Swiss or Austrians might spread out ski lifts and chalets so that they blend more easily into the mountain scenery, the French will pile apartments and condos one atop the other to ensure that everyone has ski-in/ski-out access to a handy lift.

Compared with some of the Arlberg resorts, for instance, the neon signs, bright splashy advertisements and general carnival atmosphere of a Val Thorens feel like a video arcade.

In St. Anton they play acoustic oom-pah, and here it's "Girls Just Want to Have Fun" blaring from speakers. After a slight decompression period, however, the look feels in sync with the area's character: fun-loving, sporting, and slightly outrageous. If you're looking to have a drink of wine and a laugh with the locals—frequently at your own expense—then you'll fit right in. If you want to be waited on and pampered by lift attendants and polite locals alike, better to book St. Moritz.

Courchevel

This is perhaps the most cosmopolitan of the four villages. It was France's first real jet-set resort, created to cater to the upper crust and becoming the darling of those in the Riviera group who didn't flock to Megève.

Courchevel itself is really a series of smaller villages whose names reflect their heights in meters—Courchevel 1850, Courchevel 1650, Courchevel 1550 and so on. Courchevel 1300, also called Le Praz, is the quaintest, but its lower altitude may mean a sacrifice of snow for charm. There is another village, Saint-Bon on a fifth level but with no lifts. Courchevel 1850 is the highest and priciest, but it's also where most trails run right outside your hotel or apartment door. It is where the best restaurants are found and where the nightlife continues until the sky begins to lighten with coming day. Built for ski-in/ski-out, Courchevel 1850 really works. Its lift system covers both sides of the valley. The world's largest cable car, heading up to La Saulire (8,885 feet), connects Courchevel to the rest of the Les Trois Vallées area.

Méribel

Méribel has been developed into a first-rate ski resort but has taken pains to retain a semblance of the traditional mountain architecture of the French Alps. From a skier's point of view, the resort has two sections. There is Méribel that basically stretches from La Chaudanne, at 1,450 meters elevation with traditional village atmosphere with a major lift center and the tourist office, to the Altiport at 1,700 meters. About four km. up the valley is Méribel-Mottaret, a smaller village with a larger lift hub, and more ski-in/ski out accommodation. These villages are set in the central valley of Les Trois Vallées. There are 57 lifts in the valley, 18 of them that start in the village and link up with another 150 lifts in Les Trois Vallées.

Old Méribel center, called La Chaudanne was virtually founded by the British; it still retains many of its British trappings, and English seems to be spoken almost everywhere. Above this original center rises the rest of Meribel with 750 vertical feet of the new hotels and chalets built up the side of the valley toward Courchevel with excellent ski slope access—this has names such as La Renard, Les Chalets, Rond Point des Pistes, Belvédère and Le Plateau. It is about a ten-minute ride from the Altiport and Rond Point des Pistes down to the tourist office.

Half as old and still growing, Méribel-Mottaret is higher up in the same valley. It has more direct lift access to Les Menuires, Courchevel and Val Thorens via the new Cote Brune chair lift. Méribel-La Chaudanne is about a ten minute ride from Meribel-Mottaret. They are linked by a free bus.

The lift to La Saulire provides the best access to the Courchevel valley and the lifts to either Roc des Trois Marches (8,868 feet) or Mont de la Challe (8,448 feet) provide the best connections to Val Thorens and Menuires.

Val Thorens

None of the villages is more attuned to the single-minded pursuit of winter sport than Val Thorens. From the moment you park your car in indoor parking near this cluster of high-rise apartments and hotels, you can feel the hum of activity. At 2,300 meters, Val Thorens is designed for the young and restless, or at least for the young-at-heart and active. Besides some of the best year-round skiing offered anywhere, there's a huge indoor sports complex where you can play tennis on one of three courts, work out in the gym, or try your hand at squash.

Outside, the crowd is one teeming mass of rainbow-colored movement: snowmobilers, skiers, snowboarders, para-sailors, and mono-skiers.

Although there is a four-star hotel, the impression more toward video arcades, pizzerias, indoor shopping, a few flashy bars and discos and moderate hotels. The real claim to fame is not luxury, but the atmosphere of sport and lofty location of this fun town.

Les Menuires

From a distance Les Menuires' original buildings look like a misplaced spaceship resting on the snow. This isn't a judgment of good or bad, the resort works wonderfully, but never-the-less the resort has been making dramatic strides in blending the resort into the environment. Giant pines were planted at the entrance to the area to improve the first impression and covered wooden arcade now connect the buildings adding a natural feel to the compound and inside the decor has been made much more Savoyard with plenty of wood and farm influences.

This resort is home to the region's only Club Med and all accommodations have immediate access to the slopes. The village has been created to keep cars out of the way and with its apartments it offers the best family spot in the Trois Vallées. Recently, however, Les Menuires has also quietly assembled eleven two- and three-star hotels. The base of Les Menuires unfolds onto the crescent boardwalk of the central La Croisette shopping mall. Here reasonable prices attract skiers from other valleys who return to their apartments with bulging backpacks.

The newer satellite section of Reberty-Les Bruyeres has concentrated on smaller buildings built in community clusters. Here you will find skiers traveling with families and those looking for the steeps. The skiing is wide open on the west-facing slope, with lifts running up toward Val Thorens. An abundance of beginner and intermediate runs pass picturesque shepherd huts on the way down the valley toward St. Martin de Belleville. The east-facing side of the valley offers more challenging skiing from Pointe de la Masse (9,213 feet), which can be reached rapidly by riding a combination of two high-speed lifts. In the afternoon the area is deserted as skiers follow the sun. The off-trail skiing from here and nearby Cîme de Caron is exceptional, especially in spring when skiers can drop over the backside of these mountains with certified guides.

The lifts taking skiers to the Roc des Trois Marches and to Mont de la Challe provide the best connections to Méribel and the rest of Les Trois Vallées.

The traditional village of St. Martin de Belleville with its Baroque churches and pastoral aura, 8 km. down-valley from Les Menuires, offers pension accommodations and plenty of apartments. It is now connected with the entire Trois Vallées area.

Mountain layout

If you have ever thought about hiring a ski guide to learn the intricacies of an area, we suggest that your first visit to Les Trois Vallées is an excellent time to do it. The area is so vast, with so many hidden treasures the average skier might not explore on his own, that it begs for a knowing hand. The chance of avalanches is another compelling reason to take a guide when heading off-piste.

That said, each of the three valleys has its own character. As befitting the highest resort in the Alps, above Val Thorens and neighboring Les Menuires it's wide-open, bowl-type skiing above the tree line. The Funitel of Péclet cable car takes skiers up to the Péclet glacier, offering year-round skiing for intermediates and above. While most of the skiing in the bowl-shaped area above Val Thorens is intermediate, experts and advanced intermediates should not miss the cable car ride to the top of Cîme de Caron, the highest point in the three valleys. The view is worth the trip, the rocks on top make a perfect picnic spot and the runs ain't bad either. From here you can take a black run straight down, or a slightly easier advanced intermediate. True experts will want to ski over the ridge to the little-used fourth valley and the lone Rosael quad chair that will bring you back.

Further down the valley, in the Les Menuires area there's excellent expert and intermediate skiing from the top of La Masse. These runs are often less crowded owing to the inconvenient lift system here. On the other side of the valley above both Les Menuires and Val Thorens, the runs are generally intermediate, rather wide-open cruisers with an expert run named after Marielle Goitschel, the Olympic darling of the valley. One of our absolute favorite runs for intermediates is the mogul-studded connector path leading down to Méribel from Mont de la Chambre above Val Thorens.

The skiing on both sides of the Allues valley, home to Méribel and Méribel-Mottaret, ranges from easy to fairly difficult. One of the key advantages to this area is most in evidence in this section of the mountain: bottom-to-top cable cars that not only take you to long, undisturbed cruises, but also can get you across the valley and the entire area very quickly. Experts and advanced intermediates shouldn't miss the very worthy runs and wide-open off-piste opportunities down both sides of Mont Vallon. Mow down Mont Vallon early in the morning, then for gut-sucking action, mogul-busters should try the short drop under the third stage of the Plattieres lift. Advanced beginners and intermediates will find the run below the final two sections both gentle and extended. Off-piste possibilities for intermediates abound in the area between Roc de Fer, site of the Olympic downhill, and St. Martin de Belleville.

The skiing above the various levels of Courchevel varies widely. Experts will enjoy all of the runs winding down from La Saulire, especially the one that wraps around the far side of the telepherique and the one that shoots down into Les Creux from the opposite direction. On the other side of Chanrossa and Roc Merlet (2734 meters) intermediates will find this whole area—much of it below the tree line—to their liking. Beginners will enjoy the wide-open pasture surrounding the Saulire cable car. A truly gorgeous run through the trees can be had by starting at the Col de la Loze, and skiing down to Le Praz.

Off Piste: Always-present avalanche danger makes skiing with a guide very advisable and with a friend a common-sense requirement. Experts who want to explore the path less traveled should head for the Val Thorens/Les Menuires valley. Besides the aforementioned fourth valley, there is also excellent off-piste skiing above the Pointe de Thorens.

At this point, be prepared to shed your skis and hike up to the glacier du Bouchet in one direction or in the other direction toward either the Glacier de Gébroulaz or to the Aguille de Péclet.

The summits of La Masse and Cîme de Caron, also in the Val Thorens/Les Menuires valley, are the richest sources of off-piste skiing in the entire Three Valleys circuit. From the top of both there are long off-piste trails down by Lac (lake) du Lou. Take particular notice of the ski hut at the peak of La Masse—a steep initial descent from this hut intimidates most and conceals desolate, expert terrain leading more directly toward Lac du Lou than the itinerary routes. From the top of La Masse there is more serene off-piste skiing to be found by heading down to La Gratte via either the Les Encombres route or the Le Chatelard route. Advance arrangements for a taxi or a car to pick you up and bring you the short distance to the St. Martin de Belleville lift should be made.

In the Méribel valley the best off-piste skiing is in sectors between Mont de la Chambre and Les Plattieres as well as from the top of Mont Vallon. Watch out, however, for the national wildlife refuge surrounding Mont Vallon. Skiing is now prohibited here and skiers have been given merciless fines since enforcement began in July 1990.

Mountain rating

C'est magnifique! This area is so vast and varied that no skier should have trouble finding the perfect slope for his ability.

The best expert skiing is in the Val Thorens/Les Menuires valley. Here, on the Cîme de Caron and descending from Pointe de la Masse, experts can find the best steeps, the best powder, and the smallest crowds. There are also good expert runs dropping from the ridge separating this valley from that of Méribel. Méribel has some expert runs, the most noted being a straight shot from La Saulire into town. Courchevel is not known for expert terrain except for several chutes dropping from the Méribel ridge beside La Saulire. Otherwise, the best you can find in that region is under La Vizelle, running from Col de la Loze (7,480 feet) into Courchevel 1300, or the runs dropping from Col de Chanrossa, which will test any expert.

Intermediates can ski almost anywhere because all expert trails have good escape routes. The area around Courchevel is wide open and good for intermediates.

Beginners will find plenty of trails for learning and will probably leave feeling that they have conquered the entire Trois Vallées area.

 ## Ski school (97/98 prices)

All of the area's resorts have excellent instructors and offer skiing, cross-country and snowboarding. There are more than 450 instructors in Courchevel speaking English and at least seven other languages, 120 English-speaking instructors in Les Menuires, 140 in Val Thorens and 280 in Méribel. The prices vary from resort to resort and even from section to section of the resorts. The following examples provide an idea of the range of prices.

Courchevel 1850 (479 08 07 72) private lessons are FFr1,350–1,450 per seven-hour day and FFr400–500 for half days. Group lessons cost FFr145 for a morning for adults and FFr125 for children; FFr120 and FFr105 for afternoons; FFr245 for an adult full day and FFr220 for a child's full day; and FFr1,125 for six consecutive days for adults and FFr875 for children. Snowboard lessons are FFr630 for five mornings or afternoons and FFr700 for six mornings or afternoons.

Other Courchevel ski schools are E.S. F. 1650 (479 08 26 08); E.S.F. 1550 (479 08 21 07); Ski Academy (479 08 11 99); The British School (479 08 27 87); and Ski Cocktail (479 08 39 81).

Méribel has three ski schools. **The French Ski School** (479 08 60 31) is exceptional with children and lessons from provate to group and cross-country to powder skiing. Group lesson costs are FFr210 for a full day lesson or FFr987 for five days. Private lessons cost FFr190 for one or two skiers or FFr230 for three to four skiers. A full day private instructor will cost FFr1,500. **Ski Cocktail** (479 00 56 88 or 479 00 44 15) features a complete range of lessons. **Magic in Motion** (479 08 53 36) features multilingual lessons with private instructors speaking English, French, Spanish and Czech.

Val Thorens has five different ski schools. The French Ski School or E.S. F. (479 00 02 86), Pro-Neige (479 01 07 00), Ski Cool (479 00 04 92), and Ski Surf Nature l'Ecole (479 00 01 96). Depending on the ski school, private lessons cost FFr180–220 per hour. There are various prices for group lessons FFr700–910 for six full days and FFr540-700 for a week of half days.

Les Menuires: (479 00 61 43)

Private lessons are FFr175 per hour for one to two persons; FFr225 per hour for three to four skiers; and FFr1,320 for a full day.

Group Lessons	Adults	Children under 12
morning lesson	FFr142	FFr116
afternoon lesson	FFr116	FFr96
six mornings	FFr750	FFr650
six afternoons	FFr580	FFr500
six full days	FFr930	FFr790

For skiers looking for a guide, the ski school forms groups that ski all day Monday through Friday. The cost for the full week group is FFr930. This is highly recommended. You will be put into a group with similar skiers to get the most from your experience.

Special lessons for powder skiing, snowboarding, mono-skiing, ski ballet and freestyle skiing are available. There are also racing clinics and a ski kindergarten. A special accompanied ski adventure through Les Trois Vallées and another tour through the 12 valleys of the Tarentaise—including the resorts of Val Thorens, La Plagne, Les Arcs, Val d'Isère and Tignes—are also offered.

Lift tickets (97/98 prices)

Each area offers three lift-ticket combinations: one covers only the lifts in the resort area, the second covers lifts in the individual valley; and a third is a full Trois Vallées lift ticket.

Skiers who are staying for a week or more will want to purchase the Trois Vallées combination ticket. This combination ticket gives unlimited access to all the lifts and runs in the region. It also entitles holders to a day in another Olympic resort—Val d'Isère, Tignes, La Plagne or Les Arc.

Prices for Les Trois Vallées combination pass are:

	Adults	Children (11-16)	Children (6–10)	Seniors (60+)
one day	FFr220	FFr165	FFr143	FFr176
three days	FFr634	FFr476	FFr412	FFr507

	Adults	Children (11-16)	Children (6–10)	Seniors (60+)
six days	FFr1,080	FFr810	FFr702	FFr864
seven days	FFr1,188	FFr891	FFr772	FFr950
13 days	FFr1,903	FFr1,427	FFr1,237	FFr1,616

Children under 5 ski free. Seniors 60–69 save 20% on the adult rate, skiers 70–75 save 50% and skiers over 75 skis free.

 ## Accommodations

These resorts have every type of lodging from luxury chalets to dormitories. Accommodations in the Courchevel villages all fall in the same price range, except for Courchevel 1850, which is slightly higher. Even though its prices are higher than the other resorts, Courchevel 1850 still offers somewhat reasonably priced accommodations in luxury surroundings, but you must be very careful to make arrangements for low season. The tourist office will send a complete list of hotels with information about White Week periods, and details of making reservations.

$$$ is in the FFr800–1,100 per night range; $$ is in the FFr600–800 range; $ is less than FFr600 per night.

Courchevel

Bellecote (479 08 10 19) This hotel is more Alpine, cozier and exclusive than the Byblos, described below. Its wealthy guests have had their fortunes for some time and are not interested in letting the world know their every activity. Much of the furniture was imported from the Himalayas; that which is in the lobby is leather and very soft. Heated pool and a well-equipped exercise room. $$$

Le Byblos (479 08 12 12) The mountain version of the world-famous Byblos in St. Tropez, this was conceived as an all-encompassing hotel. The soaring wooden archways, the heavy wooden columns in the bar, the secluded pool and the luxury rooms cater to hedonism at its best. Here you rub shoulders with the winter jet-set elite. $$$

Hotel Trois Vallées (479 08 00 12) This, for our money, the best of the four-star properties in Courchevel. The hotel itself is delightful with excellent light pine decor. Its designers paid special attention to the bathrooms, which are at the leading edge of design, featuring giant tubs—some marble, others black, brass fittings and every amenity. The hotel is only steps away from the finest restaurants, as well as the wildest nightlife. $$$

Les Ducs de Savoie (479 08 03 00) This is the best of the three-star lot with spacious rooms, a great swimming pool and lots of wood. The hotel is a bit out of town but right on the slopes and within easy reach of the gondola during normal operating hours. At night you'll have to walk 10 minutes to get back to the hotel or take a cab. $$

New Solarium (479 08 02 01) This hotel has some of the best views over Courchevel, the dining room shares these views with the higher-priced rooms. Across the street from the Byblos, a 10-minute walk from the town. $$

Courcheneige (479 08 02 59) A good two-star find. with 84 rooms, sauna, Jacuzzi and terrace on the slopes. $$.

L'Aiglon (479 08 02 66) This recently renovated hotel is perhaps the best two-star property in town, with exceptional rooms for comparatively low rates. Its location near the slopes is excellent, with only a short five-minute walk into town. People who stay keep coming back. $

Chanrossa (479 08 06 58) In "1550," this hotel offers good access to 1850 for everything except nightlife. The hotel food is excellent. This is the best low-priced alternative to Courchevel prices. $

Ski Chalets: Crystal, Inghams/Bladon, Simply Ski, Chalet World, First Choice, Thomas Cook/Neilson (go to page 27 for phone, fax and internet addresses).

Méribel

From a resort that was originally primarily designed around apartment living, Méribel has developed an extensive and excellent hotel base over the past decade. Today there hotels for every type of skier from the luxury concious to the bargain hunters.

Le Grand Coeur (479 08 60 03; fax 479 08 58 38) This hotel is filled with fine antiques, paintings and furnishings. There is normally a list of returning clientele, so make reservations early. The lounge, built around a large stone fireplace and the dining room have sweeping views. $$$

L'Antarès (479 23 28 23; fax 479 23 28 18) The top of the line in a modern luxury hotel. Everything the rich can wish for—indoor/outdoor pool, Jacuzzis, underground parking and Michelin-starred restaurant. A long way from the center of town but ski-in/ski-out. $$$

Le Chalet (479 23 28 23; fax 479 00 56 22) Associated with L'Antarès and just across the road and uphill from that modern hotel. Le Chalet has a traditional warm Alpine wood decor which contrasts with the cooler decor of its sister property. Ammenities are similar. $$$

Allodis (479 00 56 00; fax 479 00 59 28) This beautifully decorated hotel features a combination of modern color and design, with traditional classical architecture featuring arches and columns. But while the hotel may be perfectly located for skiing, it is not close to town. $$$

Mont Vallon (479 00 44 00; fax 479 00 46 93) In Méribel-Mottaret, this is a real luxury hotel with rustic lodge-like flavor. You have everything here: pool, exercise room, Jacuzzi, sauna, squash courts and spectacular rooms. Walk out the door and onto the lifts, but take a shuttlebus or taxi to the center of town. $$$

Alpen Ruitor (479 00 48 48; fax 479 00 48 31) Beautiful lobby and modern rooms with a new emphasis on the hotel meals and a larger dining room. Ask for a room with a view of the valley rather than the parking lot. $$

Marie Blanche (479 08 65 55; fax 479 08 57 07) A small intimate hotel in a residential district only steps from the slopes and a stairway from the center of town. $$

Adray Telebar (479 08 60 26; fax 479 08 53 85) This hidden treasure has a distinct mountain lodge feel. The 26 country-style rooms are all unique, the owners charming and the food out of this world. Worth a visit for the food even if you're not staying here. $$

l'Hotel du Moulin (479 00 52 23; fax 479 00 58 23) A one-star hotel on the outskirts of Méribel with seven rooms in an old flour mill. You'll have to take the bus to the slopes, but its the best bargain you'll find. $

Hotel La Tarentaise (479 00 42 43; fax 479 00 46 99) In Méribel-Mottaret, right on the slopes with a big British clientele. Enjoy great barbeque on the terrace. Bland rooms but great location. $$

Les Arolles (479 00 40 40; fax 479 00 45 50) Also in Méribel-Mottaret on the slopes, this hotel also has a large group of British skiers, especially families. Basic modern rooms, nice pool and on-slope location. $+

Hotels l'Eterlou/Le Tremplin/La Chaudanne (479 08 61 76; fax 479 08 57 75) A complex of hotels and condos smack in the middle of the Méribel-La Chaudanne section and steps from the lifts. Rooms are decorated in warm wood, the restaurants are very good, all ammenities are shared between the properties. Even the deep leather couches set in the Chaudanne lobby offer a thrill. $$.

l'Orée du Bois (479 00 50 30; fax 479 08 57 52) This hotel provides good value; it is on the slopes but is far out of the center of town for nightlife and restaurants. $

Le Merilys (479 08 69 00; fax 479 08 68 99) This is a cosy B&B with an Alpine flavoe at the upper reaches of the resort near the Altiport. Great slope access, but a long walk to nightlife and the downtown shopping. There is a public shuttle service however. $

le **Yéti** (479 00 51 15; fax 479 00 51 73) Good value hotel with small rooms which has been expanded in the past years. Near the previous two hotels—steps from skiing and a shuttlebus ride from the center of town. $

Ski Chalets: Crystal, Inghams/Bladon, Simply Ski, Chalet World, Ski Mark Warner, First Choice, and Thomas Cook/Neilson (see page 27 for phone, fax and internet addresses).

Val Thorens

Le Val Thorens (479 00 04 33, fax 479 00 09 40) For American tastes this is perhaps the best hotel in town. The breakfast is not the usual croissant and coffee but a full buffet complete with eggs. Walk out your door and onto the slopes. $$

Fitz Roy (479 00 04 78, fax 479 00 06 11) *The* luxury hotel in town. Meals are a quantum leap above those of the Val Thorens. $$$

Novotel (479 00 04 04, fax 479 00 05 93) The resort's biggest with 104 rooms complete with most ammenities but no pool. $$

Hotel Bel Horizon (479 00 04 77; fax 479 00 06 08) Right on the edge of the complex with south-facing rooms, this hotel offers good-sized rooms but a very French atmosphere and limited English. The food is excellent. $$

Le Sherpa (479 00 00 70, fax 479 00 08 03) It is family-run and offers Val Thoren's best value for money, with excellent food. $$

La Marmotte (479 00 00 07; fax 479 00 00 14) Sparsely furnished and very basic. $

Les Trois Vallées (479 00 01 86, fax 479 00 04 08) More basic accommodations with a good bar. $

Ski Chalets: Crystal, Inghams/Bladon, First Choice, Thomas Cook/Neilson (go to page 27 for phone, fax and internet addresses).

Les Menuires

This resort, formerly only a complex of apartments with hotels squeezed into what should have been more apartments, now has eleven two- and three-star hotels.

Hotel l'Ours Blanc (479 00 61 66; fax 479 00 63 67) is run by a young English lady and her French husband who does the gourmet cooking. The interior woodwork was finished by the father and child care is free for guests. $$

Hotel Le Menuire (479 00 60 33: fax 479 00 60 00) This is a small, clean hotel on the road entering the complex. It isa good upscale motel and is close to the lifts. $

Hotel Le Skilt (479 00 76 54; fax 479 00 63 16) This hotel was just renovated. $

Hotel Latitudes (479 00 75 10; fax 479 00 70 70) This is Les Menuires' first real upscale hotel capable of supporting meetings. Located in the Reberty-Bruyeres area next to the new 12-person gondola. $$

Hotel Carla (479 00 73 73; fax 479 00 73 76) This is a new two-star hotel in the Jettay quarter of the village. $

Hotel Le Piolet (479 00 73 81; fax 479 00 68 83) A two-star hotel in the Jettay quarter with 34 rooms. $

The traditional town of St. Martin de Belleville has the **Alp-Hotel** (479 08 92 82; fax 479 08 94 61) which is a bit out of the way but connects with the entire Trois Vallées system and offers a nest of traditional architecture rather than the modern forms that fill Les Menuires and Val Thorens. $

Also in St. Martin de Belleville try **l'Edelweiss** (479 08 96 67; fax 479 08 90 40) for simple accommodation and good food. $

Apartments

Apartments are the French choice for accommodation. In fact, apartment beds outnumber hotel beds by at least 5 to 1. What you get is the ability to schedule off-slope life at your own pace and the only way to avoid the high hotel prices. Apartment rates are slightly higher in Courchevel 1850.

During all-in-one package periods in Les Menuires, for example, a two-bedroom apartment with a six-day Trois Vallées ski pass costs FFr1,400 per person. For four-person apart-ment in February high season, expect to pay FFr4,300.

The tourist office will send more information and a registration card, and will help make reservations.

Dining

Get ready for sticker shock in restaurants, both downtown and on the slopes. Make to sure to check out a few places before settling in for dinner or lunch. For bargains try pizza spots, then Tex-Mex restaurants and raclette/fondue places.

Courchevel

This is considered to have the best food of any French mountain resort. The **Chabichou** (479 08 00 55) maintains a friendly rivalry with the **Le Bateau Ivre** (479 08 36 88) for the top restaurant in town. Both will end up costing about $70–$100 per person. A meal in the **Bergerie** (479 08 24 70) shouldn't be missed. Come with money.

Le Bistro du Praz (479 08 41 33) in Courchevel 1300, serves some of the best local specialties in the area. The French country atmosphere eatery adds a special flavor to the experience.

So much for high prices. For the more reasonable restaurants, try **La Saulire** (479 08 06 52) with good local specialties and an owner who likes Americans thanks to years of living in Canada. Expect to pay FFr220–350 per person for dinner. **La Mangeoire** looks almost Western with cowhides, wagon wheels and lanterns. The food is simple but the crowds in the evening are great. Expect to pay FFr150–200.

l'Arbe (479 08 26 03) is where the locals eat. It seems to be crowded from lunch time on, first with the lunch crowd and then with the après-skiers, then with the dinner folk.

Le Fromagerie (479 08 27 47) has the best fondue in town. **La Strada** (479 08 02 07) serves all-you-can-eat spit-roasted meats at long Viking-style tables. On Thursdays, the evening normally ends with wild dancing and music.

Méribel

This town doesn't have anywhere the range of restaurants enjoyed by Courchevel. The best is **Le Grand Coeur** (479 08 60 03) with a view over the chalets of the town. The experience is hard to beat, with excellent fish as well as local specialties. Expect to spend FFr250 per person.

The restaurants in **Hotel L'Antarès** (479 23 28 23) are among the best in the valley. The gastronomic restaurant holds a Michelin star and the Savoyard restaurant serves local specialties. You'll spend FFr250–280 per person.

La Petite Rosière (479 00 41 46) between Méribel and Méribel-Mottaret is small informal gem, with 15 tables set around a fireplace in a small chalet. You need a car to get here for the hearty meals. Try the lamb chops with mountain mushrooms. Expect FFr200–250 per person.

If you have a car, make the effort to dine at the **Hotel Allodis** (479 00 56 00). The restaurant, especially during lunch, is wonderful. The evening dining room offers meals in an architectural harmony of modern and classic lines. Expect to pay FFr250 per person.

Chez Kiki (479 08 66 68) is the Méribel version of Courchevel's original Bergerie. The rustic atmosphere is cozier downstairs near the fireplace. For an adventure during the meal find the Alice in Wonderland door in the basement. Meal costs about FFr250 apiece.

Le Cave is a traditional fromagerie where cheese and wine is kept at the perfect temperature in the basement. Head here for the best fondue and raclette in the valley.

For more economical dining try Moroccan food in **Marrakech** in the new Aspen Park Hotel (479 00 51 77). **Ski Rock Cafe** in the town center is another option. For pizza and the least wallet damage try **Scott's.**

In Méribel-Mottaret try **La Baleine** where you can have a wonderful duck fondue for two for only FFr120. The reasonable prices attract the locals. **Chez Patrick** in the center of Mottaret has crepes for around FFr60.

Les Menuires

With the emphasis on apartment living, one would expect only mediocre meals, but Les Menuires is a pleasant surprise. **La Bouitte** (479 08 96 77) in St. Marcel is probably the best restaurant in the valley and the only real stand-out in the immediate area of Les Menuires. Next on the list according to locals is the restaurant of the **Hotel L'Ours Blanc** (479 00 61 66) with excellent gourmet cooking.

La Marmite du Géant (479 00 74 75) serves excellent food in modern, rustic setting near the pool and skating rink. **Auberge de Lanau** (479 00 62 96) serves excellent grilled meats and fondue. It is in the basement of the Hotel l'Oisans. **La Mousse** (479 00 69 06) has a wonderful stone-and-wood interior as well as the best fish in the valley.

Les Menuires also has several good restaurants on the slopes above the main village. Try **Chalet des Neiges** (479 00 60 55), where you'll get simple good food for FFr80–100. In the evenings the restaurant sponsors fondue dinners, and a guide takes skiers down to the lower village with torches.

Les Roches Blanches (479 00 60 22) on La Masse is a rustic chalet serving a menu of the day, pizza and spaghetti. Just above La Croisette and reached by a short walk is the **L'Etoile** (479 00 63 25) with tables around a giant fireplace. It has one of the region' best chefs. Staff will pick up guests in snowmobiles if they make prior reservations.

Val Thorens

In Val Thorens, lovers of fine French food should head for the **Fitz Roy Hotel** (479 00 04 78). The atmosphere is romantic, the surroundings plush, and the price steep. For local specialties, try the **Galoubet**. **La Taverne du la est** (479 00 01 15) serves meals in a Bavarian atmosphere. For basic French bistro fare check out the **Chalet de Glacier**. **La Fondue** (479 00 04 33) has cheese fondue and raclette. Our personal favorite for a full menu at reasonable prices was the **Taverne de Lou** (479 00 01 15). This spot is tastefully woodsy in the style of a Bavarian *Gasthaus*, the service is friendly, and the raclette and fondue superb (fixed-price menus FFr85-168). **El Gringo** waiters decked in cowboy gear serve the highest altitude Tex-Mex dinners in Europe with killer margaritas. The best pizza—and for that matter the best deal—in town is at **Pizzeria Gianni/Scapin**.

Après-ski/nightlife

Courchevel is considered to have one of the best balances between nightlife and skiing of any European resort. It can be just as glitzy and upscale as Megève, Gstaad or St. Moritz. Après-ski entertainment here is varied and you will be sure to find a bar or disco to your taste, but expect everything to start late. Be prepared to fork over lots of money—this is some of the most expensive nightlife to be found in the Alps. Cover to get into a disco will run at least FFr80 and every drink after costs the same.

The immediate après-ski centers in **Le Tremplin** at the base of the slopes, then seems to move to **L'Arbe** just before dinner, and afterward to **La Bergerie**. **La Grange** opens as the slopes close and serves drinks until midnight, then everyone heads to a disco, such as **Caves** with its transvestite show.

Méribel-Centre now has a Trois Vallées version of the famous and successful **Dick's Tea Bar** from Val d'Isère. That spot promises to be hoppin' just like in Val d'Isère. It will be staying open until 4 a.m. Another late night spot is the **L'Artichaud**. Try **The Pub** or **Scott's**—they seem to be filled often, or try **Capricorne**, **Le Refuge** and **Le Taverne**, all a few steps from one another. Méribel-Mottaret has **La Rastro** for dancing and in Méribel-1600 head to the **French Connection**.

Les Menuires has three small discos, packed with the very young, tucked into the basement of the massive apartment buildings. The best is **Leeberty** in Reberty.

The nightlife in Val Thorens used to be limited, but now you can choose from three discos which don't start until after midnight and keep on throbbing until 4 a.m., or you can drink in one of ten pubs. Those hot to trot head for **L'Agora** nightclub, which has a $15 cover (one drink included), and is decked out in a cross between decadent disco and Egyptian crypt. Prepare yourself for outrageous prices, by U.S. standards, if you plan on drinking much. **Bar Malaysia** just outside the tourist office is a surprise. Don't let the small entranceway fool you: the bar itself is underground, and very classy. The live music tends toward the avant-garde, and there are pool tables (FFr40–85 per drink, no cover). More laid back and casual is **Pub Lincoln**, where Val Thorens' considerable English clientele gathers for drinks and darts.

Child care

The tourist office, your hotel or apartment manager can put you in touch with qualified private baby sitters who provide child care services at any time of the day or night. Each resort also offers child care programs. Here's a resort-by-resort rundown.

Courchevel has six ski schools for children. Children's lessons are offered by the E.S.F. 1850, E.S.F. 1650, E.S.F. 1550, Ski Academy, The British Ski School and Ski Cocktail. Phone numbers are listed in the ski school section. Ages accepted are about 3–12. Prices will be about FFr720–960 for six days of lessons, about FFr165–190 for a morning, and aproximately FFr140–150 for an afternoon.

Two nursery programs for children from age 2 are available in Courchevel 1850 at Le Village des Enfants (479 08 08 47) and Courchevel 1650 at Les Vacances des Petits (479 08 33 69). Both are open from 9 a.m. to 5 p.m. Prices are FFr235–255 for a day with lunch and the six-day program at 1650 costs FFr1,190.

Méribel has a highly respected child care program. **Le Club Saturnin** accepts children between 1-1/2 and 3 years. It is associated with the ski school and ski lessons are offered to children ready to ski (479 08 66 90). Also associated with the ski school, the **Jardin des P'tis Loups** accepts children three to five years of age for child care and has a ski playground to encourage beginners.

Val Thorens has two Mini Clubs associated with the ski school (479 00 06 74 and 479 00 03 09). These **Mini-Club** kindergartens accept children three months to 12 years of age. Ask about discounts for three children or more from the same family. Costs for the mini clubs are FFr1,350 for six full days and FFr600 for six half-days. The older group gets ski lessons as well FFr1,350 for six days with lunch or FFr750 for six half-days with lunch. There is a discount for the third infant and additional children from the same family are free.

Marielle Goitschel, former world champion skier, has a children's program in Val Thorens (479 00 00 47, fax 479 00 06 10). The children's programs are open from 9 a.m.– 5:30 p.m. A full day costs FFr260 without meals or FFr295 with meal, six days costs FFr1,450 without meals and FFr1,600 with meals. Lift tickets, rentals and insurance are extra.

Les Menuires has the best possibilities for children. The **Schtroumpfs' Village** is divided into two sections: three months to two and a half years and two and a half to eight years. An introduction to skiing is provided for children of 3 to 6 years; different programs are offered to each group. Reservations are suggested (479 00 63 79). A second kindergarten, called **Les Marmottons**, in the Les Bruyères area takes children 3 months to 8 years (479 00 61 43).

The ski school also runs special programs for kids five and older. The lessons are coordinated with the Schtroumpfs' Village to allow children to spend the time after and before lessons at the child care facility.

Rates for the kindergarten in Les Menuires will be FFr197 for a full day; FFr560 for six half-days; and FFr820 for six full days.

Getting there

The closest airports are Geneva (135 km.), Lyon (185 km.) and Chambéry (95 km.). Buses and trains leave daily from the Geneva airport. Société Touriscar (450 43 60 02) charges about FFr360 round-trip. Weekend bus service connects the region with Lyon for about FFr300 on Philibert Bus Lines (78 98 56 62 in English). the Chambéry bus with Transavoie Transport (479 24 21 58) costs FFr260.

Rail reaches Moutiers, 27 km. away (a 40-minute drive). Buses and taxis are available from the station. The charge to Val Thorens for example is FFr77.

If driving, follow the signs to Chambéry and Albertville, then take the four-lane road to Moutiers and up to the Les Trois Vallées.

For those piloting a private plane or helicopter, Courchevel and Méribel have small mountain airports as well as heliports with charter service.

Once at the resorts, shuttlebuses move you efficiently within each valley, but moving between valleys is inconvenient and expensive. For example, a taxi from Courchevel to Val Thorens is over FFr750 or a time-consuming bus via Moutiers would cost FFr140.

Other activities

Val Thorens Facilities include an indoor swimming pool, whirlpool baths, saunas, squash courts, six indoor tennis courts, a gymnasium and an outdoor skating rink. Hang-gliding and aerobics are offered.

Les Menuires There are two heated outdoor pools, one in Reberty and one in Le Croisette, and an outdoor skating rink. The resort also has two fully equipped fitness centers called Espace Tonic and Capricorne. There are 28 km. of cross-country trails surrounding the resort as well.

Méribel facilities include an indoor swimming pool, bowling alleys and an ice skating rink. Mountain flying lessons are offered.

Courchevel has a bowling alley, hotel indoor swimming pools, saunas, squash courts and an Olympic-size skating rink, hang-gliding, ski jumping, paragliding, deltagliding and mountain flying courses.

Tourist information

Courchevel Office du Tourisme, La Croisette, B.P. 37, 73122 Courchevel, France; 479 08 00 29; fax 479 08 15 63. Internet: www.courchevel.com

Méribel Office du Tourisme, 73550 Méribel, France; 479 08 60 01; fax 479 00 59 61. Internet: www.meribel.net; E-mail: meribel@laposte.fr

Val Thorens Office du Tourisme, 73440 Val Thorens, France; (479 00 08 08; fax 479 00 00 04). Reservations is handled by Val Thorens Tours; 479 00 01 06; fax 479 00 06 49. Internet: www.valthorens.com E-mail: valthorens@compuserve.com

Les Menuires Office du Tourisme, 73440 Les Menuires, France; 479 00 73 00; fax 479 00 75 06. For reservations only, call 479 00 79 79; fax 479 00 60 92. Internet: www.les-menuires.com

Saint Martin de Belleville Office du Tourisme, 73440 Saint Martin De Belleville, France; 479 08 93 09; fax 479 08 91 71. Internet: www.skifrance.fr/~stmartin

Tignes

Tignes, Val d'Isère's sister resort, appears to be nothing more than a group of concrete apartment buildings huddled at the foot of one of Europe's largest glaciers. Upon closer examination, the large cluster is really a series of modern villages at altitudes from 5,000 to 6,900 feet. The main village, Tignes le Lac, lies at 6,825 feet. The highest village is Val Claret, and it is from here that the cable car leaves for La Grande Motte glacier. The other villages are Lavachet, Les Brévières and Les Boisses.

The big news in Tignes is the opening of a new funicular that links Val Claret with the Grande-Motte glacier. The new underground funicular will almost double the uphill capacity to the summit, carrying 3,000 skiers per hour. This reduces the time to the top of Le Grand Motte from 20 minutes to only six, and it will operate in all weather conditions.

The entire area is modern, built after the original village was flooded in the early 1950s by the lake created by the Chevril dam. Tignes is linked with Val d'Isère to form a massive ski area called "l'Espace Killy." The combined network features 300 kilometers of runs linked by 102 lifts, with continuous vertical drops of over 5,000 feet. Snow and skiing are a certainty 365 days a year.

The skiing at Tignes is fantastic. The resort rates as one of the best in the world for intermediate cruisers, experts, beginners, sun worshipers, people who don't like to ski the same trail twice, and people who travel with children. What more is there?

The lift system offers 24 different ways up, starting from different parts of town. You'll never have to walk very far to start skiing. The area peaks at the 11,995-foot La Grande Motte, site of year-round glacier skiing.

 ## Mountain layout

The ski area can be broken into five main sectors. If La Grande Motte is directly in front of you, La Tovière/Lavachet is on your left and the Palet/Aiguille Percée/Palafour areas rise on your right. A few lifts rise from the villages of Les Brévières and Les Boisses, 1,640 feet lower.

The skiing in La Tovière/Lavachet area is a steep 1,950-foot vertical drop back into town. There are some great off-trail runs over the back side of Lavachet into Val d'Isère, or around the cliffs back into Tignes.

At Le Grande Motte, skiing on the glacier is wide open and relatively mellow—this sector offers the only lower intermediate terrain. The run under the cable car is a good intermediate test of stamina, and experts can go off the trail over the Rochers de la Grande Balme into the Palet sector. Many skiers come to Tignes and never leave this section of the mountain since there is so much variety. On the expert slopes there is often avalanche danger, so check with guides.

The Palet/Aiguille Percée offers relatively mellow terrain under the Col du Palet, with relatively tough intermediate runs down from the Aiguille Percée. Experts have a wide swath of off-trail possibilities, as well as itineraries over the Col du Palet, or over the back side of Aiguille Percée down Vallon de la Sache to Les Brévières.

Mountain rating

It's easy to see why the area has been rated as tops in every category. Just the expanse of snow is mind-boggling. With a vertical drop of more than a mile and a third, coupled with 30,000 acres of terrain, there is something for everyone. Beginners and intermediates can cruise all over the upper reaches.

Experts can test themselves on extensive off-trail and powder skiing. It is best, at least for a day, to take a guide along who will show you the best places to test your skills. Before skiing off-piste, check with the ski school for the latest information on snow conditions.

 ## Ski school (97/98 prices)

The French Ski School in Tignes has 220 instructors who can teach any level of skier. English is spoken by many of the instructors, so mention that you'll need an English-speaking instructor when signing up.

Private lessons

A lesson (three skiers maximum) for one hour costs FFr180, half day is FFr620, and a full day FFr1,400.

The services of a certified guide for powder and off-piste for a group cost FFr1,400 per full day.

Group lessons

Three-hour courses are given mornings or afternoons. Five days or half-day lessons with video are FFr600 for adults and FFr530 for children 4–12. A week of full-day lessons costs FFr920 for adults and FFr870 for children.

The ski school has four offices:

In Tignes le Lac, call 479 06 30 28; in Val Claret, call 479 06 31 28; in Lavachet, call 479 06 39 73; and in Rond Point des Pistes call 479 06 56 08.

There are two other ski schools at the resort. **Evoultion 2** with offices in Le Lac, 479 06 43 78; Val Claret, 479 06 42 46; and Lavachet, 479 06 35 76. **Tignes Ski School International** is in Val Claret, 479 06 36 15.

Lift tickets (97/98 prices)

The prices below are for l'Espace Killy, which includes both Val d'Isère and Tignes areas. Children's prices are for five to twelve years, seniors prices for those over 60.

	Adults	Children	Seniors
half day (from 12:30)	FFr151	FFr112	FFr129
one day	FFr217	FFr158	FFr189
three days	FFr555	FFr395	FFr475
six days	FFr1,005	FFr705	FFr850
14 days	FFr1,890	FFr1,320	FFr1,605

Accommodations

A special low-season-only program has been organized by the tourist office and hoteliers. Low season normally runs from the end of September to Christmas week for most of January except New Year, and late April and May. Check with the office for exact dates.

The program cost is based on a two-star hotel with half board and type of package (with or without ski lessons) selected by the skier. To book, contact the Tourist Office Booking Service, 73320 Tignes, France; (479 06 35 60; fax 479 06 45 44). The office will send information. A 25 percent deposit reserves your space.

Ski D'Or (479 06 51 60) is one of the best four-star hotels in the Tignes/Val d'Isère area. Ask for Room 23 if it's available. Each of the rooms is tastefully and uniquely decorated, and the restaurant may be the best in the area.

The Curling (479 06 34 34) across the street from the Ski d'Or, is considered the next best, but is far behind its classier counterpart. Rooms are simple, and the hotel has all such amenities as telephone, TV and dryer. **The Alpaka** (479 06 32 58) a three-star hotel, is in Tignes Le Lac.

Of the two-stars, we recommend **Paquis** (479 06 37 33); **Aiguille Percée** (479 06 52 22); **Campanules** (479 06 34 36); **Gentiana** (479 06 52 46); and **Nevada** (479 06 50 33). Paquis and Campanules are the best for families.

For rock-bottom prices, try a hotel in the traditional village of Les Brévières, the **Relais du Lac** (479 06 40 03). It is very quiet and out of the way, but a gondola takes you to the middle of Tignes' lift system.

Ski Chalets: Crystal, Inghams/Bladon, Thomas Cook/Neilson (see page 27 for phone, fax and internet addresses).

Apartments

When you learn that Tignes has only 1,200 beds in hotels but almost 15,000 in apartments, you realize the importance of the rental system. The tourist office acts as a clearinghouse, providing a listing of rental apartments.

A typical sample of apartment rates, per week per apartment in Tignes, is provided below. The centrally located units are only about 100 meters from the lifts.

	high season	mid season
studio: two to four persons	FFr3,800	FFr2,150
four to five persons	FFr5,450	FFr3,600
six to seven persons	FFr9,310	FFr7,150

In many cases, linen is not included, but can be rented from the apartment owners or agencies. The normal linen fee is FFr100 a week per person.

Most agencies and individual owners offer apartments in a similar price range. Note the differences between high and mid seasons—even in high-season lodging costs will only be about $35 a day per person, based on four people sharing a two-bedroom apartment. Cable TV is available, with CNN, Sky Channel and the BBC.

Dining

There are 64 restaurants at the resort. The best in town are **l'Arbina** in Hotel Arbina (479 06 34 78) and **Le Clin d'Oeil** (479 06 59 10). Make reservations or get there early. As mentioned, the restaurant in the **Hotel Ski d'Or** (479 06 51 60) is exceptional and relatively expensive. The restaurant **Le Caveau** (479 06 52 32) in Val Claret is also excellent. There is a Japanese restaurant, **Myako** (479 06 34 79). For Savoyard decor and food try **Grattalu** in Val Claret (479 06 30 78).

In Tignes le Lac, try **La Troika** (479 06 30 24) and **L'Eterlou** (479 06 33 53). **Carlings,** is very English, in the Hotel Alpaka (479 06 32 58) or test the restaurant **Escale Blanche** (479 06 45 50).

Après-ski/nightlife

Nightlife can be found, but is not this resort's focus because most people are either "there to ski" or partying in their own apartments. Most English-speakers seem to hang out at the **American Bar**. But there are several other discos and pubs in town where true après-skiers gather. For discos try **Les Chandelles**—the most popular in town—in Val Claret, and **Playboy**, also in Val Claret. The **Bar Du Curling** is the upscale spot for a drink, and don't dream of showing up in your ski boots.

Xyphos, in Tignes Le Lac, is a disco and **Café de la Poste**, also in Tignes le Lac, is a nightclub open late. Key West also has après-ski from 5 to 8 p.m. then opens as a disco at 10 p.m. The **Embuscade Café**, with a gregarious owner, gets most of the locals' business. In Lavachet, try **The Snooker Bar** that runs snooker tournaments.

Child care

Les Marmottons, in Tignes le Lac (479 06 51 67), accepts kids 2½–10 years for one week, a day or a half day. Those over four are taught to ski. **Les Petits Lutins**, in Tignes-Le-Lac and Val Claret (479 06 51 27 or 479 06 37 90) is for children from three months to six years. It's open daily, 8:30 a.m.–5 p.m.

The ski school children's program (479 06 30 28 or 479 06 31 28) accepts those from 4 to 12 years. Packages cost FFr470 for six days of three-hour lessons.

Another children's course, **Stage Mini Champion**, teaches children technical skills and racing techniques.

Getting there

The closest international airports are Lyons (150 miles from the resort) and Geneva (about 86 miles) A smaller airport that offers some flights is Chambéry. A daily bus to Tignes from Geneva airport and weekend service from Lyons airport operate in winter.

TGV trains now run directly from Paris to Bourg-St. Maurice in 4 1/2 hours. A bus connection gets you to Tignes. A joint rail/bus ticket is available at the railway station or from travel agents.

If you drive, the best route from Geneva is autoroute A41 to Annecy and then N90 to Albertville. From there, follow signs to Bourg-St. Maurice and on to Tignes. From Lyons, take autoroute A43 to Albertville, then follow the signs to Moutiers, Bourg-St. Maurice, and on to Tignes.

Other activities

Hang-gliding lessons are offered for FFr450 a flight. Special scuba diving courses are conducted under the ice in the lake in March and April. Bowl at the highest bowling alley in Europe, with twelve lanes; FFr45 a game. Ice skating on the lake is on tap daily from 2 to 8 p.m.

The Lac du Tignes Sports Center (479 06 57 97) has weights, saunas, Jacuzzis, steam baths, squash and indoor golf simulation. There are two indoor tennis courts. There is also a fitness club in Val Claret (479 06 43 70) with more extensive body-building equipment; it's a bit more exclusive. Costs are FFr100 per activity.

Tourist information

Office du Tourisme, BP 51, 73321 Tignes Cedex, France (479 40 04 40; fax 479 06 45 44).

For hotel and apartment booking, call 479 40 03 03; address is the same as above.

Val d'Isère

Val d'Isère has long been one of the true European meccas of skiing. Although the professional ski world knew Val d'Isère, the average skier began to hear more about it after native Jean-Claude Killy won his Olympic gold in 1968. The town was also home to three other Olympic champions who won a total of nine gold medals.

The town lies at 6,012 feet and the ski area rises to 11,336 feet, with working verticals of more than 3,250 feet in all sectors of the resort. Skiers looking for the best on- and off-trail runs in the world need look no further.

Unlike many French purpose-built resorts, Val d'Isère is actually a town. Unfortunately, when it was initially being developed, architects opted for functionally square, flat-topped hotels. Recently, though, new buildings have been constructed in the Savoyard Alpine chalet style, and many of the unprepossessing buildings have been dressed up with facades to create more of a mountain atmosphere.

The ski area is linked with Tignes, creating "l'Espace Killy," with 186 miles of marked runs for every level of skier, tried-and-true off-piste itineraries for serious experts and 104 lifts, including an underground lift with an uphill capacity of more than 3,000 skiers per hour.

Mountain layout

An area as enormous as Val d'Isère/Tignes is virtually impossible to describe in words. Even the trail map, on a relatively small scale, gives no feel of the immensity of the area. Your first clue will be when you exit from the Funival or Bellevarde cable car and look out over the seemingly endless fields of snow.

The Val d'Isère share of l'Espace Killy is divided into four sectors corresponding with the three main ridges dropping into the town and the glacier area.

Le Fornet sector is reached by Le Fornet cable car, which rises the first 380 meters. From the top of the cable car, skiers can drop back down into the town on a steep and narrow expert run directly under the cables, or loop to their right around an advanced beginner trail. There are also two choices of lifts further up the mountain. The gondola leaving from the cable car building reaches the Col de l'Isèran area, which provides access to skiing on the Glacier de Pissaillas or allows skiers to take the connecting lift to the Solaise sector. The very long Signal drag lift will take you to just under the Signal peak, at 10,633 feet. From there you can take a tough intermediate trail back to the cable car or drop into the off-trail Le Vallon powder fields which then drop more than 3,000 feet back to the base of the Fornet cable car. This skiing is some of the most beautiful in the world.

The Solaise sector is also reached by cable car from the village center. This area is a wide-open beginner and intermediate paradise. About 1,500 vertical feet wait for open slope cruising. There are good off-piste itineraries from the Solaise that will keep any expert happy.

The Bellevarde sector has the best access, with three methods of getting to the top of Rocher de Bellevarde and two additional lifts serving intermediate and beginner runs from La Daille. The Funival, a high-speed subway, rises from La Daille through the rock to the top of Rocher de Bellevarde. Beginners have a series of runs at higher altitudes and a choice between two long runs with more than a 2,900-foot vertical back to La Daille. Intermediates have their choice of two more challenging drops back to La Daille. Intermediates can drop down La Face or into the valley back to the town. There are also excellent off-piste itineraries from the top of the Bellevarde sector. Take Le Kern around the front side of the rock cliff and drop through powder back into town, or take the drag lift to the side of the Charvet rock cluster and ski around the backside of the formation entering the valley, eventually returning to town, or drop down to La Daille off-piste.

Mountain rating

There is something for everyone; the upper reaches of the mountains are excellent for any skier level. Experts can test themselves on the steeps that sail into town, as well as extensive off-trail and powder-skiing pockets. It's a good idea to take a guide along, at least for a day, to find the best places to test your limits. Also, if you plan to ski off-trail, check with the ski school before you leave for the latest information on snow conditions.

Ski school (97/98 prices)

The Val d'Isère French Ski School boasts Jean-Claude Killy as its technical adviser. Its ski instructors are among the most qualified in the world: three former world champions and many members of the national ski team serve on the staff. In total, there are 250 instructors including 19 mountain guides who can teach any level of skier, from the basic beginner to the Olympic caliber racer. English is spoken by many of the instructors. (If required, ask for an English-speaking instructor.)

French Ski School (ESF) offices are in the Village Center (479 06 02 34) and in La Daille shopping center (479 06 09 99).

Private lessons

A lesson lasting an an hour and a half will cost FFr290. Private lessons are limited to five students. Instructors or guides can be hired during high season for the full day from 9:30 a.m. to 5 p.m. for FFr1,500 for up to four people and FFr1,700 for five to seven.

Morning lessons from 9:30 a.m. to 12:30 p.m. cost FFr920; afternoon lessons, 2 p.m. to 5 p.m., are FFr820.

Group lessons

February courses cost FFr1,070 for six full days of lessons, which run from 9:30 a.m. to 12:30 p.m. and from 2:30 p.m. to 5 p.m. and FFr159 for a single day.

A Grand Ski class that takes place every morning from 9 a.m.–1 p.m. allows you to ski in a group with an instructor on most of the off-trail itineraries. Six days will cost FFr1,530, and a single day will cost FFr308. This course is worth every franc.

On Tuesday and Thursday, area discovery groups are launched into the Espace Killy for FFr265 per person.

There are also powder skiing lessons for a six-day course and day trips to La Plagne, Les Arcs and La Rosière/La Thuile for expeditions.

There are several other ski schools and guide organizations in Val d'Isère. Instructors are bilingual speaking English and French. You can sign up with the English section of Snow Fun, the largest non-EFS school, at the Solaise Gallery (479 06 19 79). Altimanya Ski School specializes in moguls, Alpine Experience focus on off-piste powder instruction, Surf Rider Club is a snowboard school and Top Ski has instruction in extreme skiing.

Heliskiing is offered. The helicopter drops you into Italy for backcountry skiing. Call 479 06 04 53 for prices.

Europe is at the leading edge of snowboarding, which they call "le surf," as well as monoskiing. Check with the tourist office and the ski school for a half-dozen opportunities to learn or improve on technique.

 ## Lift tickets (97/98 prices)

These prices are for the entire l'Espace Killy, including the Val d'Isère/ Tignes area pass. There are reduced prices for children five to twelve and seniors over 60.

	Adults	Children	Seniors (60-69)	Seniors (70-74)
one day	FFr217	FFr158	FFr189	FFr109
three days	FFr555	FFr395	FFr475	FFr280
six days	FFr1,005	FFr705	FFr850	FFr505
seven days	FFr1,140	FFr805	FFr965	FFr570
14 days	FFr1,890	FFr1,320	FFr1,605	FFr945

Children under five ski free. A photo is needed for all tickets two days and over. The ticket is valid for one day of your stay on La Plagne and Les Arcs ski lifts. Six to 21 day tickets are also good for a day at Trois Vallées and a day at Valmorel.

All lift tickets are offered with insurance for an additional charge starting at FFr14 for a single-day adult and varying based on the length of your lift ticket and the age of the person buying the ticket.

Val d'Isère has created a loyalty club that provides any skier returning to the resort with a copy of their lift ticket from any of the last three seasons a 5 percent discount off high-season tickets and a 10 percent reduction from low-season tickets. Children will receive a 20 percent discount.

The lift company will refund part of your lift ticket price if extreme weather forces closure of the lifts when you have a three- to 15-day lift ticket. Apply to the ticket office for the prorated refund.

Accommodations

The tourist office and the hoteliers have organized special weekly discount programs organized for the blue and white periods. Costs for the program are based on the category of hotel chosen and the package being offered. Packages come in four categories, each with half board and breakfast-only options. There are also less exspensive packages with apartment accommodation which have no meals, a six-day lift ticket and no pool entrance.

Packages include seven nights accommodation with bath or shower, seven-day lift ticket and pool pass.

These prices are per person for Winter 1998 based on double occupancy with half board.

Blue zone periods are November 29–December 12, 1997, January 3–24 and April 18–May 4, 1998.

	Half board	B&B
★★★★ hotel	FFr5,645	FFr4,160
★★★ hotel	FFr4,665	FFr3,330
★★ package	FFr3,700	FFr2,735
★ package	FFr2,610	FFr1,940

White zone periods are January 24–February 7, March 21—April 4, and April 11–18, 1998.

	Half board	B&B
★★★★ hotel	FFr6,415	FFr4,930
★★★ hotel	FFr5,300	FFr3,965
★★ package	FFr4,150	FFr3,185
★ package	FFr2,965	FFr2,295

Guests on these programs may rent skis and boots for FFr490.

Hotel Grand Paradis (479 06 11 73) This three-star hotel enjoys perhaps the best location in the resort—downtown and just across the street from the lifts. The lobby has recently been redecorated in elegant dark wood, Tiffany lamps and mirrors. The hotel has underground parking.

Hotel Latitudes (479 06 18 88) This is a recent four-star built in the village center. The lobby and bar step up several levels. Rooms are very businesslike, with little of the Alpine charm the exterior of the hotel promises.

Val d'Isère (479 06 08 30) A four-star hotel built directly above the tourist office that is convenient and modern.

Hotel Christiania (479 06 08 25) Chalet-style, four-star hotel two minutes from the lifts and full of atmosphere. The suites available on the top floor are among the best in the resort, with beautiful bathrooms, antique country furniture and rough-hewn appointments.

Hotel Mercure (479 06 12 93) A three-star modern hotel in the center of the village that would be the perfect businessman's hotel—clean, convenient and efficient.

Hotel Savoyarde (479 06 01 55) This is our favorite hotel in Val d'Isère. This three-star is chalet-style and has a cozy sauna and an excellent restaurant. Its best feature is being in the center of town, only steps away from the lifts.

The Kandahar (479 06 02 39) This is a relatively new three-star lodge built over the now new Taverne d'Alsace.

Hotel Samovar (479 06 13 51) Another three-star oozing with charm, this hotel is out of the center of town at the base of the Funival and the other La Daille lifts. Its restaurant is consistently rated as one of the best in town by locals, but its best section remains reserved for hotel guests or outsiders who often wait two weeks for reservations. The rooms are weathered but comfortable. The owner says he wants to create the atmosphere of a chalet rather than a hotel. Room 10 is nice if you can get it. Breakfast is a sumptuous affair.

Hotel Sorbiers (479 06 23 77) This is a beautiful three-star hotel built in modern chalet style. The interiors are rich with golden wood and rooms are cozy. The hotel offers only B&B arrangements.

Hotel Altitude (479 06 12 55) This hotel has one of the coziest restaurants of any hotel in the village. The rooms have been recently renovated.

Chamois d'Or (479 06 00 44) This two-star hotel is filled with old Alpine charm. The restaurant has a giant fireplace. The rooms vary in size, but all have ample space. The hotel is only steps away from the cable cars up to the Solaise and the Bellevarde. If you want atmosphere, this is the place.

For a quiet change of pace outside of the town try **Le Chalet du Lac** (479 06 25 47), a new hotel alongside the lake a few kilometers outside of La Daille. This hotel offers, for those with a car, a position between Tignes and Val d'Isère.

The central reservations system is run by Val Hotel, which can make arrangements in any of these hotels unless noted otherwise. The agency will also provide more information on the packages. Contact: Val Hotel, BP 73, 73153 Val d'Isère Cedex, France; (479 06 18 90).

Ski Chalets: YSE, Crystal, Inghams/Bladon, Simply Ski, Chalet World (see page 27 for phone, fax and internet addresses).

Apartments

In the French apartment rental system, the tourist office acts as an information clearinghouse. It maintains an extensive list of individuals and agencies who will rent apartments in the resort area at extremely low rates.

In many cases, linen is not included but can be rented for the week from the apartment owners or agencies.

Val d'Isère now can combine apartments with hotel service. The most elegant of these new establishments are the **Les Domaines du Soleil** which has a swimming pool, and the **Residence Squaw Valley** right at the base of the lifts near the ski school. Two similar new apartment complexes are **Jardin Alpin** and **Eureka Val**. The **Alpina Lodge** also offers similar condominium arrangements with daily maid service. Apartment prices are FFr1,820–4,000 for a studio in mid January, and FFr2,800–6,100 for a two-room apartment during the same period. In late February and early March the rates jump to FFr2,900–4,500 for a studio sleeping two to four, and FFr6,090–8,300 for a two-room unit which will sleep five to six.

Normal apartment costs in Val d'Isère are provided below. Most units are only 100 meters from the lifts. The blue-zone prices will be FFr1,300–3,580 for a studio; and FFr2,340–4,800 for a two-room condo. In the white zone prices will be FFr1,770–4,250 for studios and FFr3,160–6,250 for two-room condos. In the red zone, (high season), prices are FFr2,425–5,980 for a studio and FFr4,400–8,110 for two-room condos.

Most agencies and individual owners offer apartments within similar price ranges.

Note the differences between various seasons or "zones." For more information and a complete list of rental apartments, write to the tourist office. It will send listings of both agencies and individual owners along with prices.

For apartment accommodation in the region contact **Val Location** (479 06 06 60, fax 479 41 45 59).

 ## Dining

Surprisingly, Val d'Isère has no nationally recognized restaurants. The smaller places that have traditionally offered the top meals are being pressed by the hotel dining rooms, which offer excellent meals at reasonable prices.

Le Grande Ourse (479 06 00 19) still reigns as the top restaurant in Val d'Isère after decades in that position. The interior is the most beautiful of any restaurant in the region. It's almost worth the price just to eat in such surroundings. Meals here are as gourmet as they get in Val d'Isère. Expect to pay FFr220–300 for meal with wine.

Hotel Savoyarde Restaurant (479 06 01 55) is consistently mentioned as the second-best eatery. The dining room has a beautiful wooden ceiling, a warm Savoyard atmosphere, and a menu that will allow you to walk out for FFr200–250, including wine.

The Hotel Bellier Restaurant (479 06 03 77) serves excellent fare. Menu prices are about FFr175 with wine. The dining room is an elegant and cozy Alpine spot. Reservations are recommended unless you're a hotel guest.

All three of the following restaurants are within a stone's throw of one another in La Daille, serving good meals in some of the resort's most rustic settings.

The Samovar (479 06 13 51) in La Daille serves wholesome meals. The real atmosphere is upstairs, where the hotel guests eat as well as those lucky enough to have reserved one of the two tables allotted to outsiders.

Crech'Ouna (479 06 07 40) also in La Daille, serves regional cuisine around a giant fireplace under massive beams and stone walls.

La Vieille Maison (479 06 11 76) also in La Daille serves Savoyard specialties with the atmosphere of a flickering fire, whitewashed walls and flagstone floors.

These restaurants serve up less costly meals:

Restaurant La Corniche (479 06 02 05) tucked between the old stone buildings of the old part of the village, is a new spot with an atmospheric dining room. Stone walls alternate with wood—this is how a modern Alpine restaurant should look. Expect to spend FFr100–120.

Restaurant Le Kern (479 06 06 06) is in a small two-star hotel and has genuine old Alpine charm. Meals are excellent and reasonable. Prices will be about FFr90–120.

Taverne d'Alsace (479 06 02 39) serves up German-Alsatian cuisine, including a potent onion cake, in a very cozy bar setting.

Restaurant Florence, across the street from the tourist office, is a good, inexpensive restaurant where you can get away for less than FFr100.

For pizza, try **Perdrix Blanche** and **Pacific Espace**. Cheese fondue (FFr78), fondue bourgogne (FFr120) and raclette (FFr70), are best sampled in **La Raclette** in Hotel Avancher (479 06 02 00) and **Restaurant Arolay** in Le Fornet (479 06 11 68).

On the slopes, try **La Folie Douce** and **La Fruitière** at La Daille midstation and **Bellevarde** at the top of the funival. Also try **Cabaret des Neiges** at the midstation at

Solaise; **La Datcha** at Solaise; **Les Tufs** at the base of La Daille.

You can be sure that locals will promote their favorites, so ask them for other recommendations.

Après-ski/nightlife

Val d'Isère has some of the best nightlife in France for Americans and British.

For après-ski head to **Moris Pub, Pavillon** or **G-Jay's** as well as **Dick's Tea Bar.** Check out the various happy hours 4–7 p.m.

For nightlife, **Dick's Tea Bar** is the main English-language hangout. Dick's Tea Bar also has good immediate après-ski with happy hour, videos and then jazz, before the disco scene cranks in. New bars in town are the **Café Face** in the Christiania Hotel and **St. Hubert Pub** under the St. Hubert Hotel. Avoid these places if you are searching for a quiet spot to talk. For real French discos, try **Club 21, Aventure** in the Sofitel and **Blue Night** in the basement of the Hotel Latitudes.

Perdrix Blanche is normally packed with a young crowd after skiing and **Taverne d'Alsace** offers a very rustic bar and quieter après-ski for a slightly older crowd.

Child care

There are many alternatives for child care in Val d'Isère. The hotels and the tourist office can put you in touch with private babysitting services (479 06 06 60).

Le Petit Poucet (479 06 13 97) and **Garderie Isabelle** (47941 12 82) are for children between three to ten. Costs are FFr220 a day and FFr1,185 for seven days. They open from 9 a.m. until 5:30 p.m. and Le Petit Poucet offers bus service that picks up the children. **Les Boutd'choux** (479 06 13 08) takes children from three months to 2 1/2 years.

The third facility is the French Ski School, which has an extensive children's program for kids from four years all the way up to twelve. There is the **Children's Corner** with 30 instructors and the **Snow Fun School Solaise** (479 06 11 79), which conducts a 30-hour program of English-language lessons. Other ski school opportunities are the **Eterlou Club** for more advanced child skiers. It costs FFr1,715 a week without meals. Call the ski school at 479 06 02 34 for more information.

Other activities

The town0 offers good, but limited activities for non-skiers. There is a covered, heated swimming pool open from 3 p.m. to 8 p.m., with a daily entrance fee of approximately FFr25 for adults and FFr18 for children (free to holders of seven-to15-day ski passes). Cards for ten entries are available.

Visitors interested in bubble-bath treatments, underwater seaweed massages, exercise rooms and regular massage can get the full treatment at Hotel Sofitel (479 06 08 30). A six-day relaxation package with massage, sauna, whirlpool and gymnastics costs FFr1,560. The six-day Fitness Cure costs FFr2,840. The Fitness Club offers health club facilities for FFr60 a visit. Call 479 41 13 51.

Paragliding courses are offered for FFr1,500 per day, including equipment and insurance. Flight with an instructor costs FFr350. Contact G.R. Sports: 479 06 11 37.

Viking Snowmobile offers night snowmobile rides on the Tovière plateau. Rides cost FFr300 per hour. Contact Viking Snowmobiles at 479 06 05 27.

Snowshoeing walks and lessons are organized by Pascal Bertres (479 41 10 01) for FFr120 per person.

A new late spring skiing spree will be organized for late April. Approximate rates with ski test, hotel, lifts and instructor is FFr4,280 in four-star hotel; FFr3,615 in three-star hotel; and FFr2,755 in two-star hotel.

Getting there

The closest airports are in Lyons and Geneva. Geneva is about 112 miles and Lyons is 137 miles from the resort. Rail transport via TGV is quick and easy from Paris to Bourg-St. Maurice, where a bus takes you on to Val d'Isère.

Driving from Geneva, take A41 to Annecy; then N90 to Albertville, where you follow the signs to Bourg-St. Maurice and on to Val d'Isère. From Lyons, take autoroute A43 to Albertville and on to Val d'Isère. Direct bus service leaves from Geneva airport three or four times a day, and there is weekend service from Lyon Airport to Val d'Isère.

Tourist information

For information, contact Office du Tourisme, BP 228, 73155 Val d'Isère, France; 479 06 06 60; fax 479 06 04 56.

For hotel accommodations, contact Val Hôtel, BP 73, 73150 Val d'Isère, France; 479 06 18 90; fax 479 06 11 88.

Garmisch-Partenkirchen
Germany

Garmisch-Partenkirchen, at the base of the Zugspitze, the country's highest mountain (9,721 feet), is less than an hour's drive from Munich. As Germany's best and most famous ski resort, combining the twin towns of Garmisch and Partenkirchen, it attracts an international group of ski enthusiasts and ranks as one of Europe's friendliest and best-organized, with activities for visitors of every age. When considered with the neighboring slopes in Mittenwald and across the border in Austria—on the other side of the Zugspitze—this is an excellent destination resort. The exchange rate for the Deutschmark when these prices were received was DM1.8 per US$1; DM2.9 for UK£1; and DM1.32 per Cdn$1 .

Mountain layout

Garmisch offers nearly 75 miles of runs, but the rugged Alpine landscape prevents any sort of continuous ski circuit between the seven different slopes. You ski in one of two large areas. One is on the high slopes of the Zugspitze plateau. You can get to the top by cable car from Lake Eibsee above Garmisch or from the Zugspitze cog train; the cable car is more scenic, the train more direct. Skiing here is at its best in early November and December, and in spring—April and May—when other resorts are closing. Best of the trails is the two-mile run from the Schneefernerkopf at 9,427 feet.

Garmisch hosted the Winter Olympic Games in 1936, and its facilities are well maintained. The World Cup runs on the Kreuzeck and the neighboring Hausberg provide several difficult turns, but overall it's perfect terrain for intermediates.

Our favorite runs are from the Osterfelderkopf. From here you can make the only real skiing circuit in Garmisch, linking up with lifts from the Hausberg below.

For Zugspitze fans there is a new double chair to the glacier at 9,186 feet. A tunnel from the cog railway eliminates walking and climbing, and allows direct access to the slopes. During the past years, the resort has established many new and more difficult trails on the Zugspits. According to locals, the plateau is now great for all levels of skiers rather than only intermediates and beginners as was the case several years ago.

One more suggestion: for another ski adventure and often shorter lift lines, take the border highway past Grainau into Austria. On the other side of the Zugspitze, less than a 30-minute drive away, you can try the slopes of Ehrwald: when Garmisch's weather is bad, the sun will sometimes be shining here. Neighboring Lermoos and Biberwier, in Austria, are popular with local skiers.

In the other direction, at Mittenwald, the Damkar run from the 7,822-foot Karwendel summit is challenging and the mountain panorama superb.

Mountain rating

Garmisch is intermediate country but with new trails is becomming a good spot for advanced and expert skiers. The challenging parts of red runs might be considered black in other areas, the Zugspitz has added advanced terrain and the difficult World Cup sections on the Kreuzeck and Hausberg provide upper-level skiers with a test.

The advanced beginner and intermediate will find it the place to be. Beginners could not come to a better place for outstanding ski instruction.

Garmisch has excellent cross-country trails. There are 45 miles of maintained trails in the area.

Ski school (97/98 prices)

Garmisch's ski school program includes off-trail touring instruction and an outstanding climbing school. Eight schools offer instruction in the area. Rates for the various schools are all within a few DM of each other.

Private lessons for one hour are DM70 (DM15 for extra person); for two hours, DM100; for one day, DM240 (four hours).

Group lessons for one day cost DM 60 (three hours); for three days, DM 150; for five days, DM 190.

All the following ski schools have good reputations, but their locations may play a role in your choice. The schools also offer cross-country instruction.

Skischule Sprenzel (1496) near Hausberg.

Skischule Garmisch-Partenkirchen (4931) At the Hausberg slope.

Skischule Wörndle (58300) At the Hausberg cable car station.

Olympia Skischule (4600) Near the Osterfelder.

Skischule Hohenleitner (50610) Near the Zugspitze railway station.

Skilanglaufschule (1516) Cross-country school at the Olympic stadium.

Bergsteigerschule Zugspitze (58999) Mountain climbing and ski touring instruction with skins and ice climbing.

Lift tickets (97/98 prices)

For years, the least attractive aspect of Garmisch skiing was the mishmash of tickets you needed to move around the area.

Now one ticket, called the Happy Card, is available—good for transport on all 101 lifts in the region, including the Zugspitze.

three days	DM141
four days	DM187
five days	DM226
six days	DM260
seven days	DM291

A day-ticket for the Wank area (W Tageskarte) costs about DM33; for the Eckbauer area (E Tageskarte), DM28.

If you want to ski the Zugspitze, you need the Z Tageskarte, which costs DM60 daily.

Accommodations

Fortunately, the lift-ticket confusion is not carried over into accommodations. You can quickly find a place to stay, anywhere from a farmhouse or an ultra-luxurious hotel.

The tourist office offers a series of inclusive one-week vacation plans that combine hotel, lifts and local transportation. Prices range from about DM540 for a room in a private home without private bath, to DM1,220 for lodging in a luxury hotel.

Hotel Sonnenbichel (7020; fax 702131) DM140–240 per person per night with half pension. This is considered the best hotel in town by many.

Best Western Hotel Obermühle (7040; fax 704112) DM150–190 per person per night with breakfast. It has what many visitors feel is the resort's best restaurant.

Hotel Boddenberg (93260; fax 932645) DM80–95 per person per night (B&B).

Alpen-Hotel Forsthaus Graseck (54006; fax 55700) DM90–145, half pension per person per night.

Aschenbrenner (58029; fax 4805) DM70–100, (B&B only).

Hotel Hilleprandt (2861; fax 745448) DM75-90, quiet, family-run hotel within walking distance of the Hausberg ski school. Lower priced rooms begin at approximately DM350 a week. A good choice for the budget plan.

Haus Tanner (54647) is run by a great family. They have wonderful rooms and speak excellent English.

Haus Schell (95750; fax 957540) DM40–80, B&B. No bath in rooms—go down the hall. Very close to the station.

Apartments

The popularity of apartments has increased in Garmisch in recent years and many hotels now offer them. The Garmisch tourist office provides an accommodations booklet, which not only lists available apartments but also includes pictures of some of them. Most interesting of those we saw were the apartments in the Husar section with furnished apartments for two to six people. Prices are approximately DM75–150 a day.

Child care

Larger hotels provide day care services. In addition, check with the tourist office for a listing of babysitters in the area. Ski kindergarten and ski courses for youths are available.

Ski kindergarten prices:
half day including lunch
 (9 a.m.-noon or 1 to 4:30 p.m.)   DM9
one day including lunch
 (9 a.m.-4:30 p.m.)   DM21

A five-day children's ski course with four hours of instruction daily, including lunch, is DM210.

Dining

The **Obermühle** in the hotel of the same name is where you'll be served excellent Bavarian specialties and suprisingly good fish. Another excellent Bavarian meal can be enjoyed at **Husar** (tel.1713). The **Post Hotel** in Parten-kirchen on Ludwigstrasse 49 also serves excellent fare.

You need walk only as far as yet *another* **Post Hotel** (7090) in Garmisch's Marienplatz for dining in the Poststüberl.

You can eat less expensively, surrounded by an international group at the **Chapeau Claque** bistro (71300). Other restaurants recommended by locals include:

Grand Café, (79699) with international cuisine, vegetarian menus and a quaint bar; **Café Max** (2535) with excellent German cooking as well as international dishes; **Mukkefuch Bistro** (73440) that serves wonderful salads, sandwiches on long bagettes and good pasta; **Werdenfelser Hof** (3621) has typical Bavarian food and oom-pah music; **Da Elia** (73740) serving creative Italian and French bistro foods; and **Bruno's Pizza Flizza** (1209) has affordable food mixed with great music during the friday night jam sessions, plus they deliver to the hotels.

We were partial to the bountiful, tasty dishes at another **Hotel Post** (08825-211) in Wallgau, about 12 miles from Garmisch. Traditional Alpine decor, massive wooden tables and chairs and extra-friendly service complement the food.

Après-ski/nightlife

Garmisch rocks when it comes to après-ski. Naturally you are in Bavaria, home of great beer and of knee slapping oom-pah-pah fun. For a basic Bavairan floor show try dinner at **Fraundorfer** in Partenkirchen (2176), or head to **Werdenfelser Hof** (3621).

Otherwise, après-ski means a trip to the **Irish Pub** at the corner of the Hauptstrasse and Bahnhofstrasse (78798) with a great international crowd and plenty of suds and singing. The **Rose'n Crown** at Zugspitz 70 (51282) has a British pub flavor with good pub grub. For a late-night spot to party with a good bar crowd and live music, duck into the Zirbelstuben at Promenade 2 (71671).

Other activities

After a hard day of skiing head for **TAO** at Mohrenplatz 7 (79547). TAO sells Aveda natural hair and body care products from America, Thursday Plantation Tee Tree products, and an eclectic selection of clothing, jewelry, gifts and music. It is run by an American and a Brit.

Within an hour's drive are world-famous attractions. Chief among them is Munich, the Bavarian capital. Above all, visit the Deutsches Museum, the German technical museum that rivals the Smithsonian. Central Munich, around the Marienplatz, should be included on any tour. Best view of the city is from the 1,000-foot television tower on the Olympic grounds.

Oberammergau, site of the famed Passion Play, is about a half hour away by bus or car. Visit dozens of woodcarving shops displaying the work of artisans, many of them trained in Oberammergau's woodcarving school.

Along the road to Oberammergau, take a trip up the Graswang valley to Schloss Linderhof, the ornate palace built by Ludwig II, the Mad King of Bavaria. Also consider a full-day trip to Neuschwanstein, the most famous of Ludwig's castles (near Füssen) and to Berchtesgaden.

Getting there

Munich's Airport II is only an hour away by car on the autobahn. Innsbruck is less than an hour's drive. Rail travelers will find connections to Garmisch from Munich excellent.

Tourist information

Verkehrsamt, Richard-Strauss-Platz, D-82467 Garmisch-Partenkirchen, Germany; (08821-1806; fax 180755).

☎ *Telephone prefix for Garmisch-Partenkirchen is 08821; for Germany the code is 0049.*

Italy

Italy, geographically, has more of the Alps than any other country. Mont Blanc, the highest mountain in Europe, straddles the French-Italian border, and the Matterhorn is right on Switzerland's border with Italy.

Italy also has the entire Dolomite range, which many consider the world's most spectacular. Italian ski areas here are world class, and the skiing is augmented by the Italian love of life and matchless cuisine and wines. If the weather changes, there is always a beautiful city such as Milan, Turin, Verona or Venice just a few hours away from the slopes.

This border region of Italy has distinct influences from both the French and the Germans. The cooking in the northwest has distinct French overtones and the wines of Piemonte are more like beefy French reds than the lighter Italian wines. In the far northeast, the Italian and German languages share the limelight—both are spoken with ease. The cuisine is a pleasant mixture of German and Italian taste as well. Here, the locals work with German efficiency and live life with Italian enthusiasm.

This is a land where the people go out to enjoy life as much as they can in the mountains. No one seems to take skiing seriously, even the Italian Olympic and World Cup champions. Relax. Enjoy long, long lunches. Or, if you aren't into massive midday meals use the time to ski—the slopes empty between 1 and 3 p.m.. Once you get into the Italian swing of skiing, you will have the time of your life. Remember, you can always squeeze that next run in tomorrow, or next year for that matter.

A note on prices

Most of these prices are for the 1996/97 or 1997/98 season. Since prices do change, they should be used as a guide only.

All prices are given in Italian lire (L.). The prices were assembled when the exchange rate was L.1,600 to US$1; L.2,880 to UK£; and L.1,288 to Cdn$1. Any adjustment to the exchange rate will be the biggest factor affecting prices.

When are the seasons?

Some Italian resorts have adopted a rather complicated series of mini-seasons. Basically, the high and low seasons remain, but are in some cases separated now by in-between seasons. If you follow these season breakouts for planning you will not go too far wrong:

High season: Christmas and New Year holidays, and all of February to mid-April.
Low season: January after New Year holidays.
Pre-season: 6 December to Christmas.

☎ **Telephone country code for Italy is 0039.**

Cervinia

Walt Disney's film "Three Men on the Mountain," about the dangerous climb of the Matterhorn, had an image of grandeur that characterizes the best of the Alps. It, along with many works in all media, added to the mystique of the Matterhorn and Zermatt, but there is another side to the mountain—the Italian side. Cervinia, Zermatt's Italian opposite number, is the prototype purpose-built resort in Europe. When Mussolini decreed that a ski resort should be developed where the town of Breuil stood, energetic Italians enthusiastically took up *Il Duce's* mandate. However, unlike other purpose-built resorts, which have a semblance of central architectural control, Cervinia is the child of a score of fathers. Its outward appearance shows the worst of the Italian square-apartment style, in haphazard combination with large stark circular and triangular objects.

Despite being ravaged by architects and developers in infancy, Cervinia manages to delight skiers year after year. The wide-open slopes, the reliable snow and the chance to ski Zermatt on the cheap bring Germans, British and Americans who zip across the slopes during the week until the weekend hordes from Milan and Turin arrive for their days in the snow.

One other important point to note is the quantum improvement of the lifts from the village to Testa Grigia. Once sone of the worst lifts in Europe, the old cable cars have been replaced by a sleek six- and twelve-person gondolas and a 140-person cable car.

Mountain layout

To the Italians the Matterhorn is *Il Cervino*, and the village at the base of the Italian side of the mountain is called Cervinia. Cervinia, without the old charm and beauty of Zermatt, nonetheless has hotel and lift prices about 30 percent lower. Its lift system has been connected with Val Tournenche, a nearby village, to provide more than 100 km. of prepared ski runs, served by seven cable cars, three gondolas, ten chair lifts and 17 surface lifts. The longest run covers more than 20 km.—from Plateau Rosa to Val Tournenche—with a vertical drop of

1,500 meters.

One problem affecting where to ski is the poor trail map. There are at least two or three versions circulating around the resort, but none is useful except very broadly. Don't expect to find well-marked trails either, but fortunately you can feel comfortable, thanks to relatively easy slopes and a focused effort required for access to anything difficult.

The descent to Zermatt starts from Plateau Rosa. Special lift tickets for use on the Swiss side should be purchased before you go up the mountain; otherwise, expect to pay double for the lifts back up the Swiss side. The Zermatt side has much steeper terrain and narrower trails. An expert can have a field day on the Swiss side, while the beginner and intermediate can find enough easy runs to make the trip enjoyable.

In the Cervinia area experts candrop from Plateau Rosa, or try out the lifts above the Cristallo Hotel for a few bumps. Cervinia is really paradise for beginner and lower intermediate skiers—the gentle, wide-open snow fields above Plan Maison build confidence.

Mountain rating

The Cervinia/Val Tournenche slopes support beginner and intermediate skills. Wide open and excellent for practice, they offer an adequate number of challenging steeps.

Expert skiers may enjoy several great days of cruising the wide slopes, but may also become bored. However, should a group of experts invest in the services of a ski instructor, they'll find the most challenging slopes Cervinia has to offer. Experts will also have a great time on the Zermatt side, and this is part of the allure of Cervinia as a resort: it lets you take advantage of the savings made possible by staying in Italy and skiing the wilder-and-woolier Swiss side.

Ski school

There are two excellent ski schools in Cervina (949034 or 948451). Make arrangements at any hotel reception desk, or visit one of the schools. Ask for an English-speaking instructor.

Private lessons cost L.50,000 an hour for one; L.53,000 for two persons; L.58,000 an hour for three, and L.64,000 for four.

Group lessons (include three hours a day of instruction with about six to 10 skiers per group). One day, L.58,000; six days, L.190,000.

An instructor for an entire day costs about L.225,000.

Lessons are available for cross-country, racing (six-day course), off-piste skiing and summer skiing.

Lift tickets (97/98 prices)

half day	L.39,000 (96/97)
one day	L.50,000 (96/97)
three days	L.132,000 (96/97)
six days	L.260,000
seven days	L.293,000
14 days	L.415,000

The supplement added to the Cervinia ski pass to ski in Zermatt costs L.40,000. If you do not have a Cervinia pass and want to ski to Zermatt you will have to pay L.60,000 for an international lift. If you want to try to ski all of Zermatt in a day, forget it. But realize that the supplementary ticket you buy in Cervinia is good only for Zermatt's Klein

Matterhorn. You may also want to strike out for Gornergrat or Sunnegga; if so, wait and buy a full-day lift ticket in Zermatt.

A Valle d'Aosta ski pass good for the entire region costs about L.136,000 for three days; L.255,000 for six days and L.288,000 for seven days.

Accommodations

These hotels and pensions have been visited by a *Ski Europe* representative and offer good value for the money. Prices are 1997 maximum prices per person and include half board in a double room with bath during low season (with the middle season—February and March— price fol- lowing in parentheses).

Hermitage (948998, fax 949032) L.200,000 (L.320,000). This beautiful hotel is the best choice in Cervinia. Everyone who stays here loves it. Make reservations early because it is very popular.

Cristallo (943411; fax 948377) L.160–185,000 (L.230–295,000). Up the hill from the main part of town. A hotel shuttlebus takes guests to town and to the lifts in the morning. Ski directly back to the hotel in the evening. This is a modern luxury hotel, comfortable but by no means cozy.

Europa (948660, fax 949650) L.80–140,000 (L.100–200,000). In the center of town, just a few minutes' walk from the lifts; clean and modern with parking.

Breithorn (949042, fax 948363) L.70–100,000 (L.70–125,000). Furnished in knotty pine, this hotel is about 200 meters from the lifts and has one of the better restaurants in town.

Bucaneve (949119, fax 948308) L.60–130,000 (L.110–230,000). Center-of-town location.

Excelsior Planet (949426, fax 948827) L.80–120,000 (L.100–165,000). Plain and with little atmosphere, this hotel is nonetheless modern and convenient to the slopes.

Lyskamm (949074; fax 948692) L.80–95,000 (L.105-130,000). Small; perhaps the closest to the skiing.

Mignon (949344, fax 949687) L.70–125,000 (L.110–170,000). Very small and cozy, just minutes from the lifts. Its rooms have recently been renovated and the restaurant has a good reputation.

Perruquet (949043; fax 940013) L.90–180,000. Bed & Breakfast only. In town center; clean and roomy.

Apartments

Cervina's stock of apartments are somewhat limited but often offer bargains. The rental agencies in town are Il Cervino, tel/fax 949510; La Maison de Vacances, tel/fax 948267; Nuova San Grata, 949442, fax 949644; and Valtur, 948381 or 949242, fax 949881 or 949732.

Dining

Cervinia's best and most typical restaurants, such as the **Cime Bianche** and **Les Clochards**, are on the slopes just outside town. Have your hotel call for a van or jeep to pick you up free of charge. Both these restaurants serve excellent food, so even if your hotel arrangement includes meals, make an effort to dine in one of the two at least once during your stay.

Try *bagna cauda*, vegetables covered with an anchovy sauce; *tomino*, a delicate riccota, normally covered with parsley or peppers; *bresaola*, smoked ham from the mountain regions; *lardo d'Arnaz*, a fatty bacon that has been cured in a secret mountain concoction.

Other recommended eateries: **Matterhorn, Serenella, Nuovo KL** and **Les Neiges d'Antan**, a bit out of town but with a menu well worth the taxi ride. **Copa Pan** was recommended by plenty of tourists but not by one Italian.

Après-ski/nightlife

Cervinia does not have a lot to choose from; however, there is a growing English-speaking clientele at the few spots in town.

The town has four discos—**The Chimera**, with a younger crowd, the **Etoile**, which attracts an older group, and the **Blow Up** and the **Cristallino**. The two most popular bars are the **Yeti** and the **Dragon Pub**. All the bars are within five minutes' walk of each other. There are a total of eight pubs with live music.

Child care

Babysitting services and special ski classes for children are available. Contact the tourist office (949136).

Getting there

You can drive here easily from either Geneva or Milan airport. From Geneva come through the Mont Blanc tunnel. From Milan and Turin, take the autostrada; the Cervinia exit is only 27 km. from the resort.

Buses make the trip between Aosta and Milan five times a day with a change in Chatillon. It is not a simple trip. For connections to Malpensa airport there is now a bus leaving at 7:15 a.m. and arriving at Malpensa at 10:30 a.m. The bus from Malpensa to Cervina leaves at 12:30 p.m. and arrives at 4:05 p.m.

Other activities

An Olympic-size pool in the Hotel Cristallo is open to the public.

Cervinia has a bobsled run, an ice-skating rink and bowling alleys.

Day trips can easily be made to Geneva, Lausanne, Milan or Turin.

The ski trip over the Alps to Zermatt is a must-do side trip.

Cervina also has night skiing open 24 hours a day.

During the last weekend in January, the Feast of Sant'Orso, one of the largest craft fairs in Italy, takes place in Aosta. Fantastic wood carvings and other crafts can be purchased at great savings.

During *Carnevale* the town of Ivrea is one of the wildest places in Italy. Costumed residents and a "Battle of the Oranges," in which a castle defended by bad guys is besieged by good guys hurling more than a ton of oranges, make for pre-Lenten fun.

Tourist information

In Cervinia: Via J.A. Carrel, 11021 Cervinia, Italy. 0166-949136 or 949086; fax 0166-949731.

☎ *Telephone prefix for Cervinia is 0166.*

MUSEO ALPINO

Courmayeur

At the Italian end of the Mont Blanc tunnel, Courmayeur enjoys one of the best European ski resort locations. Mont Blanc, the highest mountain in Europe, guarantees snow; the Alps here are among the most spectacular in the range; and Courmayeur lies at the junction of Switzerland, France and Italy. If a skier tires of skiing the Courmayeur slopes, Cervinia and La Thuile in Italy are within striking distance; Chamonix in France and Verbier in Switzerland can also be reached for a full day of skiing.

Courmayeur is a small picturesque Italian village with the ski area across the valley. The village provides a cozy atmosphere with a warren of narrow cobblestone streets, small bars and fabulous restaurants. For skiing, the slopes are reached by cable cars stretching across the valley, and the short return to town is by bus. During the past three years the resort has invested heavily in snowmaking to insure good snow conditions on the Val Veny side of the resort. But, its star quality is found in the restaurants, where Italians seem to spend far more time than on the slopes.

 ## Mountain layout

The major ski area is on the opposite side of the valley from Mont Blanc. This area is centered around the Plan Checrouit, a transfer point for the cable cars that carry skiers up to an area serviced by 26 lifts and covering terrain that will keep all skiers happy. Unfortunately, skiers will have to return to town via this cable car unless they loop around the back of the Cresta Arp to Zerotta and then down to take a shuttlebus. It's a hassle.

The highest lift arrives at Cresta Arp at 8,954 feet. However, the skiing from that point is for experts only, and at that only with guides. The highest skiable point for the run-of-the-mill skier is the Cresta Youla, at 8,528 feet. From here you can ski a good, tough, intermediate run, finishing at Zerotta at 4,940 feet. Another good off-piste adventures drop from Cresta d'Arp to Dolonne or Pré-St-Didier. Or those with a guide and return transportation can strike out down to La Balme and end up near La Thuile.

Otherwise expect to have a bland intermediate and beginner playground. Real beginners will be a bit cramped with limited facilities at Plan Checrouit. They may be happier at one of the other baby slopes in Val Veny or below at Dolonne.

The second major skiing area at Courmayeur is Mont Blanc itself. A cable car carries skiers in two stages to almost 11,000 feet. They can ski back down to Courmayeur over the mountain to Chamonix or take some time skiing on the glacier. This side of the mountain is connected to Chamonix by a cable car, which makes getting back to Courmayeur fast and easy. If for some reason a skier manages to arrive at Chamonix after the lifts have closed, it is relatively inexpensive to take a taxi through the tunnel back to Courmayeur. Normally there are others in the same situation: team up and save some francs.

Mountain rating

If you an absolute beginner this is probably a mountain you should avoid. Although there are some beginner areas, the terrain is steep enough to take the fun out of skiing if you are over your head. For the intermediate this is heaven. There are plenty of semi-steeps to make the intermediate feel like an expert and enough moguls to keep his head from swelling. The expert can find some challenging slopes off-piste. The ski instructors can take experts down slopes that will keep them coming back for more. Even the marked trails are good enough for a good day of cruising.

Lift tickets (97/98 prices)

	Low Season	High Season
half day	L. 27,000	L. 35,000
one day	L. 38,000	L. 50,000
three days	L. 123,000	L. 136,000
six days	L. 221,000	L. 255,000
seven days	L. 248,000	L. 291,000
14 days	L. 397,000	L. 491,000

Lift tickets valid for more than five days include one day of skiing in Cervinia and Chamonix, France.

Ski school (96/97 prices)

The ski school of Mont Blanc has over 100 instructors. Many speak English—be sure to ask for one who does. Lessons are given every day. These are high season prices.

Private lessons for one or two costs L.50,000 per hour and L.5,000 for each additional person.

Group lessons (three hours a day of instruction with about six to 10 skiers per group). Six days cost L.190,000.

A ski instructor for a day costs L. 340,000, and L. 30,000 per additional person.

Lessons are also available for cross-country, ski competition (six-day course), and off-piste skiing .

The ski school is on Strada Regionale, just up the hill from the Val Veny cable car.

Accommodations

The recommended hotels and apartments in Courmayeur are all close to the town center.

Hotel Pavilion (846120) The best in Courmayeur, with indoor pool, sauna, garage and TV. Only 100 yards to the lifts and ski school.

Hotel Les Jumeaux (846796) A first-category hotel, brand new and closest to the lifts. Sauna, TV and exercise room.

Hotel Palace Bron (846742)

Hotel Cresta Duc (842585)

Hotel Cristallo (846666)

Hotel Lo Scoiattalo (846721)

For Bed & Breakfast, try the **Bouton d'Or, Croux** or **Vittoria.**

Ski Chalets: Inghams/Bladon (go to page 27 for phone, fax and internet addresses).

Apartments

This is a relatively new development for Courmayeur. There is one very basic group of apartments in town—**Bon Souvenir** (8428800; fax 841390).

In St. Didier, **Residence Universo** (887066; fax 87087) features several types of rooms, including a studio for two or three people and two-room apartments for up to five. All are equipped with TV and complete kitchen equipment. A free shuttlebus takes guests to the lifts. **Checrouit** (844477; fax 842120) is a simple group of condos in the same town. In La Thuile head to Planibel (884541; fax 884535). This large apartment grouping sit at the base of its own ski area that connects to France.

Dining

This is a town dedicated to eating. On the slopes you can't go wrong at any one of 24 different restaurants. Even the self-service at Plan Checrouit is good, filling and cheap. The Christiania (843572) has wonderful fish high on the slopes and Chateau Branlant (846584) is worth the dining experience for only its tasty desserts. Dropping down into the Val Veny try to find La Grolla (869095) at Peindeint for an great (and expensive) meal.

Most of the hotel restaurants are good. If you want to get out and explore the local restaurants, follow the old rule: if it is crowded with locals, then it must be the place.

This a diner's delight. Try **Cadran Solaire** on the main street (844609). La Palud serves excellent fresh fish (89169) and Pierre Alexis (843517) on Via Marconi also has fine dining. Or try the very reasonable **Mont Fréty** at 21 Strada Regionale, just down from Hotel La Jumeaux (841786). The Mont Fréty food is every bit as good as the Cadran Solaire, and it may be the best place in Courmayeur to try regional specialties. **Pizzeria Tunnel** has great pizzas and is packed.

Outside of town Maison de Filippo (869797) in Entrèves, where for a fixed price you are served some 40 courses. The stream of food seems never to end, with servings of antipasti, pasta, sausages, contorni, salads, various meats, and baskets of nuts and breads. Another enjoyable restaurant, **Chalet Proment** (89947), is next to the cross-country area **La Val Ferret**, and known locally as **Da Floriano**. The owner prides himself on his local specialties of *boudin*—blood sausage with beets, fontina cheese, marinated smoked pork and excellent wines. **Le Petite Bouffe** meal includes entrace to Clochard disco.

The local red wines are excellent. Try *Donnaz*—a strong heavy dry wine; and *Enfer d'Arnier*—lighter and fruitier. A good grappa or *genepy* finishes off the meal in style.

Après-ski/nightlife

The English-speaking crowd hangs out in the **Bar Roma** on the main street, and a few can be found in the **American Bar** and the **Red Lion**. The main street is the best place to wander—keep an ear and eye alert for the signs of a good bar and go on in. The most popular discos are **Le Abatjour** and **The Tiger Club**, which also has a good restaurant. The **Clochard**, in Dolonne, is also an excellent disco.

Child care

Hours for the children's program are 9 a.m.–4 p.m. and children as young as six months are accepted. Those between six months and 2 years pay the hourly rate of L.18,000. Call 842477 for information.

The ski school runs an all-day ski course, which starts at 9 a.m. at the ski school and lasts until 4 p.m. The children's ski school cost for one day is L.60,000, for six consecutive days L.190,000.

A kindergarten offers a combination of day-care, lunch and ski school for five days costing L.390.000 and for six days at L.440.000.

Getting there

The closest airports are Geneva and Milan. Both are within a two-hour drive. Train and bus services connect Milan with Courmayeur, and there is bus service to Geneva. Car rentals are available at both airports.

Other activities

Geneva, Milan and Turin offer excellent sightseeing and museums. The Val d'Aosta is spectacular in itself and features one of the best collections of castles in Italy, as well as excellent Roman ruins in Aosta, the capital city.

On the last weekend in January the Feast of St. Orso is held in Aosta. It is one of the largest crafts fairs in Italy, with fantastic wood carvings and other handicrafts.

During *Carnevale*, the town of Ivrea is one of the wildest places to be in Italy. The residents are decked out in costumes reminiscent of "Star Wars." They participate in the Battle of the Oranges, which features a castle defended by the bad guys being assaulted by the good guys who hurl over a ton of oranges during the siege.

Courmayeur has grown dramatically in the past four years with new swimming pools, tennis courts, horseback riding, ice skating, hang gliding, dog sleds, squash, fitness club and more.

The valley has a casino in St. Vincent. Milan, in addition to its sights, features La Scala, the largest opera house in Italy and one of the best opera companies in the world.

Tourist information

For any additional information, contact: Tourist Office (Azienda di Promozone Turistica Monte Bianco) Piazzale Monte Bianco, 11013 Courmayeur, Italy; (0165) 842060 fax 842072.

☎ *Telephone prefix for Courmayeur is 0165.*

Cortina d'Ampezzo

Since hosting the 1956 Winter Olympics, Cortina's wide, sunny valley in the eastern Dolomites has been one of the world's top ritzy ski resorts, attracting celebrities of all types.

The town's picturesque square is framed by two massive mountain ridges: to the east lies the connected area formed by Cristallo (9,613 feet) and Faloria (7,690 feet); to the west, Tofana (9,317 feet) and Pocol and Socrepes (7,487 feet) form another connected area, accessible from the town. Further to the west, approaching the Falzarego Pass (6,906 feet), the areas of Cinque Torri (8,438 feet) and Lagazuoi (9,009 feet) beckon the adventurous skier.

These areas are loosely connected by a system of buses and taxis, none of which is very expensive.

Mountain layout

One approach to Cortina is to ski Faloria in the morning, then down to Tre Croci in the afternooon and take the lift up to Son Forca or Staunies for the rest of the day. Day Two could be spent at Tofana, or at Pocol and Socrepes. Day Three might be the Falzarego area, and subsequent days could be selected repeats. Also, because Cortina is interconnected by the Dolomiti Super Ski lift ticket, you might go down the opposite side of the Lagazuoi, skiing the Corvara area and returning to Cortina by taxi or bus at an extra charge. Whatever your choice, there is plenty of skiing.

Mountain rating

This area is an advanced intermediate's paradise. With the exception of just a few slopes, it is probably a bit too challenging for most beginners, and it will push most intermediates.

The intermediate will find Tofana, Faloria and Cinque Torri enjoyable areas. Beginners should stick to the Pocol-Socrepes area and the lower lifts on Cristallo, as well as several at Faloria. Experts will enjoy shooting down the Lagazuoi; the cable car ride to the peak is a thrill in itself. Other good expert areas are the Tofana and the last lifts of the Cristallo section. The off-trail skiing is exhilarating, although it should be done with a good guide or instructor along to get the most out of your day.

Ski school

Cortina has 250 instructors, and there are courses for all skill levels. The ski school is at Piazza San Francesco, 2 (2911 or 3495). Ask for an instructor who speaks English—they are at a premium. Low season for lessons is the January after the New Year holiday.

Private lessons

These cost L.62,000, with L.15,000 for each additional skier in the Christmas/New Year season, L.60,000, with L.14,000 for each additional skier in high season, and L.50,000 and L.10,000 for additional skiers during the low season in January.

Group lessons

Single morning lessons (9:30 a.m.–noon) cost L.55,000 in low season and L.60,000 in high season. Six consecutive days of mornings cost L.270,000 in high season and L.220,000 in January.

Lift tickets (97/98 prices)

Local area lift tickets can be purchased. However, the difference in price between these tickets and the Super Ski Dolomite pass is small (about 10 percent). The prices listed below are for the Super Ski Dolomite lift pass.

	Low Season	High Season
one day	L.50,000	L.58,000
two days	L.98,000	L.113,000
three days	L.142,000	L.162,000
six days	L.249,000	L.286,000
seven days	L.264,000	L.303,000
fourteen days	L.453,000	L.521,000

Note: Children and seniors get 11 to 30 percent discounts. Make sure you have proper identification and be sure to ask for the discount. Ski passes for eight days or more will require a photograph. Long lines are the norm for obtaining these passes on Saturday—it's quicker on Sunday afternoon and Monday morning.

Cortina-only passes cost about L.1,000 a day less.

Accommodations

Cortina is a mature resort. The quality of room size and furnishings can be uneven: when checking in, be sure you see the room before accepting it. If you already have a reservation, ask to see several rooms to choose from.

The hotels listed below are centrally located, offer good value, and have been visited by a Ski Europe representative. All rates are based on double occupancy. $$$ indicates luxury hotel with high-season prices over L.220,000 and low-season prices more than

L.160,000 per person for half-board. $$ notes hotels with with most high-season prices from L.,150,000 and low-season prices starting from L.120,000 per person for half-board. $ indicated hotels and pensions with high-season prices starting at less than L.150,000 and low-season prices leas than L.120,000 per person for half-board.

Hotel Miramonti (4201; fax 867019) $$$ The most luxurious and elegant hotel in Cortina, a bit out of the center of the town.

Hotel Ancora (3261; fax 3265) $$$-$$ Our favorite hotel in Cortina is directly on the central square. There are more luxurious hotels, but staying at the Ancora is an experience you will savor long after your vacation. Make sure to meet the proprietress, Signora Flavia, who speaks good English and will make sure your stay is memorable.

Europa (3221; fax 868204) $$$-$$ Good basic hotel in the center of town.

Hotel de la Poste (4271; fax 868435) $$$ Right in the middle of town with great food.

Parc Victoria (3246; fax 4734) $$$-$$ has wonderful antiques.

San Marco (866941; fax 866940) $$ An absolutely beautiful hotel that was recently restored with fantastic woodwork. Don't let the inexpensive price fool you.

Hotel Aquila (2618; fax 867315) $$ Still family-run, is great value for money.

Hotel Italia (5646; fax: 5757) $ This two-star serves hugh portions of well-prepared food.

Hotel Impero (4246; fax 4248) $ B & B only; some rooms have kitchenettes.

Apartments

There are beds for 18,000 visitors and a special rental apartment list. Prices for rooms are L.25,000 to L.35,000 per person in low season, L.40,000 to L.50,000 per person in high season. For more information, contact the tourist office.

Dining

The following restaurants, recommended by several local residents, have good food at relatively low prices—around L.20,000 in a pizzeria and about L.90,000 in the top restaurant, including house wine.

Tivoli Lacedel, 34; (866400). Overlooking Cortina, and rated as one of the best in town with prizewinning, home-made pasta. Call for reservations. Closed Monday.

The Petite Fleur (3261) in the basement of Hotel Ancora has wonder gourmete Italian fare in a small beautiful room.

Baita Fraina Fraina; Fraina,1; (3634). Closed Monday.

Lago Scin; At Lago Scin; (2391). Closed Wednesday.

Som dei Prade, Som dei Prade; (2540). Closed Tuesday.

Da Basilio, Grava di Sotto, 2; (867533). Closed Monday.

El Toula, Ronco 123; (3339). A once-upon-a-time hayloft converted to cozy restaurant. Closed Monday.

Ra Stua, Via Grohmann 2; (868341). Closed Wednesday.

El Zoco, Cadamai, 18; (860041) gets good reviews. Closed Monday.

For pizza try **Croda Caffé, Corso Italia, 163** (866589, closed Tuesday); or **Cinque Torre, Via Stazione, 3** (866301 closed Thursday).

Après-ski/nightlife

For all its jet-set reputation, Cortina is relatively quiet at night after the *passeggiata* where Italians dressed to the hilt in furs and the latest styles stroll to see and be seen.

An old wine bar, the **Enoteca,** is normally packed with merrymakers or head to Jerry's Wine Bar. Another later-night meeting point is the **Hyppo American Bar,** which fills up nightly with foreigners and ski school instructors.

Dinner and carousing in the basement of the **Hotel Ancora** when Signora Flavia is there, is always an experience in hospitality. The Hotel Savoia has the **Ballads Piano Bar.** In the Hotel Miramonte those seeking late night dancing can head to the **Tiger Club.**

The disco at the Europa hotel, **VIP Club,** seems to be the main action place. **Limbo, Metro Club** and the **Bilbo Club** are discos that mainly cater to a young crowd earlier in the evening and an older group later on. These discos are erratic as to clientele—it really depends on hitting them on the right night.

Child care

Child care in Cortina is not a school affair. There are scores of private babysitters and services available through the hotels or private homes where skiers stay. Child care services are relatively inexpensive, and children seem to get more than their share of affection from the Italians who take care of them. The ski school also runs a children's ski course for those old enough to begin skiing.

Getting there

We suggest going by car. The nearest airport is Venice (about a two-hour drive). The closest train station is in Calalzo, with a regular bus service to Cortina. Trains from Innsbruck and Munich arrive at Dobbiaco, a 50-minute bus ride from Cortina. A daily bus service also connects Cortina with Venice and takes about four hours. Check with your travel agent, because there are some packages that include meeting incoming skiers at Milan and Venice airports, and busing them directly to Cortina.

Other activities

Regular tours to Venice and other towns are scheduled most days. There is also excellent ice skating, bobsledding, horseback riding in the snow, curling championships, World Cup ski races, ice hockey, indoor tennis, and more. The tourist office publishes a list of activities, and the local paper, *Il Notiziario di Cortina*, provides daily activity summaries in Italian.

Tourist information

The main office is located on Piazzetta S. Francesco 8, 32043 Cortina d'Ampezzo, Italy. A second, smaller information office is on Piazza Roma. Call (0436) 3231 or 2711; fax (0436) 3235.

☎ *Telephone prefix for the Cortina area is 0436.*

Madonna di Campiglio

One of the jewels of the Brenta Dolomites in Trento is Madonna di Campiglio. This elegant resort is packed with hotels and situated at 5,085 feet amid beautiful, easy-to-ski terrain. Long before Madonna di Campiglio became famous as a winter playground, it was a favorite summer vacation spot of Austrian royalty, providing a stunning backdrop of mountain flowers and crystal-clear lakes.

This massif is typified by wild limestone rock formations and multicolored rocks that are as stark and beautiful during the winter as they are in the summer. The Val di Genova is one of the most beautiful in the region and is only minutes from Madonna di Campiglio. When the road is open, a trip up to the 300-foot-high Nardis waterfalls is worth the effort.

The Campo Carlo Magno gets its name from a reported visit from Charlemagne while he was Holy Roman Emperor. Today it is part of the extended lift ticket area. The Great Rock (*Pietra Grande*) is impressive.

 ## Mountain layout

One of the best parts of skiing here is that the majority of the folk here come to see and be seen rather than for all-out skiing. This translates into very few places where skiers will have to wait at lifts. In fact, even when the town seems packed, the slopes can seem deserted with a few slow-lift exceptions.

This is one of the best-groomed group of trails in Italy. Here the clientele demands pool-table smooth slopes that help them look beautiful when the slip down the trails.

The skiing areas surround the town. Start at one end of town and ski around the village—only a short walk is needed to complete the circle. Most of the hotels are at the base of the slopes, making them convenient both for lunch breaks and quitting time.

The immediate area is linked with two others, Folgarida and Marilleva. The area has 27 lifts and more than 90 km. of prepared runs. The Folgarida and Marilleva areas add another 24 lifts and 60 km. of prepared slopes.

The highest lift-accessible point is Groste at 8,235 feet.

Cross-country skiers will find this region a Mecca. Pinzolo is only about 20 minutes away, and the Campo Carlo Magno boasts one of the world's best expert cross-country courses.

Madonna has most of its slopes covered with snowmaking.

Mountain rating

The area is good for beginners and intermediates. There is a lot of mountain perfect for learning from top to bottom and intermediates will feel like experts. Let's call this ego-booting terrain for everyone. While the 3 Tre, Fortini and Spinale runs will give experts some good exercise, the area deserves an overall rating of Very Mellow. Experts ski off trail or go ski mountaineering, but there really isn't enough expert or advanced skiing to make a trip worthwhile.

Ski school (97/98 prices)

Individual lessons (per hour)

one person	L.53,000
two persons	L.62,000
three persons	L.72,000
four persons	L.88,000
five persons	L.100,000

Check with your hotel for recommendations of the best English-speaking instructors. There are a total of 150 instructors.

Group lessons are given two hours each day for six days for L.168,000 for up to eight persons.

Children's lessons are given three hours each day for six days. Maximum of ten per group. Cost: L.234,000

Lift tickets (97/98 prices)

The Madonna high-season lift pass prices follow. Low-season prices are approximately 10 percent less.

	Adults	Children/Seniors
one day	L.50,000	L.46.000
three days	L.146.000	L.135.000
six days	L.250,000	L.230.000
seven days	L.270,000	L.245.000

Note: Tickets over three days require a photo. Children are those born after January 1, 1989. Seniors are those born before January 1, 1937.

The Skirama Pass includes skiing in Folgarida and Marilleva. It costs L.54,000 a day, L.300.000 for six days, and L.310,000 for seven days. A tour pass is also available allowing limited use of Folgarida and Marilleva plus Pinzolo lifts for several days as well.

Accommodations

Madonna's hotels are for the most part modern. Hotels listed here were visited by a *Ski Europe* representative. Prices listed below are ap-proximate for seven days' stay in low season, with full pension (break-fast, lunch and dinner). High-season prices are given in parentheses.

Hotel Des Alpes (440000) L.1,901,000 (L.2,148,000). The best hotel, built around the former hunting lodge of the Austrian emperors.

Hotel Golf (441003) L.1,285,000 (L.1,680,000). Elegant hotel with all amenities.

Hotel C. Magno (441010) L.840,000 (L.1,190,000).

Hotel Cristallo (441132) L.1,050,000 (L.1,428,000).

Miramonti (441021) L.1,050,000 (L.1,400,000).

Hotel Palu (441695) L.700,000 (L.1,050,000). Half-pension.
Madonna's best value; a beautiful hotel.

Majestic (441080) L.815,000 (L.1,050,000).

Touring (441051) L.700,000 (L.931,000).

Ariston (441070) L.686,000 (L.980,000).

Gianna (441106) L.665,000 (L.875,000).

Ski Chalets: Crystal (see page 27 for addresses, phone and fax).

Apartments

Residence Roch (440100; fax 440409) has apartments for three, four or five people. In low season, expect to pay approximately L.250,000 a week per person; in high season, L.490,000. The price includes daily maid service (except kitchen cleanup). Garage space rents for L.50,000. Both sauna and solarium are available.

The tourist board can provide additional listings of apartments in the same range. There are five other flat rental agents in Madonna.

Dining

Madonna di Campiglio isn't up to par with resorts such as Courmayeur when it comes to on mountain dining. The refugi serve good risotto and meat you can grill on hot rocks, but don't have a gourmet flair.

With that said, one of the best experiences at this resort is taking a snowcat ride for a dinner up on the mountain at Malga Montagnoli (443355) or Boch (440465). Another good spot for this mountain dining experience is Cascina Zeledria (440303).

Down in the town recommended restaurants are: **Artini** (440122) with perhaps the best cusine in the village. **Belvedere** (440396) and **Pappagallo** (442717) both also have good food. **Golden River** (441270) serves an Italian version of Tex-Mex. Two good pizzerias are **Le Roi** (443075) and **Antoco Focolare** (441686).

Après-ski/nightlife

This town is very Italian in terms of après-ski—excentric and vary late. It all starts with the see and be seen scene at Bar Suise of Josef's Stube.

The **Grand Hotel Des Alpes** has a pricey disco, as well as a very cozy piano bar where you can nurse a drink for as long as you want. Evening cabarets are presented in the restored Hapsburg ballroom. Less refined and more of a blast is the **Stork Club** with a full-blown disco down below which is packed with jail bait (even in Italy). You'll find many English and Scandinavians here. The **Zangola** with male strippers and dancing babes all in a restored cow-bar atmosphere is legendary in Italy.

Child care

There are children's ski classes. The ski school office has details.

Getting there

By car

Madonna di Campiglio is two hours north of Verona. The closest airports are in Milan, Verona and Venice. All have rental car services. From Milan take the Brescia exit and follow the signs for Lago Idro, Tione, and Campiglio.

By train

Go to Trento and transfer to a bus (about 50 yards from the Trento station), which runs on a regular schedule.

Other activities

For ice skating call 440707.

Once you are in Madonna, it is not an easy task to get out of the region—the drive to the autostrada is torturous at best. But if you insist on breaking away, you can get to Venice in about three-and-one-half hours. Verona, with its giant Roman amphitheater and Romeo and Juliet balcony, is about two hours away. Vicenza with the wonderful Paladian villas is also about two hours away.

During the drive to Madonna, enjoy the multitude of castles that dot the Trentino countryside. The town of Trento has the Castello del Buon Consiglia (Castle of Good Counsel) that used to be home to prince-bishops. Today it is the Privincial Art Museum. The Cathedral towers over a cobbled square and the Via Belenzani is lined with Venetian-styled palaces.

There is an organized cultural tour. Call 801166 for details.

During *Carnevale* just before Lent, Madonna di Campiglio hosts many costume balls and special events.

Tourist information

The tourist information office, or *Azienda di Promozione Turistica*, in Madonna di Campiglio is located in the center of the resort in the Centro Rainalter. Its staff is well organized with information. Reservations for you at local hotels can be made through Campiglio Holiday Travel Agency, 38084 Madonna di Campiglio (TN), Italy; (0465) 442222.

Tourist Office, Centro Rainalter, 38084 Madonna di Campiglio (TN), Italy; (0465) 442000, fax (0465) 440404.

☎*Telephone prefix for Madonna di Campiglio is 0465.*

Val Gardena

While a trip through the spectacular Italian Dolomite mountain range is worthwhile in itself, when combined with the experience of skiing one of the largest interconnected lift systems in the world, a vacation in the Dolomites rates as tops. The natural panoramas found in the Dolomites around virtually every bend in the roads and ski trails are hard to properly describe. And Val Gardena, with some of the best prices in Europe, is hard to beat.

The Ladin culture is centered in the four main Dolomite valleys, in eastern Switzerland and in Italy's far northeast. Val Gardena is a stronghold of the culture, and its residents speak Ladin, a Latin derivative, as their first language. They also speak German and Italian.

As well as speaking Italian and Ladin, the residents of this region speak German as readily as they speak Italian. The people of this region have a Germanic passion for detail and hard work, so everything works perfectly; and they also have the Italian love of life, so they play as hard as anyone in the world enjoying great music and food. The cooking is a wonderful marriage of Italian creativity with pastas and wines and German meat and potatoes.

The Gardena valley has three main villages. The first and largest, coming from Bolzano, is Ortisei. The second is St. Christina, and the third, just at the start of the Gardena Pass, is Selva Gardena. St. Christina is spread out along the highway and does not have much of a town center to congregate in after skiing, so book your accommodations in Ortisei or Selva Gardena if après-ski is a priority. Ortisei, further away from the interconnected ski areas, has a more active nightlife. Selva Gardena, smaller and closer to the other Dolomite slopes, is quiet but you can still have a good time. They report that nightlife is improving. The atmosphere in the entire valley is more German than Italian, with a beer-hall flavor.

Whichever resort you choose you will have a great vacation and you will have the opportunity to move easily between the towns on a shuttle service which links Ortisei, Selva Gardena and St. Christina.

Mountain layout

The interconnected Super Ski Dolomite lift system, with 464 lifts, reaches more than 1,180 km. of prepared slopes, and hundreds of kilometers of off-piste skiing through rocky crags and spectacular mountain scenery.

Seceda, directly above Ortsei, is the highest elevation on the lift system in the Gardenaregion at 7,740 feet.

Perhaps the biggest draw for the region, besides the panoramic views, is the Sella Ronda, a 26-km. section of interconnected runs with 20 km. of lifts, allowing you to ski around the Sella mountain group. This full-day expedition involves visiting eight different ski areas. The runs are well marked and the Sella Ronda can be skied either clockwise or counterclockwise. Any reasonably competent skier can complete the basic circuit. Better skiers will find many opportunities for adventurous detours.

The major requirement for doing the entire Sella Ronda in one day is stamina. Intermediates should allow about 5 1/2 to 6 1/2 hours of skiing time, starting early enough to get back over the last passes before the lifts close from 4–5 p.m. If you are planning to do the Sella Ronda the best day according to locals is Saturday, when most vacationers are either leaving of arriving.

Cross-country skiers will find a paradise up on the Alpe di Siusi, one of Europe's highest Alpine meadows with an altitude ranging 6,500–7,150 feet.

Mountain rating

Judged solely on the extensiveness of its skiing opportunities, this area might be considered one of the best. However, expert skiers will have to go off-piste for real excitement. While there are some hair-raising runs above Arabba, Selva Gardena and St. Christina, experts in search of off-trail action should hire the services of a good guide. Try the Langkofel or the Passo Pordoi at your own risk. If you decide to go without a guide, be sure to check in with the ski school for a word about your proposed route, snow conditions and avalanche warnings.

The intermediate and the beginner will find ample suitable terrain—when skiers tire of one area, they can just head over to another for variety. The Alpi di Siusi above Ortisei is a beginner's paradise.

Ski school

The Ortisei Ski School (706153) is in the public swimming pool building. St. Cristina (795156) and Selva Gardena (796153) also have ski schools, bringing the number of instructors in the valley to over 200.

Prices are relatively uniform throughout the valley. Most ski instructors speak a little English, but make sure to ask for an English-language instructor.

High-season prices may be a bit higher as well.

Private lessons (per hour)

one person	L.55,000
two persons	L.65,000
three persons	L.75,000

Group lessons

six days	L.230,000
five of six days	L.215,000

Children's Ski School

half-day	L.40,000
full day including lunch	L.50,000
five full days with lunch	L.210,000

Lift tickets (97/98 prices)

Local area lift tickets can be purchased. However, the difference in price between these tickets and the Super Ski Dolomite pass is small (about 10 percent). The prices listed below are for the Super Ski Dolomite lift pass.

	Low Season	High Season
one day	L.50,000	L.58,000
two days	L.98,000	L.113,000
three days	L.142,000	L.162,000
six days	L.249,000	L.286,000
seven days	L.264,000	L.303,000
fourteen days	L.453,000	L.521,000

Note: Children and seniors get 11 to 30 percent discounts. Make sure you have proper identification and be sure to ask for the discount. Ski passes for eight days or more will require a photograph. Long lines are the norm for obtaining these passes on Saturday— it's quicker on Sunday afternoon and Monday morning.

Accommodations

The following hotels and pensions come recommended by locals who have also traveled extensively in the United States. They are listed in descending order of luxury. Prices are per person daily, half pension (breakfast, with either lunch or dinner) with bath (confirm when making reservations). Low-season prices are noted first, high season in parentheses. The prices do not include lift tickets.

Aquila-Adler (tel. 796203) L.130,000 (L. 280,000). One of the best, in the center of town.

Grien (tel. 796340) L.102,000 (L.280,000).

Hell (tel. 796785) L.120,000 (L.200,000). Via Promenada.

Cavallino Bianco (tel. 796392) L.120,000 (L.260,000). Via Rezia. Right in the middle of town.

La Perla (tel. 796421) L.95,000 (L.170,000) Via Digon. Our favorite in the area. Beautiful; a bit out of town, but there's bus service to the lifts and a pool.

Gardena (tel. 796315) L.100,000 (L.230,000). Via Vidalong.

Cosmea (tel. 796464) L.70,000 (L.150,000). Via Setil.

In Selva Gardena, try the **Antares**, **Gran Baita**, and **Aritz** which are among the best. **Des Alpes** is a bit less expensive. For an inexpensive B&B try the Eden and Somont.

Ski Chalets: Crystal (see page 27 for phone, fax and internet addresses).

Apartments

The tourist office has an extensive listing of vacation apartments that can be rented for a minimum of one week.

General descriptions included in its brochure indicate TV, garage, balcony, etc. The apartments all have fully furnished kitchens, but not all provide bedding, which may entail a small extra cost. Prices listed below vary according to the level of furnishing and apartment location (Christmas-New Year's rates are higher and require a minimum two-week stay):

two beds	L.300,000–1,300,000
four beds	L.400,000–2,000,000
six beds	L.600,000–2,100,000

Private rooms

A great chance to save money and get to know the natives awaits skiers who speak either German or Italian. Rooms rented in private homes include breakfast. Once again, the prices vary depending on the room. The price ranges for a room with bath (per person, per day) are:

Low season	L.30,000–40,000
High season	L.35,000–60,000

Dining

For an authentic Ladin meal, head off to the **Stua Catores** on Sacunstrasse 47. The food is hearty and the atmosphere rustic and unpretentious. Don't be afraid to ask among the restaurant patrons for someone who speaks English and can help you with the menu selection. Another typical Ladin restaurant is **Stua Zirm** on Stafanstrasse 123.

Some of our suggestions are *crafuncins*, a type of ravioli; *panicia*, a barley soup with a kid of bacon; *jufa*, a puréed version of polenta; *patac cun craut*, potatoes and sauerkraut; anes enzucredes, pancakes with anis and sugar; *ribl da furmenton*, a buckwheat pancake; *bales da furmenton*, a buckwheat dumpling; and *crafons* for desert.

Other recommended restaurants:

Concordia Romstrasse 41 (tel.796276).

Waldrand Furdenanstrasse 9 (tel. 796385).

Hotel Tyrol in Selva has won prizes for their local fare (tel. 795040)

Hotel Adler Stuben Reziastrasse (tel. 796203).

Hotel Gardena Vidalongstrasse (tel. 796315).

Sarteur (for great pizza), Bahnhofstrasse 60 (tel.797663).

Mar Dolomit has local and traditional Italian specialties with an open wood-fired pizza oven in Ortisei (tel. 7973 52).

In Selva head to **Sal Fëur** for Pizza (tel. 794276).

Bargain meals can be found at the self-service **Dopolavoro FF.SS** in Selva at 46 Plan (tel. 795165).

Après-ski/nightlife

Nightlife in Val Gardena is rather tame, but there is a collection of good bars with some local music, and several small discos crank up late at night. In Ortesei try the **L'Igloo** next to the ski school for immediate après-ski. **Purger's Pub** and **Siglu Bar in the Hotel Adler** often have an early crowd as well. Later head to the **Old England Pub, Mauriz** and **Cianél**.

In S. Cristina try Sa Doss and L Tublà which start cranking about when the lifts close. Sa Doss has live music. Yeti's Ombrella Bar is also popular.

The Selva crowds can head to their version of the **Igloo**, to **Laurinkeller, Luislkeller** and the **Speckkeller**. Later bars are Dali, **La Bula** and **La Stua**.

Child care

The ski schools accept children from the age of 4 and offer a course that runs 9:30 a.m.–4 p.m. with midday supervision. Prices are slightly lower than those for adults. Register at the ski school office.

A ski kindergarten is available both for children who want to ski and for those who are not interested in skiing.

Getting there

The closest airports are in Verona (about three hours' drive), Milan (about four hours' drive) and Munich (about three to four hours' drive). Major rental car companies have offices at the airports.

Trains come to Bolzano and Bressanone, connected to Val Gardena by five buses daily. A taxi to Val Gardena from Bolzano costs a maximum of about L.120,000 but may be less with negotiating.

Other activities

Val Gardena is a woodcarving capital with thousands of artisans. Browse through the stores for earvings of everything from figurines to bowls and utensils.

The music society schedules concerts in the winter.

Horse-drawn sleigh rides glide on the Alpe di Siusi.

There is a swimming pool, a new public sauna and steam bath in Ortisei. Covered tennis courts and ice skating are found in Ortisei and Selva Gardena.

The tourist office or your hotel will provide a free schedule of events, including folk nights, band concerts, film evenings, ice hockey games and toboggan races.

Tourist information

Ortisei/St. Ulrich

Tourist Information Office, Reziastrasse 1, 39046 Ortisei/St. Ulrich,; tel. (0471) 796328, fax (0471) 796749.

S. Cristina

Tourist Information Office, Chemunstrasse 9, 39047 S. Cristina,; tel. (0471) 793046, fax (0471) 793198.

Selva Gardena

Tourist Information Office, Mëiseles 213, 39048 Selva Gardena,; tel. (0471) 705122, fax (0471) 794245.

Internet: www.DolomitiSuperski.com/gardena

E-mail: gardena@DolomitiSuperski.com

☎ *Telephone prefix for Val Gardena is 0471.*

Switzerland

For many, Switzerland *is* the Alps—Switzerland *is* skiing in Europe. Of course, only part of the Alps is in Switzerland and Europe has other places to ski, but as the heart of the Alps and the home of Alpine skiing, Switzerland deserves all its superlatives. Its skiing is excellent, its resorts efficient, its tourist offices well organized, its lift systems well run and its hotels exceptional.

A note on prices

Most of the prices listed are valid for the 1997/98 winter season. Prices given here were researched carefully, but they change, so use them as a guide only. Ask for the latest prices before making any arrangements.

All prices are given in Swiss francs (SFr). When they were received, the exchange rate was approximately SFr1.50 to US$1; SFr2.4 to UK£1; and SFr1.1 per Cdn$1. Any subsequent change in the rate will probably be the biggest factor affecting prices.

When is high season?

High Season: Christmas and New Year holidays and all of February through mid-April.

Low Season: January after New Year and late April.

Pre-season: December 6 to Christmas holidays

Switzerland's romantic mountain railways

The visitor whose timetable is not completely filled with skiing adventures can take a scenic ride on one of the most advanced mountain railway systems in the world. The regional Swiss railroad lines and the postbus have organized three spectacular Alpine routes.

The Glacier Express: Perhaps the most famous of the Swiss rail trips, this is advertised as the world's slowest train. Indeed the trip, some 90 miles as the crow flies, lasts seven and a half hours—spanning more than 291 bridges and burrowing through 91 tunnels—on its way from St. Moritz in Switzerland's southeast corner to Zermatt.

Trains run in both directions, leaving in the early morning and arriving in late afternoon. In their elegant dining cars a complete three-course lunch is served on the Chur-to-Andermatt leg. The meal costs approximately $27, excluding beverages, and reservations are required. (Your wine glass on the Glacier Express has a tilted base to keep the wine from spilling on the route's many steep turns and gradients—turn it now and then to keep it tilted in the right direction.)

Bernina Express: The Bernina Express, which crosses into Italy over the Alps in Switzerland's southeast corner, is Europe's highest transalpine railway. The train trip follows the same route as the Glacier Express from Chur to St. Moritz, then strikes southward for the Bernina Pass, Poschiavo and on to Tirano in Italy.

Along one eight-mile stretch the track passes through two straight tunnels, negotiates five corkscrew tunnels, and crosses eight viaducts. The train crosses the Bernina Pass at 7,405 feet, climbing the steepest gradient of any non-cogwheel train in the world.

The Engadin Express: This train and postbus route connects St. Moritz with Innsbruck, Salzburg and Vienna. The trip from St. Moritz to Landeck, done mostly by post-bus, lasts almost three hours and is generally felt to be one of Europe's most romantic trips.

After leaving St. Moritz, the train chuffs alongside a beautiful Swiss national park, through the village of Scuol; then the post bus takes travelers past the famous castle of Tarasp and on to Vulpera. This is the home of the fourth language of Switzerland, Ladin. The express ends in Landeck, Austria, in the Tyrol district.

Making reservations: These train trips can be booked in the United States through the Swiss National Tourist Office (tel. (800) 223-0048; in New York (212) 757-5944); in Britain through the Swiss National Tourist Office (tel. (01) 734-1921); in St. Moritz at the Rhaetic Railway station; in Chur at the main train station; and in Zermatt at Zermatt-Tours.

The Swiss ski experience

The Swiss consider skiing more as an enjoyable cultural endeavor rather than a competitive race to measure vertical feet achieved in any certain day. They are fascinated and a bit amused by the high-tech watches that measure vertical feet skied worn by many aggressive North American skiers. The Swiss tend to measure skiing in terms of restaurants and chaise lounges, not numbers of fast runs.

Being in the mountains on vacation means enjoyment to these hard-working Swiss. They work hard and they take advantage of the sunshine and low-keyed atmosphere in the mountains to really give themselves a break.

The Swiss take advantage of sunshine by renting lounges on the mountain and enjoying the slow pace of a long, leisurely lunch. Lunch is their main daily meal and it is traditionally large and takes up to a couple of hours to consume. It might include numerous courses, beer, schnapps and coffees. They then take off to ski through the afternoon finally stopping on the trail back to the village for a late coffee and schnapps at one of the many private bistros and restaurants along the trail.

After skiing you won't fine wild exhuberance in the bars. The Swiss take their après-ski with restraint. Not that there's nothing going on, but the Austrian-style tea party drinking and dancing will be hard to find.

Swiss fondue and raclette

Fondue and raclette are cultural customs with an economic base. One of the Swiss mainstays is dairy farming and this country is home to some of the best cheeses that can be found. There are more than a hundred different types of cheese.

Here in Switzerland, fondue and raclette is more than just a meal. It is part adventure and part ritual. This is a quick meal that can be enjoyed by large groups of singing tourists or intimately by candlelight.

Raclette spread from the Valais canton of Switzerland and now can be found throughout the country. With raclette cheese is melted in front of an open fire or under a broiler and then scraped off the wheel onto a plate. It is then served with potatoes and pickled onions and eaten immediately before the cheese sets.

Cheese fondue can be considered by many to be the national dish of Switzerland. Emmentaler and Gruyère cheeses are melted in a big pot and combined with wine and various seasonings. Then hard-crust mountain bread is cut into squares and dunked into the melted cheese.

Two other fondues without a cheese base are relatively widespread and very popular. Fondue bourguignon is made with meat and vegetables which are speared on fondue forks and then cooked in oil at the table and served with various toppings. Fondue chinoise is created from thinly sliced beef that is cooked in a broth then dipped in Oriental sauces.

The wine of choice, and normally the most affordable on the menu is Fendant a local light white wine. Trust us. It seems to go with everything. It is the wine to order when eating out. You can't go wrong.

Traditional recipe for Swiss Fondue

2 to 3 large cloves of garlic
800 gr. or 20 oz. finely grated Switzerland cheese (half Emmentaler, half Gruyère)
2 + cups dry white wine
1 to 2 jiggers of Kirsch Schnappsmixed with
1 teaspoon of cornstarch
dash of pepper
plenty of crusty, chewy one-inch bread cubes

Mince or crush garlic and rub the inside of your fondue pot. Leave remains in pot. Pour in white wine and 1/3 of the grated cheese. Place over medium heat on stove. Start stirring in a figure-8 motion, gradually adding the rest of the cheese. Cook over moderate heat, stirring all the time until the mixture starts to bubble. Add the cornstarch mixed with kirsch and bring once more to the boil. Season with pepper and bring to the table. Adjust the heating flame so that the fondue will simmer throughout the meal.

Spear a cube of bread and dip it into the pot, giving it a figure-8 stir each time. Serve with a dry white or sparkling white wine or tea. During the meal it is customary to drink a jigger of Kirsch Schnapps to help digestion.

☎ **Telephone country code for Switzerland is 0041**

Arosa

A long-established Swiss ski resort, Arosa played a part in the development of skiing as a popular winter sport. Today it is known for relatively easy, wide-open skiing and good off-slope activities. The town is tucked into a circle of mountains at the end of the Schanfigger valley, above Chur.

Everything in Arosa is within easy walking distance. If you drive a car to the resort, you can park it in the public area and forget it, unless you decide to escape to some other area during your stay.

Mountain layout

At 6,000 feet, Arosa's lifts fan out to reach the two major peaks in the area, the 8,241-foot-high Hörnli and the Weisshorn, at 8,704 feet. While there are only 16 lifts, their combined capacity exceeds 21,000 skiers an hour. With the entire resort above the trees and some 43 miles of runs, long and spread out, there's plenty of wide-open skiing and perfect cruising. There are also nearly 16 miles of groomed cross-country trails.

Mountain rating

Arosa is Eden for beginners and intermediates because of its long, wide runs. When it hasn't snowed for several days, and skiers have broken new trails between the normally prepared runs, you can virtually ski across the entire mountain.

One run that does require an expert—sort of—is the descent from the top of the Weisshorn to the Carmennahütte. This very steep run is wide enough to allow a gutsy intermediate to traverse and make his way down the slope, but it also offers expert-level practice on the steeps with plenty of room for error.

Ski school (97/98 prices)

The Swiss Ski School in Arosa (3771150; fax 3771996) has more than 100 qualified instructors, most of whom speak English. The ski school has special courses for children, deep-snow skiers, snowboarders and telemarkers. The also organize other events, including torchlight descents accompanied by fireworks, descents by full moon and ski races.

Private lessons cost SFr110 for two hours and SFr275 for six hours per person.

Group lessons cost SFr29 for two hours (half day); SFr80 for three half days; SFr125 for five half days; and SFr185 for five full days (Monday through Friday).

Note: Reductions for children are available.

Cross-country courses are also available for SFr32 a half day, SFr62 for two half days, and up to SFr115 for five half days. A half day is two hours. Private instruction is SFr55 an hour for one to two persons.

There are also two **snowboarding schools** in Arosa. The Swiss Ski School operates one set of courses for SFr40 per half day; SFr 115 for three half days; and SFr185 for five half days. Call 3771150.

The Bananas Snowboard School (311591) is private with introductry courses held every Monday, Wednesday and Saturday for SFr68. Freestyle and halfpipe courses are given as well. Rates are SFr40 for a half day (2 1/2 hrs.); SFr110 for three half-days; and SFR180 for five half days. Private lessons will run SFr70 per hour or SFr 130 for two hours, with additional boarders paying SFr10.

Lift Tickets (97/98 prices)

All lift tickets for five days or more require photos.

	adults	children (to age 16)
one day	SFr49	SFr25
three days	SFr137	SFr69
six days	SFr219	SFr110
seven days	SFr239	SFr120

For the first two weeks of De¢ımber, lift tickets are reduced 15 percent. Senior citizens receive a 15 percent reduction on lift passes throughout the season.

Accommodations

Arosa has a hotel for everyone—from the most luxurious to the bargain one-star. **Ski Week** with prices starting from SFr316 for one-star to SFr756 for five-star properties, includes four days of lodging, private bath or shower and toilet, and lift tickets. The low season (December 1 to 16, January 6 to 20 and April 8 to 14) prices per day for half pension with private bath are noted for the hotels listed below. For high season (Christmas and most of February and March), add 15 to 25 percent.

Recommended four-star hotels: **Kulm Hotel** (3770131) SFr275; **Tschuggen Grand Hotel** (3770221) SFr290.

Our recommended four-star hotels are: **Hohenfels** (3770101), SFr145; **Posthotel** (3770121) right in the center of the town near the train station, SFr150; **Sporthotel Valsana** (3770275) by the lake, with a good restaurant and child care, SFr185; **Waldhotel National** (3771351) a bit back in the woods, nevertheless considered excellent, SFr230; **Hotel Eden** (310261) SFr225.

The three-star hotels most convenient to the lifts are: **Alpina** (377165) recently restored and beautiful, SFr135; **Anita** (377110) SFr137; **Astoria** (3771313) SFr138; **Hohe Promenade** (3772651), SFr135; **Obersee** (3771216) SFr130.

Our recommended two-star hotels: **Erzhorn** (3771526) SFr126 and the **Hold** (311408) SFr136.

Apartments

Arosa is well organized to handle tourists who want to rent apartments during the ski season, normally for a minimum of one week, Saturday to Saturday. During the Christmas and Easter seasons a minimum two-week rental is required.

The tourist office keeps track of available apartments. When writing, include the number of beds required, the preferred number of rooms, and your planned vacation dates. You will receive a quick response that lists a selection of apartments and prices. Pick your apartment and contact the owner.

Normally linen and kitchen utensils are provided. Other amenities, such as swimming pool, sauna, TV or room phone all add to the cost. Standard apartments rent for $35 to $60 per person a night. Prices vary significantly from low to high season.

Dining

The following restaurants come recommended by local Arosa residents: Stüva, Säumerstube, Hotel Hof Maran Im Stübli, Hotel Central Arven-Restaurant, Hotel Anita, Locanda, Bajazzo, Chez André and Gspan. For something different, take the sleigh ride up to the Hotel Alpenblick above Arosa and enjoy a special meat platter that is grilled at your table.

Après-ski/nightlife

Arosa is not the nightlife capital of Switzerland. The fun is where you make it, usually with groups that seem to form on their own on any ski trip. Arosa's après-ski activities center around the hotels in the evening. Here you'll find cozy bars with bands or piano players. There are approximately 20 such bars. Try the **Kitchen-Club** in an old hotel kitchen and **Nuts**—probably the hottest discos in town.

Child care

There are two public kindergartens. For more information and rates contact the tourist office in Arosa.

Getting there

The closest airport is Zürich; from there Arosa is less than three hours by train. Go first to Chur, where you catch a special train for Arosa just outside the main station entrance. The train ride from Chur to Arosa takes about one hour.

Driving from Zürich to Arosa will take about two-and-a-half hours in good weather. Follow the signs to Chur and after entering the city, follow the signs to Arosa. The road is steep and narrow and requires chains for most of the winter. Arosa has a car park for 460 cars. A free public bus in Arosa makes moving around the resort easier.

Other activities

Arosa is known for its off-slope activities. There are indoor swimming pools, ice skating on three open-air rinks and one covered rink, curling, indoor golf, chess and bridge evenings, more than 18 miles of walking trails, squash and tennis courts at Heidi's Parkhotel and the Robinson Club, horse-drawn sleigh rides, and hot-air ballooning. The town is also active in arts and entertainment.

For swimming expect to pay about SFr8–10.50 for adults and SFr5–6.50 for children.

For horse-drawn sleigh rides, contact E. and L. Messner Ritsch in Weierhof (3774196), J. Graber (3774716), or M. Moser (3771541). Costs are from SFr70–SFr120 for four persons depending on the route.

Arosa offers organized curling lessons every Tuesday, starting in January, for SFr8 a lesson.

Hot-air ballooning is available. Call 3771843.

 Tourist information

Arosa Tourism, CH-7050 Arosa, Switzerland; ((081) 3775151; fax (081) 3773135). Hours: Monday–Friday 9 a.m.–6 p.m., Saturday 9 a.m.–5:30 p.m., Sunday 10 a.m.–noon and 4–5:30 p.m.

☎ *Telephone prefix for Arosa is 081.*

Champéry

Portes du Soleil

The Portes du Soleil ski area, nestled just south of Lake Geneva and straddling Switzerland and France, claims to be Europe's biggest ski area. Though Trois Vallées makes a similar claim, the skiing in Portes du Soleil is more unrefined. Where a skier in the Trois Vallées may be able to transfer easily from valley to valley, transfers in the Portes du Soleil area take more time and effort. Where the lift system in the Trois Vallées forms a tight web linking miles of prepared slopes, the lifts through this region are gossamer strands linking far-flung pistes.

I remember breathing heavily after a long morning of continuous skiing from Champéry in Switzerland to Châtel in France. Jean, my guide, asked me, "Do you see that peak over to the right of the stand of trees?"

"Yes," I answered.

"Do you know where that is?"

"Somewhere in France? Is it Mont Blanc?" It looked far, far away.

He chuckled. "It's not that far away. That's where we started this morning." He smiled broadly.

"Oh, come on. There's no need to exaggerate. I'm already tired enough."

"No, no, no, I'm not making a joke. I just want you to know that we have a long way to get back."

I was incredulous and forgot any notions about a relaxed afternoon cruising home.

The Portes du Soleil area is made up of about a dozen different resorts. Four to six lie on the Swiss side of the border and the remaining eight or ten, depending on how one counts resorts, are in France. The key resorts are Champéry in Switzerland and Avoriaz in France. Over 50 mountain restaurants dot the slopes in this region with some of the best French cooking to be found at any resort.

Champéry is a mountain village that is waking up to the fact that it has turned into an international resort. Les Dents du Midi majestically stand watch over the valley and provide dramatic views of jagged mountain peaks, but it isn't a polished recreation. The old chalets look lived in, the odor of cow manure wafts across the main street, a plucky kid (of the goat type) prances in the back of a station wagon, the discos look like a throwback to the 1950s, and no tour buses pack the center of town.

The other main Swiss towns that are a part of the Portes du Soleil don't measure up to Champéry. Les Croset is isolated and once held promise as a resort, but today, is more fit for a skiing recluse. Champoussin has a major hotel that has changed hands almost annually which has not been conducive to building a good infrastructure. In the future with more stability, it has a chance of becoming a very convenient station. Morgins is far too quiet and most lodging is not very close to the two lifts up to the region.

Mountain layout

This is a real skier's area—over 650 km. ski trails. But not only is it challenging to ski the slopes; finding your way from resort to resort can test the skills of an Eagle Scout. The area does provide good maps outlining the 228 different lifts with suggested itineraries to make crisscrossing the region less difficult. (With such an ex panse of skiing, no one map allows sufficient detail; when you arrive in a new section, stop and pick up the local lift map that shows runs in that area.)

Note that the lift system does not perfectly interconnect. In Châtel there is a shuttlebus between the Linga and the Super-Châtel cable car.

The Portes du Soleil benefits from the fact that most of the skiable terrain is pasture land during the summers rather than rocky mountainside. This allows excellent skiing without the deep snow depth resorts such as Chamonix require. The locals claim that with only few inches of snow they can be up and running.

Experts can strike out in any direction but will most enjoy the World Cup section of Avoriaz, yo-yoing through the Plaine Dranse and Linga, and daring the Swiss Wall. No expert will feel complacent after any of these experiences. There is unlimited untracked snow for those looking for that type of adventure. Locals swear that since most visiting skiers stick to the trails, they can find untracked snow up to four days after a dump.

Intermediates should be ready for an endurance test of the first order. Forget any idea of skiing every run on a week-long vacation; it is just not possible. There are plenty of intermediate circuits that will provide a very full day of skiing. Try from Champéry to Avoriaz and back, or vice versa; on another day, take intermediate runs from Avoriaz to Châtel and return.

Beginners will not have a chance to really enjoy the expansive skiing of Portes du Soleil, but they certainly will have a beautiful place to learn.

Mountain rating

Score this one as a test for any expert, extensive enough for every intermediate on your list, and more than any beginner can handle.

Beginners taking the tram up from Champéry only have a limited area in which to ski. Champoussin may be a better bet for beginners, but then they lose the village atmosphere.

Intermediates will have a wonderful time criss-crossing the resorts on the Swiss side of the region, from Champéry to Champoussin to Le Crosets and down to Morgins.

Chavanette, also known as the Swiss Wall, between Avoriaz and Les Crosets, has lured experts for decades. Standing at the lip of the drop, skiers cannot see the slope that falls under the tips of their skis. Once dropping off the rim, it's a wide-open, expert steep with either ice of giant moguls, depending on the weather. Don't be ashamed to take the path around the Wall at this point—many skiers choose this option. The black runs above Avoriaz are good, but the lift lines on the French side can get long.

One serious recommendation for intermediates or experts is to limit your range unless you are in good physical shape. If you are already exhausted and someone in your group points to a distant mountain and announces that you have to return to that point before quitting, you will arrive very, very tired. As we all know, that's when the snow snakes seem to strike. Be careful. This is one of the few areas in the world where you *can* ski too far to get back home.

Ski school (97/98 prices)

The Swiss Ski School in Champéry offers both downhill and cross-country lessons.

Downhill group courses cost: half day, SFr35 (SFr45 for kids 3–7 with lunch); full day costs SFr60 for either adult or child; one week of half days, SFr140 (SFr190 for kids with lunch); five full days costs SFr250 for adults and SFr260 for kids with lunch.

Private lessons: SFr50 per hour for one or two persons, SFr60 per hour for three or four. Half-day private lessons for groups of one or two cost SFr140, or SFr160 for three to four skiers. Full-day lessons for groups of one or two cost SFr280; groups of three or four cost SFr300.

Snowboarding private lessons cost SFr75 per hour for one or two persons, SFr90 per hour for three or four. Half-day private lessons for groups of one or two cost SFr140, or SFr160 for three to four skiers. Full-day lessons for groups of one to four cost SFr280.

Snowboarding group lessons cost SFr30 for a half day, and SFr120 for five days.

A good way to get to know the area is through organized **Ski Excursions Portes du Soleil** groups of at least four skiers for SFr60 a day or SFr250 a five-day week. The groups, organized by the Swiss Ski School in Champéry, normally make a loop through Les Crosets, Champoussin, Morgins and Avoriaz, and then return to Champéry.

From Berra Sport in the center of town you can get ski rentals for SFr157 (6 days) SFr173 (7 days) and snowboard rentals for SFr38 (1 day) SFr145 (7 days). Rentals are also available from Holiday and Borgeat Sports

Lift tickets (97/98 prices)

The Portes du Soleil ski pass (for adults, 16 years and older) costs: one day, SFr48; six days, SFr219; 14 days, SFr397. For children under 16, rates are: one day, SFr32; six days, SFr145; 14 days, SFr272. Limited passes are available for each region in the Portes du Soleil.

Photos are required for passes of six days of more. Half-day passes start at noon and children under 6 are free when accompanied by a paying adult.

Accommodations (97/98 prices)

Champéry has only a handful of hotels but plenty of apartments. There is also an excellent weekly program called Ski Passion, which includes seven, five or four days accommodation with half board, six- or five-day lift tickets for the entire Portes du Soleil area, and free entry to the Sports Center. The special Ski Passion 97/98 price for low season for a seven-night stay is noted where offered and the daily high-season half-board rate is noted for each hotel. Note: these hotels have high season weekly programs as well.

Hotel Suisse Golden Tulip (479-0707; fax 479-0709; or through the Golden Tulip reservation system in U.S.A./Canada 1-800-344-1212; in U.K. 0800-951000). Special week: SFr980. Daily rate: SFr163. Hotel Suisse is in the centre of the village. The hotel has been expanded and modernized. All the rooms are comfortable, however they vary significantly in size. Ask for a big room when you make reservations or when you show up at the hotel. The hotel's subterranean jazz bar, Les Mines d'Or, is a popular late night watering-hole often featuring live music. The Bar des Guides has become the nightlife haven of choice for English speakers. The manager of the hotel was a member of the Swiss Olympic ski team. He makes an effort to ski with the guests whenever possible.

Hotel de Champéry (479-1071; fax 479-1402). Special week: SFr980. Daily rate: SFr163. This hotel, 50 meters up the road from the Suisse, is the largest hotel in town. The hotel's piano bar is a popular haunt for regular visitors.

Beau-Séjour (479-1701; fax 479-2336). A nice hotel with a good restaurant and reasonable prices. Special week: SFr720 (without half-board). Daily rate: SFr120.

Hotel des Alpes (479-1222; fax 479-3119). More upscale than the Paix with a fancy and expensive à la carte restaurant. Special week: SFr730. Daily rate: SFr121.

Hotel de la Paix (479-1551; fax 479-xxxx). An almost legendary hotel for young people. It's friendly, helpful and has great food and lots of it. The crowd is young and very international. Special week: SFr930. Daily rate: SFr121.

Hotel National (479-1130; fax 479-3155) Special week: SFr930. Daily rate: SFr155.

Ski Chalet: Piste Artiste runs four of these chalets right in town and also have a program that provides guides for the chalet groups. Rates based on double occupancy at these chalets including meals, guides, lodging and airport transfers are £294–323 (US$470–520) in January and £459–505 (US$735–810) in high season. Phone or fax 479-3344 in Champéry, or e-mail them at ski@pisteartiste.com.

Apartments

To reserve apartments write to the tourist office. You will receive a listing of available apartments, but you will have to make your reservations through a rental agency or directly with the owners. In Champéry the agencies are Agence Immobilière René Avanthey, 791444, Agence Mendes de Leon (791777) and Agence les Gaieuls (791885). Mendes de Leon seemed to be the most helpful.

Child care

The ski school (479-1615) has a special Mini-Club for children 3–7, open 9:15 a.m. to 16:30 p.m. daily. It includes ski lessons, games and lunch. Half-day cost is SFr35; five half days will cost SFr140. A full day with lunch costs SFr55 and five full days with lunch are SFr260.

There is a nanny service which must be booked before arrival. Rates are SFr275 for a week, SFr 45 for full-day service and SFr30 for a half day. Babysitting can also be arranged. The tourist office has phone numbers and information.

Dining

Location, location, location ... Champéry's cooking benefits from its proximity to France. For the best meals in town try the **Restaurant le Mazot** in the Hotel de Champéry (try their Pierrade where you cook your meat on a heated stone) and the **Restaurant in the Hotel Suisse**.

These other restaurants in town are all very agreeable

Café du Nord at top of the High Street near Banque Cantonale. One of the more popular restaurants in the village, especially with families. Serving up an assortment of rosti, fondue, and raclette. Bribe the stunning English owner Gill Dana to get the joint jumping with her inspiring accordion playing.

Restaurant le Sport has a famous pasta party and other specialties set in a nice atmosphere.

Restaurant National in the center of the village offers specials each day, has good fish and a rustic atmosphere.

Le Farinet has pizzas and pasta. The kitchen remains open until well after midnight.

La Vieux Chalet has lamb, fish, and meat dishes. Some nights offer music and dancing. Located at the end of High Street or top of the hill from the Téléphérique.

Le Gueullhi opened next to the cable car. For late night food try **La Farinet** with hot food until 2 a.m.

Across the Valley there is a raclette house called **Les Rives**. The raclette parties there are part of the resort's dining around program for guests taking half-board at hotels or pensions. The raclette 'wheel' is heated against an open fire by the Chef.

Restaurant Grand Paradis Located in Grand Paradis, this restaurant is renown for their Raclette room,

Chez Coquoz at Planachaux is the best on the Swiss side of the region.

Chez Gabi, on the slopes above Champoussin, also had excellent food and makes a great midday stop or a good evening meal after a ride up on a snowcat.

See the Avoriaz chapter for restaurants on the French side.

Après-ski/nightlife

The best après-ski spot in town is **Bar des Guides** in the Hotel Suisse. There are good beers on tap and the place is packed with English speakers from the U.K., Canada, U.S.A., Holland and Scandinavia. Check out "Ladies Night".

Giorgio's Sun Bar has a crackling fireplace and features live music on most weekends. This bar is a bit out of the center of town. This the perfect place to start or wind down an evening. Nachos and tacos are available from the bar.

Café du Levant is the grunge and snowboarder hangout. Things sometimes get a little out of hand, which is this establishments most redeeming value.

Min d'Or tucked beneath the Hotel Suisse, entrance around back. Late night jazz joint, doesn't open until after 10 p.m. Entrance is found in the back and opens up into a bizarre cave. Seems a little too dark and seedy when there isn't a band playing, but must be visited at least once.

For late night, a favorite is the **Bodega** under Le Farinet where Flamenco music is played. Another disco in town is **Le Farinet** (which has hot food 'till 2 a.m.).

Other activities

Champéry is just over a half-hour winding drive up the mountain from Montreux and Lausanne. Monthey, in the valley, has a covered bridge and open-air market. The town is only about two hours from the airport at Geneva.

The sports center has ice skating, curling and swimming as well as a fitness center, sauna and massage. Town visitors staying in a participating hotel have free entrance. Adult entrance to the pool for those not staying in participating hotels is SFr6.50; for children SFr4.50. Ice skating costs a franc less. Skate rentals are SFr4.

Hang-gliding or paragliding costs SFr80 per flight. Contact Vincent Marclay at 479-2408.

A visit to the thermal baths of Val-d'Illiez is a relaxing must with hourly train connection. Entrance is SFr8.

There is night skiing twice a week until 10 p.m. in Planachaux. A toboggan run is available for those athletic enough to climb the three-km. trail. Heliskiing and ski mountaineering is offered with qualified guides for SFr350 a day plus flight fees.

Tourist information

Champéry: Office du Tourisme, CH-1874 Champéry, Switzerland; 479 20 20, fax 479 20 21.

☎ *Telephone prefix for this region is 024.*

Crans-Montana

These twin villages perched high on a plateau above the town of Sierre celebrated 100 years as a ski resort in 1993. The new racing runs and ski lift improvements made for the World Championships resulted in one of the most accessible skiing areas in the world. Indeed, for the intermediate skier, Crans-Montana may be heaven on the slopes. Long, challenging trails coupled with virtually no waiting at lifts make for a combination that most skiers will find hard to beat.

This area was inscribed in skiing lore long before the 1987 Swiss medal sweep. In 1950, the first Swiss ski championships were held here. And even earlier, in January 1911, the founder of modern downhill racing, Sir Arnold Lunn, had the idea to organize a race from the highest point on the Plaine Morte glacier down to Montana. Unlike today's closely timed individual runs, in that race all contestants started together, and the first to reach the town was the winner. The race eventually developed into today's famous Kandahar, held alternately each year in St. Anton, Mürren, Chamonix, Sestriere and Garmisch.

Crans-Montana has been connected with a budding purpose-built resort, Aminona. This Crans-Montana-Aminona area is served by 40 interconnected lifts, with almost one mile of vertical and 100 miles of trails.

Crans and Montana do have some differences, although the names are most often said in the same breath. (Neither is a paragon of Alpine architecture; an architects' convention might have been given a free hand to erect as many kinds of buildings as possible. Unappealing square concrete boxes stand beside massive triangular Toblerone-box hotels, with a smattering of traditional chalets amidst the concrete and glass.

Crans has the more concentrated city atmosphere. The shop signs in Montana read simply—Cheese, Fondue, Real Estate, Restaurant. In Crans, the signs read Gucci, Louis Vuitton, Piaget, Cartier. Crans is chic and often crowded with furs, Montana more for the family, where one is more at home in a ski outfit.

Be prepared to hike up and down hills, because both towns climb the side of the mountain from their plateau above the Rhône. But this slope, although many curse it by day, provides many hotels with spectacular views of the Alps in the south.

Mountain layout

The ski area above Crans-Montana-Aminona is reached from four major lifts. From Crans, a gondola takes skiers to Chetseron (6,825 feet), which was the starting point of the World Cup men's Super-G. Another gondola goes thence to Cry d'Err (7,173 feet), the hub of the entire area. From Montana, a new six-passenger gondola whisks skiers to Cry d'Err. At Les Barzettes, a five-minute bus ride from Crans or Montana, another new, fast gondola takes you to Les Violettes (7,176 feet). From the base again, five minutes on the bus takes the skier to Aminona, where a gondola goes on to Pt. Mont Bonvin (7,836 feet); here, a wide-open, above-treeline area provides fantastic uncrowded conditions.

In the morning, the most crowded lifts are from Crans. A short, free bus ride to Les Barzettes and the Violettes or Aminona lifts will get you up the mountain faster.

The Cry d'Err sector of the mountain is the most crowded. Ten lifts go to Cry d'Err. After a long, flat traverse, the skier arrives on the Crans section of the mountain. From here the best bet is to take the Super-G/Slalom run into Crans, then catch the gondola back to Cry d'Err. The runs below Cry d'Err heading to Montana are intermediate playgrounds, but suffer from a serious bottleneck near Pas du Loup where the four trails merge through a narrow gap before widening on the way to town. At the end of the day, this bottleneck will be crowded—ski slowly and in control.

From Cry d'Err another trail traverses to the right, leading you into the Violettes section. This area is separated from the Montana section by a sheer cliff whose edge is marked generally by the Piste Nationale run on the ski map. The Violettes area is a favorite of intermediates, featuring twisting runs down through the trees to the gondola midstation, and four other lifts opening great intermediate skiing.

Across the valley from Violettes is the Aminona area and the Toula lifts, a favorite section of the resort. La Toula offers challenging expert runs, and Aminona boasts wide-open, uncrowded cruising.

The Plaine Morte trail starts atop the 9,843-foot-high Plaine Morte glacier, which also serves as a summer ski area. Sometime during your stay take the new Funitel mountain subway up from Violettes and measure your time against the Kandahar ski pioneers, whose best time was just over one hour for the run. The run is a long nine miles of intermediate terrain with expert tendencies, thanks to the chance for frequent off-trail shortcuts. The trail down from Plaine Morte is closely controlled for avalanche danger. After even a relatively light snowfall, the run from the glacier back to Violettes is often closed, but opened after the necessary precautions.

Mountain rating

Intermediates will rate Crans-Montana one of the greatest places they've ever skied, with excellent variety.

Beginners are relatively limited on this mountain. In Crans, absolute beginners start on the golf course, which is perfect, but the next step—directly onto the mountain—is a big one. Montana beginners start above the Signal restaurant. Instructors admit that the area is limited, and after a few days it is up to Cry d'Err, where the blue runs are really very wide, lower intermediate slopes. In Violettes there are no beginner slopes, and the beginner sections of Aminona are for those who have been on skis at least three or four days—even then the gentle slopes are isolated in a sea of red-rated trails.

Only experts need to worry at all about whether there are enough challenges to keep things interesting. Experts will find no really steep sections, but there is plenty of off-trail and tree skiing. The championship runs are also a good test.

Ski school (97/98 prices)

The Crans-Montana area has more ski instructors (about 200) than some Swiss ski villages have permanent residents. There's a lesson being given somewhere on the slopes from Crans to Aminona nearly every hour of the day. For information, call (027) 4811320 or 4811480.

The Montana ski school is by far the more international. It boasts qualified Swiss Ski Instructors from the United States, Australia and Britain. The Crans ski school is a relatively closed Swiss shop.

Private lessons cost SFr50 an hour for one, SFr60 for two or three students, and SFr70 per hour for three to four people.

Group lessons last three hours a day. One day costs SFr37 and seven days will cost SFr155.

Children pay SFr18 a day and SFr75 for one week.

Cross-country lessons are available, and four different trails with a total length of 25 miles are prepared during the season.

Lift tickets (97/98 prices)

The Crans-Montana area pass is available at the following rates:

half day (from 11:15 a.m.)	SFr35
one day	SFr45
four days	SFr155
seven days	SFr226
fourteen days	SFr343

(Children six to 16 enjoy a discount— approximately 40 percent.)

Note: The Plaine-Morte glacier an the upper reaches of the mountain is reached by a new Funitel, or mountain subway running from Les Violettes. It is not included in the above prices—expect to pay a 20 percent supplement to use that lift.

Accommodations

Crans-Montana can be very upscale. It doesn't claim many movie stars or much of the old rich, but it is an oasis for the corporate rich. The town boasts more five-star hotels than any other Swiss resort except St. Moritz, and a dazzling selection of prize-winning, expensive restaurants. Finding the ritziest isn't difficult—digging for the good solid values for the middle-of-the-road crowd takes a bit more time.

The following prices for the special ski week, "Ski-Soleil," which Crans-Montana offers outside of the Christmas season include four to seven days in hotels at half board or in apartments, with four to seven-day ski passes.

Crans Ambassador (tel. 4814811, fax 4819155) SFr1,301–1,575. The best hotel on the Montana side of the town. It is next to the cable cars, and has good nightlife and an indoor pool.

De la Forêt (tel. 481213, fax 4813120) SFr893–1,064. A bit of a walk to the downtown area but close to Les Violettes lift. Has a covered swimming pool.

National (tel. 4812681, fax 4817381) SFr893–1,084. This lower-priced hotel is near the Crans lifts. It is used by British tour groups, but the owner can be cantankerous.

Teleferique (tel. 4813367) SFr731–862. At the departure of the Cry d'Err lifts.

Vieux-Valais (tel. 4812031) SFr731–862. Small family-run hotel with only 15 beds.

Apartments

With 11 major rental agencies in Crans and 11 in Montana, apartment and chalet listings in Crans-Montana are overwhelming.

Expect to pay SFr700–800 per week for a two-bed studio in high season (Christmas, February and Easter); SFr950–1,160 for a four-bed, two-room apartment; SFr1,820–2,000 for a four-room, six- to eight-bed apartment.

To book an apartment, write to or call the tourist office in either town (see Tourist Information) with details of what you want and the price range. You'll get a prompt reply.

Dining

This town, as noted above, has plenty of great eateries. These are some of our favorites—from expensive to moderate to inexpensive.

For top gourmet cuisine, head to **Rôtisserie de la Reine** (tel. 4811885), renowned for its fresh fish and shellfish, and **Le Sporting** (tel. 4811177) has top French and Italian food. The **Poste** (tel. 4812745), in Montana is rated highly by Gault & Millaut.

For moderately priced meals, try **La Trappe** in the Hotel Cisalpin (tel. 4812425). Try their *Fondue la Trappe*. The **Hotel Aida** (tel. 4801111) has a beautiful rustic setting.

The budget crowd should indulge at **Le Bistro** (tel. 4811217) in Montana, and the **Brasserie "Le Green"** (tel. 4813256).

On the mountain, don't look for much in the gourmet level, but it is substantial and good basic Swiss food. We liked the lunch menu at **Des Violettes** and **Bella-Lui**. The scenery from **De la Plaine Morte** restaurant (tel. 4813626) on the glacier is the stuff of which memories are made. If everything on the slopes is crowded, try the restaurant at the lower station of the Montana/Cry d'Err gondola.

Après-ski/nightlife

By United States and British standards, there isn't much. Immediately after the slopes close, the only bars with a crowd are in Montana—the small, smokey **La Grange** and **Amadeus**. It's small and very smoky. **The Pub Geroges & Dragon** in Crans is the top English-speaker après-ski spot with reasonable beer. And **Le Green** has been recommended as a modern sleek bar. If you have the urge to go out between 9 p.m. and midnight, try some of the normally quiet piano bars. **Memphis Bar** in Crans sometimes has jazz.

Discos don't get going until midnight to 1 a.m. If you're determined and well-heeled, head for **Absolut** and **Pacha** in Crans, but expect to pay a SFr20 cover charge, which includes a drink. In Montana, the place to be seen is the **Number One.** There is SFr10 cover which includes a drink. **Constellation** is packed with young snowboarders.

Child care

The ski school for children (6 to 12) runs only half days. The cost for a half day is SFr37; five half days, SFr155.

Crans-Montana has four nurseries which can handle children by the hour, for half days, or all day. Call 4811320 in Crans and, in Montana, 4811480.

The tourist office also provides a list of babysitters.

Getting there

You'll most likely arrive at the Geneva airport. From there it's an uncomplicated car or train ride of a couple of hours around the lake and into the mountains. From Sierre, the bus departs directly in front of the railway station, the cable car from around the corner.

Crossair now flies from Zürich to nearby Sion, only a half hour from Crans-Montana by bus or taxi.

Other activities

Crans-Montana is a center for hot-air ballooning and hang-gliding, with instruction in hang-gliding available. Call 4850800 or 4850404 for information about both. A winter meeting of hot-air balloon enthusiasts is held annually, usually in February.

Tourist information

Tourist office, Crans, CH-3963, Switzerland; (tel. (027) 4850800; fax (027) 485080). In Montana, the address is Montana, CH-3962, Switzerland; (tel. (027) 4850404; fax (027) 4850460).

Internet: www.crans-montana.ch

E-mail: crans_montana@scopus.ch

☎ *Local telephone prefix is 027.*

Davos

Davos is not a small quaint Alpine resort. This is a ski city—the largest ski resort in Switzerland and the highest city in Europe. The year-round population is 12,000 and the town can fill up with an additional 23,000 tourists. Davos was one of the first ski resorts to be created and is still one of the world's best.

Set in Graubünden in the southeast corner of Switzerland, Davos is dwarfed by mountains on both sides of the valley (Davos means "behind" or "beyond" in the Romansh language). These mountains have been developed into five separate ski areas, any one of which would be enough for a U.S. resort, ensuring diversity and skiing for every skier.

The town is split into two basic sections: Davos Dorf, where the Parsennbahn starts, and Davos Platz, beneath the Schatzalpbahn. These, with several other villages—Wolfgang, Laret and Glaris—make up greater Davos.

Instead of wooden chalets, for the most part, you see square concrete hotels. But Davos maintains a sense of comfort as well. Traffic moves easily along the upper and lower main arteries without buildup. The hotels have a long and distinguished tradition for excellence, and practically every type of recreational activity is available. If you want to buy the latest in Gucci accessories, or the finest Atomic racing ski, you'll find them without any problem.

The town was started in 1860 by Dr. Spengler, a German physician who recognized the benefits of the dry, healthy climate in treating tuberculosis, a scourge of the times. Huge balconies seen on older houses were for patients to lie out in the sunshine. This type of treatment continued until about 1930. Thomas Mann's wife was treated at Davos, from which came his novel *The Magic Mountain*.

Development of Davos as a sports region began in 1955. Davos and Klosters combined offer 315 km. of runs, a variety of lodging, cable cars and even some yodeling accordion players. This resort may have been the first to turn skiing into a business with the construction of the Parsenn railway and the creation of the first drag lift.

At night the mix of people has unusual variety, from teenagers in town for the good skiing to elderly couples enjoying a walk in the crisp, clear mountain air and the restorative powers of an Alpine vacation. Nightlife is adequate, if restrained. Everything except the skiing seems to be done in moderation.

Mountain layout

Someone once complained to me that they couldn't find a decent trail map of the area. I would have to concur, but no one really needs a trail map—you can ski anywhere. What you need is a lift map, and those are easily found.

The five ski areas surrounding Davos are the Parsenn, the Schatzalp/Strela, Jakobshorn, Rinerhorn and Pischa.

The Parsenn: This is the best known area, almost the size of Manhattan and the major reason why Davos has become a premier European resort. The Parsennbahn, a cable railway, leaves every 15 to 20 minutes in ski season. It peaks at the Weissfluhjoch, where you can keep ascending to the Weissfluhgipfel, eventually arriving at 9,331 feet. From this point two expert runs drop to the spreading Parsenn, where the runs are wide open and offer beginners and intermediates a paradise for cruising. The Parsenn has 40 seemingly endless trails, including what was once Europe's longest: the 12-km. trail from Weissfluhjoch to Kublis.

Lift improvements continue with high-speed chairlifts replacing the Meierhof and Totalp drag lifts. A gondola stretching from the Weissfluhjoch over to the Schifferhut allows skiers to cruise for 20 to 30 minutes and then zip back to the top of the Parsenn on the gondola.

The toughest runs back into Davos are alongside the Parsennbahn, or down the Meierhofer Talli over moguls and advanced intermediate drops to Davos-Wolfgang, where you'll have to take a bus or train back into town.

You can also reach the Parsenn on a spectacular cable car running from the Strela sector and from Klosters via the Gotschnabahn.

Schatzalp/Strela: This small area of uninteresting, unchallenging runs has finally been graced with a new chairlift replacing the ancient gondola. You can use this area to bypass the mob scene down at the Parsennbahn if you are heading over to the Parsenn from Davos-Platz. The shortcut looks good on the map and is beautiful, with spectacular views, but requires trips on slow lifts to get up to the Parsenn. (Before trying this short cut, make sure all the necessary lifts are running.)

Jakobshorn: This is the second largest area in Davos, on the opposite side of the valley from the Parsenn. It's called "The Fun Mountain," and is ideal for snowboarding. The ISF 1995 World Snowboarding Championships were held here.

A cable car rises from the town to the lower station of the Jakobshornbahn, which peaks at 8,497 feet. Here 14 marked trails will keep a skier busy for at least a day. The area is more challenging than the Parsenn and less crowded, but trails are shorter and more limited.

You reach the Jakobshorn from Davos-Platz with a two-stage cable car or with a high-speed double chair lift. Then six more lifts open up the entire side of the mountain— 2,140 feet of wide-open vertical, all above treeline, with another 1,200 feet of trails through the trees (only one or two U.S. resorts have more vertical). Obviously, there is plenty to ski on this side of the valley.

If you are an expert, you also have the option of going off-piste and dropping into the Dischma Valley to Teufi, where a bus will pick you up and take you back to Davos-Platz.

Rinerhorn: The next area is the Rinerhorn area at Glaris, just up the valley from the main town, with 13 runs and several good advanced intermediate descents. These slopes are normally uncrowded except for the ski schools, which use the wide-open slopes for classes. This is where most of the locals ski, especially on weekends—they can do the Parsenn during the week and would rather ski than wait in line.

You'll arrive at the area first by train or bus from Davos-Platz (it's included in your lift ticket). Take the Rinerhornbahn up 1,900 feet and take your choice of three more lifts reaching up another 1,446 feet. This area, with its special children's facilities, is perfect for families.

Experts can drop down the 4.5-km. run back down to Glaris. Intermediates and beginners will have the entire upper reaches to practice and play in.

Pischa: This area, reached by a short bus ride from Davos, offers uncrowded runs down a 2,230-foot vertical. There isn't a lot for an expert here, but how many of us are that expert? Virtually everyone will enjoy skiing this area with its super-sunny slopes.

Davos has great cross country skiing—the second largest cross country ski area in Switzerland—with75 km. of groomed trails.

Mountain rating

Davos earns an A-plus when it comes to beginners and intermediates. This is perhaps the ideal terrain for learning to ski and for perfecting your technique. For experts, the upper Parsenn terrain may become a little boring (Ah, to be so jaded!), and they might ask where the most challenging skiing—normally off the Parsenn—can be found.

Locals might suggest runs on the Parsenn from the top of the Weissfluhgipfel, the trails that drop into town alongside the Parsennbahn, or the Drostobel-to-Klosters run, which is narrow and sometimes steep. The Strela area is uninteresting, but there is some good off-piste skiing down the wide bowl to your right as you look back down the mountain from the top of the Strelagrat. Rinerhorn has great tree skiing and good off-piste as well. The Jakobshorn has bumps and moguls to wear out any skier.

On days with good powder, it pays to hire, for the morning, an instructor who will take you to the special spots (off-trail) for thrills.

Ski school

The Davos ski school has more than 150 instructors. Almost all of them speaks some English. There are reductions for groups of senior citizens and for children. Inquire at the ski school to see whether such a group has been organized (081-4162454). There is a lot of off-piste skiing in good winters and many skiers come for that experience. A guide at private instruction rates is the way to go.

Private lessons

half day	SFr145
one day (five hours)	SFr250
five consecutive days	SFr230 per day
one hour (for one or two persons)	SFr55

Group lessons	Adults	Children
one half-day	SFr30	SFr21
one day	SFr52	—
five half-days (x-c)	SFr120	SFr95
five full days	SFr190	SFr154

There is a discount for lessons given in the first three weeks of December.

Five-day, "Sun and Fun" lift ticket/ski school combinations are also offered for advanced skiers.

"Sun and Fun"	Adults	Children
Dec 20 to 27	SFr347	SFr244
Jan 3 to 7 M-F	SFr347	SFr244
Jan 10 to 28 M-F	SFr327	SFr232
Jan 31 to March 18 M-F	SFr347	SFr244
March 21 to 25 M-F	SFr327	SFr232
March 28 to Apr 8 M-F	SFr347	SFr244
April 11 to end season	SFr327	SFr232

Lift tickets (97/98 prices)

Separate passes are sold for each of the five areas, although there is a combination pass for Strela and the Parsenn area.

The most convenient pass, especially if you plan to ski for a week or more, is the all-inclusive regional pass. This pass lets you ride all lifts, as well as the train through the valley from Glaris to Kublis. The only restriction is that it's sold only for two days or more.

	Adults	Children
two days	SFr113	SFr68
three days	SFr155	SFr93
six days	SFr259	SFr155
seven days	SFr288	SFr173
fourteen days	SFr464	SFr279

NOTE: Day ticket for the Parsenn area costs SFr52; for Rinerhorn, SFr40, for Jakobshorn, SFr46; for Pischa, SFr38; for Schatzalp/Strela, SFr25. Children get about a 38% discount.

Important transportation note: The shuttlebuses that carry you from your hotel to the Parsennbahn, or down to the Jakobshornbahn, ply a route up and down the *same* one-way street. If you are in Platz and want to take the shuttlebus to the Parsennbahn, go to the main street, Promenade, which is one-way in the opposite direction. Your bus will come down Promenade in a special lane—against traffic—to take you to the lifts. If you logically head down to Talstrasse, you will have to climb back up to Promenade.

Overall, the bus system has been significantly expanded in the past season. Nearly all the outlying lodging is now accessible by bus. The entire system, as well as the train between Davos and the outlying dorfs, is free to those with visitor cards.

Accommodations

Davos hotels range from plush to plain. The following are our top recommendations in each category. The approximate **high-season** daily rate is the last price quoted, per day, per person, including half pension and all taxes. Christmas holidays are slightly higher. Our recommended five-star hotels are:

Steigenberger Belvedere (4156000, fax 4156001). This is one of the grand old Alpine hotels. Some rooms don't live up to its price, but if you ask for one facing the valley the view from the balcony will beg for photography. Service cannot be topped anywhere else in town. The hotel restaurant can be excellent. We enjoyed a superb medallions of reindeer on sautéed forest mushrooms, a Norwegian salmon appetizer was dinner-sized and the cranberry sorbet with fresh cranberries sublime. The indoor pool and spa, featuring steam and sauna, are very comforting. Complimentary transfers to the train station. Davos-Platz. SFr255. For reservations from the U.S. call (800) 223-5652.

Hotel Flüela (4171221, fax 4164401). A family-run hotel conveniently located by the Davos-Dorf station with easy access to all ski areas. A lounge with plush carpets, comfy chairs and fireplace welcomes you, and the restaurant has beautifully painted ceilings. The rooms are all different. SFr265.

Our recommended four-star hotels are:

Morosani Post Hotel (4141161, fax 4131647). This hotel is especially popular with Swiss visitors, which speaks well of its quality, service and prices. Rooms are furnished in light pine and the interior is beautifully Alpine, even if the exterior appears cold and square. Davos-Platz. SFr208.

Hotel Seehof (4171212, fax 4166110). A renovated hotel in Davos Dorf next to the mountain railway within walking distance of the train station. SFr222.

Central Hotel (4141181, fax 4135212). An excellent hotel with pool and sauna in Davos-Platz. It has a cozy piano bar. SFr207.

Meierhof (4171285, fax 4163982). This is a hotel with a large Swiss clientele. The rooms are beautiful and the food exceptional. Davos-Platz. SFr200.

Our recommended three-star hotels are:

Hotel Cristiana (4161444, fax 4161621). This hotel is a clean well-lighted place; it qualifies as a place to hang your hat and rest your weary body and little else. In Davos-Dorf, it is a bit out of the way from nightlife and restaurants. SFr130.

Hotel Ochsen (4135222, fax 4137671) This hotel is rustic and in the center of the action. SFr144.

Aparthotel Richmond (4133888, fax 4136564). This is one of the bargain spots of Davos. Rooms are clean and the restaurant is cozy. In the middle of Davos-Platz. SFr100, breakfast buffet is extra, no dinner.

Our recommended one-star hotel is:

Edelweiss (4161033, fax 4161130). B&B. A quaint hotel with private baths. SFr94, breakfast extra.

The **Sports Center** in the middle of town offers budget dormitory accommodations for SFr58–70 a night for half-board.

Apartments

As at most Swiss resorts, the rental apartment business is well organized and bookings can be arranged through the tourist information office (see Tourist Information). Write to the office, and provide details about when you plan to arrive, how many people will be sharing the apartment and what facilities you desire. They will respond quickly with several apartment choices. The direct reservations number is 4152131.

It is more convenient to stay in Davos-Platz or Davos-Dorf; Davos-Laret and Davos-

Wolfgang are further out of the way. Make your selection and notify the tourist office or the individual owner, depending on the instructions from the tourist office.

Normally, linen and kitchen utensils are included in every apartment. Taxes and cleaning may be extra. Expect to pay SFr25-42 per person a night, depending on how many are sharing the apartment, where it's located and its relative position on the luxury scale.

Dining

Davos has scores of restaurants. The **Golfhotel Waldhuus** (4171131) serves one of the best nouvelle cuisine dinners in Davos. For very upscale dining try **Hubli's Landhaus** in Laret (4162121) which is also a local nouvelle cuisine shrine. The **Davoserstübli** (4136817) in the Davoserhof Hotel is elegant with upper level prices and excellent nouvelle cuisine. **Palüda-Grill** (4171166) is very rustic, expensive and refined, located in the Derby Hotel in Dorf.

For more down-to-earth fare, try **Ammann's Steakhouse** and the **Pöstli** in the Morisani PosthoThe **Bündnerstübli** at Dischmastrasse in Dorf is very local, very crowded and very reasonable. Just outside the town, try the **Gasthof Landhaus** in Frauenkirch (36335) for typical Swiss specialties.

The best pizza in town is found at **Il Padrino** in Platz.

Après-ski/nightlife

Davos-Platz is the place to be for any nightlife. For dancing, head to the **Postli Club**, open every evening from 8:30, the **Cabanna Club**, which gets started at 9, or the **Dischma**, where the band begins to play after dinner at about 9 p.m. Expect to hear lots of techno rock and to pay about SFr11 for a Coke, more for mixed drinks and beer.

The **Chämi Bar** on Promenade is where folk gather to see and be seen, drink, and little else. For a touch of oom-pah music and a few polkas with sloshing beer, dive into the **Cava Grischa** in the basement of the Hotel Europe, where the band sometimes plays on in lederhosen and the crowds are are a bit older.

Piano Bar in the Hotel Europe offers changing entertainment. During our last visit a blind black piano playera and singer from Atlanta turned out cool tunes for a middle agee comfortable crowd, some leaning on the piano, some at the bar, others in overstuffed chairs.

Child care

Two organized kindergartens in Davos offer supervision for children three to 10.

The Pinocchio Kindergarten in Bünda, Davos-Dorf (4165969), is open Monday–Friday, 8:30 a.m.–4:30 p.m. Costs are:

one half day	SFr21
five half days	SFr95
five consecutive days including lunch	SFr200

Lunch is served from 11:30 a.m. until 2 p.m. and babysitting service during lunch will cost SFr19. The charge for lunch, if the school feeds the child, is SFr10. Advanced booking is required.

Getting there

The closest airport is Zürich, nearly three hours away by train. You must change trains in Landquart.

By car, follow the signs to Chur on an excellent superhighway until you get to the Landquart/Davos exit. The drive from Landquart to Davos is through a narrow valley and passes through Kublis and Klosters before arriving at Davos-Platz. The distance from Zürich to Davos is just under 100 miles.

Other activities

A new sports center recently opened next to the ice stadium. There are indoor swimming pool, saunas and a solarium. Pool and sauna cost SFr11 a visit; a 10-visit book of coupons is SFr100. Swim only is SFr6 a session, or SFr42 for 10 visits.

There is a tennis and squash center in Davos-Platz with indoor courts (4133131).

Europe's largest natural ice skating rink is open, and rentals are available. Entry for adults is SFr4 and for children, SFr3 (4137354).

Hang-gliding courses are taught by Hans Guler in Davos-Platz (4136043 or 077-316043), and by Marco Schnell in Davos Dorf (4165666).

There is also a toboggan run down the Schatzalp with banked turns and a total drop of over 750 feet. It is open from 10 a.m. to 9 p.m. There is no charge for admission. Toboggans are available for rental at the base of the Schatzalp Funicular. Call 4135726 or 4135432.

A casino operates in the Europa Ho

Tourist information

The tourist information office is open Monday-Friday, 8:30 a.m. to 6 p.m.; Saturday, 8:30 a.m. to 5 p.m.; Sunday, 10 a.m.–noon.

Davos Tourist Office, 7270 Davos-Platz, Switzerland; 4152121, fax 4152100; for reservations call 4152131.

☎ *Telephone prefix for Davos is 081.*

Engelberg

This resort is one of the closest to Zurich. It has both challenging skiing and mellow stuff. You can find crowds on the weekends and empty runs during the week. You can come here and ski for a day or an afternoon from Zurich or Lucerne, or you can stay for a week or longer enjoying the scenery.

The region is blessed by a natural beauty found in few places. You have the meeting of three mountain ranges as well as spectacular views of Lake Lucerne on clear days. There are 24 hotels and 250 vacation homes.

Mountain layout

When you ski at Engelberg in central Switzerland, just remember that the Gerschnialp is for beginners and the Titlis is for the advanced. This will save you a few difficult moments if you're wary of the ski school of hard knocks.

At Engelberg there are two major areas. The Brunni is on the north side of the valley, with slopes all the way up to the Schonegg, at 6,691 feet. From Schonegg it's an intermediate cruise down to the village.

The finest beginner and lower intermediate skiing is on the opposite mountain, below the Titlis glacier on Gerschnialp. Ski out the doorway of the six-person gondola station at Trübsee and down to the Gerschnialp lifts.

Because it is central Switzerland's major resort, Engelberg is crowded on weekends. During the week things are far less hectic. Everyone but the beginner eventually makes it up to the 10,624-foot-high summit of Titlis. This is where the best skiers sharpen their skills. To join them, take the gondola from the valley floor to Trübsee and then the unique two-section rotating cable car the rest of the way up to Klein-Titlis, at 9,908 feet. You've spent over 40 minutes getting here, so enjoy the view all the way to the St. Gotthard Pass off to the south, and from Lucerne to the north past Interlaken to the Bernese Oberland in one grand sweep to the west.

From Titlis there is a memorable run all the way to Trübsee from what seems (on clear days) like the roof of Europe. The run crosses the summer ski area and becomes a black trail as you begin the biggest part of the 2,500-foot drop from Station Titlis to Stand. Take it easy the first time down. The glacial ice, sharp turns, and steepness of the slope can be treacherous. Follow the trail markers and don't let the nets, set out at the worst places, break your concentration.

After one run some intermediates choose to stay on the wider red run from Stand down to Trübsee. If you make this decision, take the horizontal T-bar across the frozen lake to Alpstübli, where you can go up to the 8,474-foot-high Jochstock. The red run down to Jochpass and Alpstübli is a good warmup for the Kanonenrohr.

The Kanonenrohr (cannon barrel) section is only a few hundred meters long, but you'll turn enough to keep your thighs burning for a while. Lower intermediates should opt for the blue trail to the left of the toughest section. To repeat the best part of the run, stop at the Untertrübsee cable car station and go back up. From Jochstock down to the ground station is about six miles, and it's about eight miles from the Titlis peak.

The best off-trail skiing is on the Laub above the Ritz restaurant and below Titlis. The 1,000-meter vertical drop is a challenge for even experienced skiers, and a guide (for about SFr120) is recommended.

Mountain rating

For beginners, the slopes of the Gerschnialp and Untertrübsee are best.

Intermediates will be challenged on both sides of the valley, particularly up on the glacier which tops Titlis.

Experts will discover whether they really merit that classification after several runs down from the glacier summit. In short, Engelberg is an excellent ski destination for the broadest range of skiers.

Ski school (97/98)

Two ski schools (for information, call 637-3737) with 65 instructors offer group and private lessons. These ski schools offer both skiing and snowboarding instruction.

Private lessons cost SFr59 per hour; SFr173 for a half day (three hours); and SFr298 for a full day (five hours).

Group lessons are offered in full-day blocks. The ski schools offer four hours of instruction a day. The following rates include lifts as well. A full day, SFr86; two days, SFr172; three days, SFr258; four days, SFr327; five days, SFr374.

Cross-country lessons last three hours a day. Rates are one day, SFr40; two days, SFr75; three days, SFr115; four days, SFr140; five days, SFr175.

Lift tickets (97/98 prices)

The Engelberg ticket is good for all 25 lifts in the area, opening about 32 miles of trails. There are discounts for children, senior citizens and families. Day ticket prices drop three francs per hour after 10 a.m.

	Adults	Children	Youth (16–20)
one day (Mon. - Fri.)	SFr47	SFr28	SFr39
one day (Sat. - Sun.)	SFr54	SFr28	SFr44
two days	SFr86	SFr43	SFr70
three days	SFr120	SFr60	SFr98
six days	SFr214	SFr123	SFr176
seven days	SFr229	SFr134	SFr187

Accommodations

Engelberg is a relatively small town (3,300) with a major tourist capacity. Overall, there are nearly 10,000 beds available in hotels, guest houses and pensions, plus another 6,500 in private homes and apartments.

Check with the Tourist Center for all reservations. Call 637-3737 or fax 637-4156.

The all-inclusive plan should be your first choice. The plan offers a week's accommodation and buffet breakfast, six-day ski pass, ski bus and other extras, starting at SFr570 a week during most of January in a two-star hotel; SFr635 a week during most of January in a three-star hotel; SFr940 a week during most of January in a four-star hotel;. The following hotels offer excellent accommodations:

Hotel Engelberg*** (tel. 637-1168, fax 637-3235) A pleasant hotel in the city center.

Hotel Central*** (tel. 637-3232, fax 637-3233) Ideal spot for all activities in town with its own pool and sauna.

Hotel Europe*** (tel. 637-0094, fax 637-2255)

TFEFF Hotel Regina Titlis**** (tel. 637-2828, fax 637-2392) One of our favorite hotels in town.

Hotel Hess**** (tel. 637-1366, fax 637-3538) Here you get friendly staff, traditional rooms and, excellent food.

Sporthotel Trübsee**** (tel. 637-1371, fax 637-3720) Hotel has a great location halfway up the Titlisbahn.

If the hotels in Engelberg are fully booked, as they often are in peak season, the lakeside city of Lucerne is a good alternative. It is only 30 minutes from the slopes by car. An excellent waterside hotel is **Hotel des Balances.**

Apartments

Engelberg has much to offer the skier seeking apartment accommodations. Prices start at SFr285 a week for a one-bedroom apartment. The average apartment for four costs in January about SFr460, and in February about SFr535. The tourist office (637-3737or fax 637-4156) has a computerized listing of available apartments, and an inquiry will be answeres by mail the same day.

Dining

The **Tudorstübli** restaurant at Hotel Hess (tel. 637-1366) is the best restaurant in town and offers excellent lamb specialties. Other excellent eateries are **Restaurant Spannort** (tel. 637-2626) and **Restaurant Eden** (tel. 639-5639).

Après-ski/nightlife

Drop into the **Spindle** in the cellar of the Alpenclub Hotel. It's crowded with the 18- to 25-year-old set, as is the nearby **Carmena Casino**. Our favorites were **Dream Life**, an English pub at the Central Hotel, the pub in the Hotel Engel, and **Peter's Pub**, just up the street. The **Bierlialp Chalet** disco has dancing in the center of town. Try **Yucatan** in Hotel Bellvue or **Mattes** for music.

Child care

The ski school (637-1074 or 637-3040) operates a ski kindergarten for kids three to six, from 9 a.m. to 5 p.m.

For kids three to six years of age who ski, rates are: full day, SFr61; two days, SFr122: three days, SFr183; five days, SFr280. These rates include four hours of lessons, supervision during lunch, lift tickets and ski test.

For kids 7–16 years of age who ski, rates are: full day, SFr86; two days, SFr172: three days, SFr258; five days, SFr374. These rates include four hours of lessons, supervision during lunch, lift tickets and ski test. For kids who don't ski the rates are significantly lower.

Getting there

The main international airport is Zürich, and transfers are by train or automobile. Driving time from Zürich is about one-and-a-half hours. If possible, make a sightseeing stop in Lucerne along the way.

Other activities

Engelberg is sunny most of the year. The biggest non-skiing pursuits are hiking and sightseeing.

Engelberg has a sports center with indoor and outdoor ice skating, indoor tennis courts, a fitness center, a curling competition area, billiards, darts and table tennis.

Horse-drawn sleigh rides are available throughout the winter; on Fridays, January through March, nighttime sleigh rides are a tradition.

Visit the beautiful twelvth-century Benedictine abbey at the edge of town. For more extensive touring, take the train for a tour of Lucerne and the four lakes area.

The Engelberg Talmuseum has been set up in the Wappenhaus. Visitors will get a good idea of what life is and was like in these high Alpine valleys.

Courses in trick skiing are offered (tel. 637- 10 74).

The most scenic local excursions other than the ride up the Titlisbahn, is a trip to Schwand, about five miles away, where from a vantage point above the church, you get the best view of the ring of mountains.

Tourist information

Contact the Tourist Center, CH-6390 Engelberg, Switzerland; tel. (041) 637-3737, fax (041) 637-4156.

Hotel and apartment reservations are available by calling (041) 637 3737, or fax (041) 637-4156.

Internet: www.engelberg.ch

☎ *Local telephone prefix is 041.*

Flims Laax Falera

Flims Laax Falera is still one of the undiscovered ski areas in Switzerland as far as American and British skiers are concerned, even with excellent ski club patronage. Unlike the best-known Swiss ski resorts, which were patronized by English visitors, Flims Laax Falera were discovered by the Swiss and the Germans, who know a good area when they see it. The ski area is in the southeast part of Switzerland across the valley from Arosa.

Flims is a small town in the traditional sense. The ski lifts start from the town center (about 3,600 feet altitude) and the major hotels are spread throughout the town. Laax, a couple of kilometers down the road, as far as skiers are concerned, is limited to the new hotels and apartments, purpose-built at the base of the Crap Sogn Gion cable car. Not only are the major hotels centered here but also the major nightlife. Flims is perhaps the more Swiss; Laax is a purer ski vacation experience.

It is hard to describe the incredible expanse of ski area that surrounds a skier as he gazes from the station at the top of the Crap Sogn Gion cable car that rises from Laax. This is a wide-open area that cries out for all-day skiing.

Mountain layout

One major lift from each town carries skiers to the snowfields, which are in turn linked by an extensive far-flung lift system. These lifts are not tightly packed, but they service the trails belonging to four major sections: Cassons Grat, La Siala, Crap Sogn Gion and Vorab.

After the lifts split above Flims, one continues to Cassons Grat, a spectacular snowfield surrounding the Flimserstein peak. Here, powder and off-trail skiers can have a field day. The other fork of the lift takes skiers to Grauberg, linked with other lifts under La Siala peak.

Above Laax the cable car reaches the Crap Sogn Gion, at 7,283 feet, and a second continues to Crap Masegn, 650 feet higher. From here, skiers can shoot back into the valley toward Falera or to the lower cable car station. Other runs drop into the opposite valley, where more lifts bring skiers up to the La Siala area above Flims. High-altitude buffs head to the Vorab area, which at 9,842 feet presents great panoramas and skiing.

Mountain rating

The beginner will find the best areas under La Siala and on the Vorab and on Flims-Foppa, the first stage of the way up the Cassons Grat.

Intermediates will be overjoyed with the Crap Sogn Gion section and can find more than enough challenging runs anywhere in the resort area.

The expert skiers can stay busy when the mood strikes them, especially beneath the Crap Sogn Gion cable car, the back side of the Vorab and through the Cassons Grat powder and trails. But they will have to pick their spots.

Ski school (96/97 prices)

Ski school is available in Flims, Falera and Laax. The prices are almost identical. Private instruction costs SFr135 for a half day, SFr240 for a full day

Group lessons for adults are: SFr52 for a full day; SFr135 for three full days; SFr182 for five full days.

Group lessons for children are SFr26 for a half day; SFr120 for five half days.

A private leson for carving work costs SFr140 for a half day, and for snowboarding SFr240 for one day.

The ski school offers a special Carving Academy to help intermediate skiers improve their technique with shaped skis. A half-day lesson with skis privided is FFr55; without skis FFr40.

Snowboard lessons are available throught the Swiss Ski School in Flims-Dorf (911-1438). Group lessons are FFr180 for a three-course, FFr60 for a full day with a FFr100 charge for a two-day extension to either program. Private lessons are FFr135 for one or two boarders for a half day. Full-day lessons for one or two boarders are FFr240. Extra boarders cost FFr10.

There is a cross-country school in Flims offering private lessons. It is open from 9 a.m. to 4:30 p.m. Call 911-2035.

Lift tickets (97/98 prices)

A combination ticket that allows unlimited skiing in the Flims Laax Falera area costs as follows (a photo, which they take at the lift station, is required for lift passes of six days or more):

	Adults	Children (6-16)	Youth (16–20) Seniors (60+)
one day	SFr56	SFr28	SFr45
two days	SFr104	SFr54	SFr84
six days	SFr281	SFr135	SFr219

Accommodations

The daily rates given below are the normal high-season rates with half pension, based on double occupancy. They are around 20 percent less in low season.

All-inclusive White Week packages are available throughout the winter season. They include seven nights accomodation, six days of lifts and five days of lessons.

Park Hotel Waldhaus (tel. 911-0181; fax 911-2804) The best hotel in Flims. A beautiful hotel that is almost its own small village. The buildings are interconnected by covered paths and underground walkways. You can be elegant and formal or casual in this complex in the woods. Daily rate: SFr215–235.

Adula (tel. 911-0161; fax 911-1315) In Flims, this runs a close second to the Park Hotel. In fact, many people prefer it because it is cozier and smaller. It has an indoor pool, sauna, and fitness room. Its Barga restaurant is consider-ed one of the best in the region. Daily rate: SFr115–235.

Alpenhotel Crap Ner (tel. 911-2626; fax 911-2675) Its name means "black rock" in the local dialect. Ten minutes from the lift in Flims Dorf. Excellent menu in the Giardino restaurant, and cozy atmosphere in the Tschuetta Bar. Daily rate: SFr114–185.

Hotel National (tel. 911-3923; fax 911-2420) This hotel is young and fun with an energetic owner and manager. Daily rate: SFr100–130.

Arvenhotel Waldeck (tel. 911-1228; fax 9114384) In Flims-Waldhaus this hotel is known for its restaurant. Rooms have been done in knotty pine and the ambiance is casual. Daily rate: SFr90–115.

Hotel Meiler-Prau da Monis (tel. 920-9393; fax 920-9394) In Flims and close to everything. Daily rate: SFr82–160.

Apartments

Flims, Laax and Falera are well organized to handle apartment rentals. Apartments are normally rented out for a minimum stay of one week, Saturday to Saturday; in the Christmas and Easter seasons a minimum two-week rental is often required.

The tourist office keeps a computerized, updated listing of available apartments. When writing, include the number of beds required, the preferred number of rooms, and your planned vacation dates. You will receive a quick response that lists a selection of apartments and prices. Select the apartment you want and contact Flims Tourism.

Normally, linen and kitchen utensils are provided. Other communal or private amenities, such as swimming pool, sauna, TV or room phone all add to the cost. Apartments rent for SFr30 to SFr60 per person a night.

Dining

Area restaurants are reasonably priced and most feature a good selection of international and regional specialties. The best in the region is the **Restarant Barga** (tel. 911-0181) in the Hotel Adula. Gault Millau considers it one of tSwitzerland's best.

For good basic value and Swiss tradition in Flims, try the **Fidazerhof** (tel. 911-3503); the **Crap Ner** (tel. 911-2626) is noted for its fish dishes. In Laax, the **Posta Veglia** (tel. 921-4467) is highly recommended for traditional Swiss cooking.

Après-ski/nightlife

The best meeting spot in the area is the **Iglu Bar** in Flims that caters to a younger crowd earlier in the evening. An older crowd congregates for the special shows that start around midnight.

In Laax, the **Camona** offers action reminiscent of big city discos. A live band starts at about 11:30 p.m. The **Casa Veglia** in Laax has a somewhat older crowd and is more sedate. You'll pay about SFr10 for a beer and SFr15 for a mixed drink.

Child care

Kindergartens associated with the famous Swiss Ski School operate in the area. In Flims and Laax, the children's ski school and kindergarten is open from 9 a.m. until 4:30 p.m.

Rates are SFr26 for a half day; SFr52 for a full day; SFr120 for five half days; and SFr182 for five full days.

A mid-day nursery service with lunch costs Sfr64 for five sessions. Older children can enroll in ski school.

Getting there

The closest airport is Zürich. From there you can take a train to Chur, where you must change for a postbus to Flims, Laax or Falera. The entire trip takes about three hours.

If driving, take the main road to Chur and continue until you see signs for Flims to the right. Driving time is about two hours. Do not try to approach Laax, Falera and Flims from the west—the Oberalp pass is closed in winter.

Other activities

Horse-drawn sleigh rides cost SFr30 per person. Ice skating is SFr5.50 a half day. Play tennis for SFr40 an hour in the Park Hotel in Flims and in the Hotel Signina in Laax.

Four heated hotel pools are open to the public—Park Hotel, Schweitzerhof, Adula and Crap Ner.

A public swimming pool is open in Laax Monday to Thursday from 1:30 p.m. to 9:30 p.m., on Friday it closes at 8 p.m. and on Saturday and Sunday it closes at 6 p.m. It is also open 9:30 a.m. to noon on Sunday. Entrance is SFr7 for adults and SFr4 for children.

Tourist information

Flims Tourism, CH-7018 Flims-Waldhaus, Switzerland; tel. (081) 920-9200; fax (081) 920-9201. Flims hotel and apartment booking: tel. 920-9202.
Laax Tourism, CH-7031 Laax, Switzerland; tel. (081) 921-4343; fax (081) 921-6565.
Falera Tourism, CH-7153 Falera, Switzerland; tel. (081) 921-3030; fax (081) 921-4830.
Internet: www.laax.ch/
E-mail: flims@whitearena.ch
☎ *Telephone prefix for Flims and Laax is 081.*

Gstaad-Saanenland
Super Ski Region

People associate Gstaad more with the jet set than with good skiing, and that's a mistake, because it has outstanding slopes for beginners and intermediates. This Alpine village tucked into a scenic valley just east of Lac Leman, two hours from Geneva and 90 minutes from Interlaken, is part of a thriving ski circuit called the Gstaad Super Ski Region. When you buy a lift ticket in Gstaad, or at one of the ten smaller resorts in the area, you can use any of 69 lifts opening up about 180 miles of prepared trails. The other villages lie stretched along the railway line (from east to west): St. Stephan, Zweisimmen, Saanenmöser, Schönried, Gstaad, Saanen, Rougemont, Chateau d'Oex, Les Moulins—with Lauenen, Gsteig and Reusch accessible by bus up the valleys fanning from Gstaad.

Mountain layout

The skiing in the immediate area of Gstaad is fragmented. The relatively low Eggli (5,494 feet) is the largest area, interconnected with the peak of Videmanette and the towns of Saanen and Rougemont.

The Wasserngrat (6,365 feet) and the Wispile (6,397 feet) are the two other totally separated areas. The Wasserngrat is the most challenging of the three areas, but is limited to two lifts. However, the skiing is superb and there is hardly ever a line—if the Eggli is crowded, this area offers skiing with no waiting. (It should be noted that beginners and lower intermediates may be slightly out of their league here.)

The Wispile is not as difficult as the Wasserngrat and is closer to town. This is a good intermediate area with limited lifts but long, enjoyable runs; wide stretches of the slopes are left unprepared for powder hounds. It also has short lines and is within walking distance of the Eggli lifts. The Swiss Ski School is located at its base and the drag lift is used mainly by the ski school.

The Eggli shows two black runs, although an intermediate should seldom feel anxiety here. The run through the trees from the chair lift at Eggli Stand to the ground T-bar station in neighboring Saanen has enough moguls and turns to hold the expert's interest.

There is some genuine skiing adventure above Gstaad. The finest is La Videmanette. Ski over the Eggli and down to the Pra Cluen chair lift to reach the area above neighboring Rougemont, or drive there. From Rougemont, four-passenger gondolas ascend past rocky pinnacles to the La Videmanette summit at (7,071 feet). The run down through the rocks off the back side is strictly for experts.

On the Videmanette front side, the first 300 meters straight over the edge is also an eye-opener (skittish types can take the traverse around the rim of the bowl). There's a difficult mogul field to negotiate before beginning the remainder of the 3.5-mile intermediate run to Rougemont. Alternatively, ski around the corner to the top of the Pra Cluen lift and ski the 3.5-mile schuss into the valley.

There is summer glacier skiing at Les Diablerets (10,637 feet), reached by a three-stage cable car from Reusch at the end of the valley. This glacier has also become a favorite of snowboarders.

The Hornberg section is the largest interconnected grouping of lifts in the region. It is not directly connected with Gstaad, but is easily reached by bus or train (both included with your ski pass). Take either the Horneggli lift from Schönried or the Saanerslochgrat gondola from Sannenmöser. Both lifts are opposite the respective railway stations, making it impossible to get lost. This area, a lower intermediate paradise, is served by 14 lifts, which keeps waiting time to less than five minutes.

For more challenging runs, head for the St. Stephan lifts connected with Hornberg. Take the Saanerslochgrat gondola and ski down to Chaltebrunne. Then take the chair lift up to the Gandlouenegrat, which sits at the top of the St. Stephan section. The face of the mountain from Gandlouenegrat down to Chaltebrunne is an enjoyable wide-open slope. There is something for everyone, from advanced beginner to expert. Playing here can take up half the day. Time it right for lunch and eat at the Chemi Hütte at Lengebrand on the slopes above St. Stephan, at the top of the chair lift from town.

Opposite the Hornberg section is the Rellerligrat (6,285 feet) with what many claim is the most beautiful view of Gstaad. The slopes face the sun, and so are the first to lose snow. Mornings can be icy and afternoons slushy, but skiing here on sunny days is a joy. The restaurant at the top is one of the best in the area. The runs back into the valley are long cruising trails, with a long black run under the gondola for experts.

Zweisimmen offers an unfortunately isolated ski area flanked on the left by St. Stephan and on the right by the Hornberg lifts. There is no lift connection with either. The gondola from town to the Rinderberg opens up seven prepared runs served by five lifts. It is pleasant for a day's skiing. Most of the people who stay in Zweisimmen take the train to ski the Hornberg section.

Chateau d'Oex is another area included in the regional ski pass. Here the La Braye gondola lifts skiers over a ridge behind the town to a mellow area of about a dozen runs.

Despite the relatively low-lying intermediate slopes, Gstaad enjoys good snow most years from late December to mid-April, with skiing available on the glacier through the end of April.

Mountain rating

If you are a beginner, Gstaad is an excellent destination. There are plenty of gentle inclines to practice snowplows and stem christies. The finest beginner run is the 1,253-meter-long Skilift Schopfen slope from the gondola station on the Eggli.

Intermediates will be overjoyed at the variety. Just when you think you've mastered it all, you can cut through the woods or go over the edge of a mogul field you've been bypassing and suddenly realize you have more to learn.

The expert can enjoy Gstaad if he places more emphasis on technique than thrills.

Ski school (97/98 prices)

Gstaad, with more than 100 instructors, has a good reputation for English-speaking ski instructors and for private lessons. It is open 8:30 a.m.–noon and 2:30–6 p.m.

Private lesson rates: one hour (one to four persons), SFr60; all day, SFr260.

Group lesson rates: half day, SFr29; full day, SFr51; six consecutive days, SFr195; six non-consecutive days, SFr210.

Many ski classes meet directly on the Wispile slope or at the entrance to the Wispile gondola station. Call 7441865 for information and bookings. Lessons are available for cross-country and snowboarding.

The Saanenland region has four ski schools in various towns throughout the ski area.

Lift tickets (97/98 prices)

These tickets are good for the entire Gstaad Super Ski Region area covering 69 lifts and 250 km. of runs. They are good on the railroad, on buses and for entrance to the covered pool in Gstaad.

a four-hour ticket	SFr38
one day	SFr46
three days	SFr130
six days	SFr233
seven days	SFr263
thirteen days	SFr389

Children receive a special reduced lift ticket rate.

There is a day lift ticket limited to Chateau d'Oex/Mt. Chevreuils for approximately 13 percent less than the regional pass. Separate ski passes can also be purchased for Adelboden Lenk and Alpen Vadoise.

Accommodations

All hotels in the region offer special weekly programs running throughout the season except for holiday periods. These packages include seven nights accommodation with half board, a six day ski pass, cross-country or snowboarding pass, plus entrance into the indoor swimming pool and local transportation. The price noted is approximate, per person for a double room in high season with half board. For information call 7488181.

Gstaad Palace (tel. 7485000, fax 7485001) The best in town. A chance to rub shoulders with the best of the movie, fashion and jet-set world if you can afford the entrance. Daily rate: SFr480.

Park Hotel (tel. 7489800, fax 7489808) New hotel with indoor salt-water pool, heated outdoor pool, fitness center, squash and tennis, Greenhouse coffee shop, elegant and rustic restaurants only two minutes' walk from the center of Gstaad. Daily rate: SFr340.

Grand Hotel Bellevue (tel. 7483171, fax 7442136) Traditional hotel in the town center. One of the town's best hotels just below the luxury level. Daily rate: SFr180.

Le Grand Chalet (tel. 7483252, fax 7444415) A small, charming hotel on the hill with a magnificent view of Gstaad. Daily rate: SFr210 (B&B only)

Bernerhof (tel. 7488844, fax 7488840) Centrally located with swimming pool. Spacious rooms, good service with good kindergarten. Daily rate: SFr189.

Hotel Arc-en-Ciel (tel. 7483191, fax 7443633) Best location for skiing the Eggli. Opposite the gondola station and near a ski rental shop. Quiet, with a good restaurant. Daily rate: SFr150.

Hotel Gstaaderhof (tel. 7486363, fax 7486360) Good location relatively near lifts, station and downtown. Daily rate: SFr169.

Hotel Alphorn (tel. 7444545, fax 7441790) Good location for skiers; near the lift for the Wispile. Across the highway from the Eggli gondola. Daily rate: SFr122.

Posthotel Rössli (tel. 7443412, fax 7446190) This is one of the hotel prizes in Gstaad, but is small and booked very early. The restaurant is one of the best in town. Daily rate: SFr112.

Sporthotel Victoria (tel. 7441431, fax 7446923) Excellent food; has two restaurants and a pizzeria. The most reasonable hotel in town. Daily rate: SFr112.

Saanen

Hotel Steigenberger in Gstaad/Saanen (tel. 74886464, fax 7486466) Deluxe hotel with pool, sauna, good disco and two restaurants. Daily rate: SFr225.

Hotel Cabana between Gstaad and Sannen (tel. 7483200, fax 7449473) Pool, garden, sauna, fitness and beauty center. Daily rate: SFr170.

Landhaus (tel. 7444858, fax 7448940) Good, middle-priced hotel in town center. Daily rate: SFr117 (B&B only).

Saanenmöser

Hotel Hornberg (tel. 7444440, fax 7446279) Everything a good ski hotel should be: near the lifts, pool and sauna and an owner who helps his clients. Daily rate: SFr190.

Schönried

Hotel Alpenrose (tel. 7446767, fax 7446712) This is a Relais et Châteaux property. Many claim the hotel restaurant is the best in the area. Daily rate: SFr265.

Hotel Alpin nova (tel. 7486767, fax 7486768) Centrally located with a traditional mountain atmosphere. Daily rate: SFr152

Hotel Bahnhof (tel. 7444242; fax 7446142) Includes ski school. The lowest priced major hotel in town with nice rooms and close to the station. Daily rate: SFr120.

Chateau d'Oex

This town down the tracks toward Montreux from Gstaad is significantly less expensive than the Saanenmöser-Gstaad-Saanen area. The town is in the French part of Switzerland. It is not as charming nor as "Alpine" as Gstaad. But for overall savings of about 25 percent, this might be the place to stay if you don't mind the half-hour train ride to the major slopes above Gstaad and Schönried. Good English spoken at both.

Hotel Beau-Sejour (tel. 026-9247423, fax 9245806) This hotel is very convenient, across from the train station and the cable car to the Chateau d'Oex area. Daily rate: SFr75–110.

Hotel Ours (tel. 026-9242279, fax 9242270) In the center of town about three minutes from the lift and train station. Daily rate: SFr100.

Apartments

Vacation apartment rentals are available in every village. Information on rentals is provided by the tourist offices. In middle season an apartment with one bedroom, living room and furnished kitchen costs approximately SFr700–1,300 a week. Ample room for four people is typical. Call 7488184 for assistance with apartment reservations.

Dining

Even with Gstaad's jet-set reputation, the best restaurants are just outside town. Naturally, the Palace has several world-class restaurants, but then again most of us are not up to Palace prices. **The Cave** in the Olden Hotel in the center of town provides excellent dining by anyone's standards. Expect to pay top price, but you'll never know who you're going to rub shoulders with. Still in town and considerably more reasonable is the **Rössli** across the main street from the Olden—this is typical Swiss cooking at its best. Behind the Rössli, try the **Chesery**, which is good but not as exceptional as the Rössli. The **Arc-en-Ciel** opposite the Eggli gondola station is stark but serves excellent Italian food at low prices.

Out-of-Gstaad Places

Schönried has the **Alpenrose** (tel. 7446767) with a Relais et Châteaux gourmet restaurant. This small nouvelle cuisine restaurant is one of the tops in Switzerland. An exceptional traditional Swiss restaurant is the **Bären** (tel. 7551033) in Gsteig on the road from Gstaad to Les Diablerets. Down the road from Gsteig try the **Rössli** in Feutersoey (tel. 7551012). In the tiny town of Lauenen enjoy a meal at the **Wildhorn** (tel. 7653012). Finally, don't miss the 17th-century **Restaurant Chlösterli** (tel. 7551912) just outside town on the road to Les Diablerets.

On the slopes

The best mountain restaurants above Gstaad are at the Eggli and Kalberhöni. Above Schönried, try the Hornberg restaurants—one is slightly more upscale, the other has wonderful *Rösti* and plenty of pasta . . . both have great terraces to enjoy the sun. The **Rellerli Mountain Restaurant** on the opposite side of the valley from Hornberg enjoys a storybook view of Gstaad. Try the **Chemi Hütte at Lengebrand** above St. Stephan.

Après-ski/nightlife

The place for après-ski just off the slopes is the **Olden Bar**. It's normally packed. Otherwise, even on Friday night, this town snoozes until midnight. The **Chesery Bar** and the **Stockli Bar** in the Bernerhof were recommended as the best places to have a beer or drink, but both are very quiet. **Club 95** in the Hotel Victoria is a popular disco with a young crowd. **The Grotte** in the Hotel Alpinnova is a good disco.

The well-heeled enjoy an après-ski drink in the Palace Hotel lounge above the city. Take money if you want to join them. For starters, the Palace disco cover is SFr40.

After dark there's a lively crowd and live music at the **Chlösterli** disco outside town. Also try the **Greengo** at the Palace Hotel for dancing.

Gstaad has a new casino where the rich can strut their stuff and gamble away some of their earnings or inheritances.

Child care

The Gstaad Tourist Office can help with child care arrangements. Call 7488181. The ski schools all have programs—call 7441865 in Gstaad or 7488160 in Saanen

In Chateau d'Oex, call Mme. Blati at Les Clematites, tel. (026) 9247351. She takes children from two months old. The ski school has children's lessons; call (026) 9246848.

Getting there

The most popular international airport is Zurich. From there, it is about three-and-a-half hours by train to Gstaad. Rental cars are also available in Zurich. You may also arrive in Geneva which doesn't have as convenient train connections, but is closer by rental car.

Other activities

Gstaad has an excellent covered swimming pool.

Gstaad is in a good location for train or auto excursions to Montreux, Geneva, Lausanne, Interlaken and Bern, all within approximately two hours by train.

Ballooning over the Alps provides a once-in-a-lifetime thrill. Balloon rides can be arranged through the tourist office (tel. 7488181). The price is SFr485 per person for about two hours. Paragliding is also available.

Ice skating, curling and horseback riding are available (tel. 7444368).

Tourist information

Information on the Gstaad Super Ski Region is through Gstaad Tourist Association, CH-3780 Gstaad, Switzerland; tel. (033) 7488181; fax (033) 7488183. Tourist Office Chateau d'Oex: tel. (026) 9247788.

Internet: www.gstaad.ch; E-mail: tvsl@gstaad.ch

☎ *Telephone prefix for Gstaad is 033;*
for Chateau d'Oex the prefix is 026.

Jungfrau Region
Grindelwald, Wengen, Mürren

The Jungfrau region is near Interlaken on the map; for intermediate skiers it is at the end of the Alpine rainbow. A network of 185 miles of trails spreads over a vast expanse of slopes, set in two majestic valleys about an hour's drive from Bern, the Swiss capital.

The backdrop created by the Jungfrau, Mönch and Eiger mountains is one you see on posters the world over.

The Jungfrau region has three major ski areas accessible from its twin-valley towns. For Americans, the Jungfraujoch is best known for the Eiger, a 13,026' peak made famous by Clint Eastwood's *The Eiger Sanction*, an edge-of-your-seat suspense movie that came out in 1975. Although the movie is nearly 20 years old, the view hasn't changed.

The best-known resort is Grindelwald, a picture-postcard settlement nestled at the foot of 10,000-foot peaks about 30 minutes by train or car from Interlaken. There is skiing at Grindelwald First (First, in this case, means peak), which in its day had Europe's oldest operating chair lift.

The second area is just beneath the Eiger. Here, Wengen and Kleine Scheidegg offer car-free villages on the mountain. Lauterbrunnen is in the valley on the opposite side of the Lauberhorn, and is a second starting point for the cog train up the mountain. Wengen is halfway up the mountain along the train route overlooking the Lauterbrunnen valley. Up on the ridge plateau, at the base of the Eiger, is Kleine Scheidegg, a settlement with a railway station and hotels.

The third ski area, Mürren/Schilthorn, is across the Lauterbrunnen Valley and is also reached only by cog train or cable car. Mürren is a tiny village, as perfect as a movie set. In fact it was, for James Bond in *On Her Majesty's Secret Service*.

Mountain layout

The Jungfrau Top Ski Region has 49 lifts in all, including railway routes up the mountain. Grindelwald and its surrounding hills and mountainsides are divided into seven pie-slice pieces radiating out from the center of town. Each forms a co-op for business purposes: by a plan set up in 1402, people clustered near the center have land-use rights to any land and pasture in their slice.

The ski lifts are owned by the individual co-ops. Since there is no one ski company, every time you use one of the lifts, your ski ticket is read by a scanner so that each region's ski income can be calculated. (Many of the lift attendants farm the ski runs in the summer; it is told that one farmer, many years ago, decided he'd had enough of winter and spread manure on the ski run to hasten the spring melt.)

Grindelwald First

The 9,609-foot Schwarzhorn, on your left as you enter town from Interlaken, is the backdrop for the Grindelwald First slopes. The access gondola, the three-mile Firstbahn, leaves from the city core of Grindelwald, about 50 yards off the main street.

The Firstbahn angles through two stops on the way to First. Then skiers can hop the new quad chair to Oberjoch with its huge wide groomed runs. First is great for intermediates.

Follow a group down new (to you) trails. These trails will all come out somewhere useful, such as a lift station or a ski bus stop.

For some, First is a place to work out those kinks before moving over to tackle the runs on the Kleine Scheidegg side of the valley. But First offers plenty of great skiing on its own. In the U.S. any resort would be overjoyed to have this much terrain and vertical drop (4,705 feet—more than any resort in the United States) There are 41 km. of prepared trails here, with good limitless off-piste runs.

Most skiers stay at the higher altitudes, on the runs under the Oberjoch and the trails served by the Schilt and Grindel T-bars. This area is shielded from the wind and provides the most varied skiing.

Grindelwald/Kleine Scheidegg

The cog train from Grindelwald Grund takes about a half hour to reach Kleine Scheidegg, a bit of an Alpine ski village trisected by railway tracks. Across from the parking lot of the Grund station is the Männlichenbahn, a gondola lift. In 25 minutes the gondola takes you to the Männlichen summit.

If you take the cog train you can yo-yo your way across towards Männlichen on the Arven, Hönegg, Gummi, Tschuggen and Läger lifts. The skiing gets progressively more difficult as you work your way across, until you arrive at the wide-open Männlichen area.

From the Kleine Scheidegg station you can take the lift to the top of the Lauberhorn and then either ski back toward Kleine Scheidegg or loop around to the Wixi lift and Wengen, more or less following the famous Lauberhorn downhill race course. The World Cup is held there every January. It's a delightful ski experience, with a seemingly endless variety of dips, turns, mogul fields and occasional ice patches—perfect territory for the advanced intermediate. Try the run from the Lauberhorn to the Wixi chair lift, picking your way through the mogul fields. When the snow is good, this run is exceptional.

You can also take the cog train up to the next stop, Eigergletscher, where several steep runs drop back down toward Wixi and Wengen and over-the-ridge runs also descend toward Grindelwald alongside the Salzegg lift.

At the end of your day, you'll have a marvelous 30-minute run to Grindelwald, passing the Arvengarten lift base before reaching a network of intermediate trails that offer a touch of adventure—there is always an easier way around the tough places for the less advanced. This 30-minute run to the car park of the Männlichen gondola or to the Grund cog train station may be the highlight of your stay in the Jungfrau region, unless you're counting the chills of Mürren's 007 Run as a fun experience.

Grindelwald/Männlichen

Take the gondola from Grund directly to Männlichen. You will rise 4,223 feet of vertical, which can be skied in one long expert run or one long intermediate run.

Most skiers decide to remain at the upper level of the Männlichen and play on the wide-open slopes served by the Männlichen T-bar and the Läger chair lift. From the Läger chair skiers can drop down to the Gummi chair lift and yo-yo their way over to Kleine Scheidegg. These runs between Männlichen and Kleine Scheidegg are a delight for skiers of any level.

Wengen

The town of Wengen sits at the base of the vertical cliff dropping from the Männlichen area and the Lauberhorn areas. Skiers have a choice of taking either the cable car from town to the Männlichen area, or the cog train around the Lauberhorn to the Kleine Scheidegg area.

The only way back to town without a parachute or hang-glider is around the Lauberhorn under the Wixi chair lift, down to the Bumps T-bar, then along the trails to the town.

Mürren

For ski challenges in this region, savvy downhillers head for the Schilthorn, the mountain above Mürren, across the gorge from Wengen. Take the cog train from Lauterbrunnen to Mürren and then go by cable car the rest of the way; or take a direct cable car from Stechelberg, outside Lauterbrunnen.

There is less good skiing but more challenges on the Schilthorn than at any of the other locations. Overall, there are 18 slopes with about 30 miles of runs. The eye-opener is the black run from the 9,748-foot Schilthorn. Start by quaffing an extra-strong cup of espresso or have lunch in the Piz Gloria revolving restaurant atop the Schilthorn, then tackle the famed Inferno, also called the 007 Run. The lower section, called the Kanonenrohr (Cannon Barrel), sends you hurtling down a series of narrow, steep, bumped-up, rutted and often icy trails. Actually, good intermediates can make it haltingly down the entire run. The Engetal area, approximately a third of the way down from the Schilthorn, offers plenty of wide-open skiing, with the option to take the last stage of the Schilthorn cable car up to the top for another chance to carve your way down the face of the mountain. It's below the Engetal area that the series of narrow and steep spots come into play.

If you visit in mid-to-late January, watch at least a part of the Inferno-Rennen, the traditional (since 1928) Schilthorn race that pits nearly 1,500 (as many as 4,000 apply) would-be champions against the clock and the 15.8-km. course. It takes a world-class skier almost 15 minutes. The race is normally scheduled in mid January.)

Adventurous skiers also tackle the black runs from the 7,035-foot Schiltgrat. This area has excellent bumps and some super-steep off-piste skiing. Intermediates stay on the flat top of the ridge. Connecting lifts take you to the Winteregg and Allmendhubel, the mountain's other two ski areas, where intermediate skiing—with an occasional black run—is the rule. The best intermediate run leads down to the base of the Winteregg chair, where you can lunch at an excellent restaurant.

If you are coming up from Lauterbrunnen on the train for Mürren, there is a stop at the Winteregg chair where you can start and work your way to Allmendhubel and over to the Schiltgrat and the Schilthorn.

Mountain rating

Grindelwald/First

This should present no difficulties for the lower intermediate. Intermediates will have a blast and even experts will enjoy the run beneath the gondola and some of the occasional steeps to be found above. Beginners use the two short Bodmi lifts above town with ease, while everyone from advanced beginner and above goes right to the top.

Grindelwald/Kleine Scheidegg

Working one's way around the mountain toward Männlichen from Kleine Scheidegg requires good intermediate skills, but can be handled by most intermediates. The Lauberhorn can get bumped up, but still can be skied by any intermediate. The Wengen side with the Lauberhorn run is perhaps the most challenging. The runs dropping from the Eigergletscher down to the Wixi are expert territory, and intermediates can also make the drop down the Salzegg side.

Grindelwald/Männlichen

The wide-open area at the top of the gondola is perfect for every level of skier. Intermediates and experts will have a blast playing on the trails that wend over to Kleine Scheidegg. The long run to the base of the gondola is a joy.

Wengen

The nursery slopes surrounding this town are the best in the valley. If you are a beginner or traveling with a beginner, Wengen is the best village to stay in. It's also the sunniest of the ski areas.

Mürren

Don't plan to ski Mürren extensively if you're a beginner. There are some intermediate slopes that the absolute beginner may be able to handle after a few days, but just barely. Lower intermediates will have their hands full, but strong intermediates will have a field day. Experts will find that the slopes of the Schilthorn and the Schiltgrat are the most challenging in the entire Jungfrau area.

 ## Ski school (97/98 prices)

All three major resorts in the region have ski schools offering downhill, snowboarding and cross-country instruction.

More than 80 ski instructors are available daily for individuals and groups in Wengen (552022) and Grindelwald (532021). Mürren (551247) ski school has 25 instructors giving group and private lessons.

Prices are within a franc or so of each other in all three ski areas. These prices are for the Grindelwald Ski School:

Private lessons

Half-day (2 hours)	SFr170
full day (5 hours)	SFr288

Group lessons

half-day (2 hours)	SFr32
five half-day lessons (10 hours)	SFr122
ten half-day lessons (1 week)	SFr192

Cross-country instruction is available. There is a seven-mile loop around the outskirts of Lauterbrunnen. Grindelwald has 35 km. of trails. Wengen does not have a cross-country run, but Mürren has a simple 2-km. circuit.

Lift tickets (97/98 prices)

A special Jungfrau Top Ski Region ticket for a minimum of two days includes Mürren, Kleine Scheidegg and Grindelwald First. It includes all cog trains and ski buses. Tickets good only for individual areas are also available.

	Adults	Teenagers (16–20)	Children (6–16)	Seniors (62+)
Jungfrau region				
two days	SFr100	SFr80	SFr50	SFr90
three days	SFr136	SFr105	SFr68	SFr122
six days	SFr232	SFr186	SFr116	SFr209
seven days	SFr254	SFr203	SFr127	SFr229
14 days	SFr400	SFr320	SFr200	SFr369
Grindelwald First				
half day	SFr38	SFr30	SFr19	SFr34
one day	SFr50	SFr40	SFr25	SFr45
two days	SFr90	SFr72	SFr45	SFr81
Kleine Scheidegg/Männlichen				
half day	SFr40	SFr32	SFr20	SFr36
one day	SFr52	SFr42	SFr26	SFr47
two days	SFr95	SFr76	SFr48	SFr86
Mürren				
half day	SFr38	SFr30	SFr19	SFr34
one day	SFr50	SFr40	SFr25	SFr45
two days	SFr90	SFr72	SFr45	SFr81

Accommodations

Grindelwald

Grindelwald has 51 hotels, and 47 of them are owned and managed by a family. Many of the hotels are 100 years old, and most are smaller than 100 beds. Only four Grindelwald hotels have more than 100 beds.

Prices, unless otherwise noted, are for seven days at half pension (breakfast and one meal, normally dinner), and six days of lifts in January or April with free entrance to the respective sports center. The daily rate is per person based on double occupancy, with half board, in February and March.

Hotel Regina (854-5455, fax 853-4717) SFr1,550 Grindelwald's only five-star hotel, with excellent location by the Jungfrau cog railway station is as luxurious as it gets in this town. Jacket and tie worn in the candlelit dining rooms. Old-World elegance. Daily rate: SFr280.

Hotel Schweizerhof (854-5454, fax 853-3353) SFr1,291 A chalet-style hotel with downtown location near the Jungfrau cog railway station. Daily rate: SFr172–230.

Sunstar Hotel and Sunstar-Adler (854-7777, fax 854-7770) SFr1,291 This is a modern hotel in chalet style across from the Grindelwald-First lifts. One side faces First; the other side faces the Eiger and Kleine Scheidegg. Daily rate: SFr145-160.

Hotel Spinne (853-2341; fax 853-2314) SFr1,200 Daily rate: SFr120–170.

Derby Bahnhof Hotel (854-5461; fax 854-2426) SFr1,025 Hotel with an excellent location handy to the Jungfrau cog railway station. Daily rate: SFr115–135.

Scheidegg Hotel (855-1212); No Ski Week. This grand old hotel is a bit worn, but for overall experience, the finest lodging in the area for the skier; overlooks Kleine Scheidegg station in the shadow of the Eiger. Thirty minutes by train into the mountains from Grindelwald. Reserve well ahead. Daily rate: SFr50–65.

BARGAIN NOTE: Skiers looking for very basic accomodation can stay in a dorm above Scheidegg train station.

Hotel Hirschen (854-8484, fax 854-8480) SFr1,025; Head here for an affordable hotel in town. Daily rate: SFr105–130.

Bellevue Garni (B&B) (853-1234) No Ski Week. A small 16-room B&B in town center; rooms were recently renovated. Ask for a room with bath. Daily rate: SFr55–70.

Wengen (prices with half pension)

Park Hotel Beausite Wengen (856-5161, fax 855-3010) This is now the most elegant and upscale hotel in Wengen. It has indoor pool and sauna. It overlooks the wide-open beginner slopes and is next to the Männlichen cable car. With good snow, you can ski right back to the front door. Rooms range from singles to suites and small apartments. Daily rate: SFr110-175.

Sunstar Hotel (856-5111, fax 855-3272) Yhe top choice hotel with an excellent location between the station and the lifts. All amenities necessary for a great vacation. Weekly rate with half board and ski pass: SFr1,368.

Hotel Silberhorn (855-5131, fax 855-2244) One of the first hotels in Wengen, directly across the street from the station. Recent renovations have all rooms with light pine furniture, sauna and whirlpool. Known for healthy servings at the dinner table—you can chose from four different dining rooms. Weekly rate with ski pass: SFr1,228.

Wengener Hof (855-2855, fax 855-1909) Popular with ski racers, particularly during Lauberhorn race week, but a bit out of the center of town. Weekly rate with half-board and Ski Pass: SFr1,228.

Hotel Eiger (855-1131, fax 855-1030). Behind the station. This is a locals' place too, not as Alpine-looking on the inside as it seems from the outside. Weekly rate with ski pass: SFr1,088.

Hotel Berghaus (55 21 51, fax 55 38 20) A very pleasant hotel next to the Park Hotel and the Männlichen cable car. All rooms have TV. Weekly rate with ski pass: SFr1,158.

Hotel Falken (856-5121, fax 855-3339) This rambling hotel is a step back in time. It was built at the turn of the century and may not have been changed except for the addition of an elevator fifty years ago. It has beautiful views over the beginner slopes and across to the opposite side of the valley. If you want a room with bath, be sure to specify. Weekly rate with ski pass: SFr1,088.

Alpenrose (855-3216, fax 855-1518) Noted for its quiet setting and traditional meals. Weekly rate with ski pass: SFr1,088.

Hotel Hirschen (855-1544, fax 855-3044) This is a charming mountain inn with one of the best kitchens in Wengen. The rooms are small, but each has a modern shower and toilet squeezed in. Weekly rate with ski pass, SFr1,018.

Hotel Eden (855-1634, fax. 855-3950) Inexpensive, loaded with charm, and overflowing with hospitality, but short on rooms with bath—make sure to ask for one of the few that do, or you'll be walking down the hall. Weekly rate with ski pass, SFr1,018.

Ski Chalets: available through Crystal and Ingham/Bladon (see page 27).

Mürren (based on double occupancy with breakfast rates for most of January or late-February and March; half-board surcharge follows)

Hotel Eiger (551331, fax 553931) This is the class act in Mürren as far as hotels go. The owner is delightful and the perfect hostess. This hotel can stand as a definition of excellent service. The restaurant is one of the best in town, and the bar is a gathering spot for locals. SFr130–170. Half-board SFr30.

Palace Hotel Mürren (552424, fax 552417) A grand old hotel that's been thoroughly modernized, but the great dining room and ballroom still have their Old-World elegance. It is next to the sports center, which has pool, squash and tennis courts. The Inferno disco gets packed with young teens. SFr130–180. Half-board SFr35.

Hotel Alpenruh (551055, fax 554277) As close to the lifts as you can get. This is a restored chalet with great views and exceptional decor in the old Swiss style. The restaurant presents Mürren's best nouvelle cuisine. SFr75–80. Half-board SFr25.

Hotel Alpina (551361, fax 551049) Good hotel with reductions offered for families. Excellent view of the valley and a quiet setting, but a long walk from the lifts. Weekly rate with ski pass: SFr130–170. Half-board SFr30.

Hotel Alpenblick (551327, fax 551391) Small hotel with great views, two minutes from the cog-train station but a long way to the Schilthorn lifts. SFr130–170. Half-board SFr30.

Jungfrau (552824, fax 554121) This hotel looks absolutely Gothic, with spires and peaked roof, but you step through the door into a time warp—everything is so modern guests at first may have trouble finding the elevator button. Right in in the center of town, near the sports center with its indoor pool. SFr110–135. Half-board SFr25.

For unusual places to stay higher up on the mountain, Mürren has two guest houses in the middle of the slopes that get rave reviews from those who know them. These are the **Pension Flora-Suppenalp** (551726) and the **Pension Sonnenberg** (551127). Neither of these has rooms with private baths. They have only a handful of rooms, but both have dormitory space and are filled with atmosphere. Rates for rooms per person, double occupancy with half board, are SFr62 for the Flora-Suppenalp and SFr65 for the Sonnenberg. Dormitory rates with half board are SFr47–57 and SFr52 respectively.

Hotel Regina (551421) The bargain hotel in town, in a majestic building but quite under-cared-for on the inside; it might be described as a skiers' commune. There are a handful of rooms with private bath. Everyone makes up his own room each day. Normally youngsters pack in here and share rooms, making the bargain a bit better. Food is simple and substantial. SFr128–137. Half-board SFr8.

Lauterbrunnen

Hotel Silberhorn (551471) Ten minutes' walk from the cog trains to Kleine Scheidegg and Mürren.

Hotel Staubbach (551381) Comfortable and only eight minutes' walk from the cog train.

Hotel Alpenrose In Wilderswil at entrance to Lauterbach valley, 15 minutes by car from Lauterbrunnen. Family-run hotel three minutes from ski train to Lauterbrunnen or Grindelwald and two miles from Interlaken.

Staying in Interlaken

Interlaken has begun to emerge as a hotel center for skiers planning to ski the Jungfrau area. It is only a 45-minute bus ride from the lower lift stations and as a relatively large city it has nightlife and good dining. Two reasons for staying in Interlaken may be persuasive for some visitors.

First: Interlaken hotels and ski packages are much less expensive than those of Wengen, Mürren and Grindelwald. In general, Interlaken menu prices are about one-quarter less than Grindelwald's. (Piz Paz is a satisfying Italian restaurant, in the medium price zone. At Yelp Beers & Comics on Centralstrasse, 400 brands of beers are available.) Second: If you are traveling with a non-skier, Interlaken has more to offer than the liveliest Jungfrau resort, Grindelwald, and is in a perfect position for day trips to many Swiss cities such as Bern, Lucerne, Zürich and even Zermatt.

If neither of these considerations applies, then head into the mountains. If you are a real skier, this city is probably too far from the mountains to keep you happy. If you're sharing a vacation with a non-skier, it's perfect.

Apartments

There are many apartments and chalets for rent in the Jungfrau region. The local tourist offices have prices and locations, and will assist in booking.

A typical rental apartment in Grindelwald, Wengen or Mürren with one bedroom, living room (with sleeping space for two more people), kitchen and all utensils costs about SFr850 a week in high season; SFr550 in midseason. The only extra is tax.

During the special ski weeks, Grindelwald offers an apartment option with all-inclusive seven nights accommodation, a one-week entrance into the Sports Center and a Jungfrau ski pass. During low season—January and early February, late March and April—the price is SFr430 per person. For most of February and March the price will be SFr470–495 each.

Dining
Grindelwald

In Grindelwald you can choose from more than 50 restaurants.

For a very special (and expensive) meal, try the dining room in the **Grand Hotel Regina** (554-5455); it may serve the best meals in town. Chateaubriand for two costs SFr98. The restaurant at the **Hotel Spinne** has good Swiss and international specialties, complemented by a full wine cellar. The most crowded eatery in town is normally the **Gepsi Restaurant** (853-2121) which has grilled meats, spaghetti and fondues. **Ristorante Mercato** has a good Spaghetti Rustico for SFr17. A Hopfenperle Bier brings the minimal meal to SFr 21.80. Pastas, usually Bolognese or Milanese, and pizzas are the best dining value in local restaurants. The pastas are usually SFr 12–18. Chateaubriand for two, at the top of the price scale, averages about SFr 100. A decent bottle of wine will cost at least SFr 18.

Wengen

In Wengen the best typical meal is probably at the **Hirschen** (855-1544). The best fondue in Wengen can be found in the **Bernerhof**. Restaurant **Eiger** in the Hotel Eiger (855-1131) serves good fare.

Mürren

In town the **Alpenruh** (551055) serves the best nouvelle cuisine in a beautifully rustic setting. The **Eiger** (551331) has excellent traditional Swiss fare, real U.S. cut steaks, and the best fondue—either Chinoise or Bourguignonne—in town. The **Palace Hotel Mürren** and the **Stägerstubli** both have excellent cheese fondue. The restaurant in the **Hotel Blumental** is perhaps the most rustic and atmospheric spot to enjoy Swiss specialties. For Italian meals try **Peppino** at the Hotel Palace or **Taverna**.

On the slopes

Enjoy at least one midday meal inside the **Piz Gloria**, a revolving restaurant (552141) on the Schilthorn. At a lower altitude stop in at the **Restaurant Allmendhubel**, which is tiny and cute and filled with real locals, or at the new **Winteregg Restaurant**, which has great lunches and excellent après-ski. The **Flora-Suppenalp** or the **Sonnenberg** also serve excellent mountain meals.

At the **Berghotel Männlichen**, even the cafeteria fare is served on china plates. One liter of water is SFr7 and spaghetti is SFr12. For sun worshipping, a lounge chair and blanket rent for SFr5. **Mary's Cafe** on the trail down to Wengen has a great raclette at lunch. The restaurant at the railway station at Kleine Scheidegg has excellent meals at good prices.

Interlaken

This is an international tourist center and starting point for excursions in the Bernese Oberland, one of Switzerland's most beautiful regions. No-smoking restaurants are an extreme rarity in Switzerland, and McDonald's in Interlaken is one of the few. A Big Mac is SFr 5.90, McChicken SFr 4.90 and coffee is SFr 2. Another rarity is ice in soft drinks. A medium Coke costs SFr 2.90.

 ## Après-ski/nightlife

Grindelwald

The **Gepsi-Bar** and **Mescalero** seem to be the singles meat market and the hottest immediate après-ski hangouts, where folk squeeze in and stay for the duration. The **Disco** in the cellar of the Hotel Spinne is probably the hottest spot for nightlife and dancing, but very crowded. **Le Plaza Club** disco in the Sunstar Hotel is not as packed but gets interesting, depending on which groups are in town. For Country & Western music try the **Challi Bar** in the basement of the Kreuz & Post HoThe **Bodenwald** and the **Glacier** have traditional music and entertainment. For quieter conditions, try the **Espresso Bar**—have Kaffe Fertig with Schnapps—the **Alte Post Bar**, the **Hotel Wolter Terrace** or the **Hotel Kreuz Terrace**. For apple strudel, try the **Spinnet Tea Room** in the middle of the village.

Live music for dancing and listening are offered nightly in the **Hotel Grand Regina** and the **Challi Bar**. The **Cava Bar/Spaghetti Factory**, under the Derby Hotel, has a local band for music and dancing from 9 p.m. It's closed Sundays.

The **Mescalero Club** under the Hotel Spinne and the **Plaza Club** under the Hotel Sunstar are both open to 1:30 a.m. most nights and until 3 a.m. on Saturday.

A nighttime adventure you will remember is sledding from the tiny Gasthaus at **Bussalp** back into Grindelwald. A bus will pick you up from your hotel, and sleds will be waiting after a fondue or other Swiss dinner. Call the tourist office for prices and to make your sled and dinner reservations. (854-1212).

Wengen

Check out the Eiger Hotel's **Pickel Bar,** the **Tonne Bar,** and the **Silberhorn** terrace on sunny days for good après-ski. Nightlife is more limited here, since after dark only the group staying on the mountain will usually be around, although trains run until late evening. Try the **Tiffany Disco** in the Silberhorn, **Carrousel** in Hotel Regina, or the **Paradise** at the Hotel Belvedère for dancing or head to a piano bars for a quiet evening.

Mürren

For immediate après-ski, head to the base of the **Winteregg,** to the old and rustic **Stägerstubli** filled with grizzled locals and a handful of tourists, the **Bellevue** across from the ski school, the pub in the **Hotel Belmont** for expensive beers, or hang out on the terrace of the **Jungfrau Hotel.** For later nightlife in Mürren, head to the Hotel Eiger's **Tächi-Bar.** This bar gets a crowd around 27 and up. The **Inferno Disco** has a mixed clientele ranging from 18 to 27. The **Bliemlichäller** in the cellar of the Hotel Blumental, with dozens of video games, attracts a younger virtually all-teenage crowd.

Child care

Grindelwald and Wengen

These resorts offer ski kindergarten for children from ages three to seven. The Grindelwald school begins at 10 a.m. and lasts until 4 p.m. The cost for one day is SFr42, including meals. For either morning or afternoon, the cost is SFr15 without lunch. In Grindelwald look for the Kinderclub Bodmi. The Grindelwald ski school will take care of and feed kids at lunch for SFr16.

In Wengen head for the Sport Pavillon where school begins at 8:45 a.m. and lasts until 4:30 p.m. Cost in Wengen is SFr25 per day including lunch. Wengen, with its no-traffic environment, is one of the premier resorts for families with children. It has good nursery slopes and plenty of easy tracks back to the town from all over the mountain.

Mürren

Here parents with infants and small children have to call babysitters at 553706. There is a day-care facility at the Sports Center which takes children from two years of age. Rates there are SFr25–40 for a full day with lunch. Children over four years can enter the ski school with classes taking place in the morning.

Other activities

Fully thirty percent of winter visitors to Grindelwald are non-skiers, and there is plenty for them to do. Hikers, three-pinners and snowshoers have their own trails throughout and around the ski areas. They're even groomed, to a width of about eight feet, and good for sledding. You can hike or ride a lift up. There is even a restaurant above First, to which the lifts don't even come close—you'll have to walk, but as Mark Twain said in *A Tramp Abroad,* "There is no opiate like Alpine pedestrianism."

The smart shops in Bern and the really charming Old-World center of the capital city merit a side trip.

Grindelwald offers the widest range of non-skiing activities such as ice skating, curling, hang-gliding, sledding, swimming and hiking.

The Grindelwald Winter Festival in mid-January has snow sculpture contests feature four-member teams from around the world.

The sports center, on the main street of Grindelwald, is excellent, with swimming, fitness rooms and ice skating.

The Jungfraubahn cog railway

The Jungfraubahn cog railway, which takes skiers up the mountain, is also a delightful outing for the non-skier. After dropping off most its skier-passengers, it bores through the Eiger's north face to the Jungfrau slopes. The entire route through the mountain took 14 years to build and was finished in 1912.

A stop inside the mountain allows passengers to look through windows at the precipitous mountain face. At the top of the rail line the train arrives at 11,333', the highest railway station in Europe. A spectacular building houses a restaurant, an ice palace carved into the glacier and outdoor observation platforms with views down over the glacier.

Be careful navigating your next path if you're in ski boots! It's an entanglement of pathways carved through an ice tunnel. Glittering passages, mysterious niches and stairways pass ice sculptures sprinkled along the route and end up at an ice bar where typical Swiss ice wine is served to giddy singing, playful children in adult bodies.

Piz Gloria

Piz Gloria and its revolving restaurant were chosen as the villan's lair in the James Bond movie, *On Her Majesty's Secret Service*. The movie features a wild chase on skis from the restaurant to the car-less village of Murren below.

A series of cable cars and cog trains haul you up to the Schilthorn, a 9,748-foot- tall peak surrounded by a sea of 200 spectacular snow-covered Alps. You are on top of the world with a view of France, Germany, and of course, much of Switzerland. Along with a 200 mile radius view on a clear day, the Piz Gloria restaurant offers a special local dish: rare, local mountain mushrooms or "stienpilzer" over pasta. It's as fabulous as the vista.

Getting there

The most frequently used international airports are Geneva and Zürich. Rail connections are frequent and excellent to Interlaken and on to Grindelwald, Wengen or Mürren.

Tourist information

Verkehrsbüro Wengen, CH-3823 Wengen, Switzerland; (033) 855-1414, fax 855-3060.

Verkehrsbüro Grindelwald, CH-3818 Grindelwald, Switzerland; (033) 854-1212, fax 854-1210.

Verkehrsbüro Mürren, CH-3825 Mürren, Switzerland; (033) 856 86 86, fax 856 86 96.

☎ *Telephone area prefix for the entire region is 033.*

Klosters

A small and traditional village, Klosters offers the low-key atmosphere and relative obscurity that make it the perfect hideaway. The English royal family, most notably Prince Charles, have chosen Klosters as their winter ski center for several years. They come for the excellent skiing and the relaxed elegant atmosphere—you will probably like Klosters for the same reasons. The houses surrounding the town proper are a bit more elaborate than most other places you'll visit, giving an immediate tipoff that Klosters is a cut above. The central town area is small and quaint, but packed with specialty stores.

Think of Klosters, little more than a suburb of Davos, as Davos' little sister resort, the beauty of the family who has been kept hidden. Both resorts share the Manhattan-sized, wide-open expanse of the Parsenn, but Klosters has the more challenging runs into town. Klosters also has its own ski runs and lift system in the Madrisa area, on the opposite side of the valley from the Parsenn. The entire Klosters-Davos ski area offers 200 miles of runs served by more than 50 lifts.

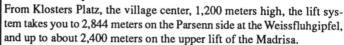

Mountain layout

From Klosters Platz, the village center, 1,200 meters high, the lift system takes you to 2,844 meters on the Parsenn side at the Weissfluhgipfel, and up to about 2,400 meters on the upper lift of the Madrisa.

The Parsenn is the best-known area and is reached by the Gotschna cable car, which leaves every 15 to 20 minutes in ski season. The cable car lets you off at the Gotschnagrat, where you can either traverse to the Parsenn or ski under the cable car to a T-bar and chair lift. The Parsenn reaches its peak at the Weissfluhgipfel (2,844 meters) where it drops with two expert runs. Here it is wide open, offering both beginners and intermediates a paradise for cruising. The Parsenn has 40 seemingly endless runs, including what was once Europe's longest—from Weissfluhjoch to Kublis. If you like carefree cruising, you will love the Parsenn.

The Madrisa area is much smaller: some 30 miles of runs served by six lifts. The area is reached by cable car from Klosters-Dorf, an outlying hamlet, which is a hike from the center of town. The area runs are mostly beginner and intermediate. When the sun is out, the Madrisa slopes are bathed with warming rays the entire day, something to remember when it's cold but sunny. The longest and most scenic Madrisa run is from St. Jaggem, 8,340 feet down to the Schlappin overlook, then down to the Madrisa cable car.

For the jaded, Madrisa is a springboard for an exciting ski mountaineering trek to Austria, which combines both skiing and climbing. The Swiss Ski School can line you up with a guide for this adventure if the snow quality is good.

Mountain rating

Klosters earns an A-plus from beginning and intermediate skiers. The Parsenn is perhaps the ideal terrain for learning to ski and perfecting your technique.

Experts may find the Parsenn terrain somewhat boring and should ask instructors where the most challenging skiing can be found. The best expert runs on the Parsenn are from the top of the Weissfluhgipfel. Otherwise, stick to the trails that drop into town alongside the Parsennbahn, or take the Drostobel-to-Klosters run, which is narrow and sometimes steep. The Wang trail, which runs directly under the Gotschna cable car, is one of the toughest expert runs in Europe. Unfortunately it seems to be closed more often than open, but if it's open and there is no avalanche danger, you're in for an experience. Watch yourself here: this is the spot where Prince Charles narrowly escaped an avalanche and his aide was killed while skiing out of bounds.

The Madrisa area is strictly for intermediates, beginners and sun-worshipers.

Ski school (97/98 prices)

The Klosters ski school is divided into six levels, and also offers special children's courses and cross-country instruction. Classes meet either on the Madrisa or near the Gotschna. Check with the ski school (422-1380) for lesson times. There is the Ski and Snowboard School at Saas in Klosters Dorf (420-2233). Both ski schools provide snowboard lessons.

Private lessons for one to three skiers cost SFr250 for a full day or SFr160 for a half day. There is an additional fee of SFr25 for each extra skier.

Group lessons are SFr35 for half days, SFr90 for three half days, SFr130 for five half-days, and SFr220 for five full days.

Lift tickets (97/98 prices)

Daily lift passes for the Gotschna, Parsenn and Madrisa are SFr52; for the Madrisa only, SFr42.

The most convenient pass (REGA) to use is the Klosters/Davos all-inclusive pass. It includes the Madrisa side of the valley, plus use of the train that runs between Davos and Klosters and as far down the valley as Kublis. It is also good on local buses in Davos and Klosters. The tickets are available only for periods of two days or more.

There are 20 percent discounts for passes purchased for the pre-season before December 19, 1997, and 20 percent reductions for six-day regional passes for January 4–25, 1998, March 15–April 4, 1998.

	Adults	**Children**
two days	SFr113	SFr68
three days	SFr155	SFr93
six days	SFr259	SFr155
14 days	SFr464	SFr279

Klosters only lift tickets for Gotschna/Parsenn and Madrisa are:

	Adults	**Children**
two days	SFr98	SFr59
three days	SFr138	SFr83
six days	SFr223	SFr134
14 days	SFr382	SFr229

Accommodations (97/98 rates)

The best time to ski Klosters is during one of its special organized Ski Weeks. These weeks are normally held in early December, the last three weeks of January and first week of February, and late March through April. Contact the tourist office for the special rates, which include lift tickets together with room and board. January Ski Week prices are SFr990–1,300.

The **Hotel Alpina** (410-2424, fax 410-2425) is the finest place to stay. It has a great location, indoor pool, nice staff, and ease of reservations through Best Western. Doubles with breakfast are SFr296–384 in low season, SFr378–500 in high season.

Perhaps the most traditional hotel is the **Chesa Grischuna** (422-2222, fax 422-2225). It is part of the Romantic Hotel chain, but though it has ambiance, the rooms are small and there is no pool. You'll pay SFr260–450 middle and high season for a double with half board.

Also available at the upper end of the scale is the **Hotel Pardenn** (422-1141, fax 422-4006). A hike from the ski shuttlebus and 10 minutes walk from town, but with plenty of five-star comfort—pool, sauna and fitness room. Rates: Low season, SFr170–240; high season, SFr300–510.

The **Hotel Vereina** (422-6191, fax 422-1539) is a large rambling old hotel popular with American tour groups. Its location is central and it has a beautiful pool. Rates: Low season, SFr270–400; high season, SFr300–450.

The less expensive hotels are located in Klosters-Dorf, which is near the lifts for the Madrisa area but a hike or shuttlebus ride from the Parsenn lifts.

Apartments

Apartments are normally rented out for a minimum of one week, Saturday to Saturday; in the Christmas holiday season a two-week minimum rental is required.

The tourist office keeps track of available apartments. Write and supply the necessary information, including number of beds required, preferred number of rooms and dates of your stay. You'll get an immediate response from apartment owners with a choice of apartments and prices. Select the apartment you want and return their forms.

Normally, linen and kitchen utensils are provided, while extras, such as swimming pool, sauna, TV or room phone all add to the cost. Standard units rent for $20 to $35 per person a night.

Dining

For good local specialties, try **Hotel Alpina** and **Restaurant Steinbock**. Other restaurants recommended by Klosters natives are **Alte Post Aeuja** (for lamb specialties), and **à Porta**. For pizza and a great lunch buffet head to the cellar **Pizzeria in the Hotel Vereina**—we recommend the Chicago-style thick crust deluxe. The Hotel Wynegg also has a good restaurant with reasonable prices.

Après-ski/nightlife

Klosters' nightlife centers around its major hotels. For discos, there are **Casa Antica**, **Kir Royal** in the Hotel **Silveretta**, **Madrisa** and **Rufinis**.

The bar in the **Pardenn** for a late evening visit is intimate and relaxing, but a bit stuffy. Better still is the bar of the Chesa Grischuna where there is quiet piano entertainment.

Child care

Babysitting service in town can be arranged for around SFr10 per hour by calling 410-2020.

There is also child care (three years and older) on Madrisa near the gondola, open every day 10 am to 12:30 p.m. and 1:30 p.m. to 4 p.m.. Cost is SFr5 per hour or SFr16 per day, without lunch. Telephone 422-2333.

Getting there

The closest airport is Zürich. Klosters is two-and-a-half hours by train, with a change in Landquart.

If you decide to rent a car, take the Zürich-Chur road as far as the Landquart/Davos exit. The drive from Landquart to Klosters is through the narrow valley and passes through Kublis before arriving at Klosters Dorf and then Klosters. The distance from Zürich is about 90 miles.

Other activities

Klosters is rather quiet. Visitors looking for other activities should take the train to Davos, only fifteen minutes away. Klosters has an open-air skating rink, cross-country skiing, horse-drawn sleighs and tobogganing. There are four covered hotel pools in town; check with the hotel for the facility rates.

Tourist information

Tourist Office, CH-7250 Klosters, Switzerland; 410-2020, fax 410-2010. Normal hours are Monday through Saturday, 8 a.m.–noon and 2:30–6:30 p.m. It is also open 9:30 a.m.–noon and 3:30–6:30 p.m. on Sundays.

☎ *Telephone prefix for Klosters is 081.*

Saas-Fee

Saas-Fee is a village of very narrow streets, chalets, small hotels and year-round skiing. It's for serious skiers—the ones who care more about the number of black-rated runs on the mountain than the number of discos in the village. Nestled in the next valley from Zermatt, Saas-Fee allows no private cars in town; you park on the outskirts and take public transportation.

The town occupies a magnificent site at 5,904 feet, ringed by 18 separate peaks of 13,000 feet or more. Snowcaps on these mountains are permanent, as is skiing on the 9,840-foot-high Felskinn.

Saas-Fee also has its own snowmaking equipment on the beginner slopes below. That, combined with the glacier runs above, means that your vacation will never be in danger from poor snowfall.

Mountain layout

Saas-Fee's nearly 50 miles of downhill trails are superbly divided between beginner, intermediate and expert. Absolute beginners start on the Saas-Fee town lifts, where they usually stay for about three days. Later they ski either the Plattjen lift or the Felskinn.

For the other levels there are three distinct areas. The first to get the morning sun is the Spielboden/Längfluh. These runs are on good intermediate to expert terrain. From Längfluh down to the chair lift, is intermediate country. If you ski past this middle station, get ready for the steep and narrow.

From the top of the Längfluh cable car there is a drag lift right on the glacier. This Feekatz lift connects the two main ski areas of Längfluh and Felskinn/Mittelallalin.

The Felskinn/Mittelallalin area is the most popular section of Saas-Fee's trails. Two small lifts tow skiers from town to the lower station of the Felskinn cable car.

Once at the top of the Felskinn cable car, you're whisked up another 1600 feet on the underground Metro Alpin to Mittelallalin. Here, stop to enjoy the magnificent panorama of dozens of 13,000-foot peaks. Intermediates, and beginners brave enough to come this far, should traverse to the left, and experts should cross to the right, in front of the revolving restaurant. Skiers have a choice of doing several runs or heading back to the Metro Alpin underground and the Felskinn area.

To the left of the Felskinn cable car, a drag lift opens to a delightful smaller area—the Egginer. Strong intermediates will be satisfied with the Egginerjoch lift. Experts will be thrilled with the drops from the Hinterallalin lift (which may be closed owing to avalanche danger).

The rest of the Felskinn runs crisscross under the cable car back toward town. The area between the middle station and the top of the Felskinn is a beginner and intermediate playground. The drop back into the village steepens considerably, and experts have a challenge on the Kanonenrohr and Bach trails.

The final section of Saas-Fee's ski domain, the Plattjen, catches the last of the day's sunshine. This area is served by only two lifts, but they are long ones. The gondola takes skiers up from town (5,850 feet) to Plattjen (8,342 feet), resulting in a run with an almost 2,500-foot vertical drop. There are trails for all abilities. This section is not normally crowded.

One interesting point for anyone searching for a place to go summer skiing, the new lifts have opened glaciers at 3,500 meters above sea level. Saas-Fee has constructed a special summer glacier snowboarding park as well with three halfpipes, two quarterpipes, rails, tables, gaps and a high jump for professionals.

Mountain rating

Experts will never complain about the runs at Saas-Fee. There's enough black to make things interesting.

Intermediates may think that the lift network and trails were laid out with them in mind: most trails above Saas-Fee start with a red or blue leg, often with the option of taking a black-rated stretch.

Beginners can work toward becoming advanced beginners on the Saas-Fee town slopes; then the slopes above the valley beckon.

Lessons (97/98 prices)

The Saas-Fee school (tel. 027-957-2348) has approximately 100 instructors. English is no problem.

Private lessons cost SFr55 an hour for one or two persons, SFr60 an hour for three to four people, SFr275 for a full day.

Group lessons (four hours a day)
one day	SFr44
five days	SFr165

Lessons for children are SFr44 for a full day and SFr165 for five days. Private lessons are at the adult rates.

Cross-country lessons are also offered, but only a five-mile loop around Saas-Fee is prepared.

Special ski mountaineering off-trail adventures have been organized in the past for climbs to the top of the Alphubel and Allalin. These treks start with a two- to four-hour climb on skins and end with long, high-altitude powder cruises through virtually virgin snow. Tours are limited by both the weather and the availability of qualified instructors. From mid-February through the end of the season the treks depart approximately once a week.

"**The Haute Route**" is a classic ski adventure tour between Saas-Fee, Zermatt, Courmayeur and Chamonix. These trips are organized from mid-April to the end of May. For this tough, physical trek participants should be in good shape and must be able to ski in deep snow. The mountain climbing school conducts a different special tour from early May until the first week in June. Contact: Bergsteigerschule Saastal, CH-3906 Saas-Fee; (tel. 027-957-4464, or the tourist office at 027-958-1858). The cost for the classic "Haute Route" is SFr1,000, which includes guides, accommodations in mountain huts, meals, hotel expenses during the tour, and mountain railway and bus.

Lift tickets (97/98 prices)

one day	SFr56
two days	SFr102
three days	SFr148
six days	SFr260
seven days	SFr290

The resort also offers a ticket for five of seven days costing SFr240 and ten of fourteen days for SFr420.

Beginners need only purchase tickets for the Saas-Fee town lifts at SFr15 for an adult half day and SFr8 for a child's half-day; SFr20 for adult full day and SFr12 for children full day.

Children 6–16 get a 40 percent discount on lift fees. Children younger than 6 ski free.

Accommodations

The first prices listed are Snow and Fun Week rates normally available in November, December (before Christmas), January, and April after Easter. They include three or seven nights in hotel with half pension, six-day ski pass, six days of ski lessons and pool fee. There is also an active entertainment program of ski racing, hiking, fondue and raclette parties and sledding. Rates for ski weeks range from SFr856–1,542 depending on the hotel selected.

The daily rate noted is the normal high-season, half-pension price based on double occupancy.

The Best

Walliserhof (tel. 958-1900, fax 958-1905) The best hotel in town. For a splurge, try the suite with round bed, white marble bath and sauna. Daily rate: SFr240–280.

Ambassador (tel. 957-1420) Renovated with new pine furniture. In town near the ski school. Has indoor swimming pool. Daily rate: SFr149–200.

Allalin (tel. 957-1815, fax 957-3115) This three-star hotel is really four-star quality. It is at the far end of town from the lifts, but has ski storage facilities at the lifts. They have some of the best food in town. Daily rate: SFr153.

Moderate

Mischabel (tel. 957-2118, fax 957-2461) At the entrance of the town, about a seven-minute walk to most lifts. Daily rate: SFr118–153.

Hotel Marmotte (tel. 957-2852, fax 957-1987) The rooms could be bigger, the decor could be more traditional Swiss Alps, and the location could be closer to the main lifts. This hotel shines because of its mad owner, Karl Dreier, who makes everyone feel at home. Karl, who doubles as the chef, cooks some of the best hotel food we've eaten. There is a free ski storage arrangement with the Waldesruh Hotel opposite the Felskinn lift, and a free baby sitting arrangement with Hotel Alphubel, good hotel for children. Daily rate: SFr113–147.

Derby (tel. 957-2345, fax 957-1246) Family place on the way to Felskinn or Plattjen lifts. Daily rate: SFr113–153.

Hotel Europa (tel. 957-3191; fax 957-2018) Small hotel for those planning to do most skiing on the Hannig. Daily rate: SFr102–132.

Hotel Waldesruh (tel. 957-2232, fax 957-1447) Near the Plattjen and Längfluh gondola ground stations. Caters to families. Daily rate: SFr118–153.

Budget

Mühle (tel. 957-2676) Small hotel offering basic accommodations. Daily rate: SFr84–109

Feehof (tel. 957-2308; fax 957-2309) (B&B only) Inexpensive. No telephone, no public restaurant and no credit cards accepted. Daily rate: SFr53–69.

All of the hotels in Saas-Fee are good. We've picked out some exceptional ones we know. The best way to select a hotel if you're traveling with a group or tour package is to decide whether being close to the main lifts or being in the center of town (and its nightlife) is more to your liking.

Near Felskinn, Plattjen and Spielboden lifts: Waldesruh, Derby, Burgener, Bristol, Ambassador, Feehof, Mistral, Mühle, Rendezvous, Saaserhof, Ambiente, Condor and Elite.

Center of town: Beau-Site, Britannia, Christiana, Dom, Gletschergarten, Grand, Mischabel, Park, Walser, Walliserhof, Zurbriggen, Metropol, Sonnenhof.

Near Hannig on the sunny side: Allalin, Alphubel, Domino, La Collina, Marmotte, Sporthotel, Tenne, Etoile.

Ski Chalets: Crystal, Inghams/Bladon (go to page 27 for phone, fax and internet addresses).

Apartments

Apartments are the way to go if you really want to save money. Saas-Fee has about 1,500 chalets and apartments for rent. Write to the tourist office and ask for apartments that will be available when you plan to be in Saas-Fee. Include details on the number of people in your party. The office will send a list of available apartments and a map showing locations. Select the apartment you want and write to the tourist board or to the owner. The reservation line for apartments is 958-1868.

The apartments normally include linen and kitchen utensils. You will be charged a visitor's tax, and there may be an extra charge for the electricity and heat you use.

Expect to pay SFr25–45 per person a night, based on location and the number of people sharing the apartment.

Dining

The best restaurant in the region is the **Fletschhorn** (957-2131), a 30-minute walk from town or a ten-minute taxi ride. It is considered one of the best in Switzerland and features nouvelle cuisine.

Perhaps the second-best eatery is the **Hohnegg** (957-2268), just about a 10-minute walk above the town (or call for its taxi service). Also nouvelle cuisine.

The **Swiss Châlet** (tel. 957-3535) is considered another of the top gourmet spots with nouvelle cuisine.

Le Mandarin Thai restaurant in the Walliserhof (958-1903) serves Asian cuisine.

For excellent traditional local Walliser food, try the **Saaserhof** and the **Schäferstube**. For cheese and Swiss specialties the top recommendations are the **Käse-Keller** (tel. 957-2120) and the **Arvu-Stuba** (957-2747).

For good, less expensive meals, try the **Hotel Allalin** (957-1815)—a rebuilt 300-year-old room with wooden beams and hand-carved chairs that make it magical by candle-light; **Hotel Dom** (957-5101) for great *rösti*. **La Gorge** (957-2641) and the **Hotel du Glacier** (957-1244) also has excellent fondue and raclette.

For pizza, try the restaurant under the **Romantik Hotel Beau-Site**; the **Boccalino**—in front of the Saaserhof—or the pizzeria in the Walliserhof. Pizza or pasta is SFr15–20.

On the slopes have at least one lunch in the revolving restaurant at the top of the **Metro Alpin** lift, the world's highest such restaurant. The prices are down to earth. The mountain restaurant **Berghaus Plattjen**, a third of the way down the National run from the top of the Plattjen lift, is great for a late lunch when the area catches the sun. It has great *Rösti*. On the opposite side along the Längfluh run, where it meets the Gletschergrotte trail cutting off from the Kanonenrohr, is the **Gletscher-Grotte**, which catches sun most of the day.

SFr22 will cover a good lunch with beer and coffee at most spots on the mountain.

Après-ski/nightlife

Saas-Fee is known as a town for young skiers and those who think young. You'll meet a lively crowd in the evening. The three main live-music places are within a stone's throw of one another. The **Crazy Night** in the Metropol also has good music but with a younger crowd (18–25). There is also a good group of bars: **Pic Pic** is a Swiss locals' spot; the **Underground** and the **Popcorn** (young crowd) normally have a good crowd; **Feeloch** under the Hotel du Glacier and the **Go-Inn Bar** (young crowd) near the Hotel Beau Site are lively.

Après-ski, as the slopes close, is an early affair because the sun drops behind the mountains quickly. If you're off the mountain at around 3 p.m., the terrace bars at the **Derby, Mühle, Rendezvous** and **Christiana** do a great business. After 4 p.m., when the sun drops out of sight, the crowd evaporates. Most gather in bars like **Chemi Stube** in the Christiana, the **Saaserhof** or the **Rendezvous**.

Child care

The ski school (957-2348) takes children from five to twelve, with a day fee of SFr50.

A guest kindergarten is run in the Hotel Garni Berghof (957-2484). A full day costs SFr60 including lunch and a half day is SFr35 without lunch.

Getting there

By train: From Zürich airport via Bern, Spiez, through the Lötschberg tunnel to Brig. At Brig you change to the postbus, which leaves from the front of the railway station.

From Geneva, trains run directly to Brig.

By car: Drive via Montreux, then up the Valais to Visp, where you turn south and follow signs to Saas-Fee.

If you are driving from Zürich or Basel, there is a new tunnel, or take the Lötschberg tunnel from Kandersteg to Goppenstein, above Brig and Visp. This tunnel requires that you load your car onto the railway. Trains transit the tunnel every half-hour from 5:35 a.m. to 11:05 p.m. The trip takes only 15 minutes. Cost per car (including 9-seat vans) is SFr25. From Goppenstein, drive to Visp, then on to Saas-Fee.

Park in the public lot at the town entrance. Call your hotel for pickup, or take a taxi. Taxis from the parking lot and bus station to town cost about SFr15 for two people, SFr15 for three, SFr16 for four.

Other activities

The Hannig area is now closed to skiers. It gets good early morning sun and is now the location of a 4-km. toboggan run. Tobaggans can be rented from the sports shops or at the Hannig cable car station.

Visit the Saaser Museum, packed with photographs of the old Saas valley, and old tools, kitchen utensils and furniture of mountain people. Open from 2–6 p.m., the museum charges SFr3 for adults, SFr1 for children to 16.

The Bielen sports and leisure center offers an 80-foot, heated indoor swimming pool, children's pool, two tennis courts, exercise room, whirlpools, steam bath and coed sauna. Tennis courts should be reserved; with the visitor's card, they cost SFr23 an hour from 9 a.m.–4 p.m. and SFr29 an hour from 4 p.m.–10 p.m. Bargain time is from 8–9 a.m. when court time is only SFr12 an hour.

Tourist information

Write Tourist Office Saas-Fee, CH-3906 Saas-Fee, Switzerland; (tel. 958-1858; fax 958-1860). Reservations: 957-1868.

Internet: www.saas-fee.ch; E-mail: to@saas-fee.ch

☎ *Telephone prefix for Saas-Fee is 027.*

St. Moritz

My ski guide was Marcello. Just before lunch one day, as we cruised down a mellow run under Piz Nair, he pulled up, extracted a cellular phone from his designer parka, and engaged in an animated conversation concluded by a thank you and good-by (*Grazie mille, Ciao!*). It could have been his stockbroker or his girl friend, but the moment was totally in character—only in St. Moritz.

Yes, when you have visited all the other great resorts, when you have enjoyed the other hotels claiming to pamper guests to the extreme, when you've seen all the mountains said to be grand and great, then and only then: journey to St. Moritz. You'll find that though there is elegance and Alpine beauty everywhere in Switzerland, nowhere is it concentrated in such huge amounts as here on the rooftop of Europe, St. Moritz, the original Swiss winter resort. Each night at dinner at the Hotel Schweizerhof it is great theater to observe the maitre d'hotel greet guests in German, Italian, French and English. After speaking with you once, he always addresses you in your native language.

In winter the great expanses of snow-covered lake provide a massive, scenic foreground for the celebrated town whose name is a synonym for quality and luxury. The most elegant aspect of St. Moritz—the great hotels—are expensive, but everything else, restaurants included, is there for nearly everyone.

The tourist office claims the sun shines 322 days a year in St. Moritz; in the winter this sunlight brightens some 250 miles of downhill ski runs, 100 miles of cross-country ski trails, 30 curling rinks, horse races and polo on the frozen lake, the Cresta and bobsled runs, an Olympic ski jumping hill and much more.

The central area, St. Moritz Dorf, is compact, really only two main streets with a few side streets and a single small main square. Sports shops abound, and prices are surprisingly low. There are actually bargains in February and March when they have sales. Movies are up-to-date, nightlife superb, moonlight strolls on the lake wonderful. The entertainment fits every pocketbook and taste. St. Moritz Bad, the less built-up section, curls around the western end of the frozen lake.

Mountain layout

Until you have experienced St. Moritz, your education in Swiss skiing is incomplete. Exclusive, exciting, this two-time winter Olympic site—1928 and 1948—is home to some of the finest intermediate skiing anywhere.

Altogether there are 150 miles of groomed trails. The setting is stunning: 6,000 feet high in the southeastern corner of Switzerland, near the border with Italy in the twin shadows of the 9,270-foot Piz Nair and the 10,833-foot Piz Corvatsch.

The main runs are clustered around the summits of the two main mountains. The Corviglia runs finish near St. Moritz-Dorf and the Corvatsch Hahnensee run drops into St. Moritz-Bad.

The finest run is the Hahnensee, a black-rated trail that is intermediate for most of the five-mile length. It boasts a vertical drop of more than 4,900 feet. It's a five-minute walk from the end of the Hahnensee run to the Signalbahn cable car, which takes you up to Corviglia.

On the second run down the Hahnensee, break off at the Mandras T-bar and climb to the Murtèl cable midstation. Here the run down the Surlej is peppered with moguls and dips, while the panorama includes the frozen lakes of Champfèr and Silvaplana. Adventurous folk work their way along the slopes via the T-bars at Alp Margun to the 9,186-foot-high Culöz de las Furtschellas. From here there is an interesting run to Sils-Maria on the Silvaplana lake shore. Be sure to have the regional lift ticket, or you pay a SFr6 surcharge for the Sils-Maria lifts.

The longest and favorite run of many is from Piz Nair, either down the front side to St. Moritz or over the ridge at the 8,154-foot level at the cable car station in Corviglia and down to Marguns. For the greatest length along an intermediate trail, climb to the top of the Fuorcia Grischa T-bar, behind Piz Nair, for the run to the valley floor.

The single most challenging run in the valley is "Il Muro," a chilling drop from the top at Lagalb on the Bernina Pass. On the other side of the pass is Diavolezza. The skiing there is average, but a stunning glacier ski trek awaits after a 25-minute walk on skis to the mountain bar run by Otto Rohner. On full-moon nights glacier skiing is a unique Alpine experience.

There is also summer skiing at Diavolezza.

Mountain rating

Beginners will start to feel at home after several runs on one of the longer trails. But this is not the best spot to learn to ski. Beginner skiers will feel limited with not too many slopes to take them from absolute beginner to lower intermediate.

Eighty percent of the slopes in the St. Moritz area are for intermediates. Corvatsch has plenty of ego-boosting trails that catch lots of sun. The Diavolezza-Langalb has some of the best intermediate trails with the thinnest crowds. When in doubt, tag behind the advanced beginners of a St. Moritz ski class for the best slope that day.

Experts will head for the toughest parts of the back side of the Piz Nair, as well as Corvatsch summit and the super challenge of the black run at Lagalb. If you are in the Diavolezza sector head to the Schwarzer Hang for some steep skiing. To ski off-piste from Corviglia or Corvatsch a guide is required for many of the itineraries.

Ski schools

St. Moritz area ski schools employ up to 350 instructors. In 1927 the world's first ski school was established here. The main ski school (tel. 081-8338090) is in the center of town next to the public parking.

Private lessons cost SFr80 an hour from noon to 1:15 p.m. with reductions for multi-hour lessons. A half day costs SFr140.

Cross-country lessons are available; they are extremely popular thanks to nearly 75 miles of well-maintained trails in the valley. Cross-country buffs will probably want to participate in the Engadin Marathon course, a 26-mile cross-country circuit. Come in March and take part along with 12,000 others in one of the world's great cross-country races.

Private cross-country lessons are SFr65 per hour for one or two skiers, plus SFr5 for each additional person.

Group cross-country lesson rates are SFr35 for a half day and SFr90 for three half days.

There is helicopter transport for off-trail skiing, powder skiing and deep-snow skiing instruction.

Lift tickets (97/98 prices)

The Engadin regional pass includes St. Moritz and Corviglia, Sils Maria, Silvaplana, Surlej, Champfer, Celerina, Samedan, Pontresina and Zuoz. The pass serves 59 lifts covering 350 km. of prepared trails.

	Adults	Children
one day	SFr54	SFr42
two days	SFr100	SFr50
three days	SFr144	SFr72
six days	SFr258	SFr129
seven days	SFr286	SFr143
twelve days	SFr410	SFr205

Accommodations

Over half of the hotels in St. Moritz are four- and five-star, the highest concentration of quality hotels in Switzerland. Prices unless otherwise noted are high season half board per person based on double occupancy.

The Engadin region also organizes special all-inclusive Sunshine Ski Weeks that include seven days half-board, six days of lifts and six days of instruction or a ski guide. Contact the tourist office for details and prices. For most of the 1997-1998 season the Sunshine rate at participating four-star rate is SFr1,595. These same week packages without the six days of lessons (called Holiday Weeks) cost SFr1,295.

The best of the best is the **Suvretta** in neighboring Champfèr. This wonderful monument to Swiss hotel expertise is overshadowed in reputation by the Palace in St. Moritz-Dorf. The Suvretta (tel. 832-1132, fax 833-8524) is a model of understatement, a great hotel with its own lift connection to Corviglia. Rates are SFr215–580.

Second in our ranking of the five five-star hotels in St. Moritz is the **Kulm** (tel. 832-1151, fax 833-2738), on the road to the bobsled and Cresta runs. Room rates run SFr235–765 per person, half pension, high season. The Kulm seems more welcoming than the Palace; it's also a center for sports, its trophy cases brimming with awards for curling, skiing, golf, tennis, and the famous Cresta run. The hotel sits high on a hill overlooking the frozen lake and offers a commanding view of the valley. Taking tea in the large lounge overlooking this spectacular vista is highly recommended.

Badrutt's Palace (tel. 837-1000, fax 837-2999) is still the place to stay if you want to be seen. It is one of the most famous and elegant hotels in the world, where if you have to ask the price you should be staying somewhere else. Prices range from SFr400–750 a night per person, half pension in high season. Come prepared with dark suit and tie or you will not be allowed to wander through the public areas after 7 p.m.

Hotel Albana, (tel. 833-3121, fax 833-3122) SFr130–225, single, with half pension. Excellent downtown location with superb staff and a very good kitchen.

Schweizerhof (tel. 837-0707; fax 837-0700) SFr190–280, single with half pension. The food is very good and the staff friendly and efficient. Four-star and one of the most comfortable hotels in town, the Schweizerhof is well located a few blocks up from the Palace on Via dal Bagn, along with Bulgari, Bugatti, Vuitton, Armani, Cartier and Versace. If you think these are ski instructors, you're in the wrong neighborhood.

Posthotel (tel. 832-2121, fax 833-8973) SFr210–280, single with half pension, high season. Four stars within a short walk of main tourist office.

Steffani (tel. 832-2101, fax 833-4097) SFr240–280, high season, per person, half pension. Comfortable midtown hotel near the parking garage. Four stars and 119 rooms.

Hotel Bären (tel. 833-5656; fax 833-8022) SFr130–150, single, high season, SFr32 for half pension. Four stars, but a bit of distance from Dorf central.

Hotel Steinbock (tel. 833-6035; fax 833-8747) SFr180–250, high season per person. Half pension SFr35 additional. Small three-star hotel (28 beds) with good restaurant and a reputation for making guests comfortable.

Hotel Nolda (tel. 833-0575, fax 833-8751) SFr160 single, SFr280 double, SFr40 each for half pension during high season. This family hotel with 70 beds has a good location at the end of the Corviglia run and close to the Signal cable car lift; sauna, swimming pool, solarium and whirlpool.

Waldhaus am See (tel. 833-7676, fax 833-8877) SFr170–200, single, high season, half pension. Three-star 85-room hotel in quiet location on the shore of St. Moritz lake; only three minutes' walk from the train station.

Hotel Bellaval (tel. 833-3245; fax 833-0406) A B&B minutes from St. Moritz-Dorf center. SFr59–76; single, SFr25 additional.

National Hotel (tel. 833-3274; 833-3275) SFr75–125, single, high season, half pension. Two stars, 45 beds.

Silvaplana offers two excellent hotels:

Chesa Guardalej (tel. 832-3121, fax 833-2373) SFr230–300 (high season per person, double occupancy, including half board) A spectacular hotel consisting of a village of small buildings connected by underground passages. The rooms are excellent. There are several different dining areas and restaurants, and the hotel is equipped with a full exercise room and swimming pool.

Albana (tel. 828-9292, fax 828-8181) High season, half-board per person: SFr155–195. Features an excellent, award-winning restaurant.

Dining

One dining experience you should enjoy is the excursion to **Muottas Muragl**, a mountain hotel restaurant near Pontresina and Samedan on the way to the Bernina Pass. You take a funicular up to the hotel, which has a truly spectacular location overlooking the valley. Take the funicular just before sunset (it runs every half hour, 8 a.m.–11 p.m.) and watch the lights come on in the valley. Reserve in advance (842-8232) and get a window seat.

The great hotels of St. Moritz, which incidentally charge SFr1,500–2,000 and up a week for half pension, boast equally famous dining rooms with the same high prices. More down to earth are the Italian specialties in the pizzeria at the **Chesa Veglia**. The full-service restaurant there is also superb, although more expensive (have lunch for the same great food without the high costs).

For one of the area's top gourmet spots try **Talvò** (833-4455), a Relais & Chateaux restaurant in nearby Champfèr. The owner, Roland Jöhri-Tanner, is considered one of Switzerland's best cooks. Reservations are very necessary and it's very expensive.

The restaurant at the Steinbock hotel has tasty, reasonably priced Swiss cuisine. The **Soldanella** hotel also has good meals and prices.

To demolish your budget and add an unforgettable dining experience, lunch at **La Marmite** (reservations required for noon and 2 p.m. seatings; 833-6355), a gourmet restaurant atop Corviglia. It's in the funicular station near the self-service restaurant.

The **Stüvetta**, a cozy corner of the restaurant building at the Marguns lift station, is great for lunches, particularly pasta dishes. And the last stop of the day should be the **Alpina Hütte**, the St. Moritz ski club hut in the shadow of Piz Nair where you should order a Café Grischa, a traditional hot coffee and liqueur-filled pot with drinking spouts for four. One of the most reasonably priced restaurants in the area is **Veltlinerkeller** (833-4009), downhill from Dorf toward Bad.

Apartments

As at most Swiss resorts, the rental apartment business is well organized and bookings can be arranged through the Interrent or the tourist information office. Rentals are from Saturday to Saturday. Give them details about when you plan to arrive, how many people will be sharing the apartment, and what facilities you desire; they will respond quickly with several apartment choices.

There are about 6,500 apartment beds, but only about 2,900 are rentals. Interhome operates an office in town, opposite the Kulm hotel (tel. 833-1520, fax 833-0440) or contact the Tourist Office (837-3399).

Après-ski/nightlife

At 1 a.m. most nights, the streets are full of visitors sampling St. Moritz's great nightlife. The most famous address is the **King's Club** disco at the Palace where SFr30 gets you in (men, bring a tie) and buys one drink. The most fun we had, by far, was at the **Stübli**, the typical Swiss wood-paneled bar in the lower level of the Schweizerhof. The ski instructors come early and stay late. There's usually so little room you are crowded, shoved and shuffled from one spot to another. The **Cava Bar** at the Hotel Stef-fani is the same style as the Stübli, but in a cave. It's open from 5 p.m. to midnight. You'll like them both.

The **Cresta Bar** in the Steffani is a good meeting place after the walk down the hill from the Corviglia funicular, but from there you might move on after 10 p.m. to the nearby **Vivai,** a disco with a young following. Nearby also is **Cascade,** a sort of combination bar and pub you'll like almost as much as the Stübli. Another disco, the **Absolut,** is near the tourist office. For a quiet drink try the bar-sitting room in the Albana after a day on Corviglia.

It's chic in the late afternoon to order a hot chocolate and whipped cream-covered slice of Black Forest cake at **Hanselmann,** the famed chocolate specialist near the Hotel Albana in the center of town.

Child care

The ski school has a child care program for those four to twelve. The program provides child pickup. During the day the children have lunch, a horse-drawn sleigh ride to the ski school and ski lessons. Child care, pickup and lunch costs SFr25 per day. The price of the normal ski school lessons is additional.

There are supervised classes for children three to six at the Suvretta Ski School. Rates are: SFr66 for a full day and SFr170 for three full days. Lunch is SFr13 per day.

Child care programs are available at the Parkhotel Kurhaus and the Schweizerhof (in ascending order of prices). At the Parkhotel (tel. 832-2111) a full day is SFr29 with lunch. At the Schweizerhof (tel. 837-0707) the full-day cost with lunch included is SFr34. You can take children to either the Parkhotel or the Schweizerhof for SFr6 per hour.

Getting there

You'll normally fly into Zürich and then catch a train to St. Moritz station. Air Engiadina has regular turboprop service, Zürich to St. Moritz, for SFr395 one way.

Train costs, Zürich to St. Moritz: First Class, SFr120; Second Class, SFr70.

If you are driving, the easiest route is Zürich-Chur-Thusis, then a 30-mile stretch over the Julierpass (chains needed only in the worst weather) or through the Thusis-Samedan car-train tunnel when the pass is closed.

If you stay in St. Moritz and not in one of the outlying towns, you'll pay a stiff fee for parking, about SFr14 a day unless you are staying for more than a week. In that case, there is a discount card available. The main garage is centrally located, however, two minutes down the hill from the Corviglia funicular.

Other activities

If you have the time, ride the Glacier Express, a 150-mile crossing of the ice-covered landscape between St. Moritz and Zermatt.

It's possible to ride the famed Cresta Skeleton sled run without risking your life. Sign on as a guest rider on non-racing days. This sledding run seems to be addictive if you are British. The fee for five rides as a passenger on the one-mile course is about SFr450; additional rides cost SFr44.

A horse-drawn sleigh ride along the lake costs about SFr100, or a trip in the Roseg

Valley is SFr24 per person or SFr130 per carriage.

The first "Skijöring" races, with horses pulling skiers on the frozen lake racetrack, were run in 1901. The competition continues. Try to see one of these events on the first three weekends in February.

For information on hang-gliding instruction, call 833-2416. You can go airborne for SFr220–290.

Excursions to Italy are easy, and bus tours are available if you are not driving.

St. Moritz has two museums, the Engadine, filled with local history, and the Segantini, an art museum.

The public swimming pool entrance fees are SFr7 per adult or SFr4 per child. There are discount booklets for repeated visits. You will also find a sauna at the pool.

 Tourist information

Check with the Kur-und-Verkehrsverein, CH-7500 St. Moritz, Switzerland; tel. 081-837-3333, fax 081-837-3366.

In neighboring Pontresina, the address is Verkehrsverein, CH-7505 Pontresina, Switzerland; tel. 081-842-6488, fax 081-842-7996.

☎ *Telephone prefix for St. Moritz is 081.*

Verbier

This world-class resort is in Switzerland's southwest corner, roughly between Zermatt to the east and Courmayeur and Chamonix to the west. Verbier itself is the major town in an area comprising four valleys that have been interconnected by a spectacular lift system. The highest peak, Mont-Fort, at 10,919 feet, is the nexus for lift systems that rise from Verbier and Nendaz. There are 100 lifts that take you to more than 250 miles of runs.

Verbier the town is upscale, chic and very well known, but reasonable accommodations can be found. There is no real town center—this is more of a sprawl of chalets and hotels. What is termed the center is something of a focus, but don't get the idea that this is a goos resort for an evening stroll.

Nendaz is as ugly as Swiss resorts get. It is connected with Verbier and has less expensive places to stay. The lower lodging costs are offset by slow and arduous lifts, which start at Nendaz and take you to the top of the Tortin, where you can connect with the rest of the Verbier lift system.

Unfortunately, none of the connected areas seem to connect easily here and the lift system is a real detriment to getting in lots of skiing during high season and on weekends. It seems that the new lifts constructed during the past few years, such as the Funispace gondola, while clearing up long lines in one spot, have only been making matters worse rather than better at others.

Mountain layout

This resort is at one end of the Four Valleys area. It links with Thyon, Veysonnaz and Nendaz. Verbier has the best skiing for experts and advanced skiers, but it does have a decent beginner area and limited intermediate terrain.

The Savoleyres area is the smallest of the Verbier sectors. A gondola takes skiers up to mellow trails. This area doesn't get too many crowds and the lift lines stay manageable for the most part. During the early season, skiing back to Verbier is relatively easy, however during the late season the snow coverage requires most skiers to download on the gondola.

The main Verbier area is on the north-facing slopes with the main lifts rising to Ruinettes and Attelas. This section gets crowded and at the lower levels skiers don't only have to watch out for each other, but deal with walkers, dogs and kids on sleds.

From the Attelas upper station cable cars rise to the Mont Fort glacier. The problems here are weather, which closes the area many days, and the lift lines which can be a pain.

One intermediate secret is the Bruson area. It is connected with the rest of the Four Valleys by a 15-minute bus trip from the lower station of the Châble cable car. The trails here are far from the maddening crowds. On powder days this is a wonderful spot to practice turns and perfect technique.

Experts and advanced skiers will have the time of their life with virtually limitless off-piste possibilities. Many of the formerly black runs have been redefined as itineraries. They are not groomed or marked, but have so much traffic, they may as well have been marked by the resort as they once were. A guide is highly recommended in this area to get the most out of the mountain.

Mountain rating

Verbier is considered tops by expert skiers. The black runs are steep and hair-raising. We don't recommend runs such as the Tortin, from Col des Gentianes, if you are not at least an advanced intermediate; if you fall, there is no stopping for at least a hundred meters. This is based on personal experience (several years ago, of course). The lift back up can be so crowded that skiers may wish they stayed at the top. Other expert steeps are not as long.

Intermediates will find challenging terrain and technique-perfecting runs. Beginners can glide down easy bunny slopes, but they shouldn't expect the rest of the mountain to be conquered by week's end.

The lifts and the runs in the Nendaz area are shorter and easier than those in Verbier (except for the expert-level Tortin). This provides a nice break from Verbier's more crowded sections. During the week Verbier is no problem, and lift lines are short. On weekends crowds arrive from Montreux, Lausanne and Geneva.

Ski school

The ski school has 170 instructors and is in the Chalet Orny (7753366).
Individual lessons

one or two persons (1/2 day)	SFr160
three or four persons (1/2 day)	SFr190
one or two persons (full day)	SFr320
three or four persons (full day)	SFr370

Group lessons Lessons run from 9:15 a.m. to 11:45 a.m.

one day	SFr34
three consecutive days	SFr102
six consecutive days	SFr123

Five full-day ski seminars or weekend seminars let skiers tour the area trails, honing their skills at the same time. They run, 9 a.m. to 1 p.m., from Monday through Friday and on weekends. The week-long program costs SFr320 and the weekend course is SFr130.

The instructor takes the skiers over mountain runs within their ability. It's a great way to spend a week, ski the entire mountain, and leave a much better skier, no matter the level at which you started.

Snowboarding group lessons meet from Monday through Saturday from 9:45 a.m. to noon. Lessons are SFr35 apiece or SFr138 for six consecutive lessons.

Lift tickets (97/98 prices)

Family vacationers should be sure to ask about discounts, because the formula that is used may result in a healthy discount for them. Similar discounts apply to single parents.

These lift ticket prices are for the entire four-valley area with Mont-Fort and only Verbier.

	Four-Valley	Verbier
half-day	SFr45	SFr39
one day	SFr56	SFr49
two days	SFr108	SFr95
six days	SFr282	SFr249
fourteen days	SFr509	SFr450

Forty percent-off tickets are available for skiers over 65 and for children six to 16. Lift tickets are discounted further in certain low-season periods.

Accommodations

Special weekly programs cost SFr1,450–964 per person depending on the hotel for a full week in mid-March with half board, six-day lift pass and free entry to the sports center.

The approximate daily high-season rate with half pension, based on double occupancy, is noted after each hotel.

Four-star hotels:
  Rosalp (tel. 7716323; fax 7711059) SFr235–290.
  Vanessa (tel. 7752800; fax 7752828) SFr175–200.
  Montpelier (tel. 7716131; fax 7714689) SFr280.
  Three-star hotels:
  Golf Hotel (tel. 7716515; fax 7711488) SFr105–190.
  Rhodania (tel. 7716121; fax 7715254) SFr120–160.
  Chamois (tel. 7716402; fax 7712712) SFr115–140.
  De la Poste (tel. 7716681; fax 7713401) SFr135–175.
  Rotonde (tel. 7716525; fax 7713331) SFr125–140.
  Vieux-Valais (tel. 7753520; fax 7753535) SFr130–175.

Two-star hotels:
  l'Auberge (tel. 7716272; fax 7713401) SFr110–140.

Bed & Breakfasts:
  Les 4 Vallées (tel. 316066; fax 313401) SFr110–158.
  Les Rois Mages (tel. 316364; fax 313319) SFr130–150.
  Bristol (tel. 7716577; fax 7715150) SFr90–125.
  Ermitage (tel. 7716477; fax 7715264) SFr105–125

Farinet (tel. 7716626; fax 7713855) SFr130–160.
Mirabeau (tel. 7716335; fax 7714806) SFr98–125.
de Verbier (tel. 7716688; fax 7714021) SFr70–143.

Ski Chalets: Crystal, Inghams/Bladon, Simply Ski, Chalet World, Thomas (go to page 27 for phone, fax and internet addresses).

Apartments

The tourist office keeps track of apartment availability. Write and give details on the number of beds required, the preferred number of rooms, and the dates you plan to be there. An immediate response with a selection of apartments and prices will follow. Select the apartment you want and contact the owner directly. Minimum stays are normally one week, Saturday to Saturday (in Christmas season the minimum is two weeks).

Bed linen and kitchen utensils are usually provided. Other communal or private amenities, such as swimming pool, sauna, TV or room phone, all add to the cost. Apartments rent for $25 to $45 per person a night. Prices vary significantly by season.

Dining

In Verbier's excellent restaurants prices naturally depend on the establishment's relative position on the luxury scale, but with the strong French influence here it is difficult to find a poorly prepared meal. The following restaurants are recommended by locals: **Rosalp**, with a Michelin star, and **Vanessa** for a splurge; also try **Au Vieux Valais, Le Mazot** and **Le Farinet.**

Head to the **Refuge** under the Hotel Rhodania for good spaghetti and other Italian food. Their "spaghetti by the meter" guarantees a good time. Other good cheap (for Verbier) Italian meals can be found at **Borsalino, Spaghetti House** and **Al Capone.**

On the slopes try **Chez Dany** at Clambin down from La Chaux is considered the best. **Les Marmottes** on the Savoleyres is also excellent. Other than those two, take your own chances. The rest of the mountain restaurants visited were over crowded or far too expensive for the low-quality meals served. Both Chex Dany and Les Marmottes have dinners with access by snowmobile and descent with torches.

Après-ski/nightlife

The most popular drinking spots are **The Pub Mont-Fort,** which is very English, **Nelsons, Fer à Cheval** with great hot wine, **Farinet** and **La Luge.** Try also **Aristo, New Club** and **Jacky's Bar.**

The best discos in town are the **The Tara,** the **Farm Club Disco** (of Fergie fame) and **Marshall's.** The **Scotch Club** is not as popular. Expect to pay about SFr20 to enter, which includes a drink.

Child care

A kindergarten, Chez les Schtroumpfs (Smurfs' Place), is located in Chalet Lesberty, just a short distance from the tourist office. Open daily 8:30 a.m.–5:30 p.m., its rates are SFr48 a day with lunch, SFr38 for a half day with lunch, and SFr28 for a half day without lunch. Call 7716585 for details.

The ski school runs a ski nursery (tel. 7716825), which offers ski lessons for children three to 10 years. These lessons cost SFr33 for a half day; SFr for a half day with lunch; SFr55 for a full day; SFr143 for three days; and SFr255 for six days. Full-day prices include lessons and lift tickets. Lunch is SFr11.

A children's ski program for good skiers runs Monday–Saturday from 8:50 a.m.–16:30 p.m. Rates are SFr240 for six days.

Getting there

The closest airport is Geneva. Train service runs from Martigny on the Simplon line to Le Chable, where you can either take the cable car to Verbier or a direct bus from the station in the winter. The drive from Geneva takes about two hours. Follow the signs to the St. Bernard Pass (home of the famous St. Bernard dogs) until Sembrancher; turn left there, up the hill to Verbier.

Other activities

Verbier has an extensive sports center, which features an indoor swimming pool, ice rink, curling rinks, squash courts, whirlpools, saunas, and solariums. The center has a swimming pool, tennis courts, sauna, indoor rink, curling rink, squash courts and fitness center. Pool entry is SFr7 for guests staying in a hotel in Verbier. An hour of tennis costs SFr23. Ice skating is SFr6 and squash courts cost SFr12–15 per half-hour.

Tourist information

Tourist office, CH-1936 Verbier, Switzerland; tel. (027) 7753888; fax (027) 7753889.

☎ *Telephone prefix for Verbier is 027.*

Zermatt

Zermatt, Switzerland's best-known ski resort, was the base for the famous first assaults on the Matterhorn in the 1860s. The killer mountain still casts its shadow over the storybook village, which has become one of Europe's premier winter playgrounds. Though the Matterhorn has presided over the valley for centuries, it was only conquered by climbers in 1865. Prior to that villagers only climbed as high as their cattle.

This fairy tale setting is augmented by a storybook village of Swiss chalets with a stream running through the middle.And, as if that is not enough transportation is by horse drawn sleighs or electric taxies.Only the doctor is allowed to have a car in Zermatt! Everyone else, since 1891, arrives by train. Unfortunately, the horse-drawn sleighs that used to carry tourists and townsfolk through the village, along with bags of groceries or ski equipment, have been largely replaced with speeding electric trucks and carts; when you hear a ringing bell, get to the side of the street.

Fortunately, Zermatt is a destination resort; that is, the village is difficult enough for weekend skiers to reach to keep most of them away. The town has about 13,500 beds and a lift capacity of almost 60,300 people an hour, with more than 143 miles of marked ski trails (including Breuil-Cervinia). Seventy percent of the guests are repeat visitors. Even in the busiest seasons lift lines are not impossibly long and uncrowded slopes can be found.

Despite constant development, new hotels, apartments, lifts, etc. Zermatt remains the world's most quintessential ski resort. No matter how many times you come here you are always charmed and amazed that the village remains part of the real world.

 ## Mountain layout

Unlike many other fashionable ski resorts around the world, most people who come to Zermatt actually ski! There are about 230 km of pistes and 73 lifts covering three separate (though partially connected) areas and the Italian resort of Breuil-Cervinia with a lift capacity of 64,500 skiers per hour. There are numerous cross-country trails between the mountain villages. All the areas have runs for beginners, intermediates and advanced skiers, though in all fairness, Zermatt is not the perfect place to come as an absolute first time skier. Intermediates should also realize that the trails will not all be groomed as they are in the States, though plenty of them and there should be no problem skiing anywhere.

Zermatt sits at the end of a long valley and is bounded by three major skiing areas. Each area will keep skiers busy for at least two days' worth of thrills. The three lift areas branch out from different sections of Zermatt and all are within walking distance depending on where you are staying. There is a ski bus connecting the three areas (SFr2.5 per ride or SFr22 per week) and taxi's can take up to six passengers to any of the base areas.

The Sunnegga-Blauherd area (7,513 feet) is quickly reached by an underground cable railway and has ski lifts that reach the Unterrothorn at 10,170 feet. This area is the least time-consuming to reach. It also gets the most sun in the valley and has recently been equipped with snowmaking facilities that stretch from the top station down to National. A quad chair now whisks skiers from National up to Blauherd, eliminating what was one of the worst lift lines in the area. A new cable car added in 1996 eases what was often quite a bottleneck. This whole area is ideal for every level of skier and has numerous ways down to different lifts with some seemingly endless trails. An excellent area for intermediates to explore is the Kumme side, where a triple chair allows almost continuous skiing, and long runs back down to Tuftern will keep advanced skiers and intermediates happy.

From Blauherd there are numerous ways down and another cable car taking you still higher up to Rothorn with its own runs and a quad to service them.

The Fluhalp trail down to the lower station of Gant initially has good skiing but long runouts at the lower levels. For those planning to hook up with Gornergrat it's the only connection, but it is not recommended for anyone below advanced intermediate.

The Gornergrat area is served by a cog railway that has been expanded in recent years with additional cars. It is convenient to get to and the ride to the upper station takes about 40 minutes. The wait in line at the Gornergrat station in town can be up to a half hour in high season. Normally, however, when the line at Gornergrat is long, walk over to Sunnegga and head up the mountain—there's almost no wait.

From here there are a variety of fun intermediate runs. There are several ways of skiing down to Riffelberg where you can get back on the train or take the t-bar back to the top. Beginners can get off on the way up at Riffelberg where there is a platter lift with its own trails or go on to Rotenboden where you can ski using the train to go up.

Conditions permitting, and usually after the Christmas season, there is also a cable car that continues from Gornergrat to Stockhorn and opens a whole new area of expert terrain served by it's own t-bar.

You can also ski down from Gornergrat to various mid stations and take the train back up. Alternatively you can ski from here to both of the other ski areas in Zermatt, Sunnegga and Trockener Steg; unfortunately, you can not get back to Gornergrat from either of them. But the ski route down to Furi where you get the cable car back up to Trockener Steg is quite scenic and great fun for any good intermediate skier and is highlighted by several mountain chalets where you can stop for lunch or a drink. This route continues right into the center of Zermatt as do all the runs down.

There is also a great route, fine for a good intermediate, that takes you to the Sunnegga-Blauherd area. It is about a one hour trail through the Alps and is a highlight of the trip. There is an opportunity here to stop in a mountain chalet for lunch before arriving in Gant, where you take the gondola up to the Sunnegga-Blauherd area.

The third ski area of Zermatt, **Klein Matterhorn (Little Matterhorn) or Trockener Steg** area. This is the largest area and it is here that you connect with the ultimate intermediate skiing experience in the world: cross-border skiing to Cervina!! This sector is reached by a series of cable cars. It is slightly out of town and slightly up hill; you might want to consider the bus or a taxi to get here; just make sure you take the one that drops you at the lift and not down by the river; the walk up is far more exhausting than the walk to get there in the first place!

It can easily take 45 minutes to an hour to reach the area's upper stations, but once you are there, skiing is good throughout the summer on the glacier. Snow-making facilities have been installed below Trockener Steg down to Zermatt in order to keep the lower sections of the summer ski area open.

From Trockener Steg one is again confronted with one of skiing's engineering marvels, the cable car to the Klein Matterhorn (Little Matterhorn). If your heart can take it, try and stand in the front of the cabin and watch as you approach to top station and try and imagine building this thing. Once you arrive you walk through a tunnel of about 100 yards and come out on what is certainly the single most breathtaking view in skiing. Unfortunately the conditions here can be cold and windy, since you are on top of the world at about 12,000 ft. The ski down is not at all difficult and any below average intermediate can handle it. This is the glacier area that is open all summer and serviced additionally by three T-bars (the old way of getting to the top).

From here you can ski back down to Trockener Steg or head over to Italy to the Italian ski resort of Cervina. There is a restaurant right on the top where the border is: a great place to stop, especially if you are not going down to Cervina.

Going down to Trockener Steg opens up another area of skiing; There are several t-bars back up and if you continue down to Furgg you can take the cable car back. One of my favorite runs is from Furgg back down to Furi (where you changed from the six passenger gondola to the cable car) and another of my favorite restaurants, Simi.

From here you can take the lifts up and end up on another area called Schwarzee. Schwarzee has only one t-bar so after a few runs you end up skiing down again to Furi. Normally Schwarzee is saved for the end of the day and the ski down to Zermatt. But there is a nice self-service restaurant here and no reason you can come back up again.

Over to Italy: Skiers shouldn't miss the opportunity for a special adventure: skiing over to the Italian side of the mountain and visiting Cervinia. Don't expect a picturesque Florence-style Italian town—Cervina has all the architectural flavor of frozen pizza. Fortunately, the cooking in Cervina is excellent. After the hour-long ascent and the one- to two-hour run into Cervina, you'll be ready to have a good Italian meal. This is an experience not to be missed by anyone with modest intermediate skills or better. The entire day can be taken up with two trips down and a wonderful lunch.

Always make sure you come with the idea in mind that you may have to spend the night if the weather changes and they are forced to close the lift. In 12 years this has only happened once to one of our staff, but the warning to bring your passport is probably a good idea.

Change your money before you strike out for Italy—the rates for changing Swiss Francs into Italian Lire are better on the Swiss side of the mountain. However, Swiss Francs are accepted freely in Italy, albeit at poor exchange rates. Remember that your normal Zermatt lift ticket is not good on the Cervinia lifts—a special lift pass purchased on the Zermatt side will allow you to use them. You can also purchase a lift ticket in Cervina, but the price is higher.

The last lift leaves at 3:20 p.m. There are gondolas all the way to Testa Grigia, so lift lines for getting back to the Zermatt side are not too bad, but they can take a while to negotiate.

Mountain rating

Skiers of every level will find thrills in Zermatt. Each area has some runs to make beginners feel like experts, and some to make experts wonder just how expert they really are.

Advanced skiers will enjoy the Kumme side of the Rothorn and some of the steeps drop back into the village from the Sunnegga area. There are a half-dozen steep, bumpy and exciting runs in the Gorner-grat section from Stockhorn, Rote Nase and Hohtälli down to Gant into the valley between Sunnegga and Gornergrat. And although the Klein Matterhorn area is wide open with gentle slopes, the runs from Schwarzsee back into town can be testing. Experts also have almost unlimited opportunities for off-trail skiing.

Intermediate skiers can be happy in any area, but should avoid many of the black runs, which are really for experts. Plus, many of the trails are not groomed. If you take the cable car over to the Stockhorn, Rote Nase and Hohtälli, be aware that there is no easy escape from the steep and bumpy.

Beginners will find easy slopes on the Gornergrat and on the Klein Matterhorn glacier. Also, the Sunnegga area has a good long beginner/lower intermediate trail network from Blauherd into town.

Lessons (97/98 prices)

The Zermatt ski and snowboard school (966-2466; fax 966-2464) has more than 175 qualified instructors and mountain guides who teach in the traditional Swiss ski school system.

Individual lessons	Adults & Children	
one day	SFr270	
each additional person	SFr10	
half day	SFr145	
each additional person	SFr5	

Group lessons	Adults	Children
one day	SFr65	SFr60
three days	SFr150	SFr170
five days	SFr200	SFr235
six days	SFr215	SFr255

Children are from 6–12 and their lessons include lunch.

Zermatt also offers a special Matterhorn Ski Week. The course includes a seven-day ski pass and an instructor for six full days (Sunday to Friday). The major difference between this program and standard group lessons is that the instructor stays with the group for the entire day instead of only four hours a day, and takes the group down almost every run within the skiers' abilities. Cross-country classes are also available.

To enroll in one of the Matterhorn Ski Weeks, write in advance to the tourist office and request enrollment forms. The price (including five-day ski pass) is SFr785–2,052 with accommodations.

There are many off piste ski programs for better skiers such as the six-day Monte Rosa itinerary for SFr292 or a 13-day tour for SFr516.

Helicopter to Theodul Glacier (Italian/Swiss border to ski to Cervina) costs SFr150 per person.

"The Haute Route" is a classic ski adventure tour between Saas-Fee, Zermatt, Courmayeur and Chamonix. These trips are organized from mid-April through the end of May. These are tough, physical treks, and participants should be in good shape for high-altitude ski-climbing and must be able to ski in deep snow. The tour is normally conducted from mid-May to the first week in June. Cost is SFr1,500, which includes guides, accommodation in mountain huts, meals, hotel expenses and mountain railway and bus fares. Contact: Franz Schwery, mountain guide, CH-3920 Zermatt, Switzerland; (672880), or the Mountain Guide Office in Zermatt (966-2960).

Lift tickets (97/98 prices)

The Zermatt lift system has fairly complicated fees. You can buy ski passes for each of the areas separately or in any combination. You can also buy coupons, which may not be a good deal if you plan to do any serious skiing: you have to purchase varying amounts, depending on the area you'll be skiing in. The coupons are designed for skiers who can spend only a limited time on the slopes. For those skiing the entire day, the best deal is the full combination pass. The prices are:

one day	SFr60
six days	SFr292
seven days	SFr308
fourteen days	SFr530

Children ski for half price.

Note: If you plan to ski to Cervinia, you must pay a surcharge to use Cervinia's uphill lift system. The surcharge for the combination ticket is SFr31. If you wait to purchase it on the Italian side, the price jumps to SFr62.

There is also a new Cervina/Zermatt lift ticket. Cost is about 20-25% more than the Zermatt-only ticket.

Accommodations

Do yourself a favor when requesting a room and ask for one that doesn't face the main street. For some reason the disco denizens feel compelled to yell and sing at the top of their lungs as they stagger down the main street from the music-filled cellars from one to three o'clock in the morning.

The following hotel rates are per person, based on double occupancy with half board.

For the best Zermatt has to offer, head for the **Zermatterhof** (966-8888; fax 967-2878) or the Mont **Cervin** (966-6600; fax 966-6699). Both cost SFr210–355.

You almost can't go wrong picking a hotel; the only thing to consider is location. The closer you are to the center of town, the easier it is to get home at night. There are three world class hotels here: the previously mentioned five star Mont Cervin and Zermatterhof, both with all the facilities you can think of including health clubs, sauna, Jacuzzi and indoor swimming pools. The most charming is Hotel Monte Rosa (967-3333; fax 967-1160) It is one of the grand hotels in the center with access to one of the best pools in town. SFr170–260.

The second group and only slightly less expensive would include the **Hotel Nicoletta** (967-0151; fax 967-5215) with its roof top bar, the **Schweizerhof** (967-6767; fax 967-6769) with numerous restaurants and a night club and the Hotel **Alex** (967-1726; fax 967-1943). The Alex is a favorite with its indoor swimming pool, indoor tennis, squash, health club, sauna, grill room and one of the most interesting disco's you'll find anywhere for the 30–60 set; actually if you didn't ski you wouldn't have to leave the Alex!

The next group includes:

Hotel Walliserhof (966-6555; fax 966-6550) First-class rustic lodgings with top restaurant. SFr122–195.

Hotel Butterfly (966-4166; fax 966-4165) In the center of town, whirlpool and fitness room. SFr110–190.

Hotel Simi (966-4600; fax 966-4605) Same owner as the lunch restaurant at Furi. SFr98–150

The Post **Hotel** (967-1932; fax 967-4114) If you can stand the activity and noise, the funkiest hotel in Zermatt (if not the whole ski universe) which really deserves a chapter to itself. SFr75–120.

Hotel Gornergrat (966-3931; fax 966-2925) A fairly modern hotel in the heart of Zermatt across the street from the train station and next to the Gornergrat terminus. SFr94–130.

Hotel Alpenhof (967-4233; fax 967-4232) By all reports one of the best hotels in town. A chalet-style hotel just across from the main Sunnegga lift and only minutes from the center of town. SFr150–195.

Hotel Admiral (967-1561; fax 967-5058) Shares the pool with the nearby Christiania. Most who have stayed here have nothing but praise for the place. SFr140–170.

Alphubel (967-3003; fax 967-6634) A relatively small, two-star hotel in the middle of Zermatt. SFr96–100.

More economical:

Burgener Pensione (967-1020; fax 967-5579) A small, traditionally rustic hotel. SFr90–120.

Testa Grigia (967-2501; fax 967-5523) This is a Bed & Breakfast. SFr65–100.

The hotels listed below feature lower rates and special packages which are available in low season: early December, January after New Year, and the end of April.

There are countless hotels in Zermatt and there are not any bad choices. Check out the B&B rate since one of the highlights of visiting Zermatt is the restaurants. This insures you won't be tied down to eating dinner every night in the same hotel.

Ski Chalets: Inghams/Bladon (see page 27 for phone, fax and internet addresses).

Apartments

Apartments are the best choice if you really want to save money in Zermatt. Not only will it cost substantially less but you will have room to spread out, the facilities of a kitchen and the option of staying home for dinner and relaxing.

A well-organized rental system offers apartments for more than 7,000 people a night. Write to the tourist office and ask for a list of apartments available when you plan to be in Zermatt. Be sure to include your requirements, such as the number of people in your party. The office will send a listing of available apartments and a map showing their locations. You then select the apartment you want and correspond directly with the apartment owner.

If you are fortunate enough to find an apartment in the Obere-Steinmatte section of town, you'll often be able to put on skis at your door and ski to the Sunnegga lifts or the Gornergrat car when the snow is still on the streets.

The apartments normally include bed linen and cooking utensils. You will be charged a visitor's tax, and there may be an extra charge for the electricity and heat you use during your stay.

Expect to pay SFr35 to SFr65 per person a night, depending on the number of people sharing the apartment and its location.

Dining
On the mountain
Here again Zermatt excels with an incredible selection of charming and wonderful restaurants. There are almost 40 different mountain restaurants in Zermatt. We start with the Sunnegga area.

One of the highlights of the Sunnegga area, and of all of Zermatt, is lunch.Few other ski areas have such a variety of Hansel & Gretel chalet restaurants and bars. Sunnegga and Rothorn both have great restaurants with large terraces (Rothorn also has an outdoor bar with music) and Blauherd has a large cafeteria. But the most charming are the restaurants in little mountain villages.Skiing down from Blauherd to the National quad is Tuftern—a simple place serving hearty soups, sausages, cheeses, etc.Further down and impossible to find is Othmar's Hutte in Ried (967-1761). Down from Sunnegga or Rothorn on the other side is Findeln, a collection of wooden huts housing several restaurants that give new meaning to the word cozy, including Anni & Toni (967-6404), Franz & Heidi (967-2588) and my favorite, Chez Vrony (967-2552). You won't understand skiing in Zermatt until you have skied down here for lunch.(There is a chair lift to take you back up.)

In the Gornergrat section there is a cafeteria type restaurant (967-2255) with a large sun terrace and a wonderful hotel with it's own restaurant and a spectacular view. (Spending a night or two here can be a very romantic experience (966-6500; fax 966-6505)!

The Kleiner Matterhorn/Trokener Steg section has Restaurant Simi (967-2695). This is an institution in Zermatt and this is one of the most popular lunch spots. This is also where you end up if you ski down from the Gornergrat area. There are numerous different restaurants as you ski down to Furi, but try Simi at least once if you can get in.

Heading down to the village is a long exciting trail with great views. Once the trail splits near Furi and you are committed to go into town you will ski by the village of Zum Zee (967-2045)—another must on the charm list for Zermatt and the quintessential après-ski stop. Within this little village is a restaurant famous for Café Garola. The tradition started in the Aosta Valley of Italy on the other side of the Matterhorn. Café Garola is served in a wooden pot (certainly not legal in the US!!) with four, six or eight spouts. It is passed around the table filled with a steaming a concoction of coffee, grappa, Cointreau, fruit and who knows what else. The tirual is to light up the alcohol and serve the drink piping hot. It goes down easy as skiers and boarders pass the wooden bowl. Just remember you still have to ski down to town!!

In town

While all of the major hotels have excellent restaurants they are mostly typical of hotel restaurants. If you want to dress up try the **Mont Cervin** or the **Zermatterhof** (the only places you would ever dress up in Zermatt). Some worthy exceptions, the **Monte Rosa, Walliserhof** and the **Alex Grill** are worth trying as are the restaurants in the **Schweizerhof** which really don't relate to the hotel.

To experience dining in Zermatt you have to sample the different types of restaurants hidden around town. There are no really bad restaurants, but here are some of our recommendations.

Maybe the best restaurant in Zermatt is the **Grill at the Alex Schlosshotel Tenne** (in the hotel, but with a separate entrance; not to be confused with the Alex Hotel across the street; 967-1801). Also for excellent meat dishes is **Le Mazot**(967-2777) in a charming old farm house by the river and where even normally taciturn Germans go out of their way to compliment the owner on great food and service. Perhaps the most romantic restaurant is the **Spycher Grill** (967-1141) on the other side of the river; perfect for that intimate rendezvous.

Don't miss the Swiss fondue. You can have either meat or cheese (or chocolate for desert). For meat fondue which can be either Bourguignon (chunks of beef dipped in boiling oil) or Chinoise (thin slices of veal cooked in consume), head to the **Stockhorn Grillroom** (967-1747) or perhaps better is **Chez Gaby** on the river just behind the Church. (If you have the Chinoise, and you should, don't forget to make sure they add some Sherry to the consume at the end and give it to you to drink.) For Cheese fondue and *Raclette* (melted cheese served with potatoes, onions and pickles) you should end up in a *Stübli* which will be downstairs in a sort of cave-like setting. Two favorites are downstairs at the **Stockhorn** or the popular **Whymperstube** (967-2296) below the Monte Rosa hotel. Cheese fondue can also be found for lunch at several of the huts mentioned.

For a variety of Swiss specialties, including the local trout try **Old Zermatt** (967-2681) with views of the river and the cemetery. For seafood go to the **Boat-House** (967-1931) in the Post Hotel.

Another "in" place to have dinner is **Restaurant Chez Heini**. It specializes in succulent home grown lamb prepared by their singing chef, Dan Daniell, the Don Ho of Zermatt. He'll even autograph his CD for you.

For Italian the best is **Tony's Grotto** (967-4454) next to Simi hotel (and one of the few places in town you can get a Café Garola after dinner) and the most fun is the **Spaghetti Factory** downstairs in the Post Hotel (967-1931); go for the 9 p.m. sitting as you will overlook the disco and be ready to go when it starts to fill up after 11 p.m. You can also go further down into the labyrinth of the Post to the **Pizza Factory** or leave this craziness and go across the river to **Pizzeria Roma** (967-3229) or **Da Mario** (967-6767) in the Schweizerhof.

At the corner of Kirshstrasse is the everyday lasagna caneloni **Pizzaria Papperla Pub**. Just to let you know what prices to expect—a Pizza Margarita is SFr12; Pizza Parma SFr13.50; Pizza Silly Willy with banana and pepperoncini SFr16; and a small Greek salad SFr 8.50 or a big one is SFr14.

For a quick snack there are numerous places to drop by, but don't miss the crêperie on Bahnhofstrasse opposite the Mont Cervin.

It is not very easy to diet in Zermatt. Most of the food is hearty, especially at lunch (and the good restaurants always give you two servings). Make sure you try the various specialties of the region. We have mentioned the Fondues and Raclette and at lunch you will find almost everything comes with Rosti, the Swiss version of hash brown potatoes but ten times better. There is also Käse-Schnitt that is bread with melted cheese and sometimes ham and/or an egg on top; delicious but not on the Slim-Fast diet. The mixed salads are great and come with all kinds of things in them including a special dressing. Bundnerfleisch is a regional specialty consisting of air dried beef.

Après-ski/nightlife

The fun starts as the lifts close. In addition to stopping on the way down for a schnapps, Glühwein (hot spiced red wine), and so on, and assuming you can still make it down, from 4–6 p.m., stop at the **Olympia Stübli** on the way back to town from the Sunnegga area. In Zermatt, try the **Papperla Pub** (younger crowd), **Old Zermatt** (slightly older and quieter) and **Elsie's Bar** (most pretentious) where the upscale crowed meets for Oysters and serious, cramped mingling. **Zum See** is also a good after-ski watering hole. The **Swiss Rock** further on along Bahnhofstrasse in the center of town is slightly less packed, though not so the bar of the **Post Hotel** across the street.

There are also many Tea Rooms along Bahnhofstrasse with fantastic pastries and hot chocolate. And the **Café in the Walliserhof** fits somewhere between bar and tea room and has great Glühwein and Cafe Fertig (the Swiss version of Irish Coffee or Austrian Jägertee).

Before and after dinner there are numerous bars worth checking out. Walk to those of the **Mont Cervin, Zermatterhof** and **Monte Rosa** Hotels, the **Schweizerhof** with its fireplace or the bar at the **Tenne Grill**. Still going strong will be the **Papperla Pub**, the **Swiss Rock** and the bars of the **Post Hotel**. For a view of Zermatt try the **Panorama Bar** on the top of the Nicoletta Hotel. There are no shortage of bars and you will find your favorite tucked away in some hidden alley.

For dancing or listening to music, the undisputed place to go is the **Post Hotel**; if it sounds like you don't have to leave the Post Hotel, you are right. Owned by an eccentric American it is a totally unique concept in the ski (and perhaps any other) world. It resembles an underground jumble of something Hieronymous Bosch might have concocted— it is THE hot spot of Zermatt. Just go, you'll understand. The disco downstairs is so confusing that on our last trip we found friends thought lost years ago! The 2nd floor **Boat-House** (mentioned under restaurants) also has a great bar with less noise and on the ground floor in the back is the **Elephant Bar**—Zermatt's premier (and only) jazz address that gets the who's who that might be in town. The **Moby Dick** in the Schweizerhof also gets a slightly older (late 20s–30s) dancing crowd, while the Pollux is for the younger set.

Perhaps one of the most interesting disco's, and perfect for anyone over 30, is in the **Alex Hotel** (they have yet to give it a name after 18 years). There are posh banquets, a great bar and numerous rooms to get lost in; don't miss it even if only for a drink. It is perfect for finding a romantic corner with someone special; and if you are alone, the bar always seems to be a happening place.

If you are here over New Years, the **Post** is the first, second and third choice with the **Alex** coming next.

Finally, and not to be missed, is the movie house:This multi-level combination of bars, art galleries and a movie theater (showing first run movies) isunique.The lower level has a theater set up more or less like some Hollywood moguls screening room complete with a bar and lounge chairs. Grab a drink and make your self at home! Like so many things in this town, you have to see it to believe it.

In the end Zermatt offers an incredible number of bars and restaurants; if you just follow the narrow, winding streets you will discover your own favorite.And remember, you can have one for the road—you're not driving!

Child care

At the kindergarten in Hotel La Ginabella (967-4535) nurses take care of children two-and-a-half to six years of age. A ski instructor gives lessons to those four years and older. Prices: Full day with lunch and snack, SFr90; half day with lunch included, SFr55. Prices change based on the age of the child.

Seiler's Paradies (967-0151) for children is at the Hotel Nicoletta. It accepts children 2 to 8; the hours are 9 a.m. to 5 p.m.

The ski school kindergarten costs approximately SFr60 per day; SFr170 for three days; and SFr255 for six days—all prices include lunch and beverages.

Getting there

By train

From Zürich airport via Bern, Spiez, through the Lötschberg tunnel to Brig. At Brig you change to the special Zermatt train at the front of the Brig station. Time from Zürich to Brig is about three and a half hours, Brig to Zermatt an hour and 20 minutes.

Trains run from the Geneva airport to Brig in two hours.

The trip from Milan is slightly shorter and less expensive, but the ride in from the airport to the train station adds easily another 60–90 minutes to the trip.

By car

From Montreux, go up the Valais pass through Sion to Visp, where you turn south and follow signs to Zermatt. The car park, just outside the village of Tasch, is about three miles from Zermatt. Buses and trains connect Tasch with Zermatt approximately every 20 minutes; the ride takes eleven minutes. Parking costs SFr7–11 per day.

If you are driving from Zürich or Basel, you can also take the Lötschberg tunnel from Kandersteg to Goppenstein, above Brig and Visp. Trains, with your car aboard, transit the tunnel every half hour from 5:35 a.m.–11:05 p.m.; the trip takes only 15 minutes. Cost per car, including nine-seat vans, is SFr25. From Goppenstein, continue your drive to Visp, then on to Tasch.

Upon arriving in the village you will be greeted with a choice of taxi to take you to your hotel or apartment.(You can also take the luggage trolleys to your hotel if it is not very far away.)The more upscale four-star hotels usually have their own electric taxis waiting for guests and the two five-star hotels of Zermatt, the Mont Cervin and Zermatterhof have magnificent horse drawn carriages to whisk you away to the hotel in truly grand style.Otherwise there are plenty of electric taxis and sleighs for hire (depending on the snow conditions the sleighs may be forced to use wheels).The taxis are relatively expensive and charge by number of people and luggage, but other than going to and from the train station you can well survive without ever using another one—though if possible don't miss the opportunity to take a sleigh ride through the village.

Taxi charges range from normally from SFr12–18 and the sleighs about SFr20. For taxis call 967-1567, 967-1603, or 967-1212.

Air Zermatt Helicopters can be called at 967-3487.

Other activities

Zermatt is up to handling non-skiers on vacation, although activities are much more limited owing to its distance from other tourist destinations and its dedication to skiing.

The town has twelve indoor swimming pools at various hotels; most can be used by non-guests for a small fee. Also available are 18 saunas, a salt-water swimming pool, two ice skating rinks, curling rinks, covered tennis and squash courts, indoor golfing, 19 miles of marked walking trails, helicopter rides, hang-gliding and cross-country ski circuits. There are also many art and cultural exhibitions.

Zermatt walking tours, in English leave from the front of the tourist office several times a week, contact them for times and dates.

The other great activity is shopping—Zermatt has one of the best collections of shops of any ski resort. Not just great ski clothes, but fine jewelry, watches, linens and wonderful local artifacts, wood carvings, pewter, etc.. For many, this is where the real après-ski takes place.

The Alpines Museum is open for two hours late in the afternoon, cost is SFr3.

Tourist information

Tourist Office, CH-3920 Zermatt, Switzerland; (027) 967-0181; fax (027) 967-0185.

E-mail: zermatt@wallis.ch; Internet: www.zermatt.ch

☎ *Local telephone prefix is 027.*

Spain

The ski scene in Spain is split between the north and the south. In the north, the rugged Pyrenees provide an effective border with France and very good skiing. The resort of Baqueira-Beret in the Valle de Arán, in the midst of these mountain, anchors the northern resorts. It is well-run with good snow conditions and acres of snowmaking coverage. The valley it calls home preserves one of the most fascinating cultures still existing in Spain. Other Pyrenees resorts such as formidable Formigal, traditional Panticosa, extensive La Molina and purpose-built Supermolina all provide good, if limited, skiing.

In the south, Sierra Nevada, rising above the town of Granada provides a study in contrasts. Within an hour of the snow-covered slopes, swimming in the Mediterranean can be found and verdant golf courses beckon.

Spain has come a long way in the last decade in terms of skiing. The biggest change is the installation of snowmaking equipment which has provided much more of a guarantee of acceptable conditions for skiing.

Spain has always provided excellent value for money. Lift tickets are reasonable, the ski schools (when English-speaking instructors can be found) are a bargain, and it is hard to beat the values to be found in Spain dining and enjoying excellent Spanish wines.

One of the biggest changes for U.S., Canadian and British skiers is the change in time zones. I'm not speaking about normal time zones, but the shift in dining and après-ski/nightlife timing. Dinner doesn't start until 9 p.m. and can easily last past midnight. And nightlife doesn't even start to flicker until at least midnight, normally by about 1 a.m. and can last until 4 or 5 a.m.

The Spainish internet web site for tourism information is: www.okspain.org

Baqueira/Beret
The Spanish Pyrenees

The remote Valle d'Arán lies tucked hard against the French border in the rugged Pyrenees range midway between the Atlantic and the Mediterranean. This Spanish valley is virtually cut off from the rest of the country by jagged mountains, accessible only by bus or car along a winding mountain road dwarfed by waterfalls and narrow canyons, and watched over by grazing goats and shaggy cattle. Though the drive is arduous, beauty unfolds with every turn as you pass a string of timeless villages and Romanesque churches with something of interest to see in each one. In the eastern section of the valley rises a modern cluster of apartment buildings: Baqueira/Beret. Though a dozen or more ski resorts have sprouted up in the Pyrenees, this is the largest. In fact, it is the most extensive European resort outside the Alps.

Don't expect too much charm. This ski area didn't slowly evolve into a resort. It was built as one. However, the valley itself oozes with charm and the restaurants are among the best in Spain. This is a valley that has developed in a cocoon of sorts. The first automobile road was only cut over the Bonaigua Pass in 1925 and a tunnel connecting the valley with the south was completed in 1948. Until those developments, Valle d'Arán was isolated. It had its own language and its traditional cuisine borrows from both the French and the Spanish.

Baqueira/Beret has a rather complex season structure. Christmas/New Year period is super high season as everywhere, but in Spain the week after New Year normally remains high season. The next weeks of January are low season, the first week of February is middle season, the remainder of February is high season, and March (except Easter) is middle season.

Any time of the season prices are a bargain (everything is relative). Lift lines are few and far between, if they can be found. Extensive snowmaking, with almost 250 snow cannons, insures excellent terrain coverage. The food in the region is excellent. This is a resort that simply put, works well.

Where to ski

The Baqueira, Beret and Bonaigua sections of this resort are in reality three separate ski areas linked by a series of lifts. The network of lifts and runs above Baqueira is dense and should keep most intermediates busy for a couple of days. The runs in the Beret section are much more widespread, and the lift system more modern than Baqueira's. The Bonaigua sector was recently opened and has direct access from the village to the Bonaigua Pass. The runs are well marked, and even without a map it is fairly easy to navigate.

The sector above Baqueira is reached by the Bosque Lift, a detachable quad, from the edge of town. This brings skiers to a lower plateau where beginners learn on what are called the "pastures" and four more lifts take skiers to the upper reaches of the mountain. Head to the left of the restaurant and take the detachable quad lift. This allows experts and good intermediates the option of dropping down to the single chair or heading to the Luis Arlas lift that will bring them back up to the Cap de Baqueira peak. Intermediates can enjoy the Isards and Mirador runs back to the lower plateau or or all the way into the valley to the De la Choza chair lift. There is also an exciting off-piste itinerary, called Escornacrabes, off the back side of the Cap de Baqueira that loops back to the front side of the mountain and eventually back to the village. Beginners should stay to the right side of the restaurant, where a chair lift and a drag lift open up a practice area.

The Bonaigua area is really an extension of the Baqueira section that drops down to the Banaigua pass. This is for the most part intermediate terrain with expert touches.

The Beret area is served by only four lifts, but its terrain allows skiers to ski virtually anywhere and choose from beginner to expert. The link with the Beret slopes from Baqueira is made by a triple-chair lift. Though the run from the top of either of these lifts is colored red on the map, it could just as well be blue. Once in Beret get ready to cruise almost anywhere. Two triple-chair lifts bracket the restaurant. The one to the right reaches inter-mediate terrain and the one on the left serves long beginner slopes but also allows a link up to the most exciting part of Beret—the bowl under Tuc de Dossau (2510 m). Most of the skiing in Beret is rather straightforward, but this bowl opens itself to infinite possibili-ties. There are intermediate drops directly below the chair or just to the right of the lift, and an adventurous skier can traverse along the ridge and choose steeps that will keep any expert happy. For those who get cold skis at the last minute, the traverse turns into an enjoyable beginner crossing piste back into Beret.

Mountain rating

For an intermediate, there is plenty of skiing and enough challenge to leave you feeling pushed beyond your normal limits. Absolute beginners have plenty of area to practice their stem-christies, then strike out for long easy slopes. Experts will find enough to keep them busy for about two days, but then may get itchy for new slopes to conquer. (However, with the right snowfall the powder below the Tuc de Dossal is hard to beat.)

Ski school

Baqueira/Beret has over 200 ski teachers, about 10 of whom speak English. Be sure to request an English-speaking instructor if you don't speak Spanish. Ski lessons start for children who are 3 and up.

Private lessons cost Pts4,500 per hour.

Group ski lessons cost Pts13,600–17,400 for 17 hours of lessons.

Lift tickets (96/97 prices)

high/mid-season prices	Adults	Children
half day (from 2 p.m.)	Pts2,200	–
one day	Pts4,100	Pts2,200
three days	Pts11,400	Pts6,300
five days	Pts18,000	Pts10,000
seven days	Pts24,000	Pts13,000

Accommodations

Lodgings are spread throughout the valley. This may appear inconvenient at first, but staying in such a beautiful valley is arguably a plus. You must have a car, though, and with plenty of parking near the lifts, the best restaurants scattered through the valley, and two relatively luxurious paradors ten minutes outside the resort town, an automobile is a real asset and not the problem it is in some resorts.

For those coming with a ski group, having a hotel in Baqueira means being able to ski when you want, not when your bus goes to the slopes. Don't make the mistake of missing your group bus to the lifts: public transportation is inadequate, making only two scheduled daily runs from Viella to Baqueira and back.

There are two paradors in the Valle de Arán. Here in the Valle de Arán the paradors are the most luxurious along with The Royal Tanau, a new five-star hotel recently opened by the Tryp chain.

Parador Nacional Don Gaspar de Portola, Arties (640-801). This Is a new four-star parador in Arties, 7 km. from the slopes. The town of Arties is the gourmet center of the valley, with some of Spain's top restaurants within a five-minute walk of the parador.

Parador Nacional Valle de Arán, Viella (640-100). This relatively modern parador is an impressive three-star hotel overlooking Viella at the entrance to the tunnel leading south. It is 14 km. from the Baqueira/Beret lifts. There is local bus service twice a day to the lifts and back. Unlike the other parador, this is a long walk from the town.

Royal Tanau (644-446). This is a full facility hotel, complete with a fine restaurant, gymnasium and pool facilities. This is complemented by a lovely view of the ski station, and a location within easy walking distance of the Esquiro chair lift.

In the resort of Baqueira there are three hotels, all clustered at the base of the runs and the lifts. The most sought-after rooms are in the **Val de Ruda**, a small three-star hotel. The **Tuc Blanc** is a big modern hotel and is closest to the lifts. **Montarto** has the reputation, among its Spanish visitors, of being the most elegant hotel.

The only other relatively upscale hotel in the valley is the **Hotel HUSA Tuca** at the base of the smaller ski area of Tuca. This hotel is convenient to Viella and 13 km. from the Baqueira slopes.

In the middle of Viella the newly-renovated **Hotel Arán**, does blockbusting business with British tour groups. Hotel Arán is very convenient to any nightlife that may be percolating.

Apartments

Baqueira/Beret has thousands of apartment beds. For the special weekly rate in middle season, including lift passes for the week, expect to pay about $45-55 per person per day.

For reservations call the tourist office in Baqueira/Beret, 644455 or fax 644488 from 9 a.m. to 1 p.m. or 3 p.m. to 7 p.m. There are offices in Barcelona and in Madrid.

Child care

There is babysitting service starting from 3 months old.

The resort has four child care centers accepting children from three to eight years of age. One is at the 1500 meter level in the town which will also take infants from three months, and there is a children's snow park at the 1800 meter level near the restaurant with supervisory personnel and others in Beret and Bonaigua. Children can learn to ski or just play in the snow and watch movies.

Dining

The restaurants in this valley are considered some of the best in Spain. The blend of French and Spanish cooking together with the mountain basics of the Valle de Arán, has resulted in a unique cuisine (Aránesa) which has been praised across Europe. Even without skiing, the trip to this valley would be worth the effort for the food.

The restaurants are all through the valley. The town of Arties is the cuisine capital of the region. Here you'll find **Casa Irene** (640900) where the King and Queen of Spain often dine. It is considered one of the premier restaurants in Spain and is very expensive.

In Baqueira 1500 you'll find **La Borda Lobato** (645708) famous for its Catalan and international dishes. In the resort of Baqueira try **La Perdiu Blanca** (645075) and **Ticolet** (645477). If you are in Viella try to visit **Era Mola** (640868).

My favorite restaurants are those enjoyed by the locals. The top rank in this category goes to **Carmela's** (645751) in the tiny village of Unha huddled above the town of Salardu. If you look in the local restaurant guide you will find it listed as **Restaurant Es de Don Juan**, but if you are trying to find it ask the natives for "Carmela's." Make reservations: this place is crowded.

One night after threading my way up the narrow road to Carmela's I was told there was no room. Despite dramatic begging and groans, Carmela sent me to another restaurant she personally recommended.

"See that church lit up on the mountain?" Carmela smiled and said, pointing, "The next town you reach is Baguergue. Park by the church and walk down the only street in town to **Casa Peru**."

I headed up from Salardu, past the left-hand fork heading to Unha, and found the church and Casa Peru (645437) and had a wonderful meal.

You will also find another cute little bodega in Baguergue, **Eth Chai D'unha**, where you can enjoy and buy a variety of wines, patés and cheeses from Spain and France.

Other recommended restaurants for good typical regional Aránese food are **Casa Turnay** and **Casa Estampa** in Escunhau, the next town up the road from Viella, **Et Restrille** in Garos, and **Borda de Benjamin** in Salardu.

Dining here is a passion. Lunch starts at about 2 p.m. and continues until at least 4 p.m. when skiers head out to catch the last hour of skiing before the slopes close at 5 p.m.

Here as in the rest of Spain the dinner is served late by English or American standards but not as late as in Andalusia. Restaurants open around 8 p.m. and most patrons show up between 9 and 10 p.m. Reservations, several days in advance, are necessary for many of them, and many have two sittings, one at 8 and another at 10:30 p.m. Don't wait till the last minute.

Après-ski/nightlife

There is just not much to choose from. The major disco in the valley is **Tiffany** in Baqueira. It attracts an older crowd (25 and up) than the **Viella** disco in Viella. No one really shows up until midnight or later and the gyrations continue until three or four in the morning. The **Elurra** disco and music pub in Viella is filled with a young crowd. Score this valley as very dead at night: bring along a friend to enjoy the good food and company.

Getting there

Valle de Arán is not one of the easier spots on the earth to reach. There are no trains or planes. That means bus or automobile. If you arrive by plane in Zaragoza or Barcelona (the nearest airports) and have a bus transfer, be ready for about a four-hour ride. If you aren't with a group I strongly suggest a rental car. The drive from Barcelona takes four hours, though natives claim they can make it easily in three. The resort is just over 300 km. from Barcelona and San Sebastian, and 290 km. from Zaragoza.

Other activities

Cross-country skiing, helicopter skiing, snow boarding lessons, guided excursions with dog sled, and paraskiing are all offered at Baqueira/ Beret. Swimming pools, an ice skating rink, movies, bowling and museums can be found in the valley at the new Palau de Gel. For the more adventurous, there are thermal baths about 45 minutes way. The are also a variety of historical treasures to be found in the Romanesque churches along the valley. The resort also organizes various concerts and après-ski parties, announced in a weekly flyer.

Tourist information

Oficina de Turismo de Baqueira/Beret, Apartado 60, 25530 Viella-Llérida, Spain; (973) 644455, fax (973) 644488. Information 9 a.m.-7 p.m. Reservations 9 a.m.–1 p.m. and 3–7 p.m.

Oficina de Barcelona, Paseo de Gracia 2, 08007 Barcelona, Spain; (93) 318 2776 or (93) 302 7812, fax (93) 412 2942. Hours 9 a.m.–1 p.m. and 3–7 p.m. Oficina de Madrid, Edificio Eurobuilding J. Ramon Jimenez 8, 28036 Madrid, Spain; (91) 350 8210 or (91) 350 8117, fax (91) 350 8650. Hours 9:30 a.m.– 1:30 p.m. and 4–7:30 p.m.

Snow information in Spanish: (973) 645062 and 645052.

☎ *The phone prefix for the Valle de Arán is 973. When calling from outside Spain dial only the country code then 73, then the phone number. From within Spain you must dial 973.*

Sierra Nevada, Spain

Hard to believe, but there is skiing in southern Spain, about a half-hour drive from Granada. The Sierra Nevada resort has skiing at an altitude of over 10,000 feet and brilliant sunshine most of the winter. When it storms life at the top of this treeless mountain top stops and visitors either drop down to Granada or curl up with a good book. With good weather the views are spectacular and almost unbelievable. From the top of the mountains skiers can see across the Mediterranean to Morocco.

The resort town itself is modern with a hint of traditional charm, basically a sparse cluster of hotels and apartments at the base of the first series of lifts. It is not a traditionally Spanish enclave, nor does it appear in any sense Alpine. But if you want to find snow in southern Spain, this is the place to be. When it does snow it comes down light and dry because of the low humidity in Southern Spain. When it doesn't snow Sierra Nevada has one of Europes most advanced snowmaking systems.

What Sierra Nevada does exude is the intoxicating Spanish love of the good life. There are lively tapas bars, quaint shops and elegant hotels climbing the mountainside. After skiing no one here forgets good food and spirited nightlife.

In preparation for the the 1996 World Cup Spain improved virtually every aspect of the village including the access road from Grenada. Even the old original hotels have been given a facelift and more of an Andalusian facade. ($1.00=Pts 150)

Mountain layout

To be honest, it would be hard to get lost on this mountain unless faced with white-out conditions. The skiing range is not that extensive, but it is wide open, and the runs are long and gentle. This is a true cruisers' delight. The resort boasts an above-treeline vertical of 3,757 feet.

The resort has just undergone a major series of improvements that has added new lifts and other amenities in preparation for the World Cup races. High-speed detachable quad chairs serve every major section of the mountain, limiting lift lines. In total, 19 lifts open this mellow mountain to skiers. Intermediates can have fun in every fold of the resort, beginners have plenty of space and only experts will find the resort limited.

Borreguiles is the hub of the mountain. Here at the mid-station of the cablecar rising from the town restaurants are grouped together with the ski school. The beginner area surrounds this midmountain station and the ski school. A new triple chair lift will serve the section of the mountain devoted to the World Cup Super G and Slalom race courses.

If you take the Veleta and ski down an intermediate bowl or traverse a little to your right and enter the Laguna de Yeguas bowl offering 2,300 vertical feet of more challenging intermediate terrain. When the snow is good, better skiers can drop down the Loma Dilar section of the resort and find some acceptable steeps or search for short steeps below the Borreguiles midstation.

Snowboarding is allowed on the entire mountain, but limited in the designated beginner ski area.

Mountain rating

Don't even imagine that you will find anything to challenge the expert. There are some provocative sections to encounter when skiing off-trail, but for the most part this is a mellow beginning and intermediate paradise. If you enjoy long mellow cruising carving big GS turns, you will think you are in heaven. You'll quickly discover that the object here is pure enjoyment, so relax and enjoy the sun.

High season in Spain occurs at Christmas/New Year, mid February, and Easter. Middle season is late January, early and late February, and March (except for Easter week). Low season is early December and most of January. In addition, Saturdays, Sundays and holidays draw premium rates.

Ski school (96/97 prices)

There are few places that are this perfect for learning to ski. The Spanish temperament makes for great initial instruction. What's more, most of the mountain can be handled by beginners after three or four days of instruction. There are three ski schools (480168, 480011 or 480142) has over a hundred instructors and has offices in the main square of the town and at Borreguiles at midmountain. Approximately one-quarter of the instructors speak English.

The group lessons for one week three hours a day costs adults Pts14,500 during high season and Pts11,300 during low season. Courses for children to 12 cost Pts12,000 during high season and Pts9,500 during low season.

Lift tickets (96/97 prices)

high/middle season prices	Adults	Children
half day (from 1 p.m.)	Pts2,600	–
one day	Pts3,500	Pts2,300
three days	Pts9,550	Pts6,150
six days	Pts17,600	Pts11,600

Low-season prices are about 15 percent less than high-season prices. Seniors over 65 receive a 50 percent discount.

Accommodations

All the hotels are relatively new. Add 12 percent value-added tax to each of these rates.

NOTE: The telephone prefix for the resort is 958 from Spain and

58 from outside Spain.

All these hotels have good rooms with bath. They are listed in descending order of luxury. Expect to pay $100–$200 for a double room in a four-star hotel with half board; $75–$150 for a double with half board in a three-star hotel; and $45–$63 for a studio apartment for two.

Hotel Kenia Nevada (480911, fax 480807) This four-star hotel provides some of the towns best accommodations all within walking distance of the slopes and most shops and restaurants.

Hotel Melia-Sierra Nevada (480400; telex 78507) This four-star hotel is located at the Plaza Pradollano and only steps away from shopping, restaurants and the ski slopes. the lobby is cozy heavy wooden beams and a stone floor give it a Nordic atmosphere.

Hotel La General (481450, fax 481014) This hotel right on the main town square provides all the comforts of home if you are used to living in a small room. This hotel does an excellent job of catering to families with children.

Other hotels to consider in descending order of luxury are: **Casa Alpina** (480600, fax 480506), **El Lodge** (480600), **Hotel Melia-Solinieve** (480300, fax 480458), **Hotel Nevasur** (480350, fax 480365), **Rumaykiyya** (481400, fax 480032), **Hotel Ziryab** (480512, fax 481415) and **Hotel Telecabina** (249120, fax 249122) B&B.

There are also a series of Apartment-Hotels. These are basically condos with cleaning service. The two most luxurious are **Aparthotel Cumbres Blancas** and **Aparthotel Ginebra** (480456, fax 480438).

Cheap student lodging can be found at **Albergue Universitario** (480122), **Albergue Juvenil Sierra Nevada** (480305), **Albergue Militar** (481227) or **Residencia Pradollano** (480114).

Dining

This tiny village has plenty of restaurants indicating the importance put on a good meal. Make reservations if you are planning to eat anywhere between 10 p.m. and midnight—these places can get packed.

Ruta del Veleta (486134) is a favorite of Spain's King Juan Carlos and features excellent Andalusian cuisine. Traditional Spanish cooking can be found at **Casablanca** (480830), **Rincón de Pepe Reyes** (480394), and **Restaurante Mesón Alcazaba** (480129).

Tito Luigi (480882) serves excellent and inexpensive Italian cooking. **Creperie La Gauffre** (tel.480445) has a Spanish version of French crêpes. For Chinese food try **Restaurante Chinatown** (480433).

On the slopes, the best place to head for lunch is **Restaurant Borreguiles**.

Nightlife

This is a small resort, so you should be able to find out if anything is going on rather quickly. Though the village may be small the nightlife is charged with that special Spanish spirit that takes advantage of the moment and normally stretches that moment into the wee hours of the morning.

El Golpe and **Soho Bar de Copas** both have hot action immediately after skiing. These are the spots to make contacts with other tourists that you can follow up on later in the night.

The discos start pumping around midnight but may only get crowded around 1 or 2 a.m. Try **Nevada 53** in the Hotel Meliá Sierra Nevada, **La Chimenea** in Edificio Primaverall and **La Chicle** where the yonger crowd gathers in Edificio Bulgaria.

Expect to pay hefty cover charges, but remember these cover charges normally include one or two drinks. You'll quickly learn why party folk here don't swig down drinks at a fast pace. Most nurse their drink for the entire evening.

Child care

Spanish culture revels in children—you can be sure children will be well cared for here. Child care is available at Guarderia Infantil in the new village area next to the Telecabina Al-Andalus. The facility is well-equipped and staffed by certified care providers. The guarderia has plenty of toys and videos with activities planned throughout the day. Children from three months to four years of age are accepted. Hours are 9 a.m.–5:30 p.m. Children are accepted for a half day as well. Prices are about Pts4,000 per day.

Getting there

Granada is 31 km. away. There is only one road from the city to the ski area that will take about a half-hour to drive. Traveling by car is highly recommended—it gives you much more freedom and allows exploration of Granada and the surrounding towns. Buses leave Granada from the satation near Palacio de Congresos each morning at 9:00 a.m. and return at 5:00 p.m.

The airport is 17 km. from Granada. It has connections with Madrid, barcelona, Valencia, Palma de Mallorca, Tenerife and the Canary Islands. For transportation from the airport to Sierra Nevada taxis are available. Call Tele Taxi at 280654 or Radio Taxi at 151461. Expect to pay Pts7,000–7,500 for a taxi from the airport to the resort

Other activities

The location is what makes this resort so special. Within an hour you can reach Granada and visit the fabulous Alhambra and the old center of the city. Malaga is only about two hours away, and the Costa del Sol—its chalk-white towns like Salobrena clutching small hilltops—is even closer. Excursions can be made to Jaen, with its massive cathedral and Moorish baths, or Gaudix and Purullena with their troglodyte villages. At nearby Lacalahorra castle you will have to find the gate-keeper in the town below the castle before heading up the hill.

During the spring golf is one of the major activities of this area. There are more than 30 courses lining the Costa del Sol within a two-hour drive. Call Sierra Nevada Club Agencia de Viajes at 249111 or fax 480606 for more information on the ski/golf packages.

Tourist information

For reservation center and information contact Sierra Nevada Club Agencia de Viajes at 249111 or fax 480606. General information (in Spanish) is available through telephone 249100 or 249119. Internet: www.sportec.com/ski/sierra.main.htm

The provincial tourist office in Granada has responsibility for the resort. Write Patronato Provincial de Turismo de Granada, Pl. Mariana Pineda, 10-2, Granada, Spain (958-223527).

The telephone country code for Spain is 34. The area code for Sierra Nevada and Grenada is 58 (if you are calling from within Spain the area code is 958).

European Tourist Offices

Austrian Tourist Office

500 Fifth Ave.
New York, NY 10110
(212) 944-6880
fax (212) 730-4568

1 Peachtree Center
303 Peachtree St.
Atlanta, GA 30308
(404) 522-3335
fax (404) 525-2663

1350 Connecticut Ave. N.W.
Washington, DC 20036
(202) 835-8962
fax (202) 835-8960

500 N. Michigan Ave.
Chicago, IL 60611
(312) 644-8029
fax (312) 6446526

11601 Wilshire Blvd.
Los Angeles, CA 90025
(213) 477-3332
fax (213) 477-5141

2 Bloor St. East, Toronto, Canada
(416) 967-3381
fax (416) 967-4101

200 Granville Street
Vancouver, Canada
(604) 683-5808
fax (604) 662-8528

39 St. George Street
London W1R 0AL
(0171) 780-2229
fax (0171) 499-6038

German Tourist Office

122 E. 42nd St.
New York, NY 10168
(212) 661-7200
fax (212) 661-7174

11766 Wilshire Blvd.
Los Angeles, CA 90025
(310) 575-9799

French Tourist Office

*NOTE: for tourist information
in the USA call (900) 990-0040.
Cost is 50¢ per minute.*

444 Madison Avenue
New York, NY 10022
(212) 838-7800
fax (212) 838-7855

676 N. Michigan Ave.
Chicago, IL 60611
(312) 337-6301

9454 Wilshire Blvd.
Beverly Hills, CA 90212
(213) 271-6665

1 Dundas St. W. Toronto, Canada
(416) 593-4717

178 Piccadilly, London W1V 0AL
(0891) 244132

Italian Tourist Office

630 Fifth Avenue
New York, NY 10111
(212) 245-4822

401 N. Michigan Ave.
Chicago, IL 60611
(312) 644-0996

12400 Wilshire Blvd.
Los Angeles, CA 90025
(310) 820-0098

Place Ville Marie
Montreal, Canada
(514) 866-7667

1 Princes Street
London W1R 8AY
(0171) 408-1254
fax (0171) 493-6695

Tourist Office of Spain

*for brochures and general
information call (888) OK-SPAIN*

666 Fifth Avenue
New York, NY 10103
(212) 265-8822; fax (212) 265-8864

845 N. Michigan Ave.
Chicago, IL 60611
(312) 642-1992
fax (312) 642-9817

1221 Brickell Ave. Miami, FL 33131
(305) 358-1992
fax (305) 358-8223

8383 Wilshire Blvd.
Beverly Hills, CA 90211
(213) 658-7188
fax (213) 658-1061

57 St. James's Street
London SW1A 1LD
(0171) 499-0901
fax (0171) 629-4257

Swiss Tourist Office

608 Fifth Ave. New York, NY 10020
(212) 757-5944
fax (212) 262-6116

150 N. Michigan Ave.
Chicago, IL 60601
(312) 630-5840; fax (312) 630-5848

222 N. Sepulveda Blvd.
El Segundo, CA 90245
(310) 335-5980
fax (310) 335-5982

926 The East Mall
Etobicake, Canada
(416) 695-2090; fax (416) 695-2774

Swiss Centre, Swiss Court
London W1V 8EE
(0171) 734-1921
fax (0171) 437-4577